EXPLANATORIUM

OF

NATURE

EXPLANATORIUM

OF

NATURE

Senior Art Editors Laura Gardner, Jacqui Swan
Senior Editors Sam Atkinson, Ben Morgan
Editors Shaila Brown, Steven Carton,
Emma Grundy Haigh, Helen Leech,
Sarah MacLeod, Sophie Parkes,
Laura Sandford, Amanda Wyatt
Designers Amy Child, Sheila Collins, Sunita Gahir,
Rachael Grady, Alex Lloyd, Gregory McCarthy,
Sean Ross, Mary Sandberg,
Michelle Staples, Smiljka Surla
Illustrators Edwood Burn,
Michael Parkin, Gus Scott
DK Media Archive Romaine Werblow
Picture Researcher Laura Barwick
Photography David King,
Gary Ombler, Nigel Wright
Managing Editor Lisa Gillespie
Managing Art Editor Owen Peyton Jones
Producer, Pre-Production Jacqueline Street
Senior Producer Anna Vallerino
Jacket Designers Mark Cavanagh
Jackets Design Development Manager Sophia MTT
Jackets Editor Claire Gell
Publisher Andrew Macintyre
Art Director Karen Self
Associate Publishing Director Liz Wheeler
Design Director Phil Ormerod
Publishing Director Jonathan Metcalf

Consultant Derek Harvey
Contributors Frances Dipper, Derek Harvey,
Ben Hoare, Ben Hubbard, John Woodward

DK Delhi
Project Art Editor Rupanki Arora Kaushik
Art Editors Anjali Sachar, Mansi Agrawal
Assistant Art Editors Simar Dhamija,
Sonakshi Singh
Jackets Editorial Coordinator Priyanka Sharma
Jackets Designers Juhi Sheth, Suhita Dharamjit
DTP Designer Rakesh Kumar
Senior DTP Designers Harish Aggarwal,
Sachin Singh, Jagtar Singh
Managing Jackets Editor Saloni Singh

First published in Great Britain in **2017** by
Dorling Kindersley Limited
80 Strand, London, WC2R 0RL

Copyright © **2017** Dorling Kindersley Limited
A Penguin Random House Company

10 9 8 7 6 5 4 3 2 1
001–299418–October/**2017**

A CIP catalogue record for this book
is available from the British Library.

ISBN: **978-0-2412-8684-5**

Printed and bound in China

A WORLD OF IDEAS:
SEE ALL THERE IS TO KNOW

www.dk.com

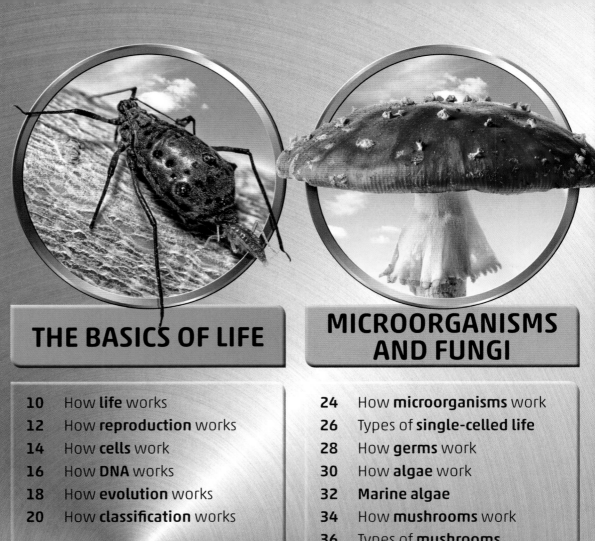

THE BASICS OF LIFE

10 How **life** works
12 How **reproduction** works
14 How **cells** work
16 How **DNA** works
18 How **evolution** works
20 How **classification** works

MICROORGANISMS AND FUNGI

24 How **microorganisms** work
26 Types of **single-celled life**
28 How **germs** work
30 How **algae** work
32 **Marine algae**
34 How **mushrooms** work
36 Types of **mushrooms**
38 How **mould** works
40 How **lichen** works

PLANTS

INVERTEBRATES

44 How **plants** work

46 How **flowering plants** grow

48 How **seeds** grow

50 How **roots** and **stems** work

52 How **trees** work

54 How **leaves** work

56 How **flowers** work

58 Types of **flowers**

60 How **fruits** grow

62 How **seeds** travel

64 **Deciduous forests**

66 How **plant defences** work

68 How **carnivorous plants** work

70 How **desert plants** survive

72 How **aquatic plants** work

76 How **invertebrates** work

78 How **snails** work

80 How **bivalves** work

82 Types of **shells**

84 How **octopuses** work

86 How **sea anemones** work

88 How **corals** work

90 **Coral community**

92 How **jellyfish** work

94 How **starfish** work

96 How **worms** work

98 How **sea worms** work

100 How **insects** work

102 Types of **insects**

104 How **exoskeletons** work

106 How **metamorphosis** works

108 How **insects** see

110 How **antennae** work

112 How **insects** hear

114 How **wings** work

116 How a **mantis** hunts

118 How **parasites** work

120 How **chemical defences** work

122 How **stingers** work

124 How **camouflage** works

126 How **mimicry** works

128 How **bees** work

130 How **ants** work

132 **Fireflies**

134 How **spiders** work

136 How **spider silk** works

138 How **scorpions** hunt

140 How **millipedes** work

142 How **crabs** work

CONTENTS

FISH

AMPHIBIANS

REPTILES

146 How **fish** work
148 How **fish** swim
150 How **fish senses** work
152 How **fish** reproduce
154 How **fish** care for their young
156 **Salmon migration**
158 How **sharks** work
160 How **fish defences** work
162 How **camouflage** works
164 **Fish school**
166 How **symbiosis** works
168 How **deep-sea fish** work

172 How **amphibians** work
174 How **tadpoles** grow
176 **Frogspawn**
178 How **frogs** move
180 How **frogs** communicate
182 How **defence** works
184 How **salamanders** work
186 How **axolotls** work

190 How **reptiles** work
192 How **scales** work
194 How **snake senses** work
196 How **reptile eggs** work
198 **Marine iguanas**
200 How **crocodiles** hunt
202 How **chameleons** hunt
204 How **chameleons** change colour
206 How **geckos** climb
208 How **tuataras** work
210 How **snakes** move
212 How **snakes** kill
214 How **snakes** eat
216 How **tortoises** work

BIRDS

MAMMALS

HABITATS

220 How **birds** work
222 How **bird skeletons** work
224 Types of **beaks**
226 How **birds** fly
228 How **wings** work
230 How **feathers** work
232 How **hummingbirds** hover
234 **Life on the move**
236 How **birds** migrate
238 How **courtship** works
240 How **nests** work
242 How **eggs** develop
244 How **birds** grow
246 How **cuckoos** work
248 How **owls** sense prey
250 How **eagles** hunt
252 Types of **bird feet**
254 How **ducks** swim
256 How **birds** dive
258 How **penguins** move
260 **Surviving the storm**
262 How **ostriches** work

266 How **mammals** work
268 How **hair** works
270 How **mammal senses** work
272 How **mammals** are born
274 How **mammals** feed their young
276 How **mammals** care for their young
278 How **mammals** grow up
280 How **hierarchy** works
282 How **pack hunting** works
284 **Ocean giants**
286 How **conflict** works
288 How **defence** works
290 How **carnivores** work
292 How **insect eaters** work
294 How **herbivores** work
296 How **rodents** work
298 How **beavers** live
300 Types of **mammal limbs**
302 How **bats** work
304 **Ceiling sleepers**
306 How **mammals** glide
308 How **gibbons** swing
310 How **mammals** burrow
312 How **elephants** work
314 **Land giants**
316 How **whales** work

320 How **biomes** work
322 How **tropical rainforests** work
324 How **temperate forests** work
326 How **boreal forest** works
328 How **tropical grasslands** work
330 How **temperate grasslands** work
332 How **wetlands** work
334 How **mountains** work
336 How **deserts** work
338 How **tundras** work
340 How **polar regions** work
342 How **rivers** and **lakes** work
344 How **oceans** work

346 Glossary
350 Index
358 Acknowledgments

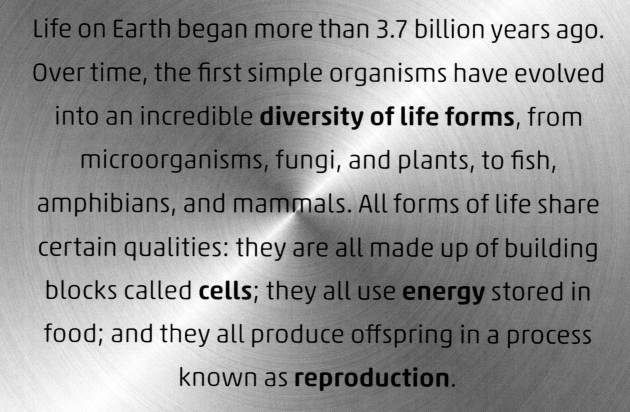

Life on Earth began more than 3.7 billion years ago. Over time, the first simple organisms have evolved into an incredible **diversity of life forms**, from microorganisms, fungi, and plants, to fish, amphibians, and mammals. All forms of life share certain qualities: they are all made up of building blocks called **cells**; they all use **energy** stored in food; and they all produce offspring in a process known as **reproduction**.

THE BASICS

OF LIFE

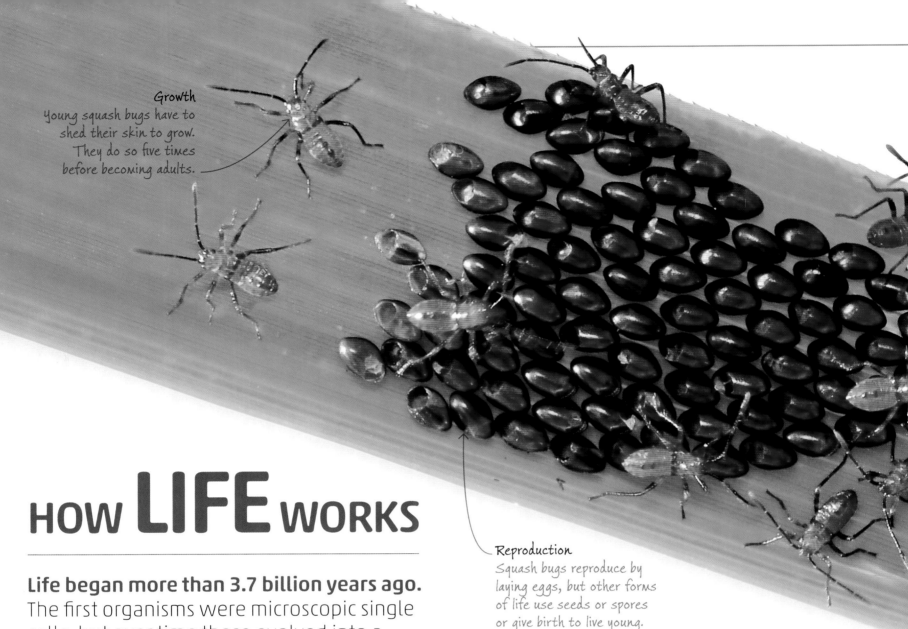

Growth
Young squash bugs have to shed their skin to grow. They do so five times before becoming adults.

Reproduction
Squash bugs reproduce by laying eggs, but other forms of life use seeds or spores or give birth to live young.

HOW **LIFE** WORKS

Life began more than 3.7 billion years ago. The first organisms were microscopic single cells, but over time these evolved into a great diversity of different forms of life. Today, living things range from bacteria so tiny that a million could fit on a pinhead, to the 150 tonne blue whale – the largest animal known to have lived. All these living things share certain key characteristics that set them apart from non-living things.

▲ CHARACTERISTICS OF LIFE
From the moment they hatch out of their eggs, squash bugs can move, sense their surroundings, feed, excrete waste, and use oxygen to release energy from food. In time, they will grow large enough to lay eggs of their own. These seven features – movement, sensing, nutrition, excretion, respiration, growth, and reproduction – are the characteristics that all forms of life share.

KINGDOMS OF LIFE
The two million or so different kinds (species) of organism on Earth are divided into seven major groups called kingdoms, such as the plant kingdom and the animal kingdom.

ANIMALS
All animals feed on other organisms. Most have nerves, muscles, and sense organs.

PLANTS
Most plants live on land and use sunlight to make food by a process called photosynthesis.

FUNGI
Mushrooms and toadstools are fungi. Many fungi absorb food from dead organic matter.

ALGAE
Algae use light to make food as plants do, but are simpler in structure and mostly live in water.

Sensing
Like most insects, squash bugs use antennae (feelers) to feel and taste objects.

Respiration
All living things release energy from nutrients, a process that takes place inside their cells.

LIFE AND WATER
The chemical reactions that sustain life take place in water, which makes water essential for all living things. Life probably began in water, perhaps on the sea floor. Some of the oldest fossils are stromatolites – rock-like mounds of bacteria growing in shallow water, like these modern stromatolites in Australia.

Excretion
All living things produce waste chemicals inside their cells. Insects eject their waste from the rear of the body.

Movement
All forms of life can move, though animals move much more quickly than plants. Young squash bugs move by walking, but adults can also fly.

Nutrition
Squash bugs use piercing mouthparts to suck sugary sap from plants.

PROTOZOANS
Members of this kingdom are single-celled but have larger, more complex cells than bacteria.

BACTERIA
These single-celled organisms are the most abundant and widespread organisms on Earth.

ARCHAEA
Archaea resemble bacteria but can survive in more hostile environments, including boiling water.

HOW **REPRODUCTION** WORKS

All forms of life strive to produce offspring. Without this process of reproduction, life would cease to exist. The rate at which different species reproduce varies enormously. A female elephant might have only five calves in her life, but some frogs can produce 20,000 tadpoles each year. Species that reproduce in great numbers face an intense struggle to survive, with only a tiny fraction reaching adulthood. There are two main ways in which living things can reproduce: sexually and asexually.

▶ **SEXUAL REPRODUCTION**
Like all mammals, spiny mice can only reproduce sexually. Sexual reproduction requires two parents, typically a male and a female. They produce special cells, called sex cells, that can combine and grow into a new organism. Sex cells form in a way that ensures every offspring has a unique blend of both parents' genes. As a result, each offspring is slightly different, which improves the chance that some of them will survive.

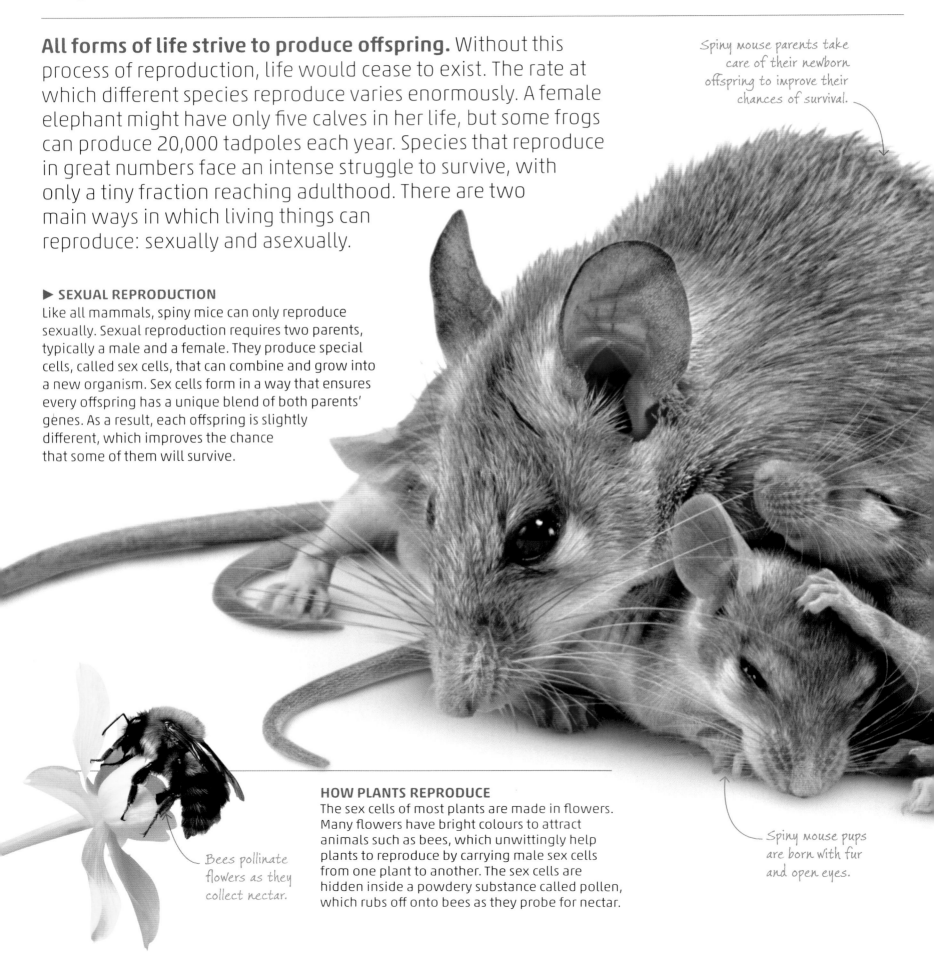

Spiny mouse parents take care of their newborn offspring to improve their chances of survival.

Spiny mouse pups are born with fur and open eyes.

Bees pollinate flowers as they collect nectar.

HOW PLANTS REPRODUCE
The sex cells of most plants are made in flowers. Many flowers have bright colours to attract animals such as bees, which unwittingly help plants to reproduce by carrying male sex cells from one plant to another. The sex cells are hidden inside a powdery substance called pollen, which rubs off onto bees as they probe for nectar.

Mating slugs dangle from a rope of slime.

The slugs' sexual organs entwine and exchange sex cells.

HERMAPHRODITES

Most plants and many kinds of animal do not have separate male and female sexes. Instead they are hermaphrodites, which means that an individual can produce both male and female sex cells. Slugs are hermaphrodites. They mate by writhing around each other while hanging upside down. As they do so, their sexual organs exchange sex cells.

ASEXUAL REPRODUCTION

Asexual reproduction requires only one parent and results in offspring that are genetically identical to the parent. It is faster than sexual reproduction, but all the offspring are equally susceptible to disease or other problems.

PARTHENOGENESIS

Aphids are insects that can give birth without mating, a type of asexual reproduction called parthenogenesis. The babies are born pregnant with babies of their own, allowing aphids to multiply with amazing speed.

FRAGMENTATION

Many plants and some animals can reproduce asexually by breaking into fragments, each of which becomes a new individual. Sponges can survive breaking into thousands of fragments and can even reassemble themselves.

DIVIDING

Sea anemones can reproduce asexually by dividing in two. This form of reproduction is common in microorganisms such as bacteria. Some bacteria can divide every 20 minutes, allowing one cell to give rise to millions of offspring in a single day.

HOW CELLS WORK

Cells are the basic units of life, the building blocks that make up all living things. The smallest organisms consist of just a single cell, but plants and animals consist of trillions. Their cells are not mixed up randomly but are organized like bricks in a wall, forming sheets or blocks called tissue. In turn, different tissues are combined to form organs and whole bodies.

▶ CELLS UNDER THE MICROSCOPE

Most cells are just a few hundredths of a millimetre wide, making them too small to see with the naked eye. However, they become visible when magnified by a microscope, as these pictures show. The cells of *Elodea*, an aquatic plant, are especially easy to see through a microscope because the delicate leaves are very thin.

LEAF TIP
Viewed at x40 magnification, the cells in the tip of one leaf become visible. The cells are arranged in rows like bricks to form sheets of tissue.

Cells

Elodea's leaves are thin and delicate because they are supported by water.

X40 MAGNIFICATION

LEAVES
A leaf is one of the organs that makes up a plant. Its job is to capture the energy in sunlight and store this energy in food molecules such as glucose (a process called photosynthesis).

INSIDE A CELL

All cells have an outer membrane that controls what can enter and leave the cell. The control centre of a cell is its nucleus, which holds all the instructions needed to operate a cell encoded in molecules of DNA. Cells are powered by energy released from small bodies called mitochondria. Many plant cells also contain chloroplasts, which absorb energy from the Sun and store it. Unlike animal cells, they also have a rigid outer cell wall and a central, fluid-filled vacuole, both of which help maintain their more rectangular shape.

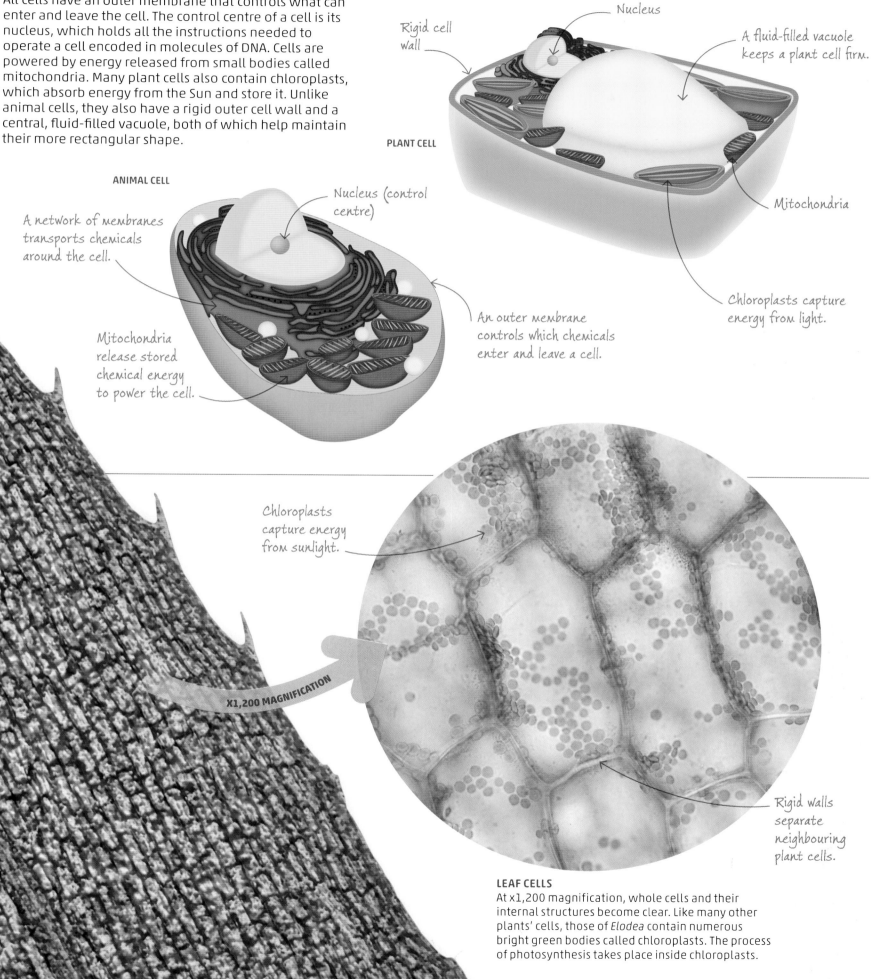

Rigid cell wall

Nucleus

A fluid-filled vacuole keeps a plant cell firm.

PLANT CELL

Mitochondria

Chloroplasts capture energy from light.

ANIMAL CELL

A network of membranes transports chemicals around the cell.

Nucleus (control centre)

Mitochondria release stored chemical energy to power the cell.

An outer membrane controls which chemicals enter and leave a cell.

Chloroplasts capture energy from sunlight.

X1,200 MAGNIFICATION

Rigid walls separate neighbouring plant cells.

LEAF CELLS

At x1,200 magnification, whole cells and their internal structures become clear. Like many other plants' cells, those of *Elodea* contain numerous bright green bodies called chloroplasts. The process of photosynthesis takes place inside chloroplasts.

HOW DNA WORKS

All forms of life on Earth are based on the molecule DNA (deoxyribonucleic acid). DNA has the unusual ability to store information in the form of a chemical code. This code carries all the instructions needed by cells to build and maintain a living organism. At least one complete copy of this information is found in nearly every cell of an animal's or plant's body.

The two strands coil around each other to form a shape called a double helix.

The backbone of each strand is a chain of simple sugars (black) joined by phosphate groups (grey).

A normal hedgehog's spines are brown because they contain melanin.

Albinos have pink eyes because their eyes lack pigment, which makes the colour of blood visible.

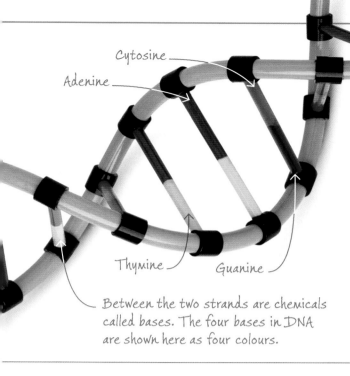

Cytosine

Adenine

Thymine   Guanine

Between the two strands are chemicals called bases. The four bases in DNA are shown here as four colours.

THE DNA MOLECULE

The DNA molecule consists of two long strands winding around each other. Connecting the strands like the rungs of a ladder are chemical groups called bases, with two bases forming each rung. There are four different bases in DNA, and each one always pairs with the same partner (adenine with thymine, cytosine with guanine). The sequence of bases running along the length of the molecule forms a four-letter code that carries genetic information.

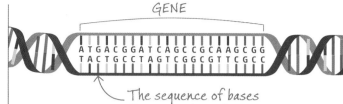

GENE

A T G A C G G A T C A G C C G C A A G C G G
T A C T G C C T A G T C G G C G T T C G C C

The sequence of bases forms a code made up of four letters.

GENES

A gene is a length of DNA that codes for a particular job. The smallest genes are just a few dozen base pairs long; the longest contain millions of base pairs. Most genes carry instructions that tell cells how to build molecules called proteins. Proteins, in turn, control the chemical reactions that take place inside cells. Some genes act as controllers, switching other genes on or off.

Albino hedgehogs have white spines because their bodies can't make the dark pigment melanin.

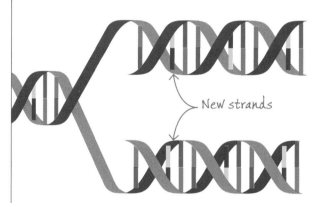

New strands

MAKING COPIES

Unlike any other kind of molecule, DNA can make copies of itself. It splits down the middle to form single strands, and each serves as a template for a new matching strand. Because each base always pairs with the same partner, the two new DNA molecules are identical. This ability to self-replicate makes it possible for organisms to reproduce and pass on copies of their genes to offspring. The very first form of life on Earth was probably based on a self-replicating molecule much like DNA.

◀ CODING ERRORS

Sometimes errors creep into the code carried by DNA. These errors are called mutations. Most do no harm, but if a mutation happens in a sex cell, it affects every cell in the body of a baby derived from that sex cell, sometimes with drastic results. For example, a mutation in a gene that helps make melanin (the dark pigment that gives animal skin its colour) can change an animal's colour. If the mutation stops this gene working, the animal has no body pigment and is born white with pink eyes – an albino.

HOW EVOLUTION WORKS

The animals and plants that lived millions of years ago were different from those alive today. Over time, species change as they adapt to the world – a process known as evolution. Most of the species that have ever lived on Earth are now extinct, but a small fraction left traces of their existence as fossils. These prehistoric remains provide a window into the past, allowing us to see the dramatic changes evolution has caused over time.

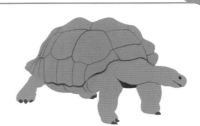

SHORT NECK
On lush Isabel Island, which has lots of grass, tortoises have short necks to feed on the grass.

LONG NECK
On Hood Island, which is drier and has little grass, tortoises have long necks to feed on bushes.

NATURAL SELECTION
When animals and plants reproduce, all their offspring are slightly different, just like the children in a human family. Because they vary, some of these offspring are better able to survive and pass on their useful characteristics to the next generation. This process is known as natural selection. Over many generations, it causes a species to adapt. On the Galapagos Islands, for instance, tortoises evolved longer necks on the drier islands where they could only find food by reaching up into bushes.

▶ ELEPHANT EVOLUTION
Fossils reveal that it took 60 million years for elephants to evolve their long trunks and tusks. Today's elephants are the last surviving members of a family known as the trunked mammals. The earliest trunked mammals had mobile snouts for handling soft plants. Over time, as their bodies grew larger, their teeth evolved into tusks and their trunks became longer, which allowed them to reach all kinds of plant foods from grasses to treetop foliage.

Shaggy fur protected woolly mammoths from the bitter cold of the Ice Age.

Unlike modern elephants, Deinotherium had tusks in its lower jaw.

Thick, column-like legs for supporting weight.

MOERITHERIUM
Early trunked mammals were no bigger than pigs. They had mobile upper lips that may have been used to grasp soft plants.

DEINOTHERIUM
Deinotherium had a short trunk and downward-pointing tusks. How it used them is unknown - perhaps they were weapons or digging tools.

GOMPHOTHERIUM
This short-trunked elephant had a set of tusks in both the upper and lower jaws.

WOOLLY MAMMOTH
These prehistoric elephants survived until a few thousand years ago. Their trunks ended in two "fingers" for plucking grass.

STEPPE MAMMOTH
Twice as big as modern elephants, the steppe mammoth roamed across cold open grasslands.

ARTIFICIAL SELECTION

Over centuries, people have changed domestic plant and animal species by breeding them and selecting certain offspring in each generation. This artificial selection works just like natural selection but is faster. The wild cabbage plant, for example, has given rise to at least six different vegetable crops since it was first harvested. Farmers who kept choosing the fattest flower buds created cauliflowers; those who chose the crinkliest leaves created kale; and so on. All these different crops originally came from the same plant species.

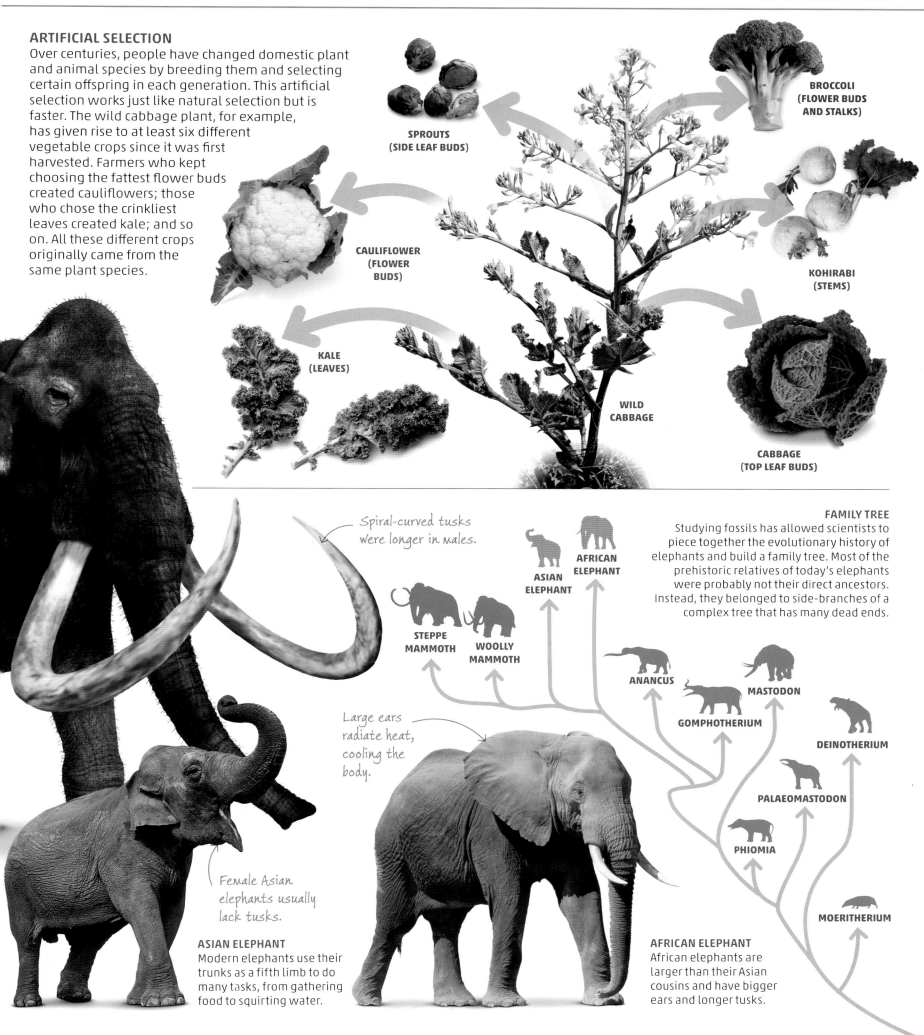

SPROUTS (SIDE LEAF BUDS)

BROCCOLI (FLOWER BUDS AND STALKS)

CAULIFLOWER (FLOWER BUDS)

KOHlRABI (STEMS)

KALE (LEAVES)

WILD CABBAGE

CABBAGE (TOP LEAF BUDS)

Spiral-curved tusks were longer in males.

FAMILY TREE

Studying fossils has allowed scientists to piece together the evolutionary history of elephants and build a family tree. Most of the prehistoric relatives of today's elephants were probably not their direct ancestors. Instead, they belonged to side-branches of a complex tree that has many dead ends.

ASIAN ELEPHANT

AFRICAN ELEPHANT

STEPPE MAMMOTH

WOOLLY MAMMOTH

ANANCUS

MASTODON

GOMPHOTHERIUM

DEINOTHERIUM

PALAEOMASTODON

PHIOMIA

MOERITHERIUM

Large ears radiate heat, cooling the body.

Female Asian elephants usually lack tusks.

ASIAN ELEPHANT

Modern elephants use their trunks as a fifth limb to do many tasks, from gathering food to squirting water.

AFRICAN ELEPHANT

African elephants are larger than their Asian cousins and have bigger ears and longer tusks.

HOW CLASSIFICATION WORKS

A particular kind of organism, such as a giraffe or a cheetah, is called a species. There are nearly 2 million known species on Earth and there are probably many more waiting to be discovered. All known species are given a scientific name that shows how they are classified in the tree of life – the family tree of all life on Earth.

▶ TREE OF LIFE

The modern system of classification is based on evolution, with species arranged in groups that evolved from a common ancestor. The tree shown here includes just a selection of the groups that make up the complete tree of life.

SCIENTIFIC NAMES

Every species has a two-part Latin name, such as *Vulpes lagopus*, the Arctic fox. The second word is unique to the species. The first is its genus – the group that includes the closest relatives. The genus *Vulpes*, for example, has over ten fox species. Every genus belongs to a succession of higher groups. *Vulpes*, for instance, is a member of the dog and fox family, the carnivore order, and the mammals class.

MAMMALS

There are more than 20 orders of living mammal, including the egg-laying monotremes, the pouched marsupials, and the (mostly) flesh-eating carnivores. All mammals share key features inherited from their common ancestor, such as the production of milk to feed their young.

SPECIES

GENUS

FAMILY

ORDER

CLASS

PHYLUM

KINGDOM

SPECIES *Vulpes vulpes* (Red Fox)

SPECIES *Vulpes lagopus* (Arctic Fox)

GENUS CANIS, DOGS

GENUS VULPES, FOXES

FAMILY DOGS AND FOXS

ORDER CARNIVORES

ORDER PRIMATES

ORDER RODENTS

ORDER BATS

ORDER DEER AND CATTLE

ORDER MARSUPIALS

ORDER MONOTREMES

CLASS MAMMALS

ORDER FROGS AND TOADS

ORDER SALAMANDERS AND NEWTS

CLASS AMPHIBIANS

ORDER WADERS AND GULLS

ORDER DUCKS AND GEESE

ORDER RAPTORS

ORDER OWLS

ORDER PASSERINES

CLASS BIRDS

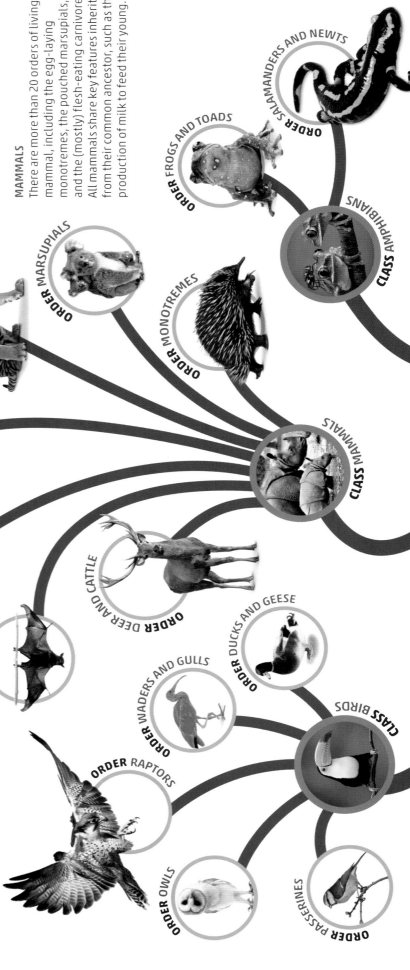

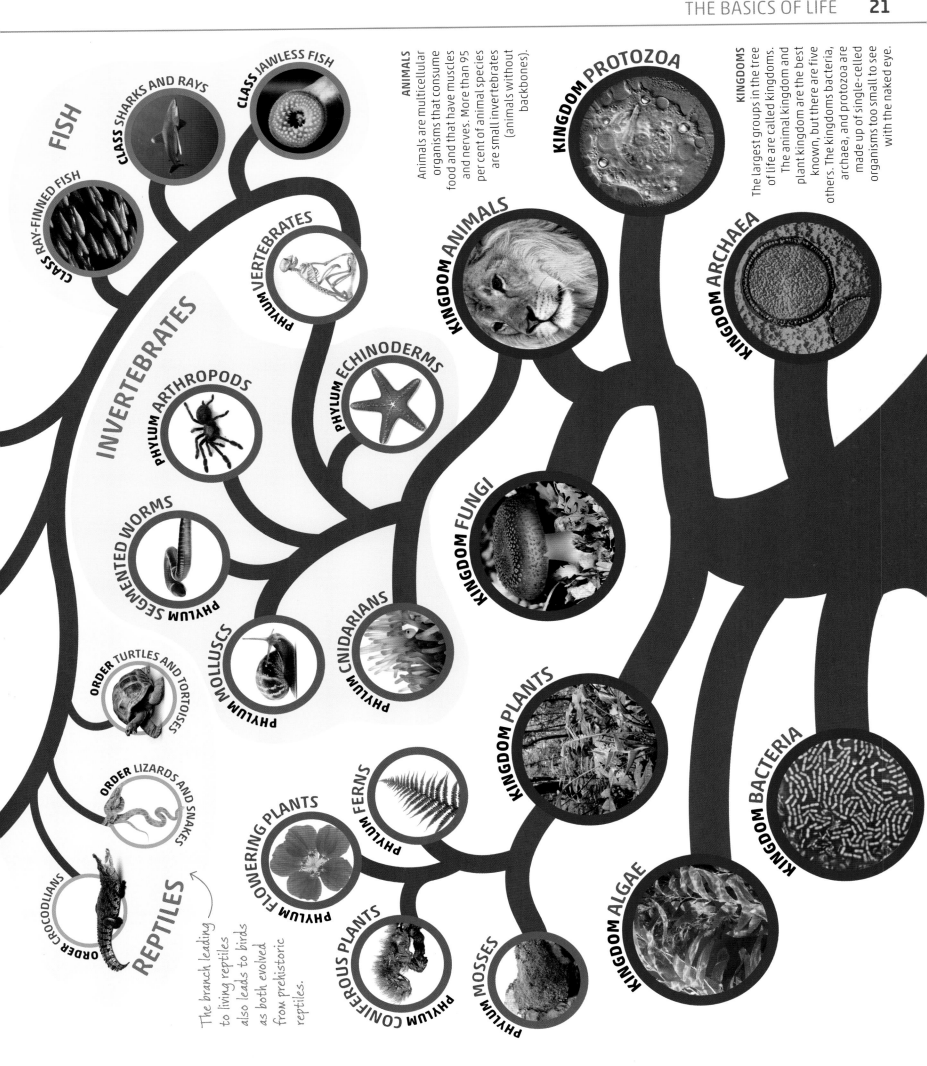

FISH

CLASS RAY-FINNED FISH

CLASS SHARKS AND RAYS

CLASS JAWLESS FISH

INVERTEBRATES

PHYLUM VERTEBRATES

PHYLUM ARTHROPODS

PHYLUM ECHINODERMS

PHYLUM SEGMENTED WORMS

ORDER TURTLES AND TORTOISES

PHYLUM MOLLUSCS

PHYLUM CNIDARIANS

ORDER LIZARDS AND SNAKES

ORDER CROCODILIANS

REPTILES

The branch leading to living reptiles also leads to birds as both evolved from prehistoric reptiles.

PHYLUM FLOWERING PLANTS

PHYLUM FERNS

PHYLUM CONIFEROUS PLANTS

PHYLUM MOSSES

KINGDOM ANIMALS

KINGDOM FUNGI

KINGDOM PLANTS

KINGDOM ALGAE

KINGDOM PROTOZOA

KINGDOM ARCHAEA

KINGDOM BACTERIA

ANIMALS
Animals are multicellular organisms that consume food and that have muscles and nerves. More than 95 per cent of animal species are small invertebrates (animals without backbones).

KINGDOMS
The largest groups in the tree of life are called kingdoms. The animal kingdom and plant kingdom are the best known, but there are five others. The kingdoms bacteria, archaea, and protozoa are made up of single-celled organisms too small to see with the naked eye.

Most of the **living things** that we see around us are animals and plants, but there are many more organisms that don't fit into these categories. Some are so tiny that we can't see them without magnification. These **microorganisms** live nearly everywhere, but only become visible under a microscope. Other organisms, called **fungi**, grow from the ground as **mushrooms**. They resemble plants, but are more closely related to animals.

MICROORGANISMS

AND FUNGI

HOW MICROORGANISMS WORK

Some organisms are so small that you need a microscope to see them. Called microorganisms, these tiny forms of life abound in every habitat on the planet. A speck of soil or a droplet of pond water can contain thousands of them. Most microorganisms consist of just a single cell. Although they lack brains, sense organs, and limbs, they can nevertheless move about, respond to their environment, and prey on each other.

Swallowed prey is trapped in bubbles called food vacuoles, where it is digested.

▶ MICROSCOPIC PREDATOR
Half the width of a human hair, *Euplotes* is a single-celled predator that inhabits freshwater habitats such as ponds. Its prey – smaller microorganisms such as algae – are visible as green patches inside it. They are swallowed by a large, funnel-shaped throat and digested alive.

Euplotes swallows prey by wafting them into its throat with a ring of beating bristles.

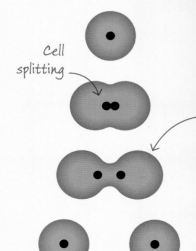

Cell splitting

Daughter cell

REPRODUCTION
Single-celled organisms such as *Euplotes* can reproduce by simply dividing in two, producing two new cells called daughters. This allows them to multiply quickly, doubling in number with each generation if conditions are ideal.

Most of the cell is filled with a fluid substance called cytoplasm.

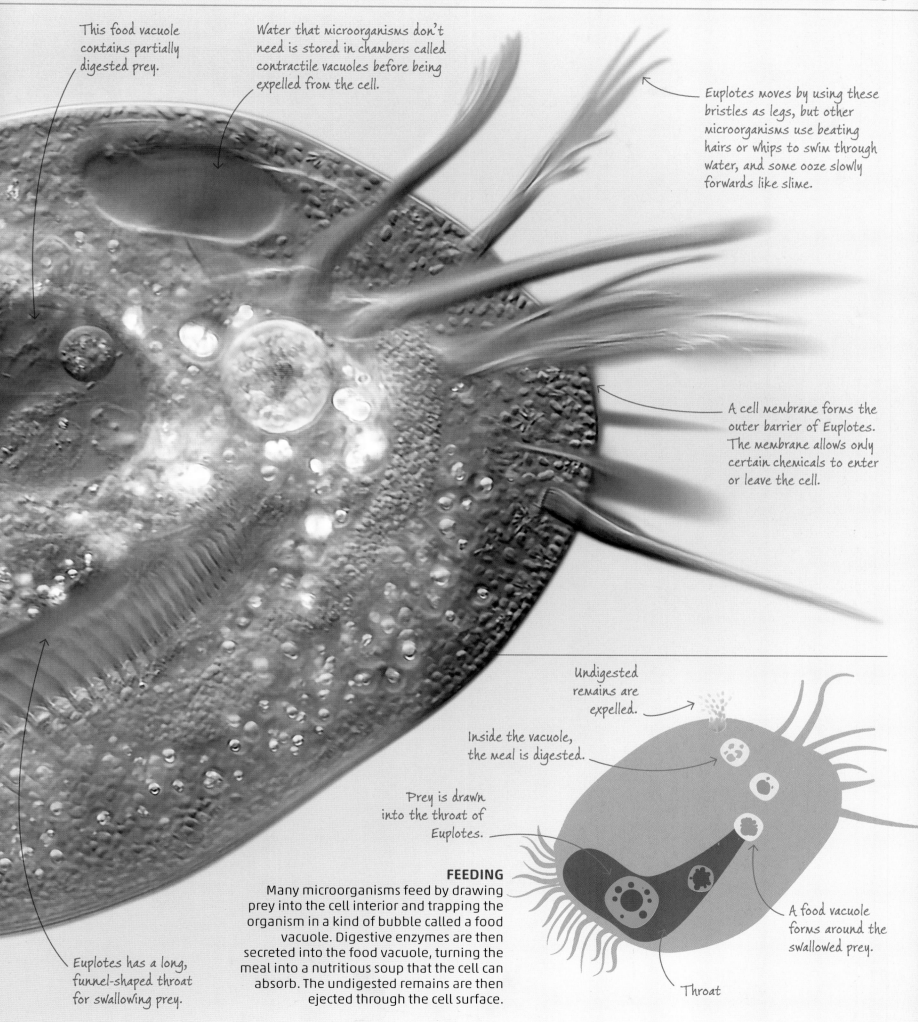

This food vacuole contains partially digested prey.

Water that microorganisms don't need is stored in chambers called contractile vacuoles before being expelled from the cell.

Euplotes moves by using these bristles as legs, but other microorganisms use beating hairs or whips to swim through water, and some ooze slowly forwards like slime.

A cell membrane forms the outer barrier of Euplotes. The membrane allows only certain chemicals to enter or leave the cell.

Euplotes has a long, funnel-shaped throat for swallowing prey.

Undigested remains are expelled.

Inside the vacuole, the meal is digested.

Prey is drawn into the throat of Euplotes.

FEEDING
Many microorganisms feed by drawing prey into the cell interior and trapping the organism in a kind of bubble called a food vacuole. Digestive enzymes are then secreted into the food vacuole, turning the meal into a nutritious soup that the cell can absorb. The undigested remains are then ejected through the cell surface.

A food vacuole forms around the swallowed prey.

Throat

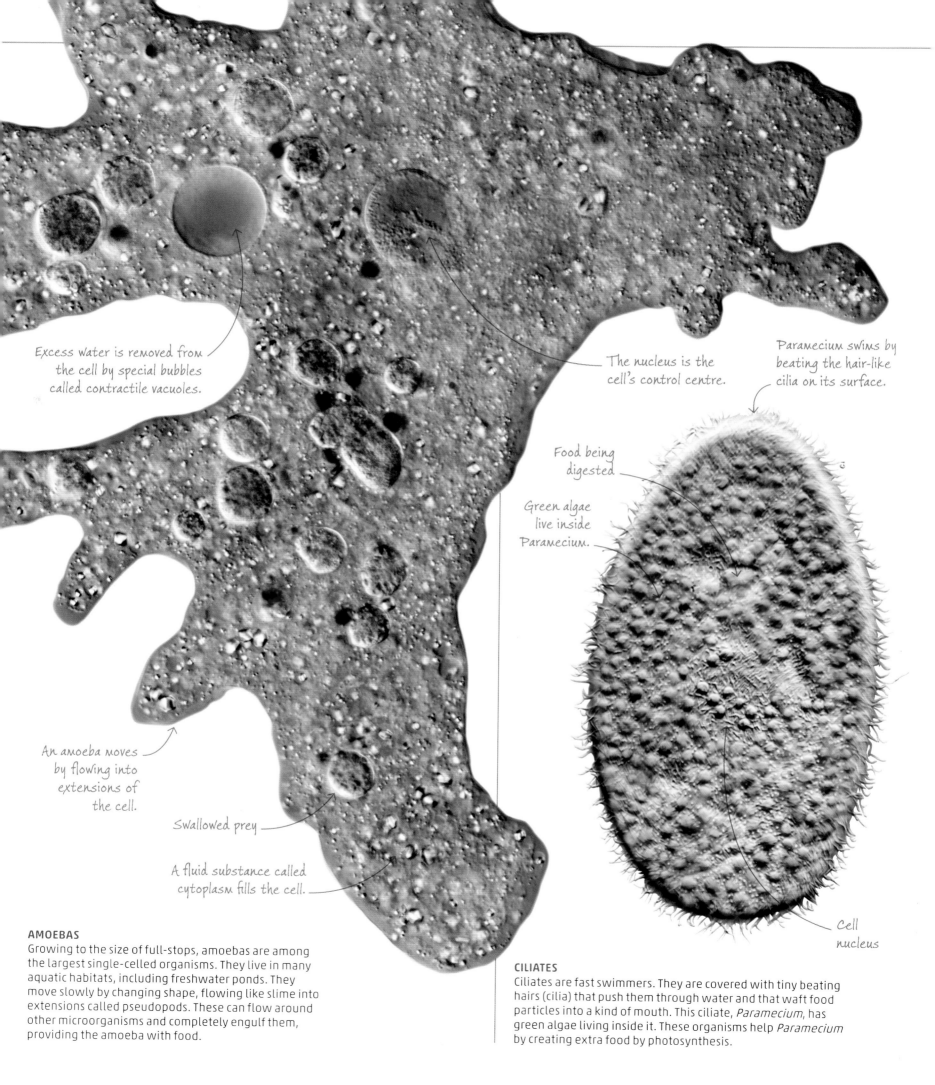

Excess water is removed from the cell by special bubbles called contractile vacuoles.

The nucleus is the cell's control centre.

Paramecium swims by beating the hair-like cilia on its surface.

Food being digested

Green algae live inside Paramecium.

An amoeba moves by flowing into extensions of the cell.

Swallowed prey

A fluid substance called cytoplasm fills the cell.

Cell nucleus

AMOEBAS

Growing to the size of full-stops, amoebas are among the largest single-celled organisms. They live in many aquatic habitats, including freshwater ponds. They move slowly by changing shape, flowing like slime into extensions called pseudopods. These can flow around other microorganisms and completely engulf them, providing the amoeba with food.

CILIATES

Ciliates are fast swimmers. They are covered with tiny beating hairs (cilia) that push them through water and that waft food particles into a kind of mouth. This ciliate, *Paramecium*, has green algae living inside it. These organisms help *Paramecium* by creating extra food by photosynthesis.

TYPES OF
SINGLE-CELLED LIFE

Most of the living things that we see around us are plants and animals, each made up of millions of microscopic cells. But these multicellular organisms are hugely outnumbered by living things that consist of just one cell each. These single-celled organisms flourish wherever water and nutrients are to be found, from puddles and ponds to the oceans and even inside the human body. To make them visible to the eye, the examples on these pages are all shown at about 700 times their actual size.

MAGNIFICATION x 5,000

MAGNIFICATION x 700

YEASTS
Yeasts are single-celled fungi that feed on sugars and are found on many fruits. Bakers use yeast to make bread. Baking yeast feeds on the sugar in flour and produces bubbles of carbon dioxide, making dough rise.

MAGNIFICATION x 3,000

MAGNIFICATION x 700

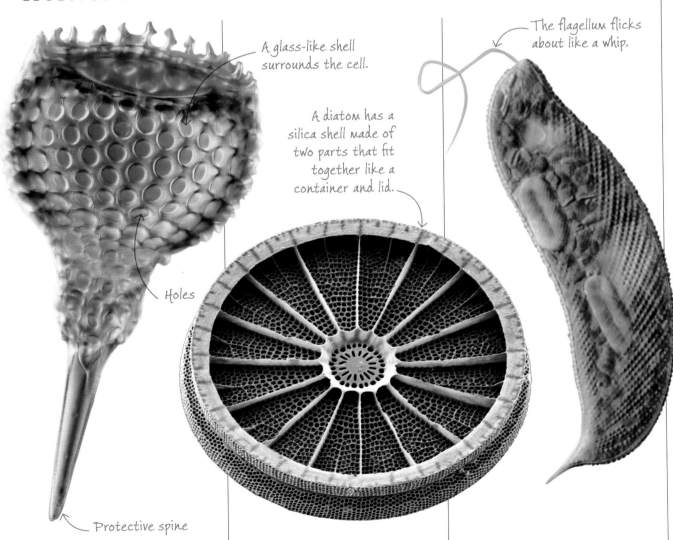

A glass-like shell surrounds the cell.

A diatom has a silica shell made of two parts that fit together like a container and lid.

The flagellum flicks about like a whip.

Holes

Protective spine

RADIOLARIANS
Spiky shells of silica (the mineral used to make glass) protect these sea-dwelling microorganisms. Like amoebas they use pseudopods to feed, reaching through holes in the shell to capture prey.

DIATOMS
About a third of the oxygen in Earth's atmosphere comes from diatoms – microscopic algae that live floating in oceans and lakes. Like plants, they use the energy of sunlight to make their own food.

FLAGELLATES
These microorganisms swim by lashing whip-like structures called flagella. This one, *Euglena*, can use sunlight to make food as plants do, but it also eats other organisms.

BACTERIA
Found nearly everywhere, these simple organisms have existed on Earth for billions of years longer than most other forms of life. Some cause diseases, but most bacteria play a vital role in life on Earth. The one shown here, *Lactobacillus*, turns milk into yogurt.

HOW GERMS WORK

Trillions of microorganisms live on and inside the human body. The majority are harmless or helpful, but some can make people ill. Harmful microorganisms, which include certain bacteria and fungi, are known as germs or pathogens. Viruses are germs that are so small and simple that they aren't considered to be living organisms.

BACILLUS MYCOIDES
Soil bacteria such as this species can easily get onto dirty hands. Certain types of *Bacillus* can also multiply in food. If swallowed with undercooked food, they can cause an illness called food poisoning.

BODY DEFENCES
Germs are infectious, which means they can pass from one person to another. The human body has many ways of defending itself from germs.

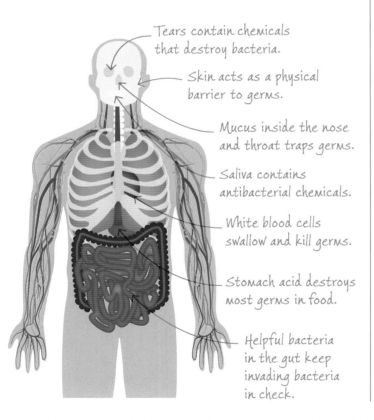

Tears contain chemicals that destroy bacteria.

Skin acts as a physical barrier to germs.

Mucus inside the nose and throat traps germs.

Saliva contains antibacterial chemicals.

White blood cells swallow and kill germs.

Stomach acid destroys most germs in food.

Helpful bacteria in the gut keep invading bacteria in check.

▶ SKIN FLORA
Every spot in this picture is a colony of thousands of microorganisms grown in a lab from a person's hand print. Each colony grew from one cell. Around 1,000 bacteria species and more than 60 fungus species live on human skin, feeding on dead skin cells, grease, and sweat. Normally harmless, they become harmful if they enter a wound and multiply, causing an infection. Our skin also occasionally plays host to more dangerous microorganisms picked up from things we touch.

Rapidly dividing microorganisms form the largest colonies.

STAPHYLOCOCCUS PASTEURI
Staphylococcus bacteria are among the most common microorganisms that live naturally on human skin. This species is normally harmless.

VIRUSES
Unlike bacteria or fungi, these tiny germs are not made of cells and consist of little more than a package of genetic material inside a protective coat. To reproduce, viruses invade and hijack living cells. The common cold virus infects the cells in the human airways, spreading itself by making us sneeze. Bacteriophages are viruses that attack bacteria.

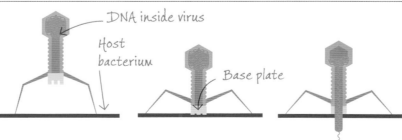

DNA inside virus

Host bacterium

Base plate

1 CONTACT
Bacteriophages identify suitable target cells by making contact with their tail fibres.

2 ATTACHMENT
The tail fibres flex, fixing the virus's base plate to the cell membrane.

3 INJECTION
The virus injects DNA into the cell. The DNA takes over the cell, causing it to make new copies of the virus.

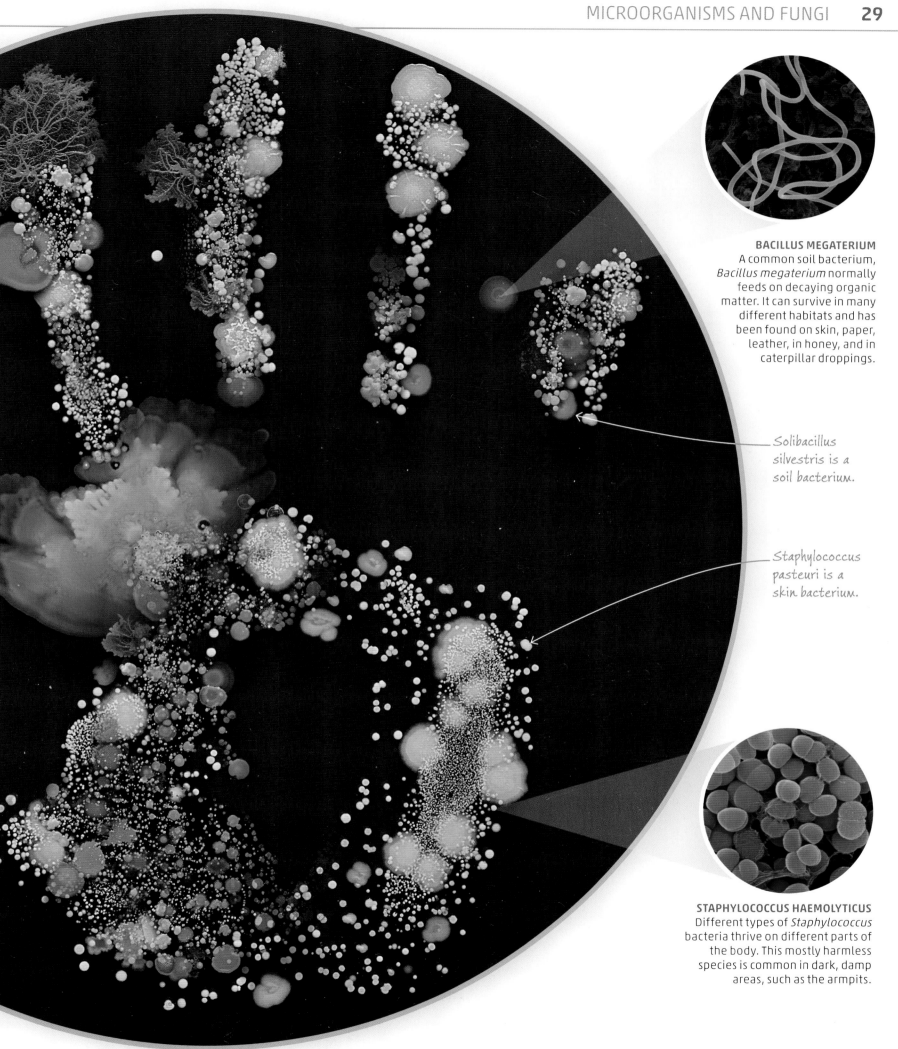

BACILLUS MEGATERIUM
A common soil bacterium, *Bacillus megaterium* normally feeds on decaying organic matter. It can survive in many different habitats and has been found on skin, paper, leather, in honey, and in caterpillar droppings.

Solibacillus silvestris is a soil bacterium.

Staphylococcus pasteuri is a skin bacterium.

STAPHYLOCOCCUS HAEMOLYTICUS
Different types of *Staphylococcus* bacteria thrive on different parts of the body. This mostly harmless species is common in dark, damp areas, such as the armpits.

TYPES OF ALGAE

There are many different types of algae, ranging from single-celled organisms to giant kelp, which forms undersea forests. Algae do not form a single related family, and their evolutionary history is complicated. As a result, they are often classified simply by colour.

SOME RED ALGAE CAN GROW IN ICE AND SNOW.

BROWN ALGAE INCLUDE MANY SEAWEEDS, SUCH AS KELP.

The chloroplast captures light energy.

The nucleus is a cell's control centre.

A layer of protective slime (mucilage) covers the cell wall.

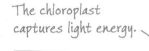

Cytoplasm

A vacuole stores water.

▼ SPIROGYRA

Some freshwater algae, such as *Spirogyra*, grow as fine threads. Such algae can look and feel like slime, but a view through a microscope reveals the beauty of their inner workings. *Spirogyra* gets its name from the single large chloroplast coiled tightly inside each cell. The chloroplast is packed with a green pigment called chlorophyll, which captures the Sun's energy so the cells can create food.

INSIDE THE CELLS

Threads of *Spirogyra* are a single cell wide. The cells of green algae such as *Spirogyra* resemble plant cells, with a cell wall, chloroplasts, and a water storage area (vacuole). However, *Spirogyra*'s nucleus is suspended in the cell centre by threads of cytoplasm, and the chloroplast has a distinctive shape not seen in land plants.

A cell wall surrounds each cell.

GREEN ALGAE GROW IN THE DAMP FUR OF SLOTHS.

Sloths hang from branches, using their hands as hooks.

The sloth's fur is stained green by algae.

A spiral-shaped chloroplast fills each cell of the alga Spirogyra.

HOW ALGAE WORK

BLANKET WEED
Filamentous algae such as *Spirogyra* are made of fine strands. Also called blanket weed, such algae can smother ponds and rivers if the water is rich in nutrients and brightly lit by the Sun.

Leave a glass of water by a window for a few weeks and it will slowly turn green as algae appear inside it. Algae are simple, plant-like organisms that flourish wherever there is water and light. Like true plants, they can harness the energy in sunlight, but they lack stems, leaves, and roots, and many are microscopic. Algae live in almost every sunlit habitat on Earth and produce more oxygen than all the world's trees combined.

MARINE ALGAE

When disturbed by movement, certain marine algae emit a shimmering blue light, a defensive tactic that can startle small animals. The display, known as bioluminescence, is occasionally triggered by waves, as on this beach in southern Australia. Microscopic algae form the base of the whole marine food chain, supporting all forms of sea life from coral organisms to blue whales. They are essential to life on land too, producing more than half the oxygen in the atmosphere and so making Earth's air breathable.

HOW MUSHROOMS WORK

Mushrooms are not plants but members of another kingdom of life, called fungi. Most fungi feed on decaying organic matter, such as soil, rotting wood, or dead animals. Hidden from view most of the time, they grow into their food as a network of threads and may only become visible when they reproduce. Many fungi reproduce by releasing millions of tiny particles called spores from "fruiting bodies" – the mushrooms we see emerging from the ground.

▼ FLY AGARIC

The distinctive red and white pattern of the fly agaric makes it one of the easiest mushrooms to recognize. Its bright colours may be a warning to animals that it is poisonous. It grows in woodlands throughout the northern hemisphere.

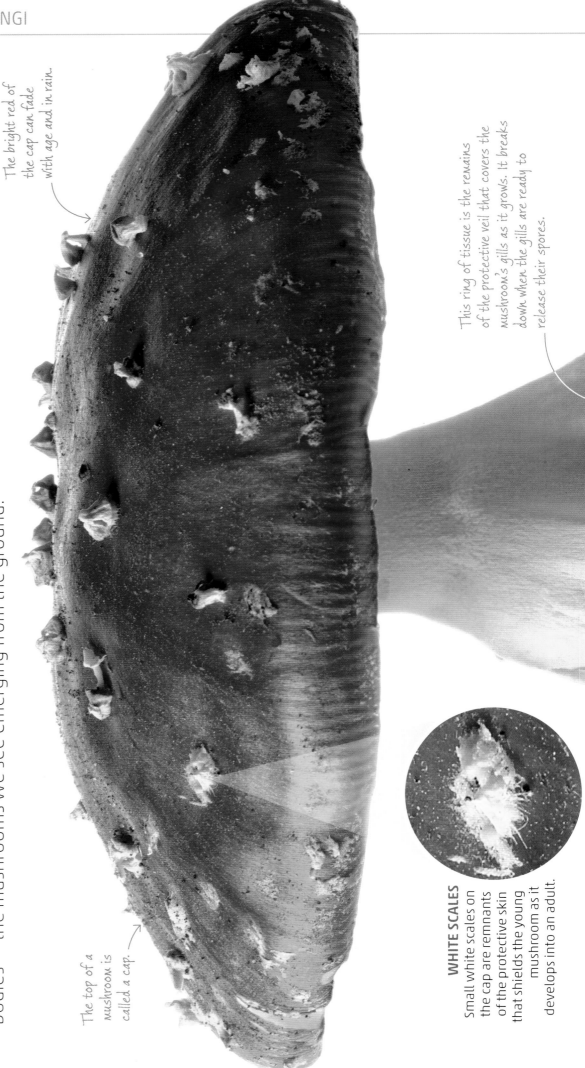

The bright red of the cap can fade with age and in rain.

This ring of tissue is the remains of the protective veil that covers the mushroom's gills as it grows. It breaks down when the gills are ready to release their spores.

The top of a mushroom is called a cap.

WHITE SCALES
Small white scales on the cap are remnants of the protective skin that shields the young mushroom as it develops into an adult.

FUNGI LIFE CYCLE

When spores land they grow into tiny threads called hyphae. Hyphae of opposite types fuse and form a network called a mycelium, from which mushrooms eventually grow.

1 SPORES LAND
The spores land in the ground and germinate.

2 HYPHAE COMBINE
The hyphae of two fungi fuse together to form a new fungus.

3 FUNGUS GROWS
The new fungus grows, bunching into knots.

4 MUSHROOM EMERGES
A young mushroom grows from a knot.

5 MUSHROOM MATURES
The mushroom grows into an adult.

6 SPORES SCATTER
The mushroom ripens and spores are released.

SPORE PRODUCERS

On the underside of the cap are hundreds of thin flaps called gills. These produce spores, microscopic seed-like units, that drop when the mushroom is ripe.

SPORES seen through a microscope

HIDDEN NETWORK

The mycelium is the main body of a fungus and is made up of thread-like structures called hyphae. It releases chemicals called enzymes to break down soil and other matter into food, which the fungus can then absorb. The hyphae are so small that they are invisible to the naked eye. If all the hyphae found in one teaspoon of soil were laid out, they could stretch to a distance of 5 km (3 miles).

Gills

Stem

Mycelium

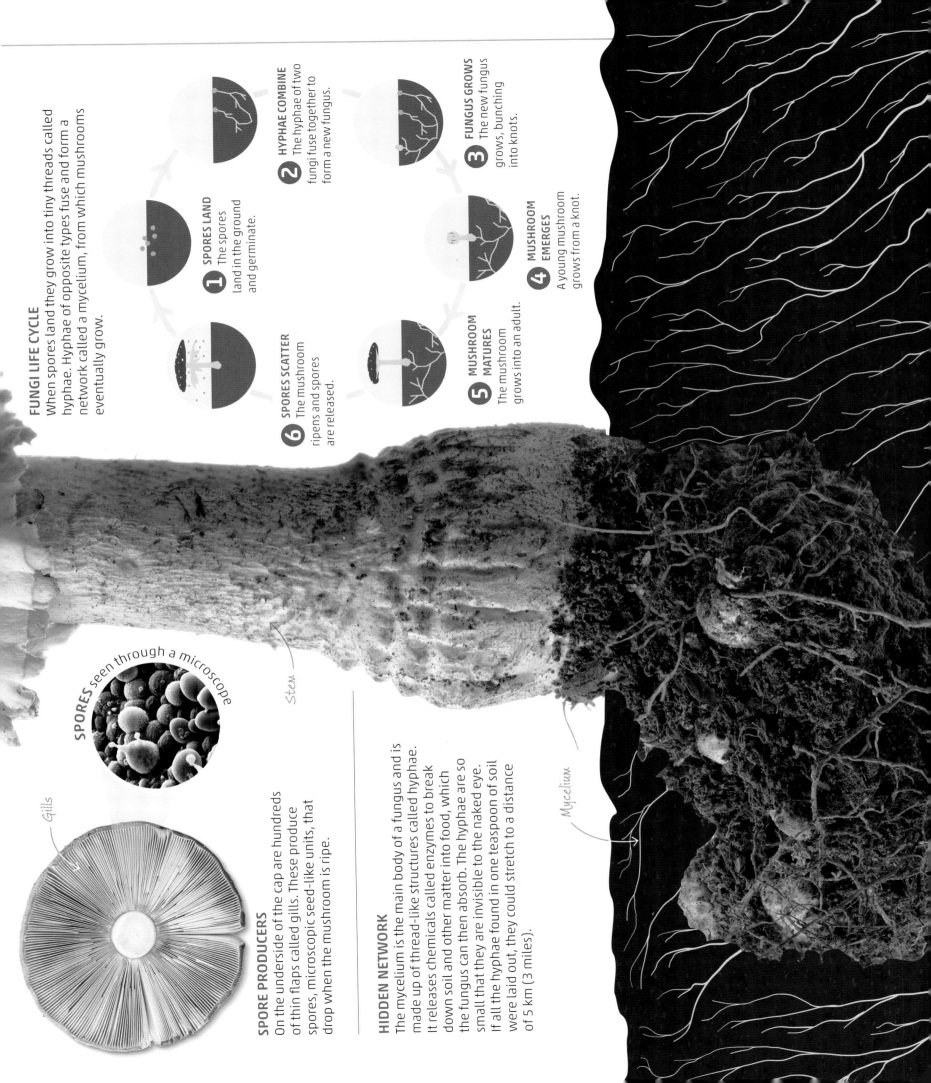

TYPES OF
MUSHROOMS

All fungi reproduce by making spores – microscopic single cells that can develop into new fungi. Spores are produced by the fruiting bodies of fungi – the structures we call mushrooms or toadstools. These take many forms and work in different ways.

Spores shoot out at high speed.

Spore tube

HARE'S EAR

The spores develop in thousands of small tubes that end in tiny pores.

Spores are expelled in a cloud.

Spores develop inside tubes in the cap.

A hole opens up as the outer surface peels away.

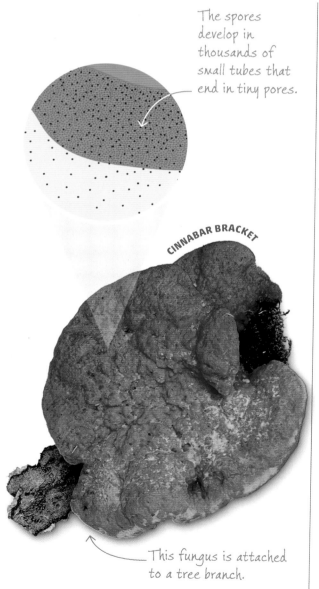

CINNABAR BRACKET

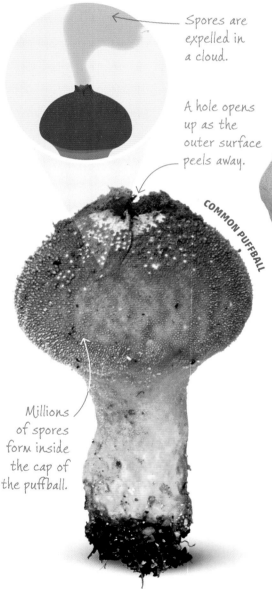

COMMON PUFFBALL

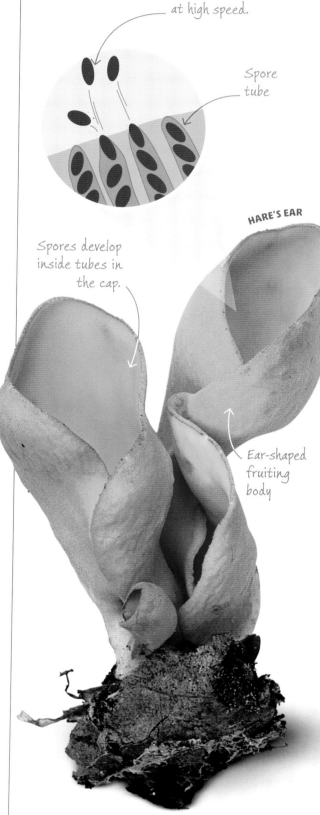

Ear-shaped fruiting body

Millions of spores form inside the cap of the puffball.

This fungus is attached to a tree branch.

CINNABAR BRACKET FUNGUS
The vividly coloured fruiting body of cinnabar bracket fungus grows on trees such as rowan, birch, or cherry. Its spores develop inside tiny tubes on its underside. When ripe, the spores fall out and are carried away on the wind.

PUFFBALL MUSHROOM
The common puffball mushroom occurs almost worldwide. Spores form inside the cap, which becomes papery thin as it ripens. When it is touched, or even struck by a raindrop, a cloud of spores puffs out of the hole in its top.

HARE'S EAR FUNGUS
Found in oak or beech woodlands, this fungus often grows near footpaths. It is named for its resemblance to the ears of a hare. Its spores grow in tubes called asci, which shoot spores out of the fruiting body with immense power.

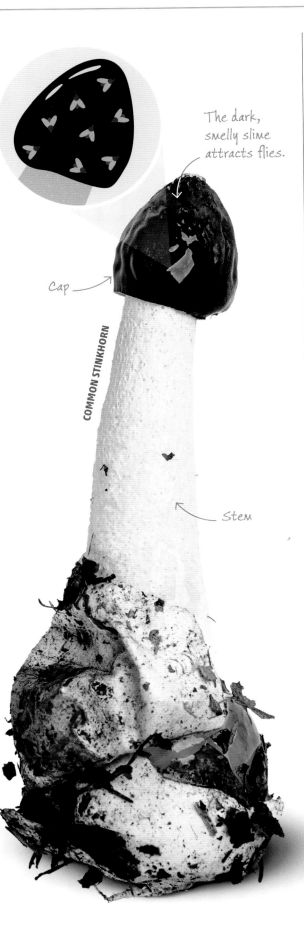

The dark, smelly slime attracts flies.

Cap

COMMON STINKHORN

Stem

The gills are arranged like the spokes of a wheel.

Millions of spores drop from the gills to be carried by the wind.

VELVET SHANK MUSHROOM

This mushroom grows in clusters on rotting wood. Its spores develop on the surfaces of its papery gills, which together form a very large area. When the ripe spores fall out they drift far and wide on the breeze.

VELVET SHANK

STINKHORN MUSHROOM

This common woodland fungus grows on the ground. Its cap is coated in slime that contains spores. The slime has a vile smell of rotting meat that is irresistible to hungry flies. Flies eat it and carry the spores away with them.

A weatherproof cap keeps the spores dry.

Mucor mould forms a fluffy surface.

Sepal

HOW MOULD WORKS

The fluffy growth that appears on rotting food is caused by fungi called moulds. Most kinds of mould feed on dead and decaying plants or animals, helping to recycle their nutrients, but others attack living organisms. Moulds spread by producing millions of spores so tiny that they float everywhere in the air.

◄ MOULD ON STRAWBERRY
The common mould *Mucor* grows quickly on fruit, bread, and other foods. The *Mucor* on this strawberry has been growing for 12 days in cool conditions.

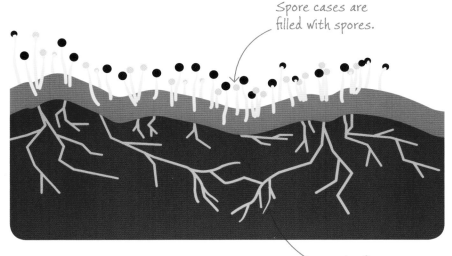

Spore cases are filled with spores.

The fungus network spreads through the surface of the fruit.

NETWORK OF HYPHAE
Moulds comprise fine threads called hyphae. These grow into decaying organisms, breaking them down. At the surface of these organisms, the hyphae form tiny cases filled with spores.

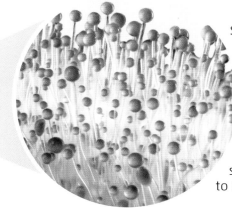

SPORE CASES
The fluffy surface of *Mucor* consists of thousands of spore cases. These turn from white to black as their spores ripen. Eventually, they burst open and release their spores into the air, spreading the fungus to new sources of food.

DECOMPOSITION
When fungi or other microorganisms feed on dead organisms, they break down the nutrients within them into simpler components. This process is called decomposition or decay.

1 DAY 1
Fresh fruit provides ideal conditions for mould to grow. Microscopic spores land on its surface, and hyphae begin to grow beneath its skin.

2 DAYS 5–7
After around a week the first signs of mould appear as furry patches on the surface of the fruit. As the hyphae grow, the fruit gets softer.

3 DAY 10
As the mould spreads, the hyphae's digestive chemicals break down the fruit even more, causing it to collapse and give off a sharp smell. The leafy sepals break down more slowly than the soft fruit.

4 DAY 12
After 12 days, the mould has consumed much of the fruit's flesh. Spore cases on the surface burst to release spores that can then spread and find new food sources.

HOW **LICHEN** WORKS

A lichen is not a single organism but a combination of two organisms living physically woven together, growing mostly on rocks or wood. One member of this close partnership is a fungus, and the other is usually an alga. Lichen can survive in some of the most inhospitable environments on Earth, from dry deserts to Arctic tundra. Lichens need so little to grow that they can even be found growing inside solid rock.

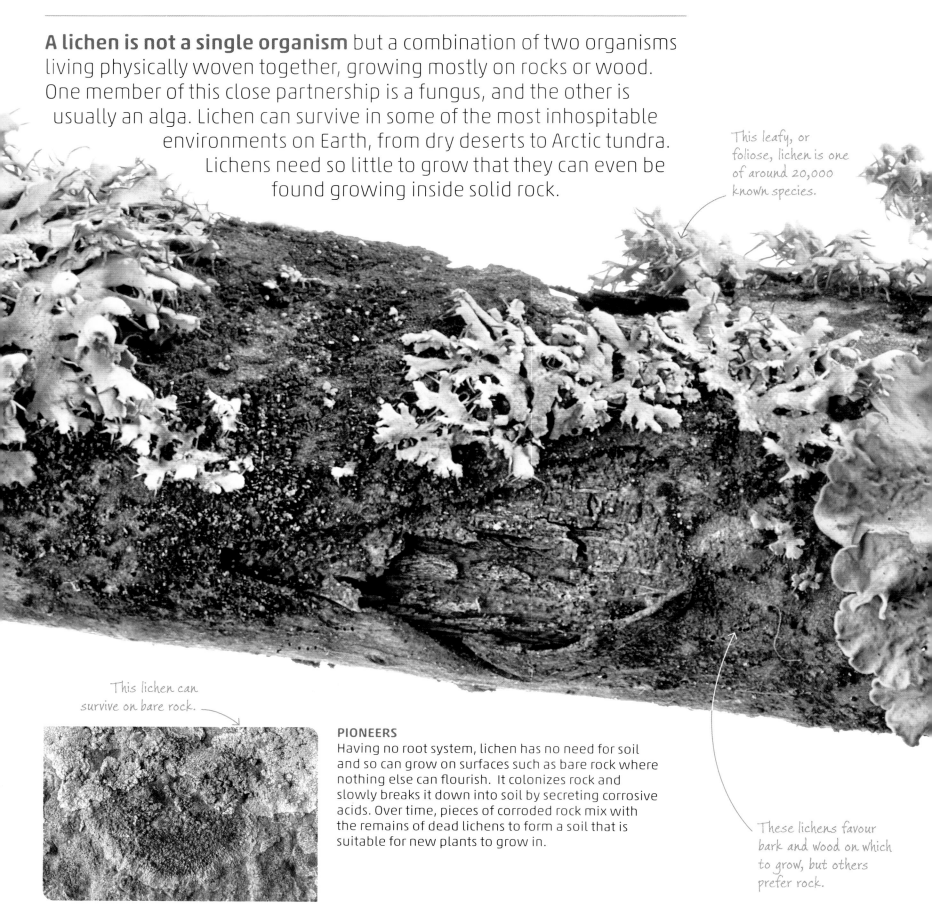

This leafy, or foliose, lichen is one of around 20,000 known species.

This lichen can survive on bare rock.

These lichens favour bark and wood on which to grow, but others prefer rock.

PIONEERS
Having no root system, lichen has no need for soil and so can grow on surfaces such as bare rock where nothing else can flourish. It colonizes rock and slowly breaks it down into soil by secreting corrosive acids. Over time, pieces of corroded rock mix with the remains of dead lichens to form a soil that is suitable for new plants to grow in.

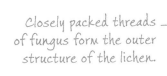

Closely packed threads of fungus form the outer structure of the lichen.

The alga lives in the middle of the structure.

LIVING TOGETHER

Both partners in a lichen benefit from a close relationship, known as symbiosis. The fungus protects the alga and helps it to absorb water and minerals from its surroundings. The alga, in return, makes food by photosynthesis, some of which is passed to the fungus. The algae in most lichens can live on their own, but the fungi cannot.

The large orange discs produce spores for the lichen to reproduce.

Hair-like structures called rhizines anchor the lichen to a surface.

▲ COMMON ORANGE LICHEN

This distinctive, widespread lichen is usually found on trees, rocks and walls. The bright orange discs are fruiting bodies, which help lichens reproduce by releasing spores.

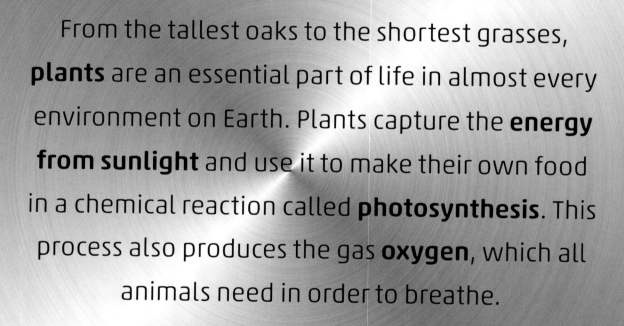

From the tallest oaks to the shortest grasses, **plants** are an essential part of life in almost every environment on Earth. Plants capture the **energy from sunlight** and use it to make their own food in a chemical reaction called **photosynthesis**. This process also produces the gas **oxygen**, which all animals need in order to breathe.

PLANTS

HOW
PLANTS
WORK

There are over 390,000 different plant species on Earth.
They have adapted to survive in some of the hottest
and coldest, wettest and driest parts of
the planet. New plants grow from seeds
that have been transported by animal,
wind, or water. Unlike animals,
plants make their own food in
a process called photosynthesis.

▶ FLOWERING PLANTS

Each part of a plant does a particular job.
Roots anchor the plant in the ground and
draw up water and minerals. A long stem
supports the plant and carries water
and nutrients between the roots and
leaves. The leaves absorb light
energy from the Sun to create
food in the form of sugars,
and flowers, seeds, and fruit
each play an important
role in reproduction.

Coloured petals attract
insects that transfer pollen
and help a plant
reproduce.

Stalks carry water
and minerals into a
leaf, as well as newly
made food to other
parts of the plant.

SEEDS
Many flowering plants
produce seeds inside
edible fruits. Once
eaten, the seeds fall
to the ground in an
animal's dung. They
can then grow into
new plants.

Ripe fruits are often
brightly coloured
to encourage
animals to eat them.

Fruits start off small and
green, but get softer
and juicier as they ripen.

Flower buds contain
developing flowers.

Veins carry water into leaves.

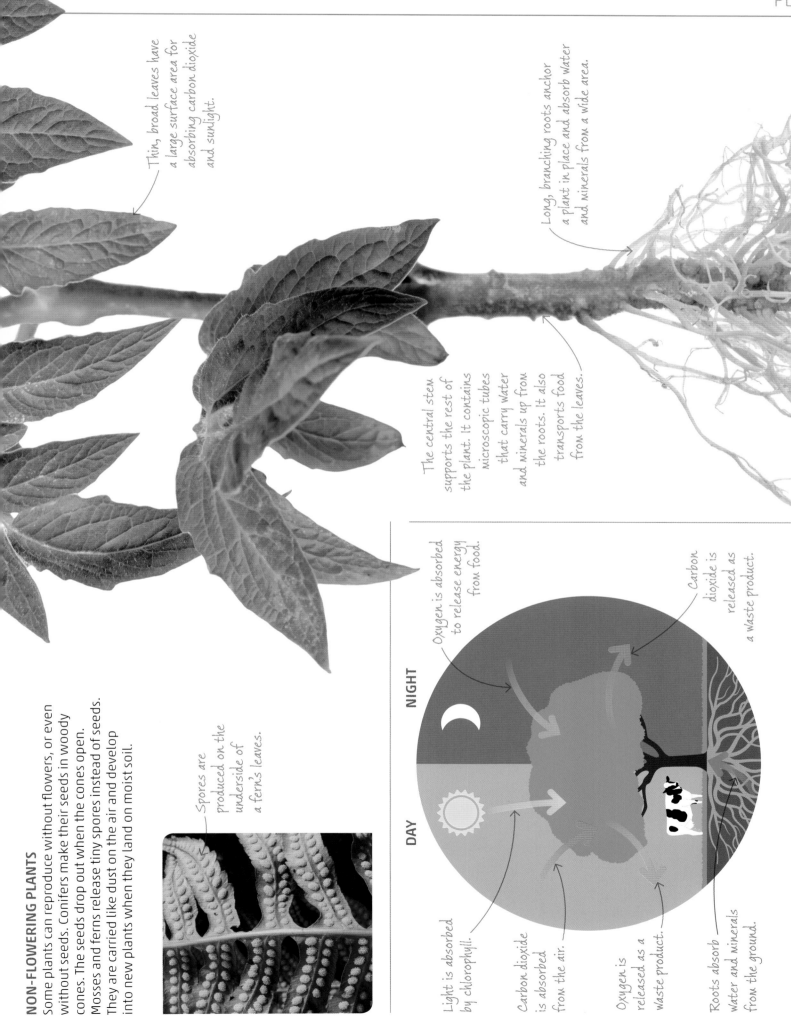

Thin, broad leaves have a large surface area for absorbing carbon dioxide and sunlight.

Long, branching roots anchor a plant in place and absorb water and minerals from a wide area.

The central stem supports the rest of the plant. It contains microscopic tubes that carry water and minerals up from the roots. It also transports food from the leaves.

NON-FLOWERING PLANTS

Some plants can reproduce without flowers, or even without seeds. Conifers make their seeds in woody cones. The seeds drop out when the cones open. Mosses and ferns release tiny spores instead of seeds. They are carried like dust on the air and develop into new plants when they land on moist soil.

Spores are produced on the underside of a fern's leaves.

HARNESSING SUNLIGHT

Leaves contain a green pigment (chlorophyll) that traps the Sun's light energy. This energy kick-starts a reaction called photosynthesis that changes water and carbon dioxide into food for the plant. Oxygen is produced. Plants can also take in oxygen and release carbon dioxide, just like animals. This happens when it is too dark for photosynthesis to occur.

DAY

NIGHT

Oxygen is absorbed to release energy from food.

Carbon dioxide is released as a waste product.

Light is absorbed by chlorophyll.

Carbon dioxide is absorbed from the air.

Oxygen is released as a waste product.

Roots absorb water and minerals from the ground.

① GERMINATION
A sunflower seed splits open and starts to grow in a process called germination. A root grows down, while a shoot and first leaves (cotyledons) emerge from the ground.

Seed casing (husk)

DAY 3

Root

DAY 1

Each seed is protected inside a hard casing (husk).

HOW FLOWERING PLANTS GROW

Seed leaf (cotyledon)

Stem

DAY 8

The discarded casing will drop to the ground.

All flowering plants begin life as seeds that develop roots and shoots when they start to grow. As they mature, bright, scented flowers form, attracting animals that carry pollen from flower to flower, which allows plants to make seeds. The seeds are then dispersed so the plant can repeat its life cycle.

The stem grows longer.

② DEVELOPMENT
The stem grows longer as the cotyledons unfurl, discarding their old fruit casing. New leaves develop, which make food by the process of photosynthesis to nourish more growth and, later, the development of a flower bud.

DAY 10

Unopened flower bud

Leaves branch out from the stem and collect energy from the Sun.

Roots spread out to absorb water and minerals.

Leaf stalk (petiole)

DAY 50

DAY 105

Seeds drop from the seedhead.

Yellow florets wither and fall.

4 SETTING SEED
Following a process called pollination, where pollen is carried from one flower to another, each tiny flower in the sunflower's head can produce a seed. Soon, the flower head is a mass of sunflower seeds, ready to be scattered so that they can continue the plant's life cycle.

Developing seeds

DAY 95

▶ SUNFLOWER LIFE CYCLE

Some plants take years to mature and produce a new generation of seeds, but others, like the sunflower, complete their life cycle in just one year. Starting from a seed that weighs only a tenth of a gram, a sunflower can reach the height of an adult human in just two months. Its flower isn't a single bloom, but a collection of many tiny flowers, known as a composite flower.

The central dark disc is a composite of up to 2,000 tiny flowers.

Coloured petal-like florets emerge as flowers open.

A composite flower opens at the top of a single tall stem.

3 FLOWERING
Much of the plant's food is transported to the flower buds to make them grow. Once the reproductive organs are mature, the flowers open to expose bright yellow petal-like florets that attract animals.

DAY 70

DAY 75

HOW SEEDS GROW

Many plants begin life as a tiny embryo enclosed inside a seed. Protected by the seed's tough outer coat and kept alive by its own food supply, an embryo waits until conditions are right for it to grow. Built to last, some seeds can survive for decades without water or warmth. When these elements are present, however, the dormant embryo may spring to life in a process called germination.

INSIDE A SEED

A seed is a capsule that contains an embryonic plant, complete with the plant's first shoot, first root, and a food supply that provides the energy it needs to begin growing. There are two main types of flowering plant seed – monocotyledons (meaning "one cotyledon") and dicotyledons (which means "two cotyledons").

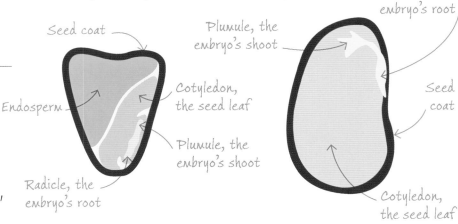

Seed coat

Endosperm

Plumule, the embryo's shoot

Cotyledon, the seed leaf

Plumule, the embryo's shoot

Radicle, the embryo's root

Radicle, the embryo's root

Seed coat

Cotyledon, the seed leaf

MONOCOTYLEDON

Monocotyledons, like this corn seed, contain one seed leaf (called a cotyledon) and get their energy from a food supply called an endosperm.

DICOTYLEDON

Dicotyledons, like this bean, contain two seed leaves (called cotyledons), which contain the food supply the plant needs to start to grow.

▶ HOW A BEAN GROWS

To germinate, a seed needs water, oxygen, and the right temperature. When a seed absorbs water, it starts to swell. Its coat splits open, and a shoot and root begin to grow. Within two weeks, a French bean transforms from a seed to a small plant.

1 DORMANT SEED
A seed remains dormant in the ground until conditions are right for it to germinate.

2 GROWTH BEGINS
The seed coat splits, and the embryo's root, or radicle, begins to grow into the soil.

3 SHOOT EMERGES
As the radicle collects water from the soil, the embryonic shoot, or plumule, starts to grow upwards.

Shoot starts to emerge.

Cress shoots lean towards a light source so they can photosynthesize as efficiently as possible.

Cress seeds

SEEKING THE LIGHT
When light shines on one side of a plant stem, a hormone called auxin moves to the opposite side. The auxin causes cells on this side to grow longer, which makes the entire stem bend towards the light.

Veins transport water and minerals from the stem into the leaf.

True leaves

True leaves

Cotyledons outgrown by true leaves

Cotyledon

4 **BREAKING THROUGH**
The plumule breaks through the soil into the light. Until it grows true leaves for photosynthesis, the plant's energy comes from the food supply stored in the two special leaves in the seed, called cotyledons.

5 **TRUE LEAVES**
The seedling's first true leaves emerge and become able to make food for the plant from light, through a process called photosynthesis.

6 **NEW LEAVES**
New leaves swell as they absorb water through a network of veins. These leaves now take over the role of supplying the growing plant with food.

HOW ROOTS AND STEMS WORK

Roots and stems are the lifeline of a plant. As well as anchoring and supporting the plant, they contain tiny tubes for carrying nutrients. The tubes that carry water and minerals from the roots are called xylem vessels, while the tubes that transport water and food from the stem are called phloem tubes.

▶ INSIDE A ROOT

Near their tips, roots are covered in tiny, brush-like hairs. These reach out between the soil particles to absorb water and minerals, which then pass through the outer layers of the root to the xylem vessels at its core, where they are carried up to the stem of the plant. Roots also have phloem tubes, which transport food and water down from the stem. Some roots, such as the edible part of a carrot plant, are enlarged for storing nutrients or water.

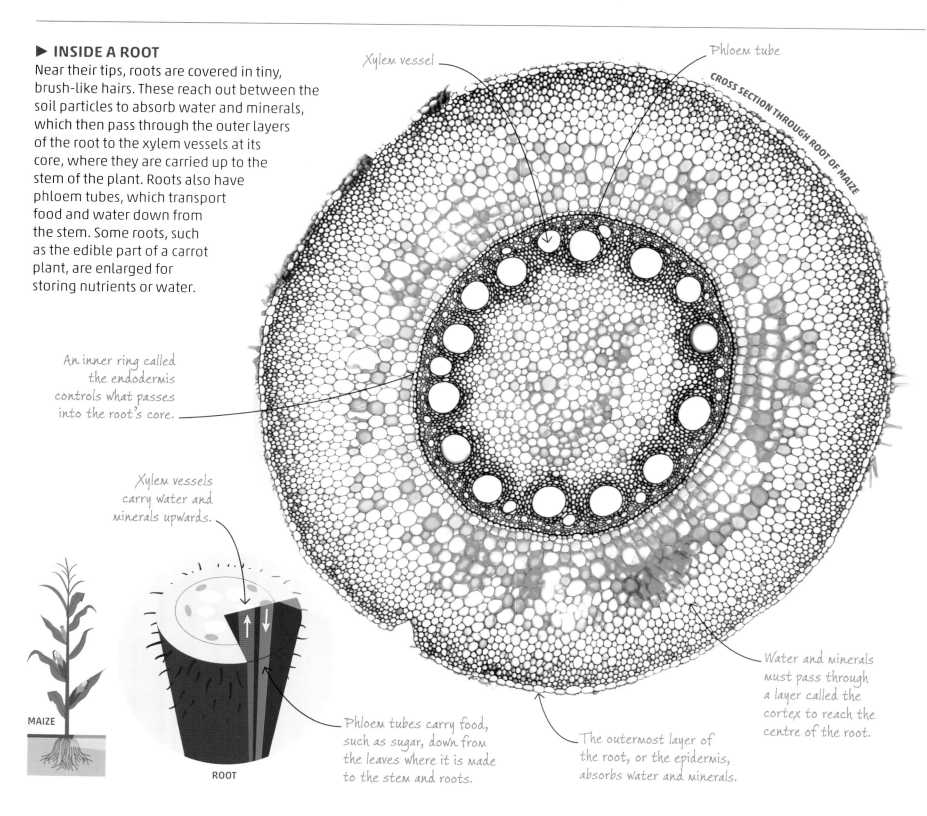

Xylem vessel

Phloem tube

CROSS SECTION THROUGH ROOT OF MAIZE

An inner ring called the endodermis controls what passes into the root's core.

Xylem vessels carry water and minerals upwards.

MAIZE

ROOT

Phloem tubes carry food, such as sugar, down from the leaves where it is made to the stem and roots.

The outermost layer of the root, or the epidermis, absorbs water and minerals.

Water and minerals must pass through a layer called the cortex to reach the centre of the root.

ANCHORAGE
Most roots branch downwards into the ground, fixing a plant into position and helping it reach water and minerals. Many plants have a large, central root that grows down vertically. This is called a taproot.

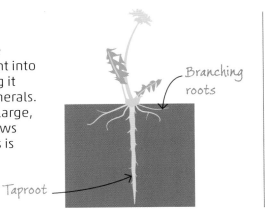

Branching roots

Taproot

UPWARD FLOW
The xylem vessels in a plant allow water to flow upwards in an unbroken column. As a result, when water evaporates from the leaves, it pulls up more water from the ground through the stem and roots. This flow of water through a plant enables plants to collect minerals from soil.

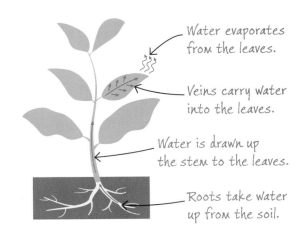

Water evaporates from the leaves.

Veins carry water into the leaves.

Water is drawn up the stem to the leaves.

Roots take water up from the soil.

◄ INSIDE A STEM
Stems branch upwards and are reinforced with a fibrous material called cellulose to stay upright. This maize stem has the strength to grow 3 m (10 feet) tall, but many other stems grow into woody trunks and can get much taller. All stems have their transport tubes arranged into bundles, with xylem on the inside and phloem on the outside. These are called vascular bundles.

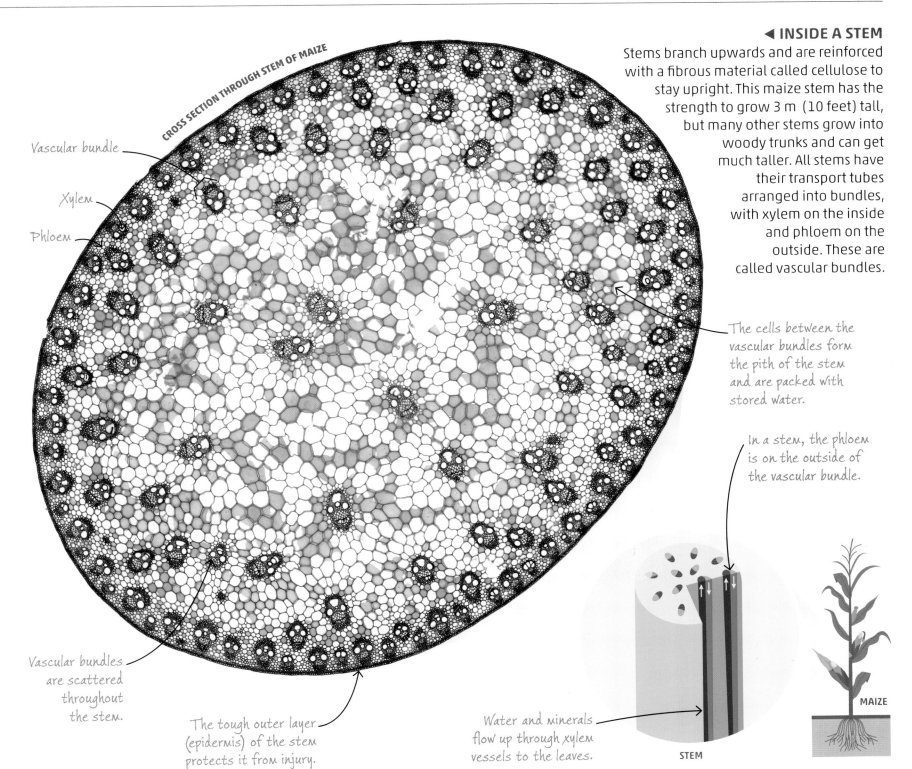

CROSS SECTION THROUGH STEM OF MAIZE

Vascular bundle

Xylem

Phloem

The cells between the vascular bundles form the pith of the stem and are packed with stored water.

In a stem, the phloem is on the outside of the vascular bundle.

Vascular bundles are scattered throughout the stem.

The tough outer layer (epidermis) of the stem protects it from injury.

Water and minerals flow up through xylem vessels to the leaves.

STEM

MAIZE

HOW TREES WORK

The tallest trees alive today stand over 30 storeys high and the oldest have lived for more than 2,000 years. Most of the giant plants that we refer to as trees have evolved stems made of wood, which allow them to tower over other plants in the competition for sunlight. A tree's large size means that it can also provide a home for many living organisms.

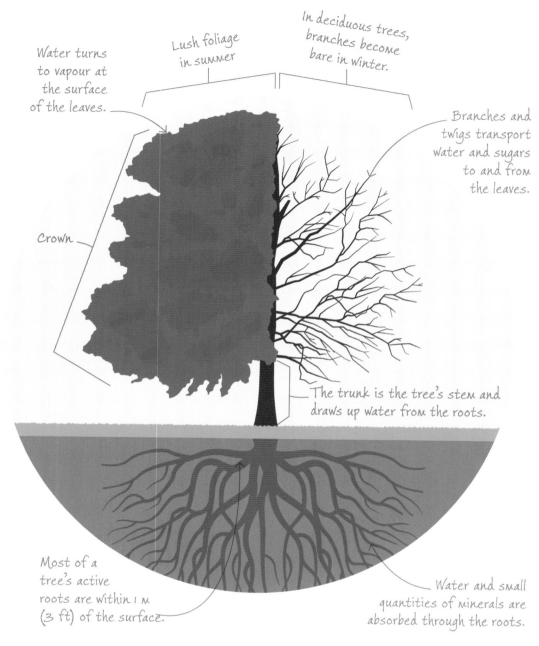

Water turns to vapour at the surface of the leaves.

Lush foliage in summer

In deciduous trees, branches become bare in winter.

Branches and twigs transport water and sugars to and from the leaves.

Crown

The trunk is the tree's stem and draws up water from the roots.

Most of a tree's active roots are within 1 m (3 ft) of the surface.

Water and small quantities of minerals are absorbed through the roots.

STRUCTURE OF A TREE
Like most plants, trees are structured so that water and minerals can be drawn up efficiently from the roots. Water moves up from the roots through the trunk, branches, and twigs to the leaves. It evaporates when it reaches a leaf's surface, drawing more water upwards.

EVERGREEN

DECIDUOUS

EVERGREEN AND DECIDUOUS
Some trees are evergreen and they replace their leaves as old ones drop. Others completely lose their leaves during seasons of cold or drought and then grow new ones when conditions improve. These trees are deciduous.

The rings are interrupted by the growth of a branch.

The paler, wider rings are earlywood, formed in the spring.

The darker, thinner rings are latewood, formed at the end of the growing season.

TREE RINGS
Tree trunks get wider each year as new wood forms just under the bark. The new layer of wood forms a growth ring. When a tree is cut down, it is sometimes possible to tell the age of the tree by counting its growth rings.

◀ INSIDE AN OAK TRUNK

More than 99 per cent of a big tree trunk is dead – formed of a dry supporting heartwood at the centre, surrounded by sapwood, which conducts water. These two layers of wood are made from a plant tissue called xylem. Wrapped around this are the living layers of cambium and the inner bark, called phloem, surrounded by the outer bark.

The supporting darker heartwood at the centre of the trunk is made of old xylem vessels that no longer carry water.

The paler sapwood is made of new xylem vessels that carry water up from the tree's roots and through its trunk.

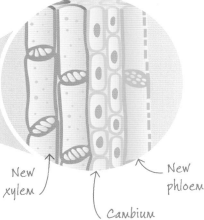

New xylem

Cambium

New phloem

NEW LAYERS

Between the wood (xylem) and inner bark (phloem), a layer of growth cells called the cambium produces new wood and inner bark. These living layers are the youngest part of a tree.

The inner bark contains living phloem cells, which carry food and water around the tree.

The outer bark has a hard surface to protect the vulnerable living inner bark underneath it, and pores to help the trunk to absorb oxygen.

HOW LEAVES WORK

Leaves collect light energy from the Sun and use it to create food for the plant in a process called photosynthesis. The energy stored in this food can be used by animals that eat plants, so this important process produces the food on which nearly all animals depend. It also releases oxygen into Earth's air, allowing animals to breathe.

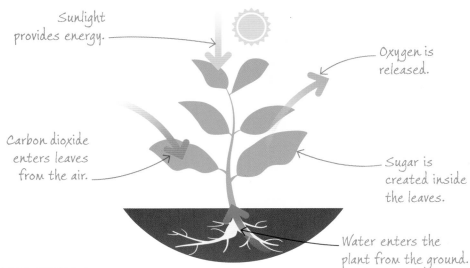

Sunlight provides energy.

Oxygen is released.

Carbon dioxide enters leaves from the air.

Sugar is created inside the leaves.

Water enters the plant from the ground.

PHOTOSYNTHESIS
During photosynthesis, a plant's leaves use light from the Sun to combine carbon dioxide from the air with water from the ground. This complex chemical reaction produces carbohydrates, such as sugar. Plants use these to store energy and to build new tissues as they grow.

SPINACH

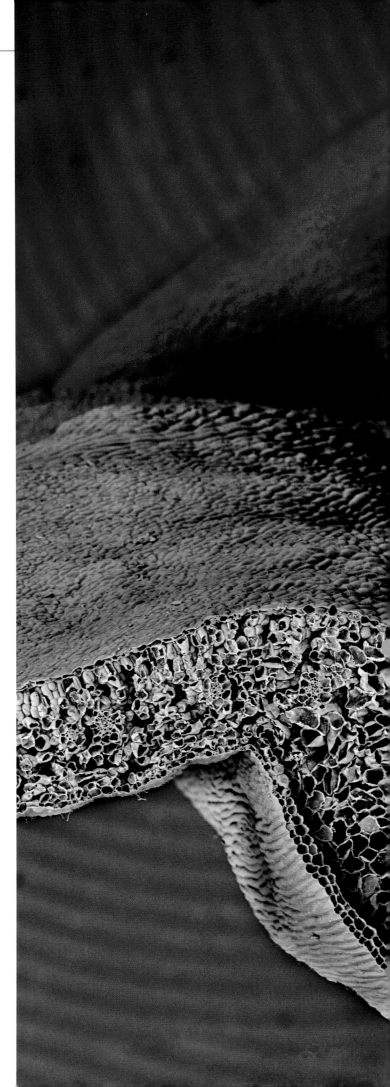

▶ **INSIDE THE LEAF**
Magnified hundreds of times by an electron microscope, this picture of a spinach leaf sliced open reveals the cells inside. Running along the bottom of the leaf is a thick vein, called the midrib, that carries water and minerals into the leaf, and newly made food out to the rest of the plant. Photosynthesis mostly takes place near the leaf's upper surface, where the Sun's light is strongest.

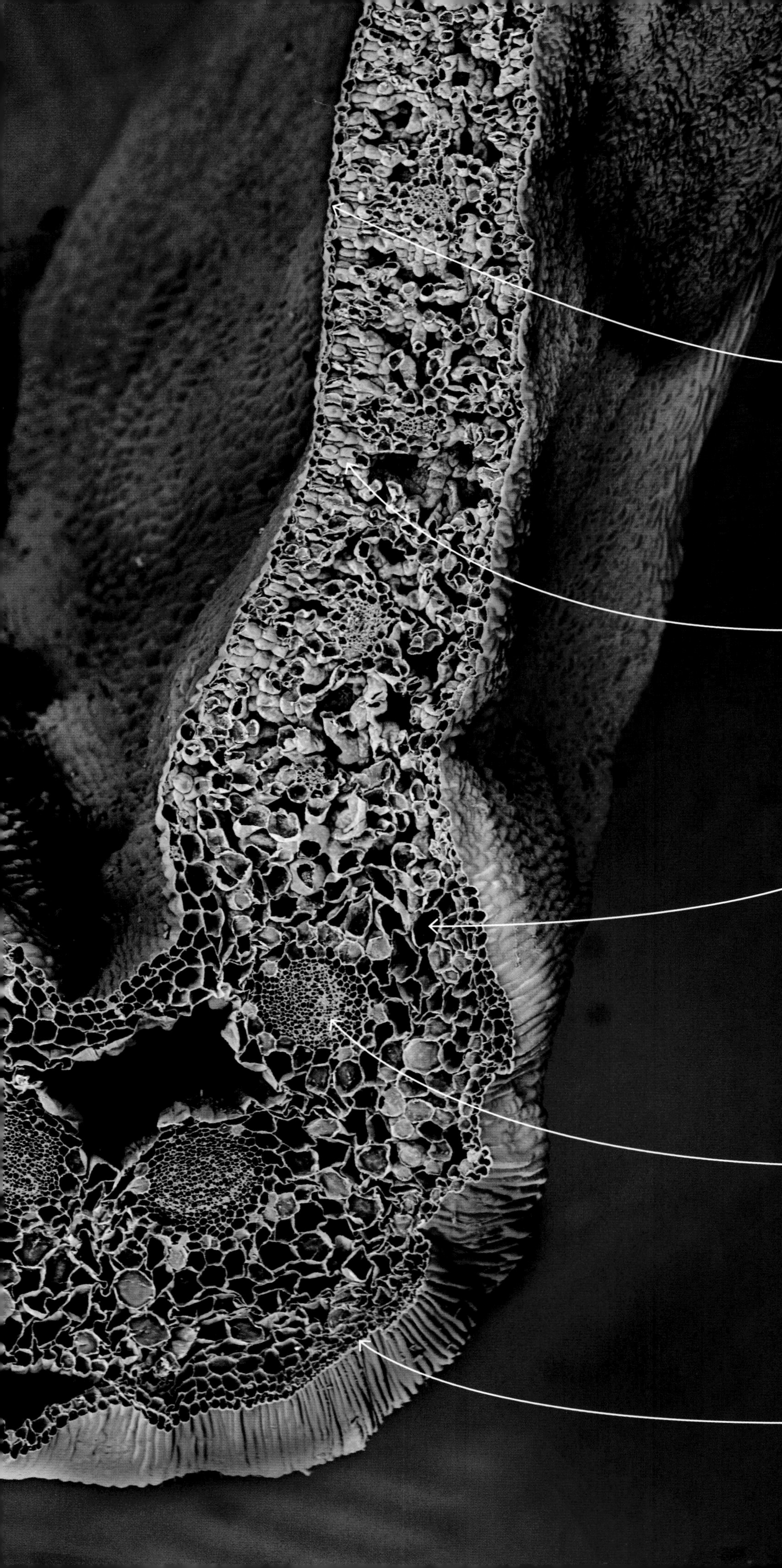

CELL LAYERS
A leaf is made up of several layers of different types of cell. Each layer carries out a particular task.

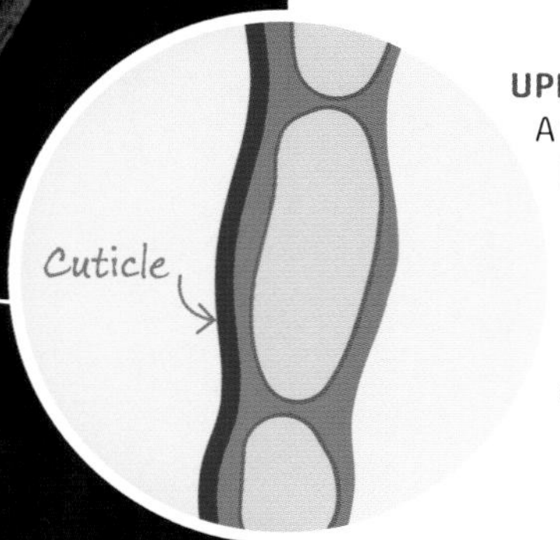

UPPER EPIDERMIS
A top layer of flat cells lets light shine right through. A waxy, waterproof coating called the cuticle stops the leaf losing too much moisture under the heat of the Sun.

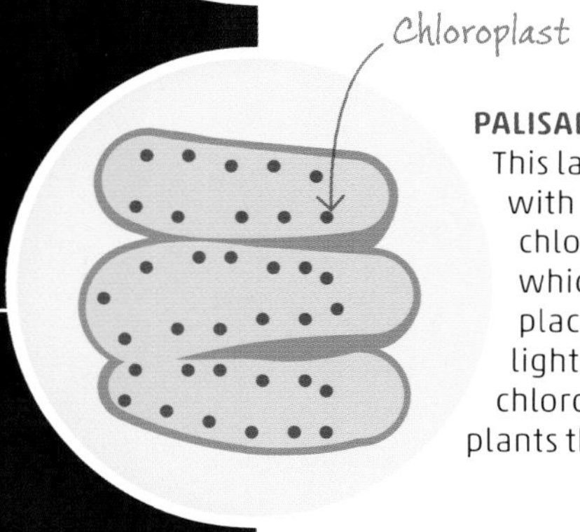

Cuticle

Chloroplast

PALISADE LAYER
This layer is tightly packed with oblong cells containing chloroplasts – tiny bodies in which photosynthesis takes place. Chloroplasts capture light with the green pigment chlorophyll, which gives plants their colour.

SPONGY LAYER
Under the palisade layer is a layer of loosely packed, thin-walled cells and air spaces. The air spaces allow carbon dioxide to reach the palisade layer.

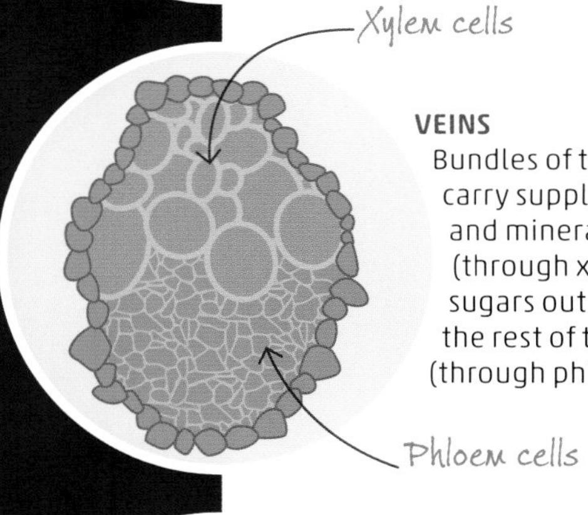

Xylem cells

VEINS
Bundles of tube-shaped cells carry supplies such as water and minerals into the leaf (through xylem cells) and sugars out of the leaf to the rest of the plant (through phloem cells).

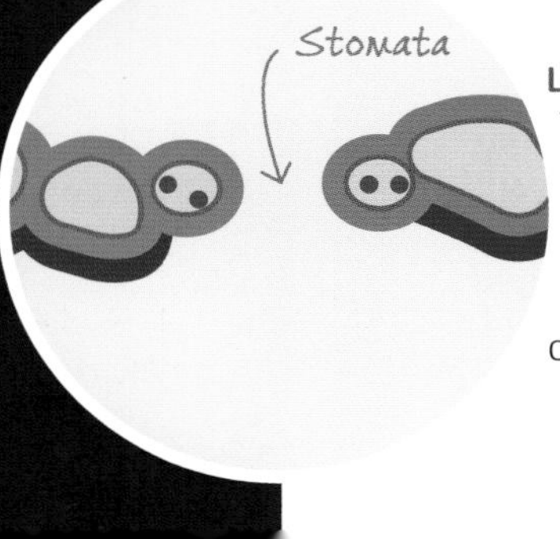

Phloem cells

Stomata

LOWER EPIDERMIS
The bottom layer of cells (the lower epidermis) has tiny openings called stomata to allow air into the leaf. They close in dry weather to conserve water.

HOW **FLOWERS** WORK

Many flowers have bright colours and sweet scents, not to attract humans but to entice animals, such as bees and bats, to visit them. When an animal travels from flower to flower in search of nectar, it unknowingly does an important job. Pollen grains stick to it and are carried from one flower to the next, helping plants to reproduce.

POLLEN on a bee's legs

BUMBLEBEE

▶ POLLINATION

All flowering plants rely on a process called pollination to reproduce sexually. The male parts of flowers make powdery, yellow grains called pollen, which contain male sex cells. When pollen is carried from one flower to another, either by wind or animals (known as pollinators), it grows deep into the flower. This allows a male and female sex cell to fuse, triggering the formation of a seed.

This flower's petals unravel in a spiral pattern.

Pollen released from stamen

Petal

Male organ (stamen)

Bright colours attract pollinators.

Flower bud

Female organ (carpel)

The top of the female sex organ is called a stigma.

Unopened stigma

Nectaries in the base of the flower produce nectar.

Sepal

Stalk

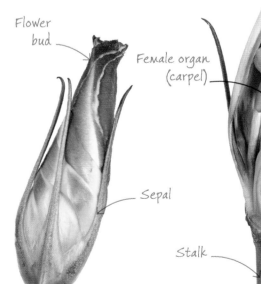

1 **NEW BUD**
Before a flower opens, its petals and sex organs are packed tightly together inside a bud. A protective case made of leaf-like structures called sepals surrounds the bud.

2 **TIME TO OPEN**
Once its sex organs have formed, a flower is ready to open. The sepals bend back and the petals rapidly expand, their cells swelling with fluids drawn from veins in the stalk. This Lisianthus has been cut open to show the sex organs inside it.

3 **OPENING BUD**
The petals unfold as they expand and eventually spread out to form a brightly coloured ring. Their colours appear even brighter to the eyes of insects than to our eyes.

4 **ATTRACTING INSECTS**
As they open, many flowers release strong scents to attract pollinators. To lure their visitors deep inside, they secrete an irresistibly sweet liquid near the base of the petals – nectar.

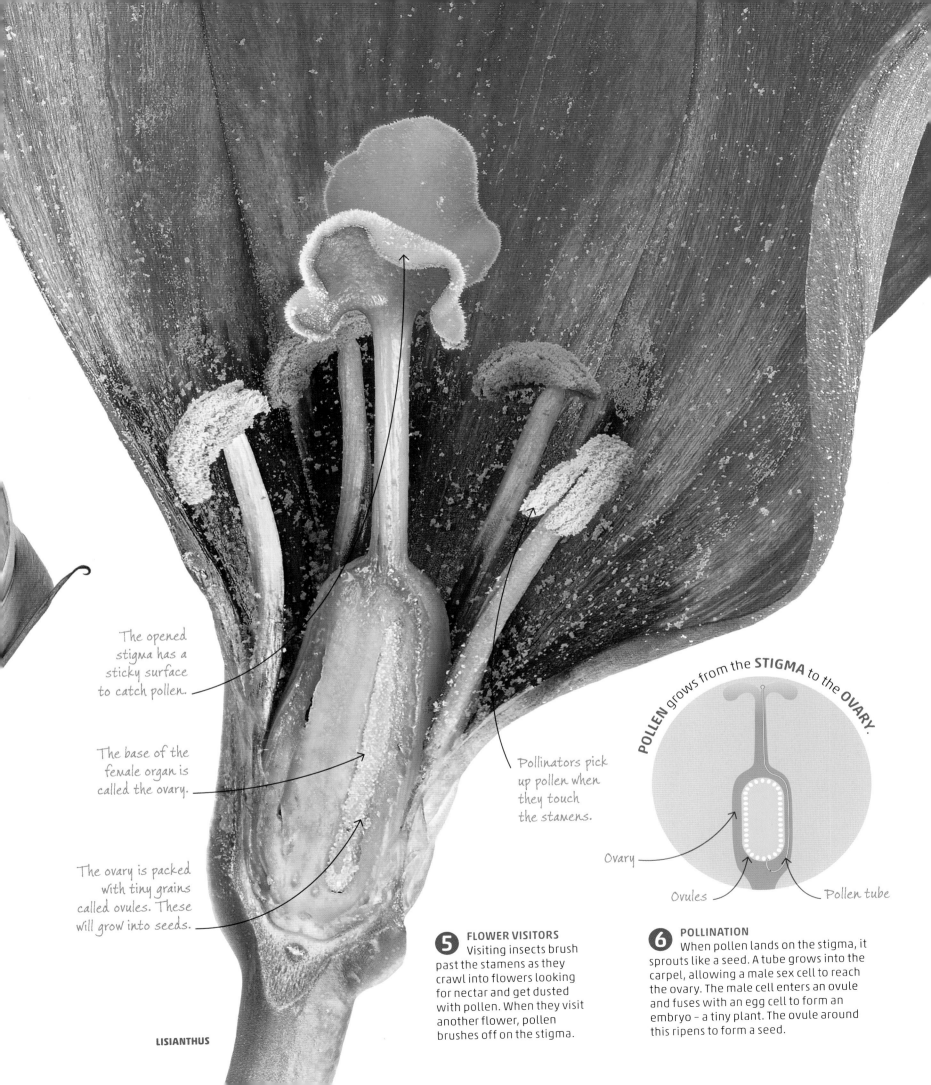

The opened stigma has a sticky surface to catch pollen.

The base of the female organ is called the ovary.

The ovary is packed with tiny grains called ovules. These will grow into seeds.

Pollinators pick up pollen when they touch the stamens.

POLLEN grows from the **STIGMA** to the **OVARY**.

Ovary

Ovules

Pollen tube

LISIANTHUS

5 **FLOWER VISITORS**
Visiting insects brush past the stamens as they crawl into flowers looking for nectar and get dusted with pollen. When they visit another flower, pollen brushes off on the stigma.

6 **POLLINATION**
When pollen lands on the stigma, it sprouts like a seed. A tube grows into the carpel, allowing a male sex cell to reach the ovary. The male cell enters an ovule and fuses with an egg cell to form an embryo – a tiny plant. The ovule around this ripens to form a seed.

TYPES OF
FLOWERS

All flowers face the same challenge, which is to ensure their pollen travels to other flowers so the plants can reproduce sexually. The way they achieve this goal varies. Some lure flying animals with rewards such as sugary nectar, dusting their bodies with pollen as they enter the flower. Others scatter pollen into the air and let the wind carry it.

BIRD-POLLINATED FLOWERS
Some flowers have evolved close relationships with specialist pollinators, improving the odds that their pollen will be transferred to the right species. Bird-pollinated plants often have tubular flowers that make it difficult for animals other than long-billed birds to reach inside and gather nectar.

BROAD APPEAL
To attract as many pollinators as possible, some plants allow many kinds of animal to reach their nectar. Such plants have simple, open flowers and strong scents. Globe thistles are a magnet to many different insects, from bees to butterflies.

MIMICRY
Orchids use many different strategies to attract highly specialized pollinators. Bee orchids, for example, have flowers that mimic female bees. Males attempt to mate with these flowers, pollinating them as they do so.

TORCH LILY

The shallow florets (small flowers) of a thistle make nectar easy to reach.

EUROPEAN DARK BEE

Birds with long bills can easily reach the nectar deep inside the tubular flowers.

MALACHITE SUNBIRD

The orchid's flowers mimic female bees.

Sticky pollen gathers on the bird's head as it probes the flower.

GLOBE THISTLE

SWALLOWTAIL BUTTERFLY

SOMBRE BEE ORCHID

WIND POLLINATION
Wind-pollinated flowers scatter their pollen into the air. Most goes to waste, so vast amounts must be produced to ensure pollination takes place. The female flowers have feathery stigmas to catch the pollen.

Male catkin

HIMALAYAN BIRCH TREE

BANANA PLANT

Growing bananas

GREEN BOTTLE FLY

Each of these female flowers will produce a banana.

The vivid colour resembles rotting flesh.

CARRION FLOWER

Large purple structures called bracts protect banana flowers.

The fine hairs resemble mould.

The wind-pollinated catkins (flowers) of birch trees release millions of pollen grains into the air.

NOCTURNAL POLLINATION
Some flowers rely on animals that are active only at night, such as moths or bats. Coloured petals are hard to see in darkness, so night-pollinated flowers tend to have strong scents and white petals instead. Wild bananas are pollinated by bats, which hang on the tough flower stalk while feeding on nectar.

CAVE NECTAR BAT

SMELLY BUSINESS
When in bloom, the carrion flower smells like rotting flesh. The stench attracts carrion flies and beetles, which normally feed on dead animals. These insects spread pollen from plant to plant, fertilizing the flowers.

TYPES OF FRUIT

As well as things like apples that are easily identified as fruits, some things we call vegetables, such as tomatoes, peppers, and peas, are actually fruits because they develop from the ovary of a flower. Many fleshy fruits, such as citrus fruits and peaches, arise from a single-ovary flower. More complex fruits, such as raspberries, come from flowers with several ovaries or even multiple flowers.

NUTS
A nut is a fruit made up of a seed within an ovary that has hardened to form a shell. Unlike other types of dry fruit, nuts don't split open as they ripen to release the seeds inside.

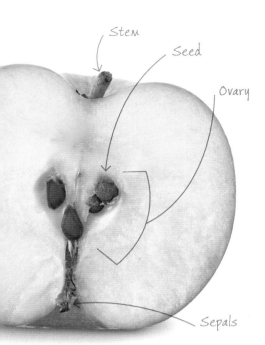

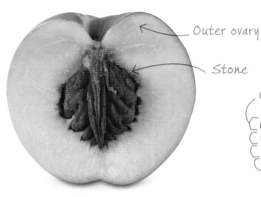

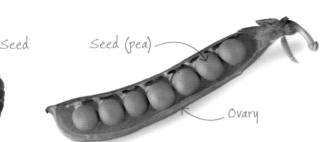

FALSE FRUITS
Some kinds of fruit do not develop from a flower's ovary and are called false fruits or accessory fruits. Apples, for instance, form from tissues that are found beneath the ovary.

DRUPES
A drupe is a fleshy fruit with a single hard pit, or stone, at its centre. A stone consists of a single seed inside a hardened case formed from the inner part of the ovary.

AGGREGATE FRUITS
An aggregate fruit develops from several separate ovaries in one flower. The ovaries join to make fruits such as raspberries and blackberries.

PODS
We think of peas in their pods as vegetables, but they are actually fruits. The pods develop from the ovary of the flower and the peas inside them are seeds.

▼ FROM FLOWER TO FRUIT

As the exposed parts of a flower wither, a fruit begins to form around the seeds. The fruit stores nutrients, such as starch, that the rest of the plant makes by photosynthesis. As the fruit swells, it ripens and becomes softer and sweeter, the stored starch turning into sugar. Tomatoes, like many fruits, change colour, turning from green to red to attract seed-dispersing animals.

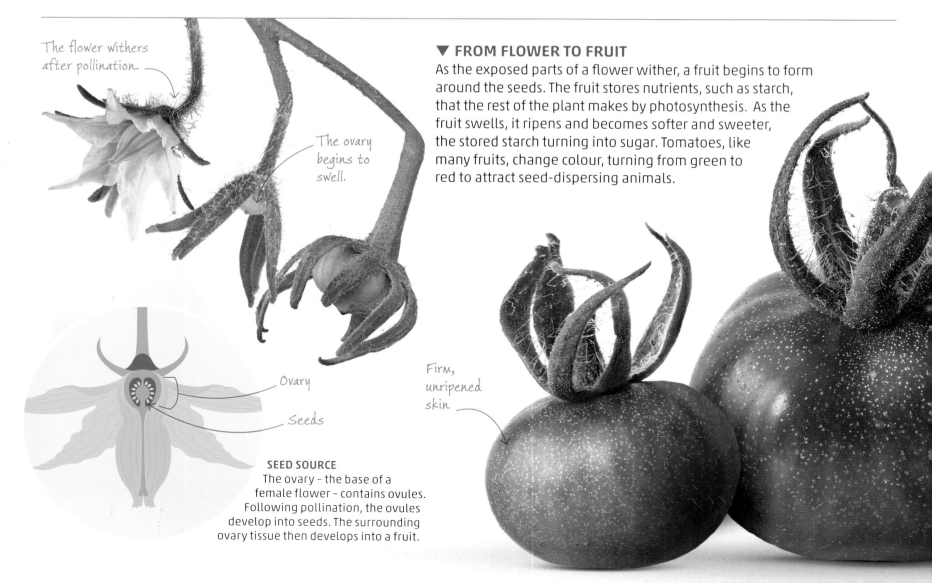

SEED SOURCE
The ovary – the base of a female flower – contains ovules. Following pollination, the ovules develop into seeds. The surrounding ovary tissue then develops into a fruit.

HOW FRUITS GROW

After a flower has been fertilized, the ovary inside it swells and ripens to form a fruit. Many fruits have bright colours and sweet flesh to tempt animals to eat them and so disperse the seeds in their droppings. Other fruits are dry and hard, and some of the things we think of as vegetables are actually fruits.

Sepal

Flower stalk

Seed

Ovary wall

The colour changes as the fruit ripens.

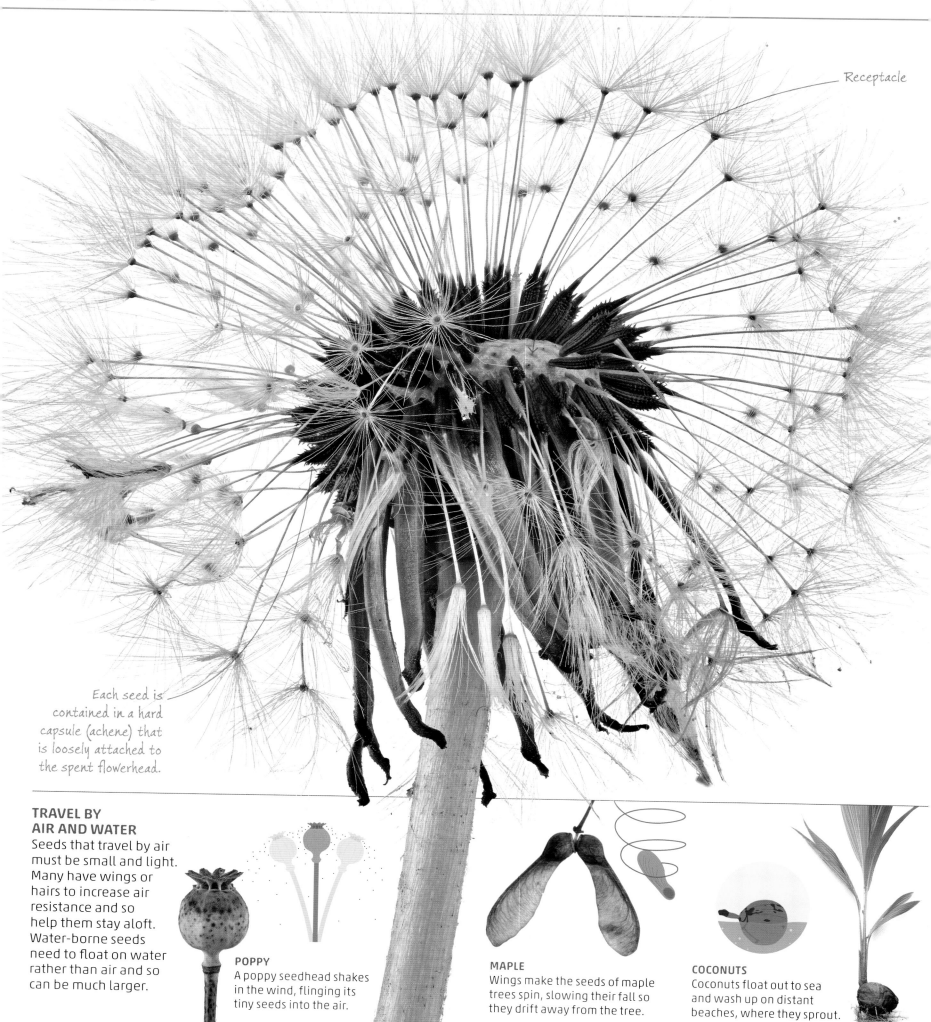

Receptacle

Each seed is contained in a hard capsule (achene) that is loosely attached to the spent flowerhead.

TRAVEL BY AIR AND WATER

Seeds that travel by air must be small and light. Many have wings or hairs to increase air resistance and so help them stay aloft. Water-borne seeds need to float on water rather than air and so can be much larger.

POPPY
A poppy seedhead shakes in the wind, flinging its tiny seeds into the air.

MAPLE
Wings make the seeds of maple trees spin, slowing their fall so they drift away from the tree.

COCONUTS
Coconuts float out to sea and wash up on distant beaches, where they sprout.

HOW **SEEDS** TRAVEL

Seeds must travel far from their parent plants if they are to find new habitats and thrive. To ensure their seeds reach suitable destinations, many plants scatter them in vast numbers and use a range of mechanisms to disperse them. Some seeds have wings or parachutes to help them travel by air. Others hitch a ride with animals, clinging to their fur or even travelling inside them.

Feathery hairs catch the wind.

◀ DANDELION SEEDS
The flowerhead of a dandelion produces 100–150 seeds. Each develops from a single tiny flower and is released encased in its own miniature hard fruit, called an achene. A parachute of feathery hairs (a pappus) helps each catch a gust of wind and float away.

The hard, capsule-like achene protects the seed.

Upon landing, small barbs catch the ground.

Hooks

TRAVEL BY ANIMAL
Seeds spread by animals don't need to be as small as the ones that are carried on the wind. As a result, they are larger and released in smaller numbers. Some stick to their carriers, but others are swallowed within fruits – ensuring they land with a heap of fertilizing dung when they reach their final destination.

BURDOCK
Hooks on the burdock's flowerhead latch onto passing animals to disperse seeds.

ACORNS
Acorns are carried away by birds and squirrels, which hide them but forget where some are buried.

REDCURRANTS
Small berries, including redcurrants, are swallowed by birds, which later scatter the seeds in their droppings.

DECIDUOUS FORESTS

As summer blends into autumn, the leaves on trees in New England, USA, gradually transform from lush greens to yellows, oranges, reds, and purples. Leaves change colour in autumn because, as the days get shorter, the green pigment that allows leaves to absorb energy from sunlight breaks down, leaving other pigments visible. Eventually, the leaves will be of no use to the tree, and will be shed for the winter.

HOW PLANT DEFENCES WORK

The leaf and stem are also covered with many non-stinging hairs.

Each tube is filled with irritants that cause a painful sting.

A solid, tubular base supports the stinging hairs.

The fragile tip breaks away easily.

Needle-like hairs called trichomes cover the underside of the leaf.

When a plant is attacked by a hungry animal, it doesn't have the option to run away or bite back. Instead, plants protect themselves with other defensive strategies, from tough bark and foul-tasting, indigestible leaves to vicious thorns and stings. The pain these weapons inflict can prevent an animal from ever touching the same plant again.

▶ **STINGING NETTLE**
A nettle's stem and leaves are covered with tiny hollow hairs called trichomes, which contain a mixture of toxic chemicals. These chemicals can cause a painful inflammation in animals for up to 12 hours.

STINGING HAIRS
Called a trichome, the hollow hair of a stinging nettle acts like a syringe. The tip breaks off when touched, leaving a sharp point that can pierce skin and inject toxic chemicals.

1 TOXIC STING
Toxic chemicals are stored at the base of the nettle's trichome.

2 TIP BREAKS
An animal bites the leaf and breaks off the fragile tip of the trichome.

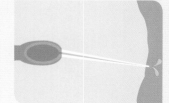

3 PIERCES SKIN
The trichome pierces the skin and injects toxic chemicals into the flesh.

4 PAINFUL RASH
A rash appears on the skin, along with tingling, burning, and itching.

PLANT WEAPONS

Plants have many ways of seeing off hungry predators. The leaves of some harmless-looking plants can contain powerful toxins. Other plants rely on sharp spines or insect partners to protect them.

SPINES

In dry habitats, some animals quench their thirst by eating plants. To prevent this, plants such as cacti protect themselves with a covering of spines.

CHEMICALS

Dieffenbachia looks like a harmless house plant, but it is highly toxic. If eaten, the leaf cells fire poisonous crystals into the predator's mouth, which can cause vomiting, paralysis, and organ damage.

ALLIES

Some plants form an alliance with animals in return for their protection. The South American cecropia tree provides a home for aggressive Azteca ants, which in turn attack predatory insects and competing plants.

RESIN

Some trees release a sticky resin to heal puncture wounds and deter or kill grazing insects. Resin can trap insects then harden and fossilize over time to become amber.

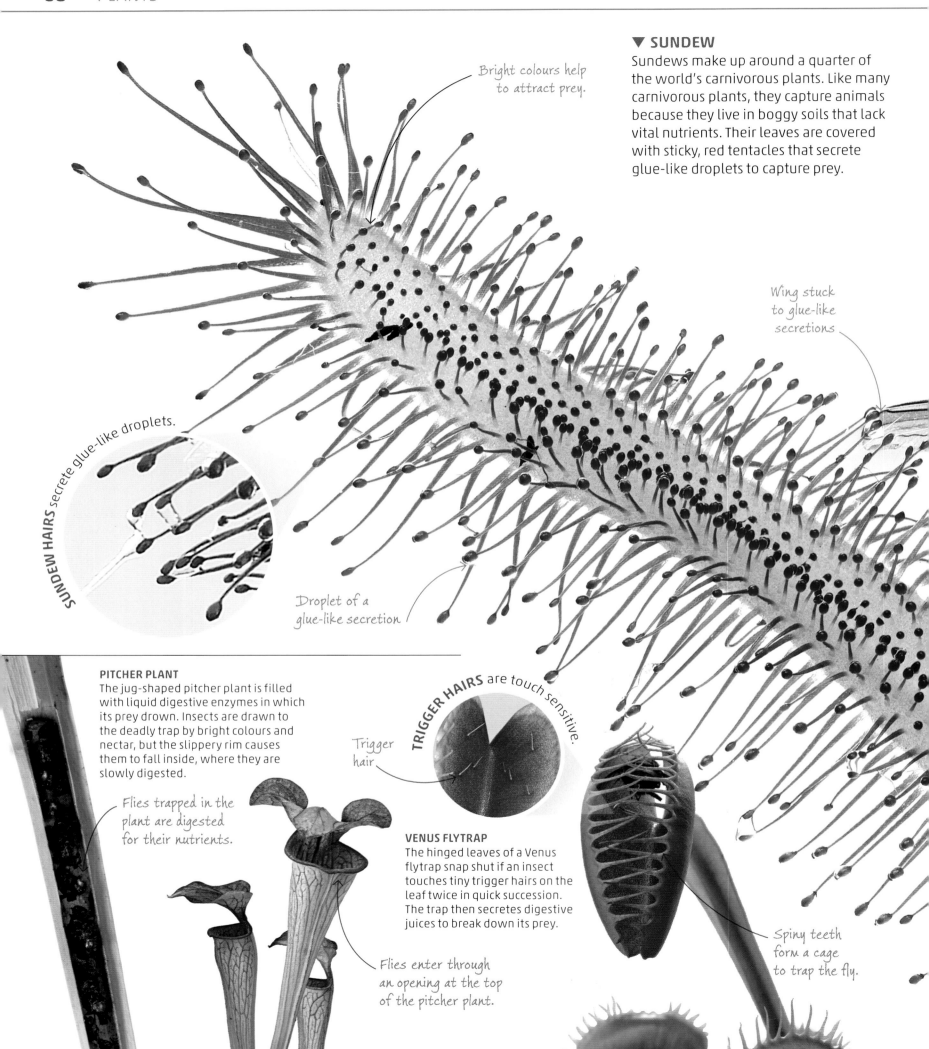

Bright colours help to attract prey.

▼ SUNDEW
Sundews make up around a quarter of the world's carnivorous plants. Like many carnivorous plants, they capture animals because they live in boggy soils that lack vital nutrients. Their leaves are covered with sticky, red tentacles that secrete glue-like droplets to capture prey.

Wing stuck to glue-like secretions

SUNDEW HAIRS secrete glue-like droplets.

Droplet of a glue-like secretion

PITCHER PLANT
The jug-shaped pitcher plant is filled with liquid digestive enzymes in which its prey drown. Insects are drawn to the deadly trap by bright colours and nectar, but the slippery rim causes them to fall inside, where they are slowly digested.

Flies trapped in the plant are digested for their nutrients.

TRIGGER HAIRS are touch sensitive.

Trigger hair

VENUS FLYTRAP
The hinged leaves of a Venus flytrap snap shut if an insect touches tiny trigger hairs on the leaf twice in quick succession. The trap then secretes digestive juices to break down its prey.

Flies enter through an opening at the top of the pitcher plant.

Spiny teeth form a cage to trap the fly.

HOW
CARNIVOROUS PLANTS
WORK

Carnivorous plants get their nutrients by catching small creatures, which die when they cannot escape. To trap prey, the plants use seductive colours and smells, snapping traps, and sticky secretions. Once caught, the prey is digested with powerful enzymes and its nutrients are absorbed by the plant.

2 STRUGGLING
To release itself from the sundew leaf, the fly begins to struggle and sticks to more hairs.

3 COILING
Within 15 minutes the fly is dead. The leaf slowly begins to curl around it.

1 STICKY TRAP
Attracted by the sweet, nectar-like scent of the sundew's sticky leaves, a fly lands and gets stuck.

4 DIGESTING
The sticky droplets contain digestive enzymes that break down the fly, releasing nutrients for the sundew to absorb.

When touched, the tentacles bend towards the insect.

5 REMAINS
The parts of the fly that cannot be digested remain stuck to the leaf until it uncurls.

HOW DESERT PLANTS SURVIVE

Deserts are the driest places on Earth and can go without rain for months or even years at a time. To endure such hostile conditions, desert plants need special adaptations. They must be able to gather water quickly after rain, store it for long periods, and protect this precious resource from thirsty animals and the relentless force of the Sun.

▶ HOW CACTI WORK

While most plants have tall, thin stems to support their leaves, cacti have barrel-shaped stems to store water, and their leaves have evolved into protective spines. This barrel cactus's roots are shallow but spread widely, ready to collect water from the damp soil surface after brief rainstorms.

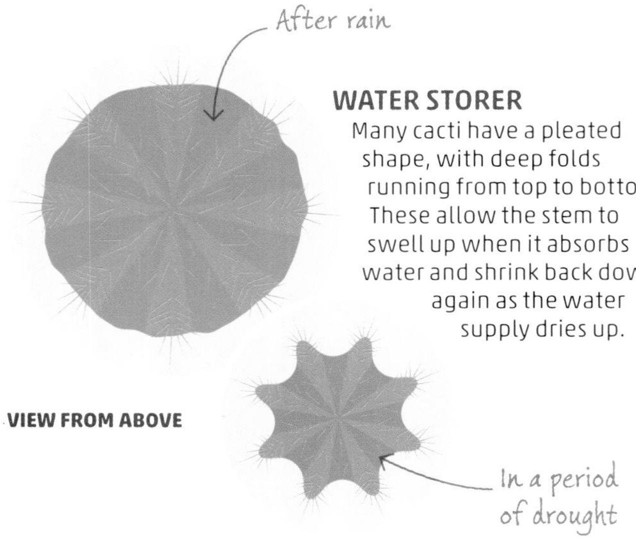

After rain

WATER STORER
Many cacti have a pleated shape, with deep folds running from top to bottom. These allow the stem to swell up when it absorbs water and shrink back down again as the water supply dries up.

VIEW FROM ABOVE

In a period of drought

Water is stored in the thick, spongy flesh.

The sharp spines deter predators.

Roots are shallow to quickly absorb rainfall.

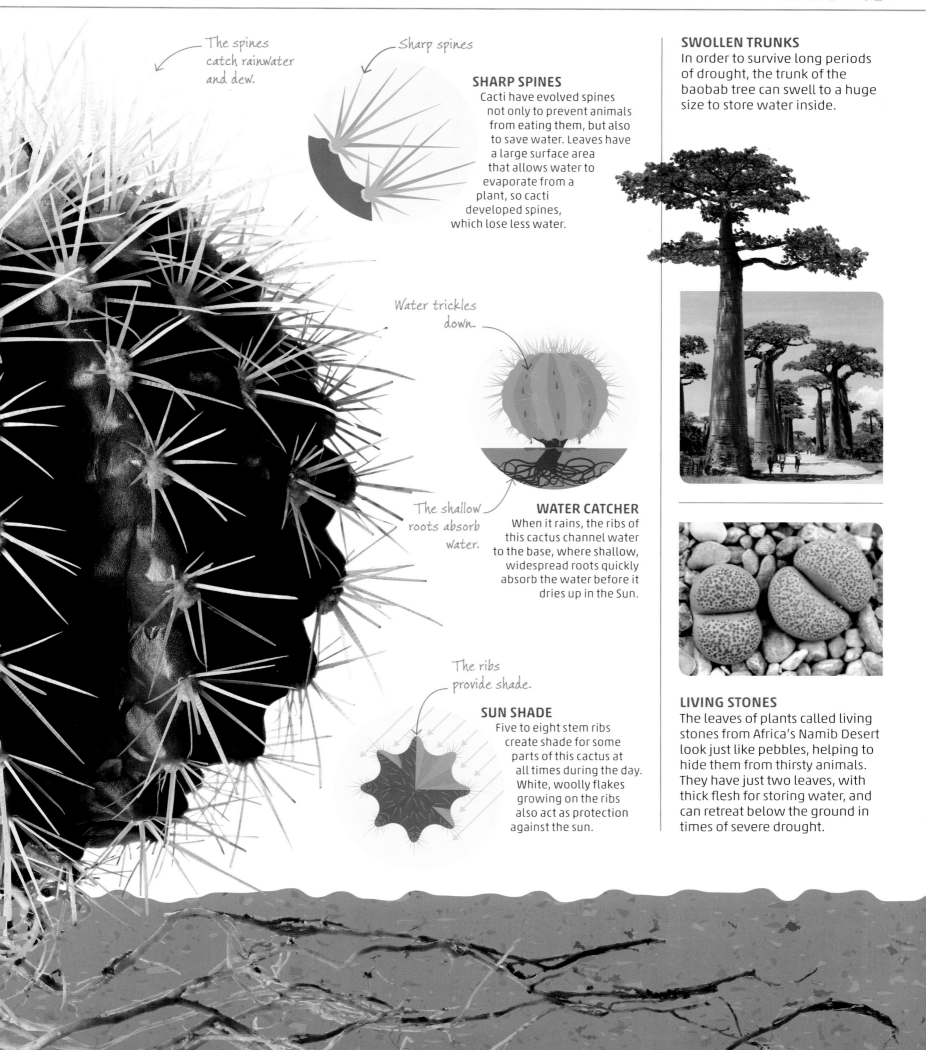

The spines catch rainwater and dew.

Sharp spines

SHARP SPINES
Cacti have evolved spines not only to prevent animals from eating them, but also to save water. Leaves have a large surface area that allows water to evaporate from a plant, so cacti developed spines, which lose less water.

SWOLLEN TRUNKS
In order to survive long periods of drought, the trunk of the baobab tree can swell to a huge size to store water inside.

Water trickles down.

The shallow roots absorb water.

WATER CATCHER
When it rains, the ribs of this cactus channel water to the base, where shallow, widespread roots quickly absorb the water before it dries up in the Sun.

The ribs provide shade.

SUN SHADE
Five to eight stem ribs create shade for some parts of this cactus at all times during the day. White, woolly flakes growing on the ribs also act as protection against the sun.

LIVING STONES
The leaves of plants called living stones from Africa's Namib Desert look just like pebbles, helping to hide them from thirsty animals. They have just two leaves, with thick flesh for storing water, and can retreat below the ground in times of severe drought.

WATER HYACINTH

WATER LILY

The strong scent of water lily flowers attracts insects, which spread the pollen.

The water hyacinth's feathery roots are not fixed to the bottom, so it can float on the sunlit surface.

HOW
AQUATIC PLANTS WORK

Surviving in water is a challenge for plants. Just like land plants, aquatic plants need the Sun's energy to make food through photosynthesis, but muddy or sandy water can block light and make this difficult. As a result, most have evolved to survive underwater or to float on the surface. Many of these plants need strong roots and leaves to avoid being damaged by moving water.

▶ **LIFE IN THE WATER**
Some aquatic plants have long shoots, so their leaves and flowers can float on the surface and capture the Sun's energy. These plants send roots deep into the water bed to keep them anchored. Others float along on the surface, with their roots dangling freely in the water. Plants growing in rivers need strong roots to hold them in place and leaves that allow water to slip past easily without tearing them apart. Some plants live totally submerged in shallow water.

ON THE COAST
Ocean coastlines can be especially challenging, because the salt in sea water damages most plant cells. Mangrove trees, which grow in coastal swamps, have strong, stilt-like roots. These keep them propped up and stable in mud, and remove salt. This helps them filter and use the water they need to stay alive.

Long roots anchor the water lily in the mud.

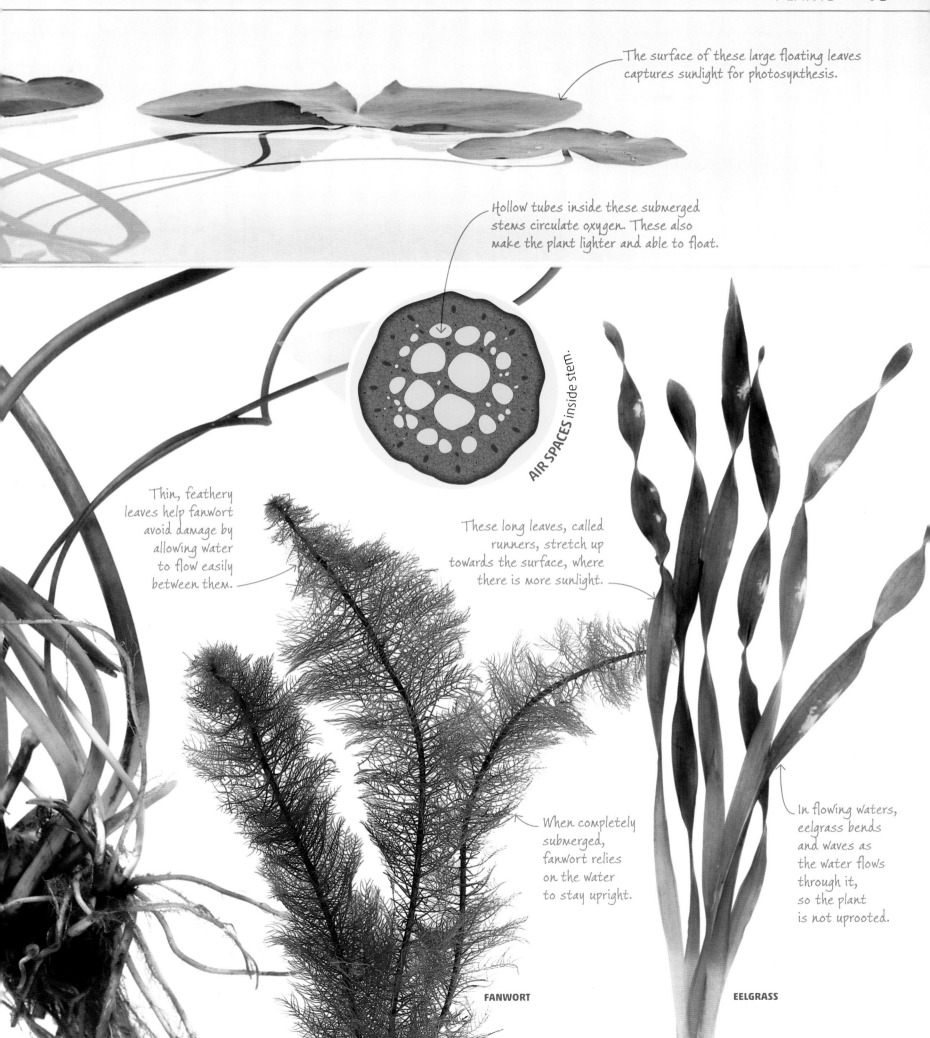

The surface of these large floating leaves captures sunlight for photosynthesis.

Hollow tubes inside these submerged stems circulate oxygen. These also make the plant lighter and able to float.

AIR SPACES *inside stem.*

Thin, feathery leaves help fanwort avoid damage by allowing water to flow easily between them.

These long leaves, called runners, stretch up towards the surface, where there is more sunlight.

When completely submerged, fanwort relies on the water to stay upright.

In flowing waters, eelgrass bends and waves as the water flows through it, so the plant is not uprooted.

FANWORT

EELGRASS

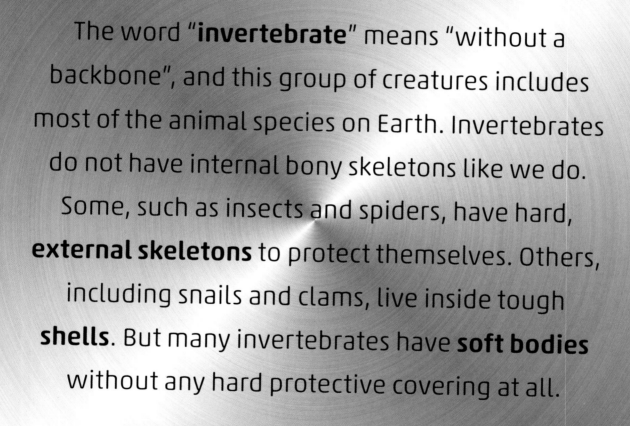

The word **"invertebrate"** means "without a backbone", and this group of creatures includes most of the animal species on Earth. Invertebrates do not have internal bony skeletons like we do. Some, such as insects and spiders, have hard, **external skeletons** to protect themselves. Others, including snails and clams, live inside tough **shells**. But many invertebrates have **soft bodies** without any hard protective covering at all.

INVERTEBRATES

HOW INVERTEBRATES WORK

More than 95 per cent of animals on Earth are invertebrates – animals without a backbone. The invertebrates don't make up a single family of animals. Instead, they include many different, unrelated animal groups that have little in common, besides the absence of a spine. They range from microscopic sea creatures to worms, starfish, and spiders. Many live only in the sea, but certain groups, such as the insects, are among the most numerous animals on land.

▶ INSECTS

Scientists estimate there are about 1 million different species of insect on Earth and that around 10 billion billion individual insects are alive at any moment. All insects have a protective external skeleton, six legs, and sensitive feelers called antennae. Most have wings as adults and eyes that allow them to see in many directions at once. Many insects begin life with grub-like bodies and go through a dramatic period of change called metamorphosis as they grow. Caterpillars, for instance, transform into moths and butterflies.

INVERTEBRATE GROUPS

There are many different types of invertebrate. Some of the largest groups include insects, echinoderms, cnidarians, molluscs, arachnids, and crustaceans.

ECHINODERMS

The spiny-skinned bodies of these marine animals consist of five equal parts, each of which has its own complete set of internal organs. Echinoderms include starfish, sea urchins, and sea cucumbers.

These strong arms can open oyster shells to expose the meat inside.

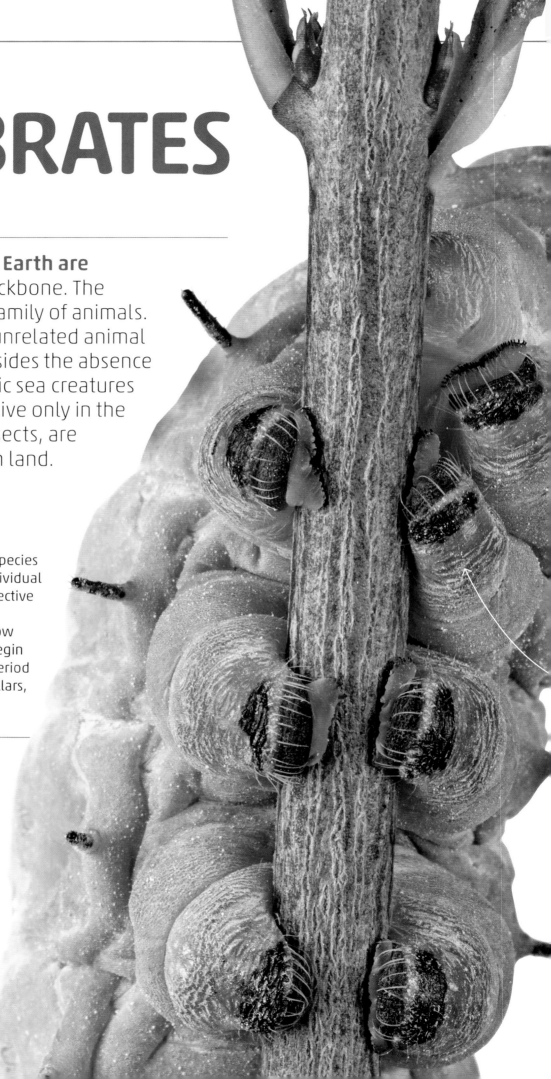

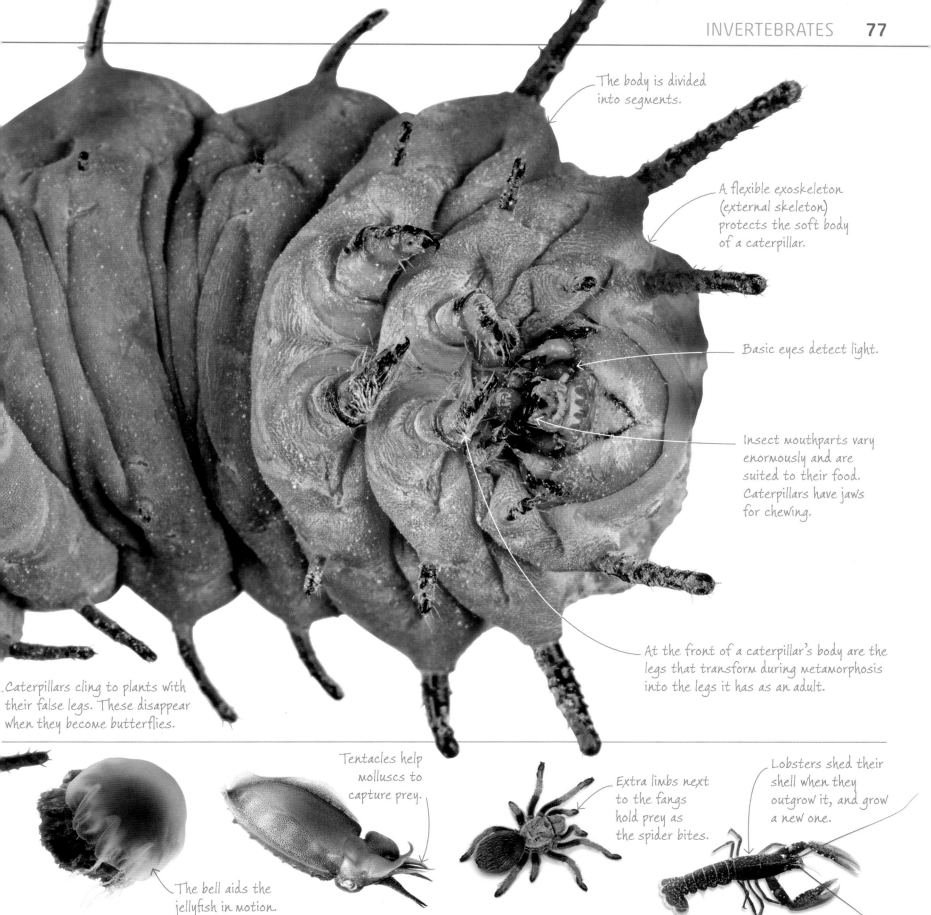

The body is divided into segments.

A flexible exoskeleton (external skeleton) protects the soft body of a caterpillar.

Basic eyes detect light.

Insect mouthparts vary enormously and are suited to their food. Caterpillars have jaws for chewing.

At the front of a caterpillar's body are the legs that transform during metamorphosis into the legs it has as an adult.

Caterpillars cling to plants with their false legs. These disappear when they become butterflies.

Tentacles help molluscs to capture prey.

Extra limbs next to the fangs hold prey as the spider bites.

Lobsters shed their shell when they outgrow it, and grow a new one.

The bell aids the jellyfish in motion.

CNIDARIANS
Corals, jellyfish, and sea anemones are all types of cnidarian. Most of these aquatic animals swim, but some spend their entire life attached to a rock. They typically have round or flower-shaped bodies with stinging tentacles, but they have no brain.

MOLLUSCS
This group of soft-bodied animals includes slugs, snails, oysters, squid, and octopuses. All molluscs have a special kind of rasping tongue, and many produce a protective shell from part of the body wall. Most molluscs live in the sea.

ARACHNIDS
Arachnids have a jointed external skeleton with eight legs, but no wings or antennae. Most arachnids, including spiders and scorpions, are predatory, but many others, such as mites and ticks, are scavengers, herbivores, or parasites.

CRUSTACEANS
Crustaceans, such as crabs and shrimps, typically have a hard, segmented outer body, four or more pairs of legs, and two pairs of antennae. Most have gills to breathe in water, but some, such as woodlice, live on land.

HOW **SNAILS** WORK

Snails and slugs belong to a large group of invertebrates called molluscs. Most molluscs have soft bodies, and many form shells to protect themselves. Snails are common not just on land but also in the sea and in fresh water. They have distinctive, coiled shells that are large enough for them to retract their body into. Slugs are close relatives of snails and use a foul-tasting, sticky slime instead of a shell to protect them against predators.

A hard shell protects the snail's soft body.

The soft body retracts under the lip of the shell when the snail feels threatened.

Glands secrete a slimy layer of mucus that helps the snail to move across different surfaces.

UNDER THE SHELL

A snail's digestive system twists to fit inside its coiled shell. At the front of the shell is a cavity, into which the body can withdraw if danger threatens. Snails do not have one single brain, but instead have several tiny brain-like structures called ganglia, made from clusters of nerve cells.

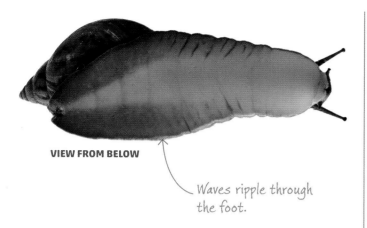

VIEW FROM BELOW

Waves ripple through the foot.

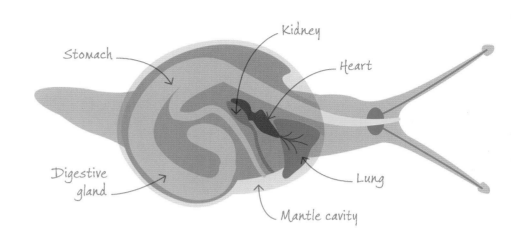

Stomach

Kidney

Heart

Digestive gland

Lung

Mantle cavity

MUSCULAR FOOT

The base of a snail is a single large muscle. The snail contracts this muscle in waves, making it creep forward. Glands in the foot release a thick liquid that helps the snail glide on the ground or stick to vertical surfaces, leaving a trail. Snails often prefer to follow trails made by other snails, as this helps them move faster – up to a top speed of 1 m (3 ft) per hour.

▼ GIANT AFRICAN LAND SNAIL

The largest land-dwelling snail in the world is the giant African land snail, which grows to a length of 30 cm (1 ft) – as long as a rabbit.

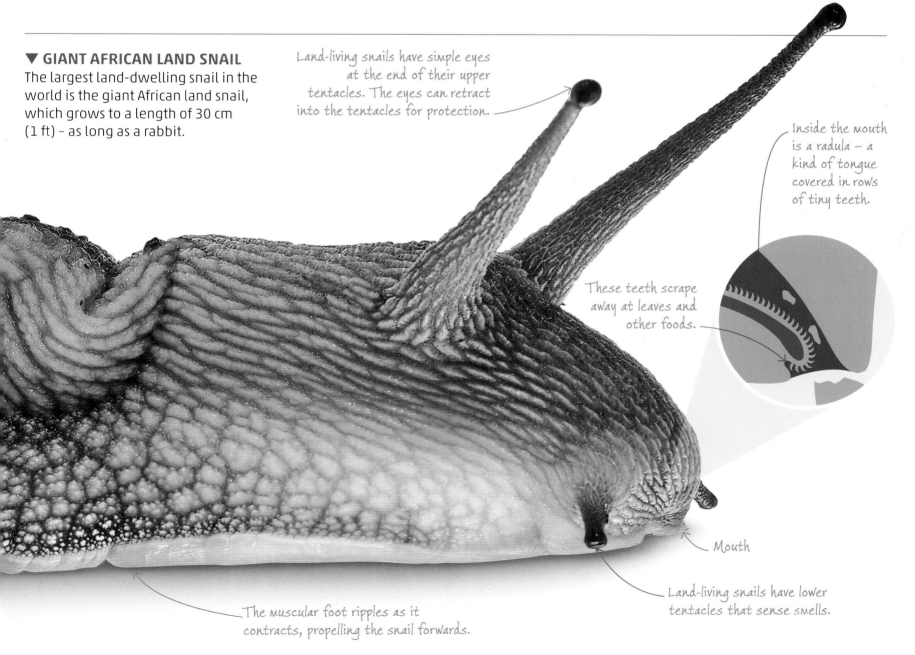

Land-living snails have simple eyes at the end of their upper tentacles. The eyes can retract into the tentacles for protection.

Inside the mouth is a radula – a kind of tongue covered in rows of tiny teeth.

These teeth scrape away at leaves and other foods.

Mouth

The muscular foot ripples as it contracts, propelling the snail forwards.

Land-living snails have lower tentacles that sense smells.

HOW **BIVALVES** WORK

Bivalves belong to the same group of animals as slugs and snails, the molluscs, but these aquatic animals have no head and live inside a hinged, two-part shell that closes tight when danger threatens. Most live buried in sand or mud, where they are hidden from predators, but some live attached to rocks or wedged into crevices. They feed and breathe using two tubes (siphons) that act like straws to suck in water, which their gills then filter for oxygen and food.

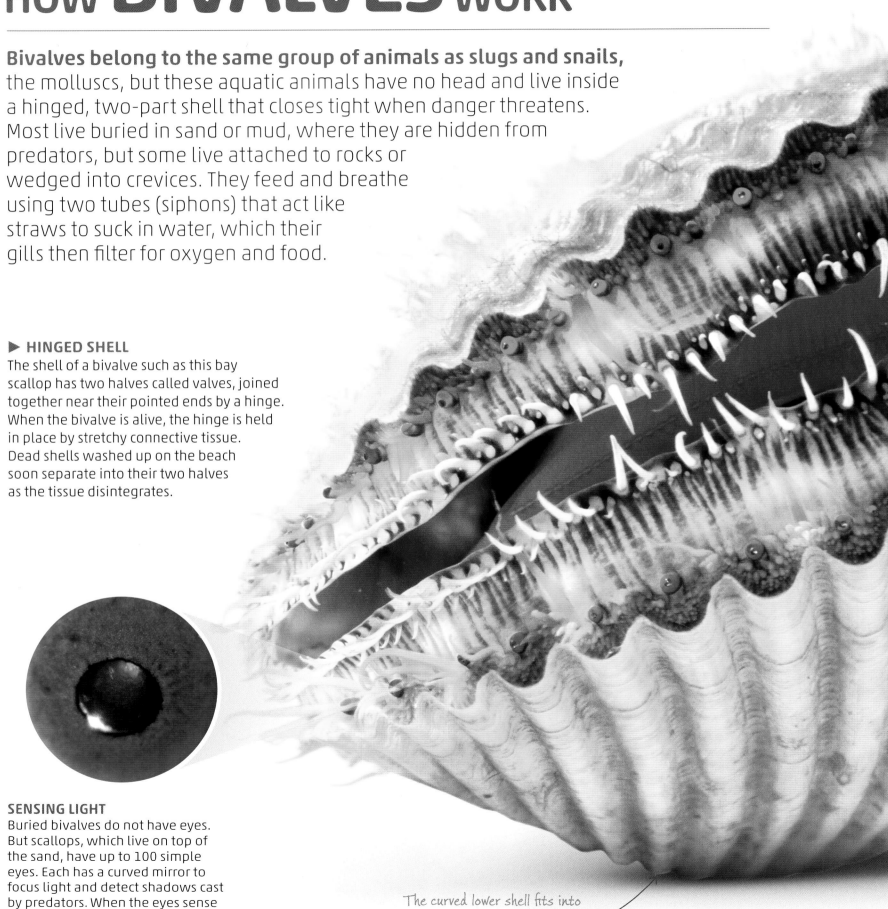

▶ HINGED SHELL
The shell of a bivalve such as this bay scallop has two halves called valves, joined together near their pointed ends by a hinge. When the bivalve is alive, the hinge is held in place by stretchy connective tissue. Dead shells washed up on the beach soon separate into their two halves as the tissue disintegrates.

SENSING LIGHT
Buried bivalves do not have eyes. But scallops, which live on top of the sand, have up to 100 simple eyes. Each has a curved mirror to focus light and detect shadows cast by predators. When the eyes sense danger, the shell snaps closed.

The curved lower shell fits into a depression in the sand.

Tentacles sense chemicals in the water or react to touch, giving warning of approaching predators, such as starfish.

Water flows in and out when the shell is held open.

A bivalve's body wall, or mantle, encloses its inner organs and also secretes the shell lining.

Each year, a new growth line forms on the shell.

MAKING PEARLS

The lining of most bivalve shells is made of a dull material. Pearl oyster shells, however, are lined with a shiny, crystal-like substance called nacre, which is secreted by the mantle and protects the oyster's soft body. Any irritating debris (such as a grain of sand) that gets into an oyster can become coated in nacre, forming a pearl.

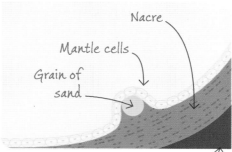

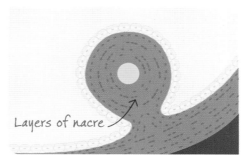

Nacre

Mantle cells

Grain of sand

Shell

1 SAND ENTERS SHELL
If sand gets trapped inside a pearl oyster, the oyster's mantle will slowly grow over it.

Layers of nacre

2 NACRE LAYERS ADDED
The mantle covers the sand grain with nacre, adding more and more layers until the sand no longer irritates the oyster.

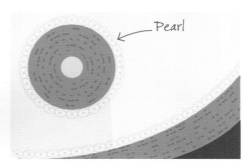

Pearl

3 PEARL FORMS
Eventually, a ball of nacre builds up around the sand grain, forming a pearl, which stays inside the shell.

MOVING THROUGH SAND

Bivalves that live buried in the sand usually stay in one place, but some, such as clams, can move downwards by using a muscular foot. They dig themselves deeper into the sand to avoid predators and move back up later to feed again. One species, razor clams, can move faster than a human can dig.

1 FOOT EXTENDS
The clam's foot extends in the direction it wants to travel.

2 FOOT ANCHORS
The tip of the foot spreads out sideways, acting as an anchor in the sand.

3 BODY MOVES
The muscular foot contracts, pulling the clam into the sand.

TYPES OF SHELLS

Most molluscs have a hard shell that protects the soft-bodied animal inside from predators and the environment. The shell is created from and maintained by the body wall, called the mantle. The shell can be made of either one or two pieces, and survives long after the animal inside has died. Mollusc shells can be found nearly anywhere, but the greatest variety is found in the sea.

The open tip allows water to flow in and out.

ELEPHANT TUSK SHELL

The sticky tentacles are used to seize prey.

Hollow chambers in the shell contain gas to help the animal float in water.

A girdle of muscle surrounds the shell.

A bivalve's shell is made of two parts that can open and close.

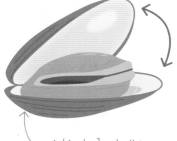

The strong foot moves the animal up and down through the sea bed.

NAUTILUS SHELL

MARBLED CHITON SHELL

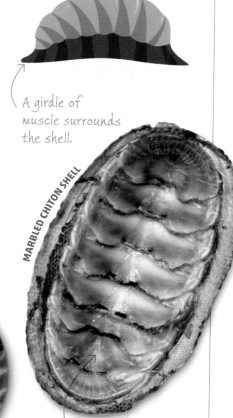

FLUTED GIANT CLAM SHELL

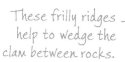

Separate shell plates allow the animal to curl up.

These frilly ridges help to wedge the clam between rocks.

CEPHALOPODS
The nautilus is a relative of octopuses and squid. It controls its buoyancy in water by adjusting the levels of water and gas in its shell. Nautiluses are known as "living fossils" as they have changed very little in millions of years.

CHITONS
The shell of a chiton is made up of eight overlapping plates that attach to the body and move separately, like a knight's armour. These plates protect chitons from predators, but also allow the animal to move freely.

BIVALVES
Bivalves have a shell made up of two separate halves called valves, joined together by a hinge and a stretchy band of flesh. In the sea, small crabs shelter in the deep, leaf-like ridges on the fluted giant clam's shell.

TUSK SHELLS
Shaped like elephant tusks, these shells have an opening at the top to let water flow in and out, providing oxygen to the creature inside. The shell is wider at the bottom, so the animal can use its foot to move through the sand.

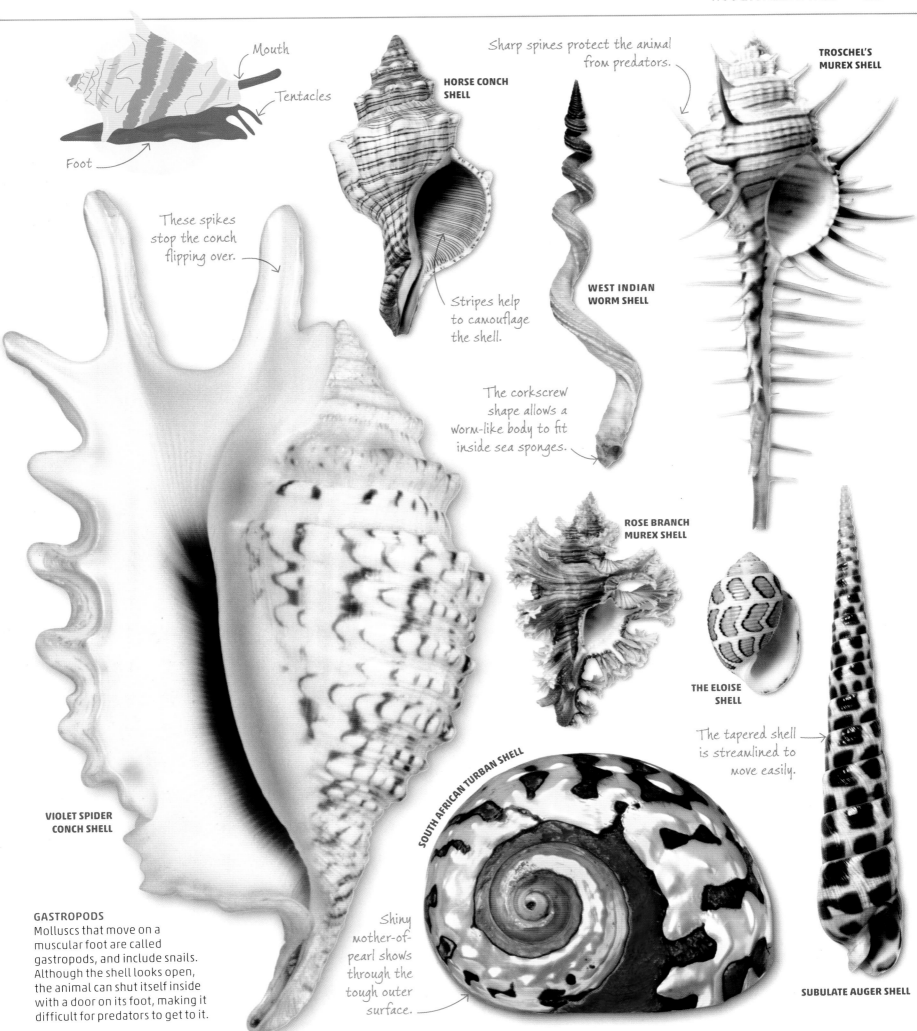

Mouth

Tentacles

Foot

These spikes stop the conch flipping over.

HORSE CONCH SHELL

Sharp spines protect the animal from predators.

TROSCHEL'S MUREX SHELL

Stripes help to camouflage the shell.

WEST INDIAN WORM SHELL

The corkscrew shape allows a worm-like body to fit inside sea sponges.

ROSE BRANCH MUREX SHELL

THE ELOISE SHELL

The tapered shell is streamlined to move easily.

VIOLET SPIDER CONCH SHELL

SOUTH AFRICAN TURBAN SHELL

Shiny mother-of-pearl shows through the tough outer surface.

SUBULATE AUGER SHELL

GASTROPODS
Molluscs that move on a muscular foot are called gastropods, and include snails. Although the shell looks open, the animal can shut itself inside with a door on its foot, making it difficult for predators to get to it.

If an arm is lost through injury, the octopus can grow a new one.

Each arm has two rows of suckers for gripping surfaces and grasping objects.

▶ **ALL-PURPOSE ARMS**

The soft fleshy body of an octopus contains its vital organs and carries eyes. Two-thirds of the animal's nervous system are devoted to controlling the eight arms' powerful muscles. These limbs are lined with suction cups that give them a firm grip. They are strong enough to wrestle sharks, but are precise enough to extract tasty lobsters from between rocks.

HOW
OCTOPUSES
WORK

Although it is a relative of slow-moving slugs and snails, the octopus is a quick-witted hunter and one of the most intelligent of all invertebrates. Its eight arms are used for crawling and hunting, while its powerful, hard beak can crack through all but the toughest shells.

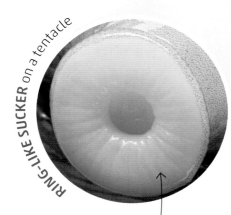

RING-LIKE SUCKER on a tentacle

As well as gripping, suckers also have receptors for tasting the objects and the water around them.

ESCAPE ARTIST

Having no hard internal skeleton or outer shell makes an octopus able to squeeze its entire body through narrow openings. In the wild it can squeeze into small caves to avoid danger, and in zoos and aquaria an octopus is a notorious escape artist.

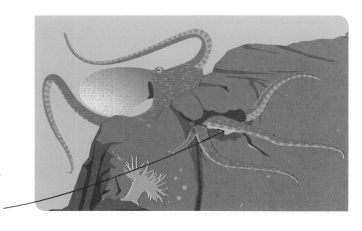

An octopus can squeeze through any hole larger than its beak, the only hard part of its body.

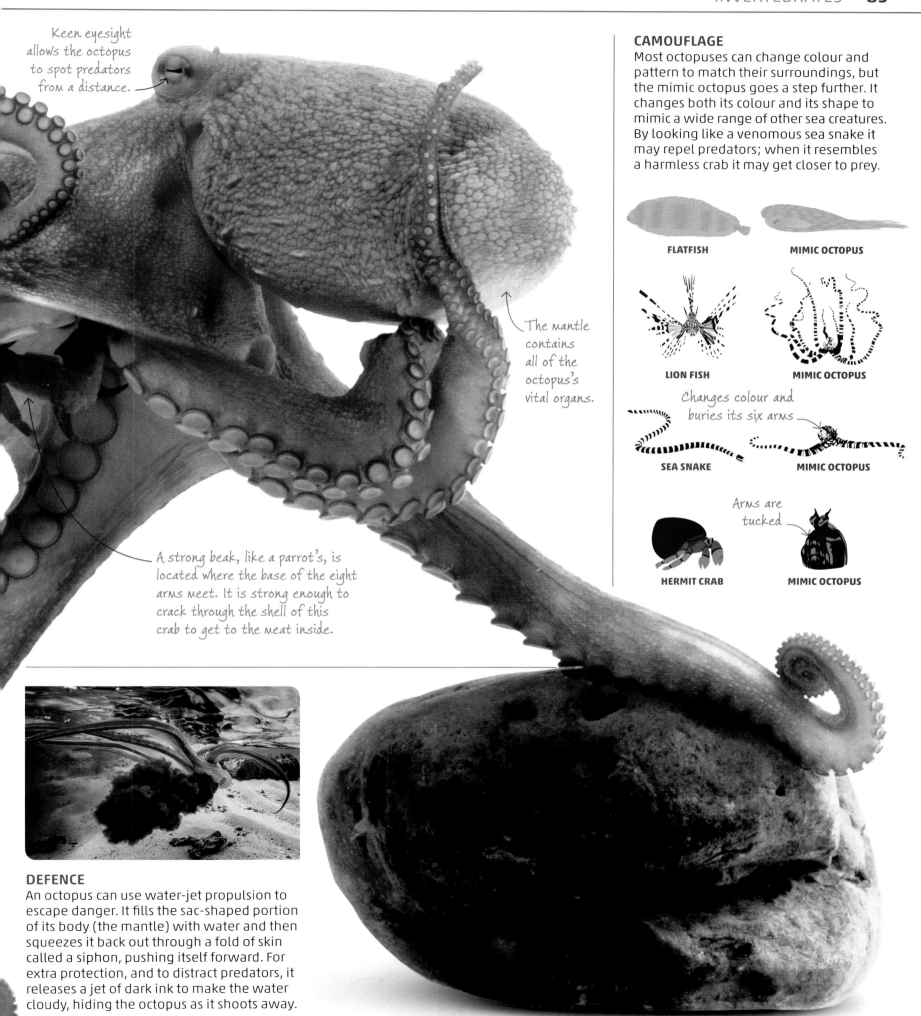

Keen eyesight allows the octopus to spot predators from a distance.

The mantle contains all of the octopus's vital organs.

A strong beak, like a parrot's, is located where the base of the eight arms meet. It is strong enough to crack through the shell of this crab to get to the meat inside.

CAMOUFLAGE
Most octopuses can change colour and pattern to match their surroundings, but the mimic octopus goes a step further. It changes both its colour and its shape to mimic a wide range of other sea creatures. By looking like a venomous sea snake it may repel predators; when it resembles a harmless crab it may get closer to prey.

FLATFISH   **MIMIC OCTOPUS**

LION FISH   **MIMIC OCTOPUS**

Changes colour and buries its six arms

SEA SNAKE   **MIMIC OCTOPUS**

Arms are tucked

HERMIT CRAB   **MIMIC OCTOPUS**

DEFENCE
An octopus can use water-jet propulsion to escape danger. It fills the sac-shaped portion of its body (the mantle) with water and then squeezes it back out through a fold of skin called a siphon, pushing itself forward. For extra protection, and to distract predators, it releases a jet of dark ink to make the water cloudy, hiding the octopus as it shoots away.

HOW
SEA ANEMONES
WORK

Each tentacle contains tiny stinging cells that paralyse prey.

Anemones may look like flowers, but they are actually animals that hold on to the sea floor with their mouths pointing upwards. Stinging, muscular tentacles wave about in the water to capture prey organisms, before transferring them to a mouth in the centre of the body. Most anemones eat small organisms that float in the sea currents and are harmless to larger creatures, but others have stings powerful enough to paralyse fish.

▶ DIVIDING IN TWO

An anemone can reproduce sexually by releasing eggs and sperm, but its simple body can also split to form two new anemones. The anemone pictured here already has two rings of tentacles around two mouths. The split will extend from the top to the base until one anemone becomes two identical clones.

Anemone

Discarded shell used by crab.

Hermit crab

BODYGUARD

Hermit crabs often place a young sea anemone on the discarded snail shells in which the crabs live. This partnership benefits both species: the anemone's stings and camouflage protect the crab, while the crab spills leftover food for the anemone to eat.

The base of the column, called the pedal disc, attaches to rock or gravel. It is not permanently rooted and can move position.

MOUTH
A single opening at the centre of each ring of tentacles is a mouth for taking in food and expelling waste.

SELF-DEFENCE
Many anemones retract their tentacles when danger threatens. This beadlet anemone, common in European rock pools, also does so when exposed to air at low tide, to keep it from drying out.

OPEN   CLOSED

Inside the main body is a chamber for digesting food and releasing sperm or eggs.

The body wall contains muscles that can contract to pull the anemone down, away from danger.

HOW
CORALS
WORK

Corals are marine animals related to anemones and jellyfish. They grow into enormous underwater colonies, many of which are supported by rock-like skeletons. The largest colonies form rocky mounds on the sea bed called reefs – Australia's Great Barrier Reef is so big that it can be seen from space. Each colony has thousands of individuals called polyps that wave their tentacles in the water to capture floating organisms known as plankton.

The polyps of a staghorn coral are embedded in stony branches that support the base of the colony.

Hard corals can grow into many different shapes.

HARD CORALS
Some coral colonies, such as the staghorn coral (above) and the galaxy coral (below), produce a hard skeleton into which the vulnerable coral organisms can retract. Made of calcium carbonate, these skeletons build up over time to form limestone reefs.

▶ CORAL ANATOMY
All corals, such as this galaxy coral, have multiple polyps, but they act as one single organism. Each polyp in the coral colony is connected at its base to its neighbours by a network of extensions of its own body. Although the polyps act as one, they each have their own stomach and a single central opening that takes in food as well as ejecting waste and sex cells.

The tentacles of this galaxy coral are usually tipped white.

Each coral polyp has a ring of tentacles surrounding a central mouth.

The tentacles paralyse prey with stings and sweep the prey into the polyp's mouth.

The mouth both consumes food and expels waste.

Thin membranes connect polyps to create a colony that acts as a single organism.

Limestone skeleton secreted by polyps

Other animals often set up home in a coral colony. These are the white feathery limbs of a filter-feeding barnacle.

Upper layer

Mesogloea (jelly-like core)

A VITAL PARTNERSHIP
Many kinds of coral contain algae that give coral their colour. The algae make food by photosynthesis and pass some of this food to the corals, helping them grow. Rising ocean temperatures associated with climate change can make polyps expel their algae, turning coral reefs white and starving the coral. This is known as "coral bleaching".

Algae live in the inner layer of cells.

Like many corals, this species contains photosynthesizing algae that help supply food.

CORAL COMMUNITY

Located off the Australian coast, this colourful coral is part of the Great Barrier Reef. It stretches for over 2,600 km (1,600 miles) and includes hundreds of islands and thousands of smaller reefs. It's a rich environment, full of fish such as sharks and rays, whales, and turtles. Coral is extremely sensitive to change. While the area shown is healthy, and teeming with marine wildlife, some regions have been damaged by severe weather and human pollution. Increasing water temperatures cause bleaching, a type of damage that drains the coral of its rich colour.

HOW **JELLYFISH** WORK

Jellyfish are related to corals and anemones, but instead of living fixed to the seabed they swim freely, propelling themselves with rhythmic pulsations of their bell-shaped bodies. Jellyfish do not have brains or complex sense organs, but they can ensnare more quick-witted animals by inflicting paralysing stings with their tentacles. A few types have venom powerful enough to kill a human in minutes.

▶ SIMPLE BODY

A jellyfish's body is more than 95 per cent water and consists entirely of only two layers of cells separated by a jellylike substance. Food is digested inside the bell, which can also contract to force water out and push the animal by jet propulsion. Trailing behind the bell are stinging tentacles and structures called oral arms, which bring food up to the mouth.

Hidden from view, the mouth leads to a simple stomach. Waste leaves the body by the same opening.

Egg-yolk jellyfish have curtain-like oral arms to engulf their prey – other jellyfish.

The tentacles have muscles so they can coil around prey.

The bell is transparent because its wall consists almost entirely of water.

The egg-yolk jellyfish gets its name from the yellow colour of its reproductive organs.

HOW JELLYFISH STINGS WORK

A jellyfish has hundreds of stings on every tentacle, each sting housed inside a single cell. A hair-like trigger activates the sting when an animal brushes it, causing a coiled thread inside the cell to turn itself inside out and shoot out violently, piercing the prey's skin. Backward pointing barbs anchor the sting in the prey's flesh while venom is injected through the tube.

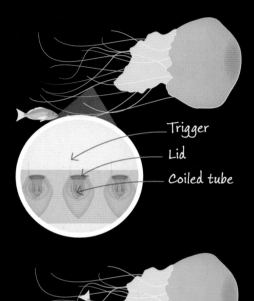

Trigger

Lid

Coiled tube

Venom flows out through the tube.

The sting turns inside out and pierces the prey.

LIFE CYCLE

The life cycle of jellyfish goes through two stages: a free-swimming stage called a medusa (the jellyfish) and a settled stage called a polyp. The polyp looks like a tiny sea anemone and feeds by catching food from the water. It divides repeatedly to produce many baby jellyfish.

A fertilized egg grows into a larva. It swims to the seabed and settles on a rock.

The larva develops a body like a coral polyp, with a ring of feeding tentacles around a central mouth.

The polyp divides horizontally into a stack of discs.

Each disc breaks free as a baby jellyfish.

Male jellyfish release clouds of sperm into the water, fertilizing eggs carried by a female.

HOW STARFISH WORK

Starfish are actually not fish at all but are slow-moving invertebrates that creep over the sea floor on hundreds of sucker-like feet. They belong to a large group of sea creatures called echinoderms, which get their name from the Greek words for "spiny skin". Unlike most animals, echinoderms have no front or back and no head or brain. Instead, their bodies typically have five or more symmetrical parts arranged in a ring.

REGENERATION
Starfish can regenerate lost arms. Some starfish can regrow from a single detached arm provided the arm still retains a part of the central disc.

This broken arm is starting to grow four new arms, to form a whole new starfish.

Tube feet are used for movement and gripping.

Seawater enters the body here.

Radial canals carry water to the arms.

Feet extend when water is forced into them.

A ring-shaped canal carries water through the digestive system.

Tube feet at the ends of the arms can sense light smells.

TRANSPORT SYSTEM
Starfish do not have a heart or blood vessels. Instead they rely on a network of seawater-filled tubes that run through the body, transporting oxygen, food, and waste. The system also helps with movement – water is pumped into the feet to make them extend as the starfish clambers over the seabed.

▲ STAR-SHAPED BODY
Starfish typically have five symmetrical arms radiating from a central disc, but some have as many has 50. The mouth is in the centre of the underside, and the anus is in the centre of the upper side. Emerging through perforations in the underside of the body are hundreds of tube feet, the sticky tips of which form cups to grip surfaces.

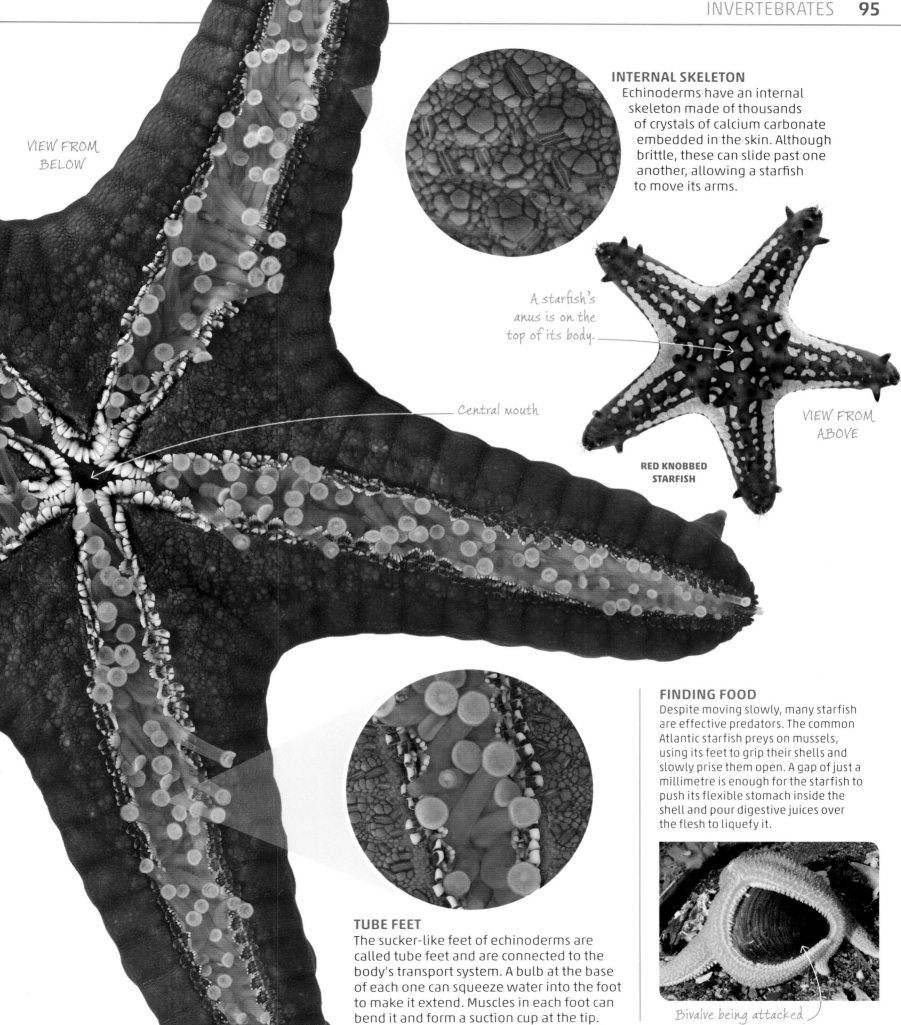

VIEW FROM
BELOW

INTERNAL SKELETON
Echinoderms have an internal
skeleton made of thousands
of crystals of calcium carbonate
embedded in the skin. Although
brittle, these can slide past one
another, allowing a starfish
to move its arms.

A starfish's
anus is on the
top of its body.

Central mouth

VIEW FROM
ABOVE

**RED KNOBBED
STARFISH**

FINDING FOOD
Despite moving slowly, many starfish
are effective predators. The common
Atlantic starfish preys on mussels,
using its feet to grip their shells and
slowly prise them open. A gap of just a
millimetre is enough for the starfish to
push its flexible stomach inside the
shell and pour digestive juices over
the flesh to liquefy it.

TUBE FEET
The sucker-like feet of echinoderms are
called tube feet and are connected to the
body's transport system. A bulb at the base
of each one can squeeze water into the foot
to make it extend. Muscles in each foot can
bend it and form a suction cup at the tip.

Bivalve being attacked

HOW **WORMS** WORK

Worms are soft-bodied invertebrates that have a long, thin body with a head at the front, a tail at the rear, and no legs. They usually live in wet places and can be found in many different habitats, including inside other animals. Worms can be flat or cylindrical, microscopic or metres long, segmented or unsegmented. It can be difficult to tell which end is the head because most worms look the same at both ends.

▼ SEGMENTED WORMS

Many kinds of animal have body sections called segments, but they are especially obvious in segmented worms such as earthworms. An earthworm's muscular body wall allows it to burrow underground, where it sucks soil into its mouth to extract food. These burrowing movements churn soil, loosening it up and mixing it with air – which benefits plant roots and other soil-living animals.

SADDLE
The bulging section of an earthworm is called a saddle. After worms mate, the saddle releases a ring of slime. As the worm slides out of the ring, it leaves its eggs inside it. The slimy ring, called a cocoon, protects the eggs until they hatch a few weeks later.

The tail looks like the head, but it is where food waste is expelled.

Earthworms do not have lungs and instead breathe through their moist skin.

Each segment has separate muscles.

INSIDE AN EARTHWORM

The earthworm's body has a fluid-filled chamber, called a coelom, that supports the body in the same way a hard skeleton does in other animals. Muscles in each segment press against the coelom to make the worm move. These muscles surround the digestive and circulatory systems, which stretch along the whole length of its body.

Food waste passes from the anus in muddy trails called casts.

A worm creates eggs in its saddle.

In the intestines, food is broken down and the nutrients are absorbed.

Coelom

Brain

Five hearts pump blood to the rest of the body through blood vessels.

Long circular muscles and short lengthways muscles in each segment contract and expand as a worm moves.

Each segment has four pairs of setae.

BRISTLES

An earthworm's body may appear smooth, but it has tiny bristles called setae. These help anchor the worm's body as it moves through the ground.

HOW WORMS MOVE

An earthworm moves in an accordian-like fashion, its segments bunching and lengthening as it pulls its back end up and thrusts its head forwards. Strong rings of circular muscles and lengthways muscles squeeze and relax against the coelom to propel the worm forwards.

Bristles prevent the worm from sliding backwards.

Head

WIDER AND FATTER

The segments become shorter, wider, and fatter when the lengthways muscles contract, pulling the rear end forwards.

Head stretches forwards.

LONGER AND THINNER

The segments become longer and thinner when the circular muscles squeeze, pushing the front end ahead.

Earthworms have no eyes, but they do have light receptors on their skin that tell them if they're in sunlight or shade.

Earthworms produce a slippery fluid that keeps their bodies moist and helps them move smoothly, even over rough surfaces.

HOW SEA WORMS WORK

Worms are as widespread in the sea as they are on land, but most marine worms look very different from earthworms. Some live in solid tubes of mud and feed by waving flower-like tentacles in the water. Others burrow into or crawl across the sea floor, or swim through the water in search of food. The most active are predators, some with biting jaws so strong they can slice prey in half.

▶ BUILDING A HOME

Tube worms use their mouthparts and tentacles to construct their homes around them as they grow. These fan worms build tubes from fine mud, held together with their own sticky mucus. Other tube worms use sand and shells or produce a chalky material that sets like a plaster cast. Newly hatched fan worms float in the sea, then settle on the seabed where they start building.

INSIDE THE TUBE

A fan worm's segmented body hangs tail-down in its tube. The worm's head and tentacles stick out of the top but can be quickly withdrawn if the worm is threatened. Bristles on each body segment helpthe worm grip the sides of the tube.

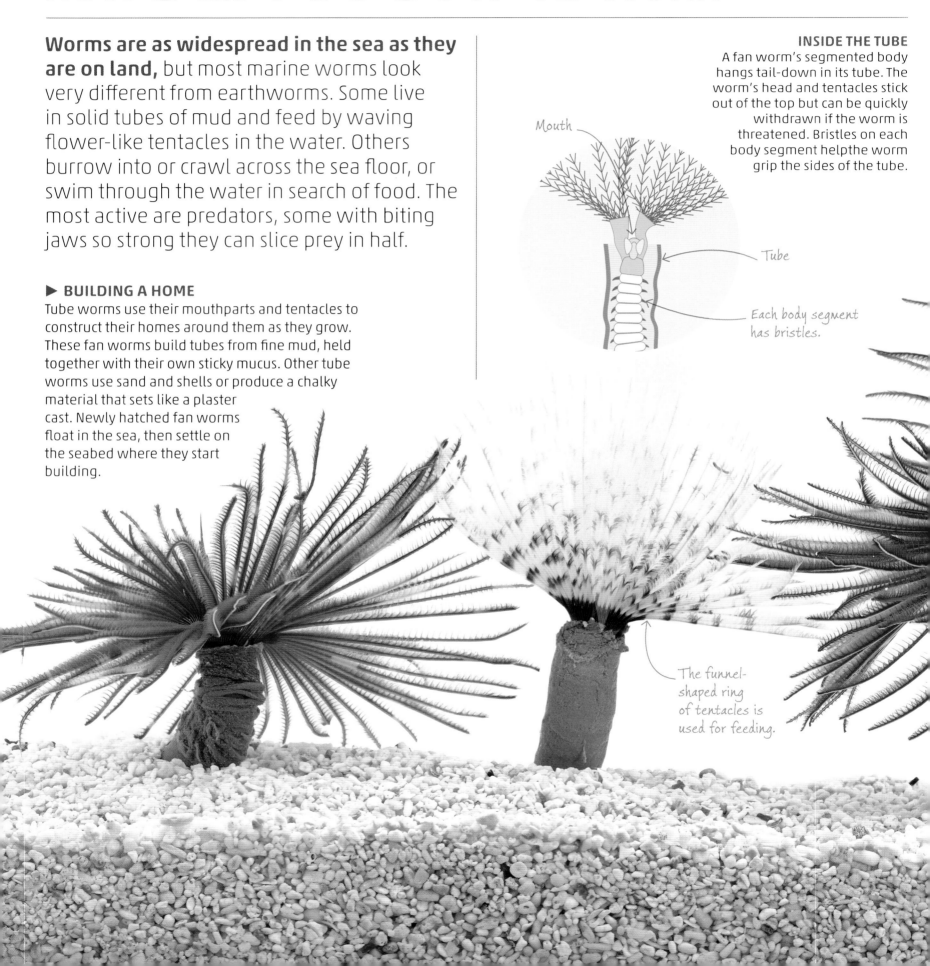

Mouth

Tube

Each body segment has bristles.

The funnel-shaped ring of tentacles is used for feeding.

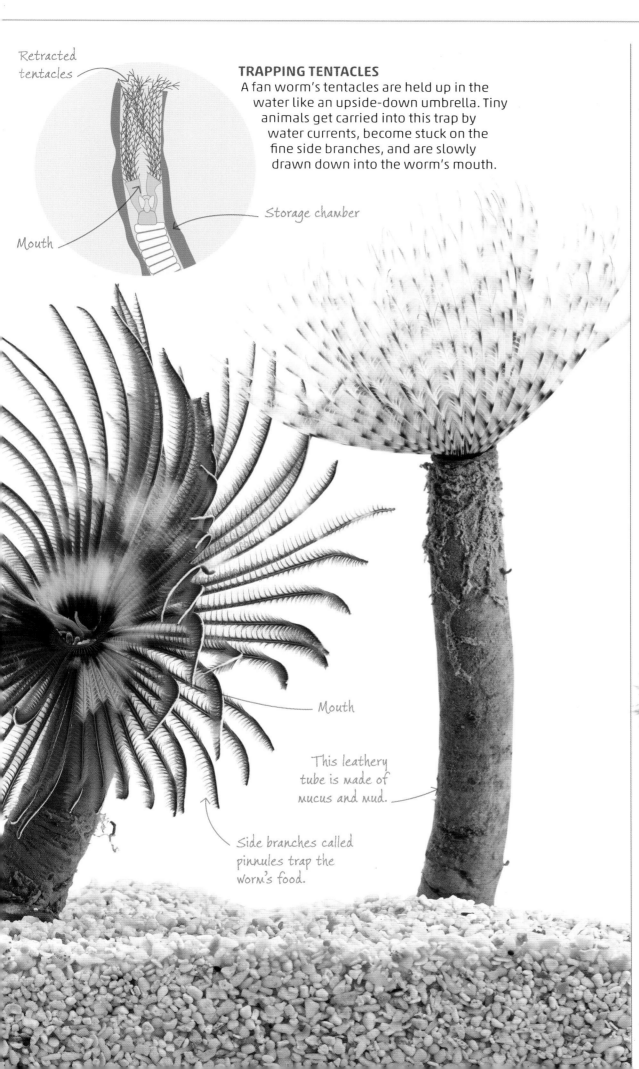

Retracted tentacles

Mouth

TRAPPING TENTACLES
A fan worm's tentacles are held up in the water like an upside-down umbrella. Tiny animals get carried into this trap by water currents, become stuck on the fine side branches, and are slowly drawn down into the worm's mouth.

Storage chamber

Mouth

This leathery tube is made of mucus and mud.

Side branches called pinnules trap the worm's food.

A WORLD OF WORMS
Sea worms come in a variety of shapes and some hardly look like worms at all. They also vary in size – some are microscopic, but others (ribbon worms) can reach 30 m (100 ft) long.

BOBBIT WORM
This predator hides buried in sand and shoots out to catch small fish in its strong-toothed jaws.

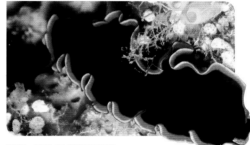

RED-RIM FLATWORM
Flatworms glide over the seabed like slugs. Bright colours warn predators that they taste bad.

BRISTLE WORM
Long, venomous bristles break off and irritate any fish that tries to eat this worm, which lives on coral reefs.

PEANUT WORM
Peanut worms are so called because when they pull their small heads back into their bodies until they look like fat peanuts.

BREATHING

An insect breathes by drawing air through a network of tubes called tracheae. These deliver oxygen directly to the muscles and other organs, and take away waste carbon dioxide.

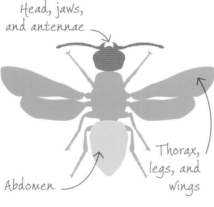

Network of tracheae

Hole in exoskeleton

SECTIONS OF THE BODY

An insect's body has three sections. Its head carries its mouthparts and most of its sense organs. Its thorax houses the muscles that move the legs and wings. Its abdomen contains digestive and reproductive organs.

Head, jaws, and antennae

Thorax, legs, and wings

Abdomen

EGGS AND YOUNG

Most insects reproduce by laying eggs. These hatch as young that often look quite different from their parents.

Stick insect about to lay an egg

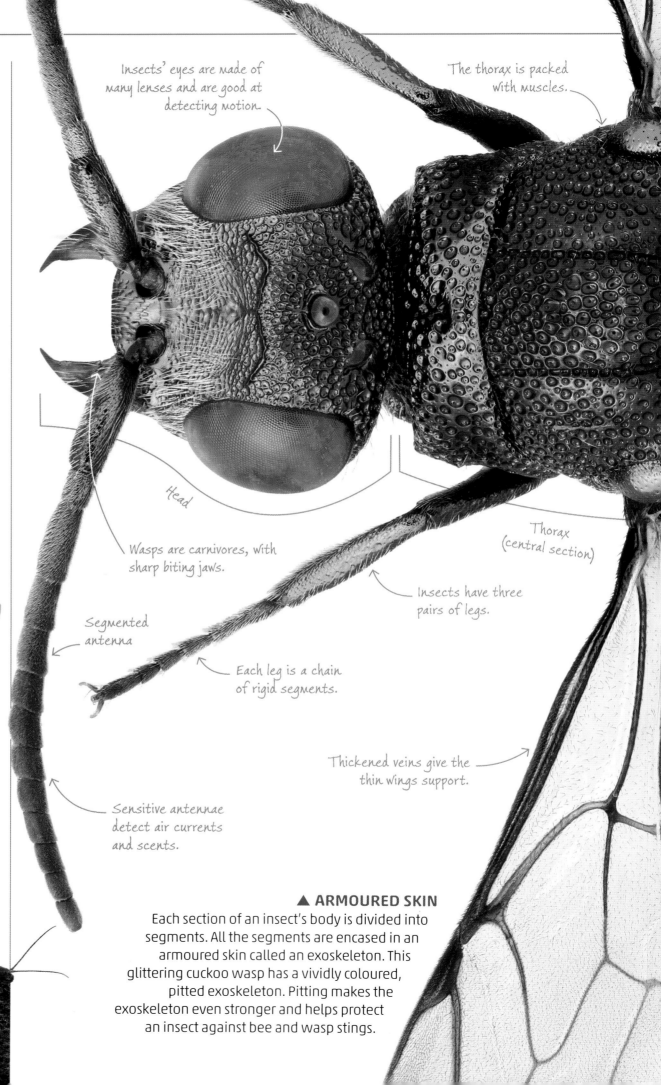

Insects' eyes are made of many lenses and are good at detecting motion.

The thorax is packed with muscles.

Head

Wasps are carnivores, with sharp biting jaws.

Segmented antenna

Thorax (central section)

Insects have three pairs of legs.

Each leg is a chain of rigid segments.

Sensitive antennae detect air currents and scents.

Thickened veins give the thin wings support.

▲ ARMOURED SKIN

Each section of an insect's body is divided into segments. All the segments are encased in an armoured skin called an exoskeleton. This glittering cuckoo wasp has a vividly coloured, pitted exoskeleton. Pitting makes the exoskeleton even stronger and helps protect an insect against bee and wasp stings.

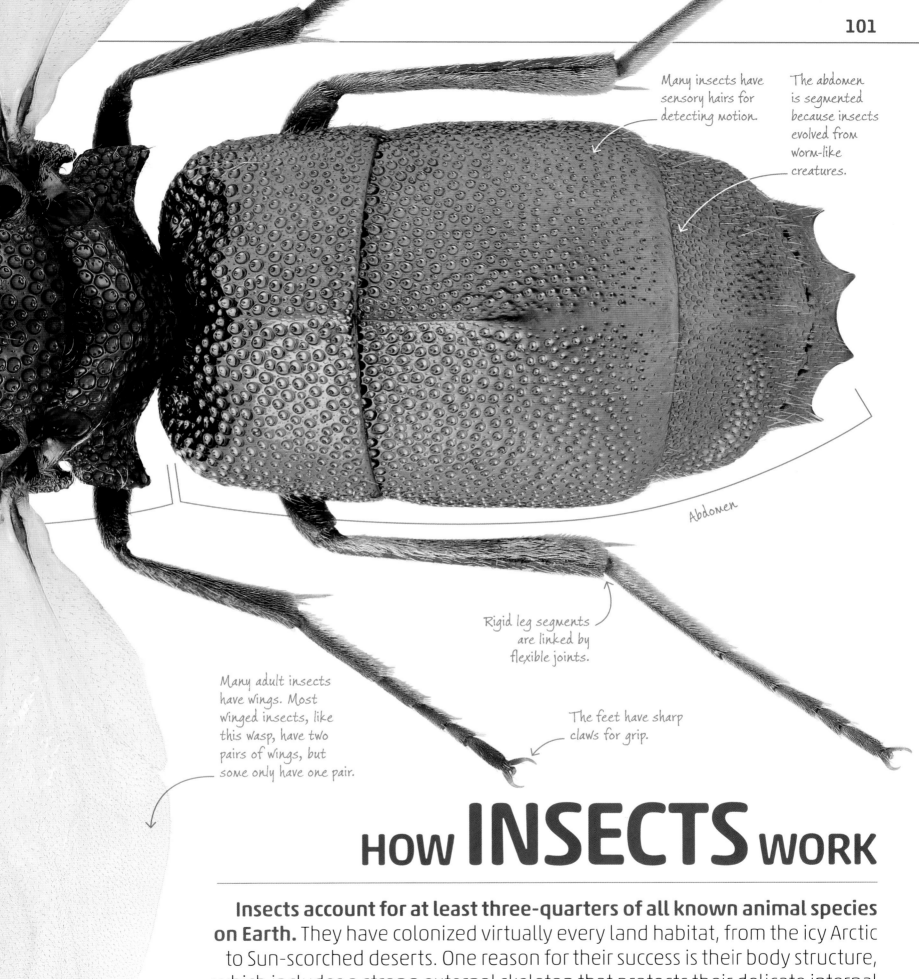

Many insects have sensory hairs for detecting motion.

The abdomen is segmented because insects evolved from worm-like creatures.

Abdomen

Rigid leg segments are linked by flexible joints.

Many adult insects have wings. Most winged insects, like this wasp, have two pairs of wings, but some only have one pair.

The feet have sharp claws for grip.

HOW **INSECTS** WORK

Insects account for at least three-quarters of all known animal species on Earth. They have colonized virtually every land habitat, from the icy Arctic to Sun-scorched deserts. One reason for their success is their body structure, which includes a strong external skeleton that protects their delicate internal organs, and a wide range of mouthparts to suit different diets. Insects were the first animals to evolve flight, and are the only invertebrates that can fly.

TYPES OF INSECTS

The only invertebrates capable of powered flight, insects are found in almost every type of habitat on land. They are the most numerous and widespread group of animals on the planet, accounting for at least a third of all animal species. There are about 950,000 species of insect, and some of the main types are shown here.

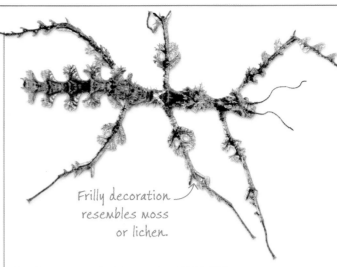

Frilly decoration resembles moss or lichen.

STICK INSECTS AND LEAF INSECTS
These masters of disguise are camouflaged to resemble sticks or leaves. Most are plant eaters.

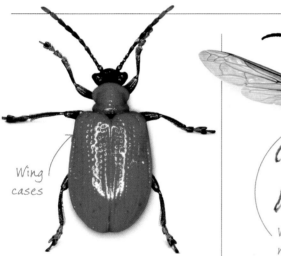

Wing cases

BEETLES
Beetles make up the largest group of insects. They typically have a single pair of wings folded under tough wing cases.

Wasps typically have narrow waists.

BEES, WASPS, AND ANTS
These insects have two pairs of wings that hook together. Many live in large colonies, and females often have stings.

TRUE BUGS
True bugs have beak-like, piercing mouthparts. Some suck plant sap; others are predators that stab other insects.

This threadwing antlion has unusual ribbon-like hind wings.

Stabilizers

TRUE FLIES
Most insects have four wings, but true flies only have one pair of wings. Behind these wings are club-like flight stabilizers, which help the fly manoeuvre.

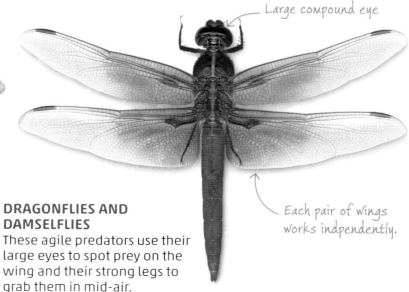

Large compound eye

DRAGONFLIES AND DAMSELFLIES
These agile predators use their large eyes to spot prey on the wing and their strong legs to grab them in mid-air.

Each pair of wings works indpendently.

LACEWINGS AND ANTLIONS
As both adults and larvae, these insects are predators that have strong jaws for chewing prey. Antlion larvae dig traps to catch ants to eat.

EARWIGS
Flattened bodies and pincers at the tip of the abdomens make earwigs easy to recognize. Most emerge at night to forage for other insects or plant matter to eat.

Pincers

BUTTERFLIES AND MOTHS
Butterflies and moths feed on nectar from flowers and have large, often colourful wings covered in powder-like scales. Their larvae, caterpillars, are leaf eaters.

Compound eye

Eyespots help to scare away predatory birds.

GRASSHOPPERS AND CRICKETS
Most grasshoppers and crickets are plant eaters with large heads, thick "collars", and powerful hind legs.

Long back legs for jumping

Scale-covered wings

HOW EXOSKELETONS WORK

The supporting skeleton of an insect is not inside the body, but forms a hard outer casing called an exoskeleton. It contains a tough substance called chitin that protects from injury and prevents water loss. An exoskeleton is rigid in some places but flexible in others to allow an insect to move its limbs, mouthparts, and antennae.

MOUTHPARTS
The mouthparts of insects are amazingly varied, and can be used for stabbing, slicing, sucking, chewing, and mopping up food.

GRASSHOPPER
Chewing mandibles are used to cut, tear, and crush leaves.

MOSQUITO
The mandibles work like needles to puncture skin and draw blood.

BUTTERFLY
A long nectar-sucking tube (proboscis) replaces biting mandibles.

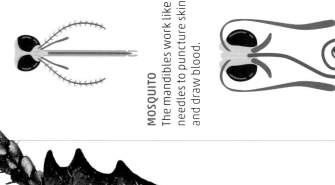

▼ BEETLE EXOSKELETON
Insect exoskeletons vary in thickness. A beetle larva has a thin, supple exoskeleton, but the exoskeleton of an adult beetle, such as this glorious scarab beetle, has the rigidity of armour and may also be brightly coloured.

The head exoskeleton forms a tough capsule that carries one pair of antennae, compound eyes, and mouthparts.

Antenna (feeler)

Compound eye

VIEW FROM ABOVE

Mouthparts

VIEW FROM BELOW

Head

The exoskeleton is thin and flexible around limb joints. In these places, the limb can bend like a hinge.

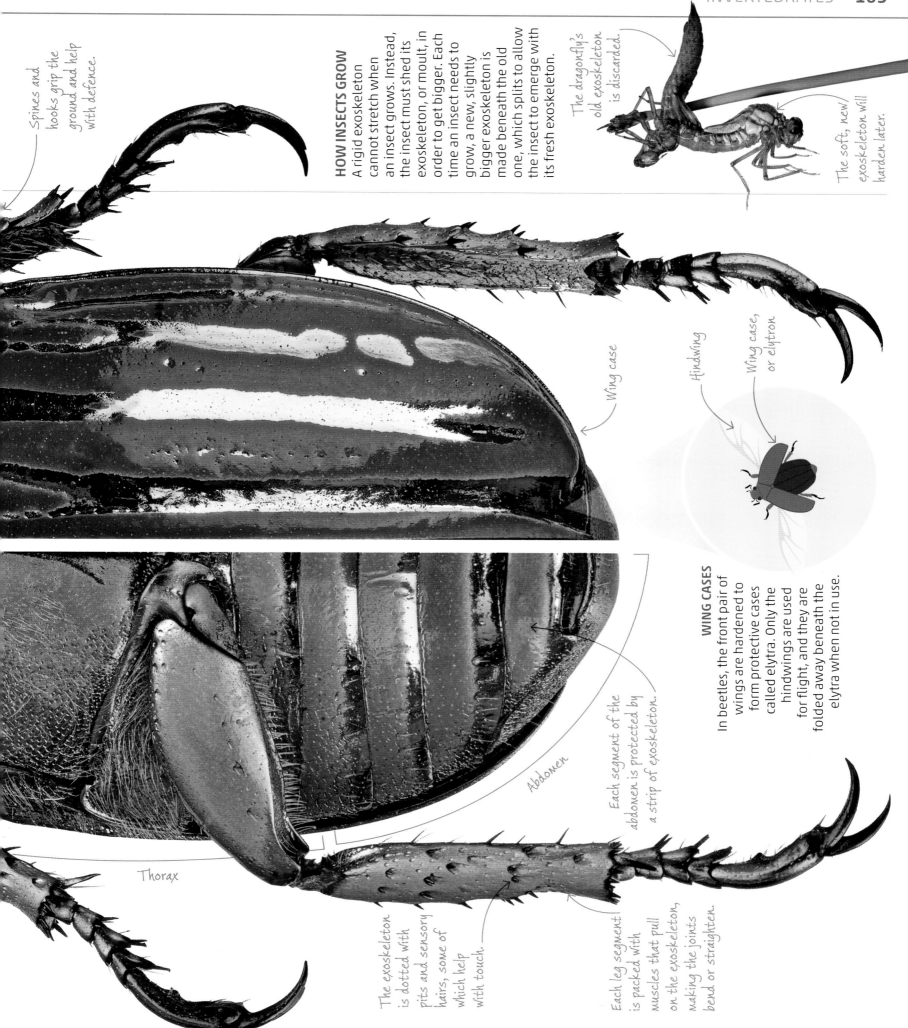

Spines and hooks grip the ground and help with defence.

HOW INSECTS GROW

A rigid exoskeleton cannot stretch when an insect grows. Instead, the insect must shed its exoskeleton, or moult, in order to get bigger. Each time an insect needs to grow, a new, slightly bigger exoskeleton is made beneath the old one, which splits to allow the insect to emerge with its fresh exoskeleton.

The dragonfly's old exoskeleton is discarded.

The soft, new exoskeleton will harden later.

Wing case

Hindwing

Wing case, or elytron

WING CASES

In beetles, the front pair of wings are hardened to form protective cases called elytra. Only the hindwings are used for flight, and they are folded away beneath the elytra when not in use.

Abdomen

Each segment of the abdomen is protected by a strip of exoskeleton.

Thorax

The exoskeleton is dotted with pits and sensory hairs, some of which help with touch.

Each leg segment is packed with muscles that pull on the exoskeleton, making the joints bend or straighten.

1 EGG TO CATERPILLAR

The juvenile forms of insects that undergo metamorphosis are called larvae. The larva of a moth is also called a caterpillar. After about 14 days growing inside an egg, silk moth caterpillars (silkworms) hatch and then feed for about 25 days, growing to 10,000 times their initial weight. They moult four times as they grow to allow their bodies to stretch.

DAY 15

DAY 5

DAY 1

Silk moth eggs are barely larger than grains of sand.

SILKWORMS only eat the leaves of mulberry trees.

DAY 17

HOW METAMORPHOSIS WORKS

The life cycle of many insects involves a dramatic change called metamorphosis, when young insects are transformed into adults. Moths and butterflies, for example, begin life as caterpillars. When fully grown, a caterpillar forms an immobile stage called a pupa. Inside, its body is rebuilt as an adult.

Silk is made by glands in the caterpillar's mouth.

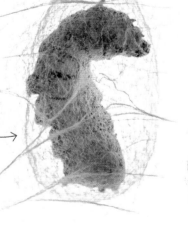

DAY 26

The caterpillar loops its head back and forth to surround itself with silk.

Dense layers of silk build up to form a hard case.

2 BUILDING A COCOON

To protect its body while it changes, the caterpillar makes a cocoon of silk. Silk emerges from its mouth as a liquid and hardens into a thread in the air. A sticky gum secreted with it helps glue the loops of silk together. The cocoon takes 1–2 days to build and consists of a single thread about 1 km (0.6 miles) long.

DAY 27

DAY 28

DAY 29

DAY 51

SILK MOTH

④ ADULT EMERGES
After about two weeks in the cocoon, an adult moth finally emerges. Adult silk moths do not eat, and live for only a few days. The males seek out females to mate with. After mating, a female moth lays 1,000 or so eggs and then dies.

DAY 50

Males have feathery antennae to pick up the scent of females.

SILK MOTH LIFE CYCLE
The whole life cycle of a silk moth lasts about ten weeks. Silk moths undergo metamorphosis inside a protective cocoon of silk and survive as adults for less than a week.

The moth makes a hole in the cocoon with saliva from its mouth and squeezes out.

Cocoon cut open

Pupa

Skin from final moult

③ INSIDE A COCOON
Hidden in the cocoon, the caterpillar moults a final time to form a pupa – the stationary stage in its life cycle. Inside, much of its body is digested to form a nutritious liquid. Clusters of cells that were dormant in the caterpillar now become active. They feed on the liquid and grow to form new organs.

DAY 35

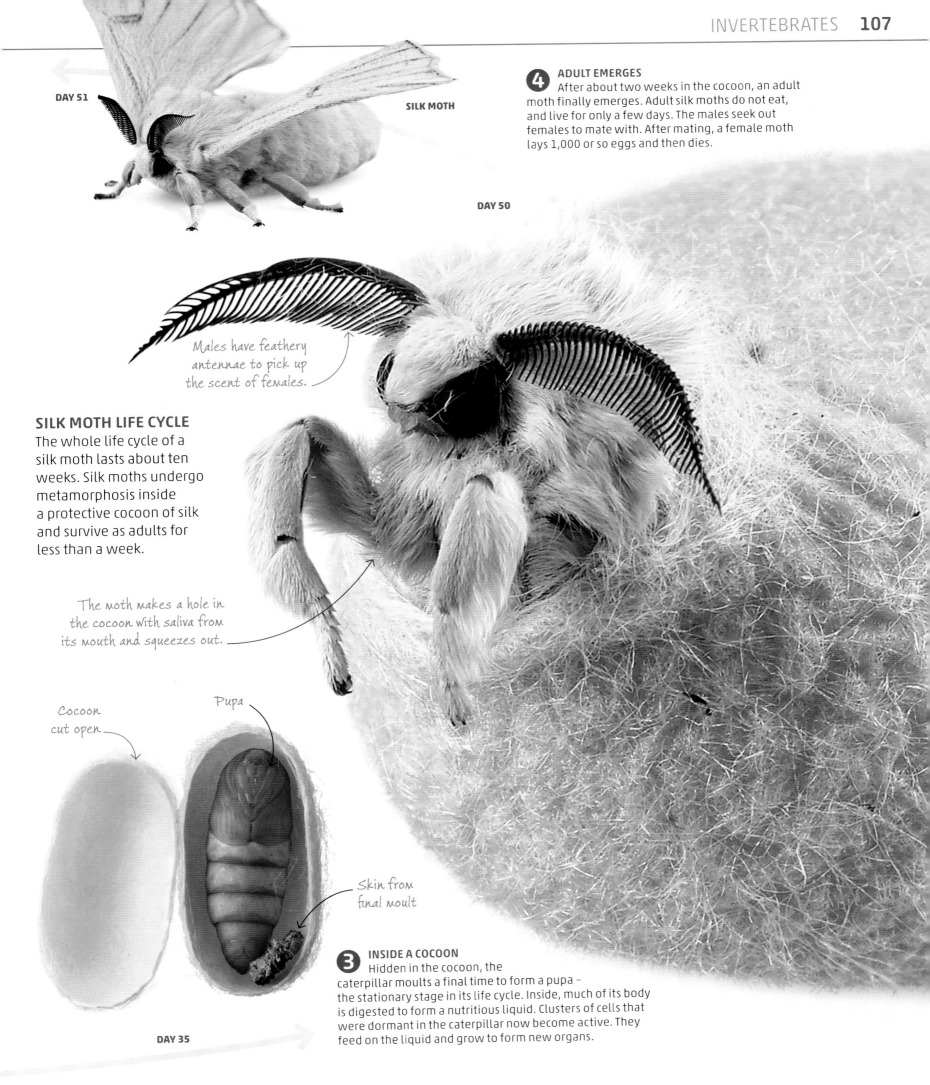

HOW INSECTS SEE

Insects' eyes are made up of thousands of tiny light-sensitive tubes called ommatidia, which are packed closely together to form two large "compound eyes". The tiny lens of each ommatidium cannot focus as well as the much bigger lens of a human eye, so compound eyes produce images that are far less detailed than those that humans see. However, compound eyes give insects a wide field of view around their bodies and enable them to spot even the slightest movement.

▼ **JEWEL BEETLE EYES**
Banded jewel beetles have large compound eyes with hexagonal light-sensitive tubes called ommatidia that fit together in a honeycomb pattern. Their eyes are specially adapted to see in colour, which is probably how the striped, iridescent-coloured beetle finds a mate.

The antennae can detect motion and odours.

Large compound eyes give the beetle a wide field of view.

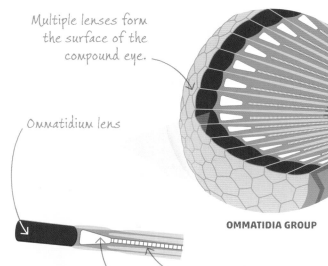

Multiple lenses form the surface of the compound eye.

OMMATIDIA GROUP

Ommatidium lens

Light receptors

Crystalline cone

SINGLE OMMATIDIUM

COMPOUND EYES
The tubes that make up a compound eye are called ommatidia. Each ommatidium is like a miniature eye in its own right. It contains a lens and crystalline cone for focusing light and receptors for detecting it.

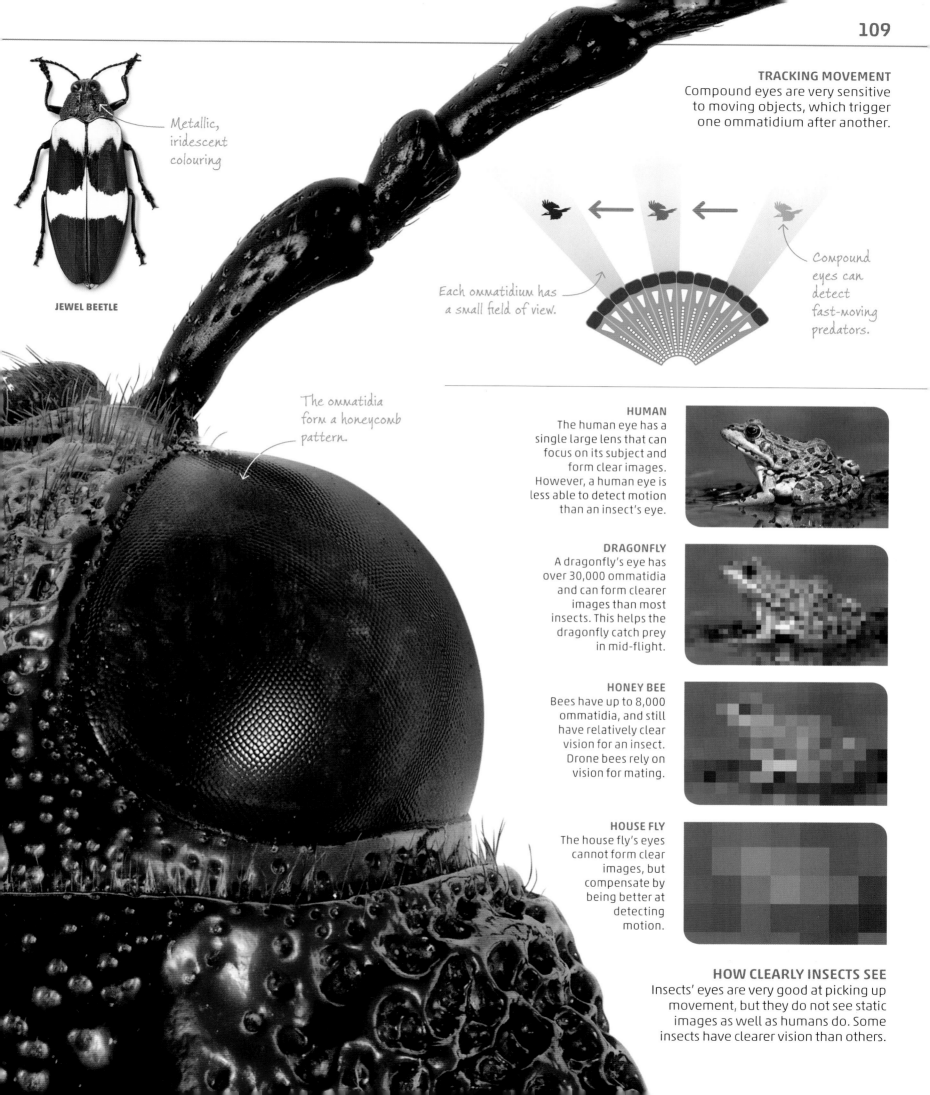

Metallic, iridescent colouring

JEWEL BEETLE

The ommatidia form a honeycomb pattern.

TRACKING MOVEMENT
Compound eyes are very sensitive to moving objects, which trigger one ommatidium after another.

Each ommatidium has a small field of view.

Compound eyes can detect fast-moving predators.

HUMAN
The human eye has a single large lens that can focus on its subject and form clear images. However, a human eye is less able to detect motion than an insect's eye.

DRAGONFLY
A dragonfly's eye has over 30,000 ommatidia and can form clearer images than most insects. This helps the dragonfly catch prey in mid-flight.

HONEY BEE
Bees have up to 8,000 ommatidia, and still have relatively clear vision for an insect. Drone bees rely on vision for mating.

HOUSE FLY
The house fly's eyes cannot form clear images, but compensate by being better at detecting motion.

HOW CLEARLY INSECTS SEE
Insects' eyes are very good at picking up movement, but they do not see static images as well as humans do. Some insects have clearer vision than others.

HOW ANTENNAE WORK

All insects have antennae attached to their heads.
Antennae are multipurpose sensory devices that allow insects to smell, taste, and feel the world around them. Tiny, hair-like sense organs on the antennae detect chemicals or movement, and extra motion detectors at the base sense vibrations in the whole antenna.

SENSING THE WORLD
Antennae don't only look different from one insect to another, but they also have many different functions. Some insects use their antennae simply to feel their way in darkness, or to help them in flight, while others use theirs to pick up chemical signals from mates.

TOUCH
The long antenna of crickets are sensitive not only to smell but also to touch. This helps crickets to feel their way in the dark, find mates, and avoid predators.

Long, thin antennae feel the way.

Some moths have as many as 60,000 scent receptors in their antennae.

▶ SCENT DETECTORS
Many male moths, like this black arches moth, are equipped with comb-like antennae that can detect the scent of females several miles away. The females lure potential mates by releasing scent chemicals called pheromones into the air.

Chemical sensors
in antennae

Pheromone
sensors

Antennae detect
air movement.

Antennae
tell the time.

GAS DETECTION
Chemical sensors in the antennae of honey bees can tell when levels of the gas carbon dioxide have risen in the hive by less than one per cent. The bees respond by beating their wings to increase circulation.

COMMUNICATION
Ants touch each other with their antennae to pick up chemical pheromones. These pheromones might, for instance, rouse the colony to attack an intruder or lead them to a food source.

FLIGHT
Sensors at the base of the hummingbird hawk moth's antennae detect the slightest vibration caused by air movement. This helps the insect to hover steadily while sucking nectar from flowers.

COMPASS
The antennae of the monarch butterfly contain an internal clock to work out the time of day. Combining this with the visual direction of the Sun helps the butterfly to navigate during its long-distance migration.

The antennae can twist
and bend at the base to
scan for scents.

The broad shape provides
a large surface area for
detecting scent molecules.

HAIRY ANTENNAE
A moth's antennae are covered with fine sensory hairs called sensilla that act as smell receptors. A single antenna may have tens of thousands of these hairs.

HOW INSECTS HEAR

Like larger animals, insects use ears to detect the vibrations in the air that we hear as sound. Unlike the ears of vertebrates, which are on both sides of the head, those of insects are located on the legs, wings, thorax, or abdomen. By listening for sounds, insects can find mates, track prey, or stay alert to danger.

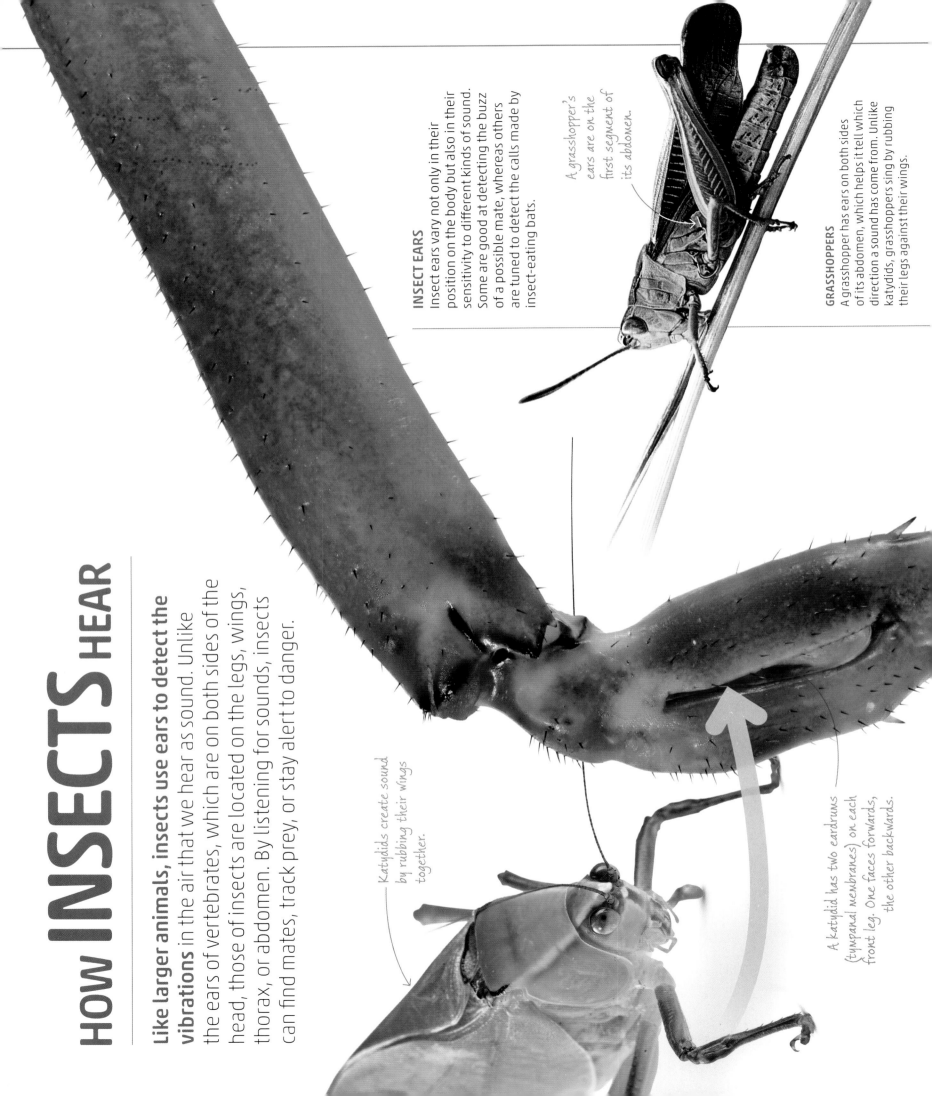

INSECT EARS

Insect ears vary not only in their position on the body but also in their sensitivity to different kinds of sound. Some are good at detecting the buzz of a possible mate, whereas others are tuned to detect the calls made by insect-eating bats.

A grasshopper's ears are on the first segment of its abdomen.

GRASSHOPPERS

A grasshopper has ears on both sides of its abdomen, which helps it tell which direction a sound has come from. Unlike katydids, grasshoppers sing by rubbing their legs against their wings.

Katydids create sound by rubbing their wings together.

A katydid has two eardrums (tympanal membranes) on each front leg. One faces forwards, the other backwards.

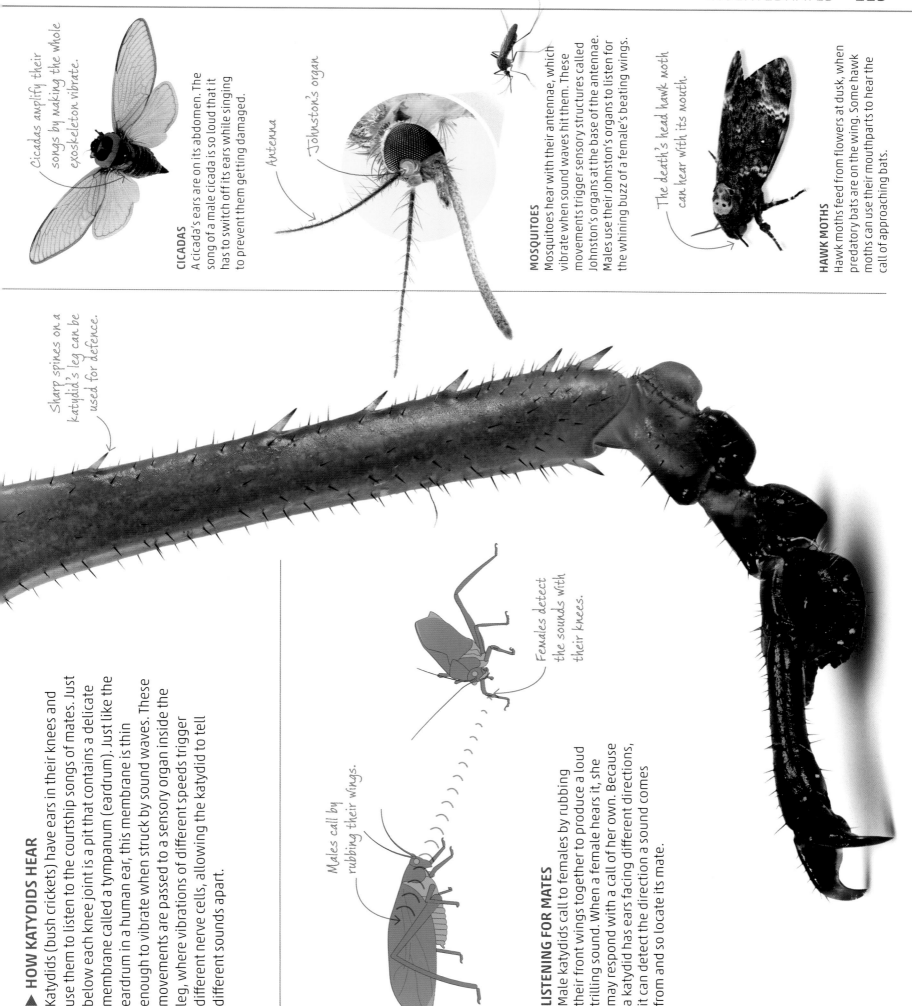

Cicadas amplify their songs by making the whole exoskeleton vibrate.

CICADAS
A cicada's ears are on its abdomen. The song of a male cicada is so loud that it has to switch off its ears while singing to prevent them getting damaged.

Antenna

Johnston's organ

MOSQUITOES
Mosquitoes hear with their antennae, which vibrate when sound waves hit them. These movements trigger sensory structures called Johnston's organs at the base of the antennae. Males use their Johnston's organs to listen for the whining buzz of a female's beating wings.

The death's head hawk moth can hear with its mouth.

HAWK MOTHS
Hawk moths feed from flowers at dusk, when predatory bats are on the wing. Some hawk moths can use their mouthparts to hear the call of approaching bats.

Sharp spines on a katydid's leg can be used for defence.

▶ HOW KATYDIDS HEAR
Katydids (bush crickets) have ears in their knees and use them to listen to the courtship songs of mates. Just below each knee joint is a pit that contains a delicate membrane called a tympanum (eardrum). Just like the eardrum in a human ear, this membrane is thin enough to vibrate when struck by sound waves. These movements are passed to a sensory organ inside the leg, where vibrations of different speeds trigger different nerve cells, allowing the katydid to tell different sounds apart.

LISTENING FOR MATES
Male katydids call to females by rubbing their front wings together to produce a loud trilling sound. When a female hears it, she may respond with a call of her own. Because a katydid has ears facing different directions, it can detect the direction a sound comes from and so locate its mate.

Females detect the sounds with their knees.

Males call by rubbing their wings.

HOW **WINGS** WORK

Insects were the first animals to evolve the power of flight, more than 400 million years ago. Unlike a bird's wings, which are limbs that are adapted for flight, an insect's wings have grown out of its external skeleton. They are powered by muscles inside the insect's body, which are either attached directly to the wings or move the wings by changing the shape of the thorax. Beating at up to 1,000 times a second, they give some insects astonishing speed and manoeuvrability.

Thickened areas stabilize the wing and help the dragonfly glide.

The long, slender wings allow fast, agile flight.

Each wing can move independently of the others, giving great control in flight.

FLIGHT MUSCLES

The wings of insects pivot on the sides of the thorax. Most insects move their wings by contracting and relaxing muscles to move the top of the thorax up and down.

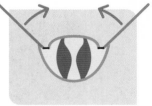

1 UPSTROKE
The wing muscles contract to pull the top of the thorax down. This makes the wings pivot upwards.

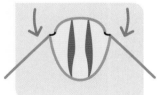

2 DOWNSTROKE
The wing muscles relax and become longer, moving the top of the thorax up. The wings spring back to their downward position.

TAKING OFF

The wings of beetles are normally hidden by modified hardened forewings that form protective wing cases (elytra). When a beetle wants to take flight, it has to unfurl its hind wings from beneath the wing cases.

1 PERCH
Perched on a bud with its wing cases closed, this cockchafer beetle uses its antennae to sense the wind speed before taking off.

2 PREPARE
The beetle's tough wing cases open on hinges near the front of its thorax, allowing the delicate hind wings to emerge and unfold.

3 LAUNCH
As soon as it has fully spread its wings, the beetle launches itself into the air. The whole process takes less than a second.

4 FLY
Once airborne, the beetle holds its wing cases above its wings, where they provide some lift, like the fixed wings of aircraft.

FLIGHT CONTROLLERS
Most insects have two pairs of wings but some flies, such as this crane fly, use just one pair. The rear wings are reduced to tiny club-shaped structures called halteres. These detect changes of speed or direction, giving the flies very precise flight control.

The long abdomen radiates excess heat generated by the flight muscles.

An insect's wings consist of chitin – the same material that its external skeleton is made of. The chitin that forms the wings is transparent, like thin glass.

The segmented, flexible abdomen can arch up and down.

◄ AERIAL HUNTER
Unlike most insects, dragonflies such as this green marsh hawk have flight muscles attached directly to their wings. This means that dragonflies can move their four wings independently of one another. It makes them spectacularly fast and agile, allowing them to hunt other airborne insects on the wing.

The wing pivots on a hinge at its root.

The wings are reinforced by thickened struts called wing veins.

The thorax is packed with powerful flight muscles.

The dragonfly uses its bristly legs to snatch other insects from the air.

The huge eyes detect airborne prey.

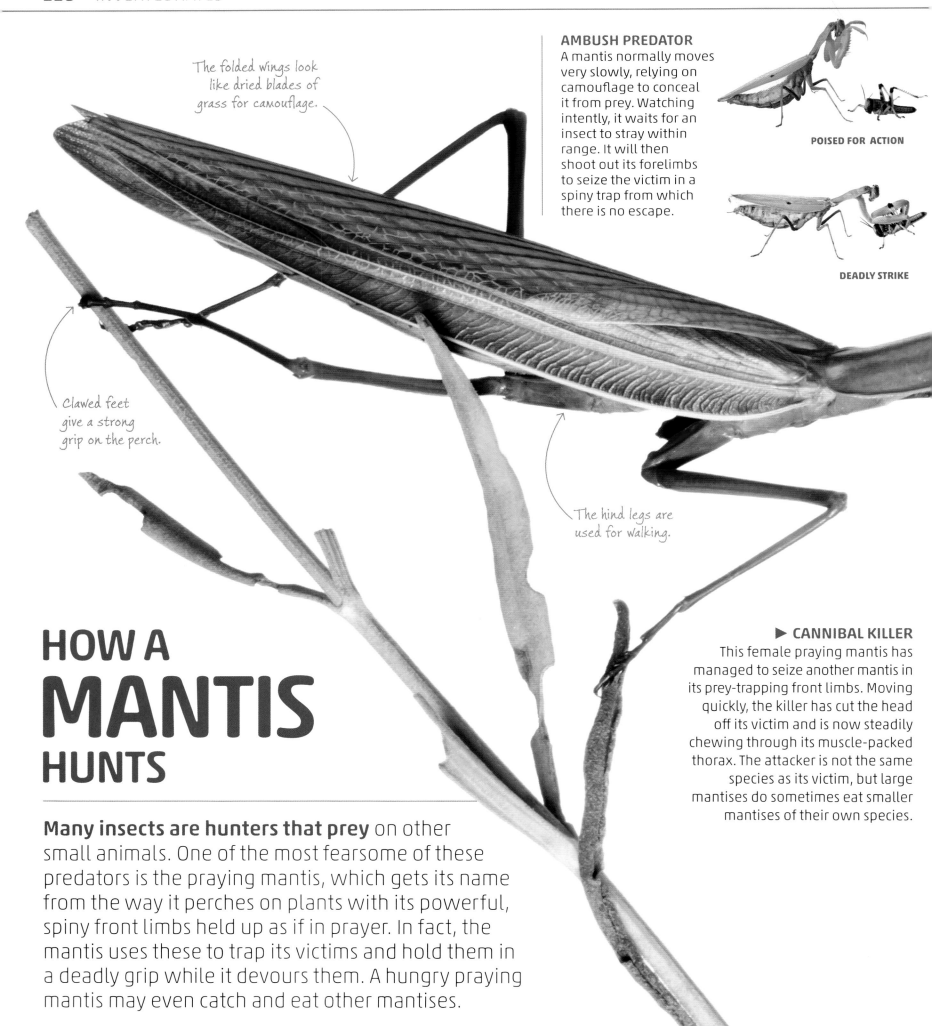

The folded wings look like dried blades of grass for camouflage.

AMBUSH PREDATOR
A mantis normally moves very slowly, relying on camouflage to conceal it from prey. Watching intently, it waits for an insect to stray within range. It will then shoot out its forelimbs to seize the victim in a spiny trap from which there is no escape.

POISED FOR ACTION

DEADLY STRIKE

Clawed feet give a strong grip on the perch.

The hind legs are used for walking.

HOW A
MANTIS
HUNTS

► CANNIBAL KILLER
This female praying mantis has managed to seize another mantis in its prey-trapping front limbs. Moving quickly, the killer has cut the head off its victim and is now steadily chewing through its muscle-packed thorax. The attacker is not the same species as its victim, but large mantises do sometimes eat smaller mantises of their own species.

Many insects are hunters that prey on other small animals. One of the most fearsome of these predators is the praying mantis, which gets its name from the way it perches on plants with its powerful, spiny front limbs held up as if in prayer. In fact, the mantis uses these to trap its victims and hold them in a deadly grip while it devours them. A hungry praying mantis may even catch and eat other mantises.

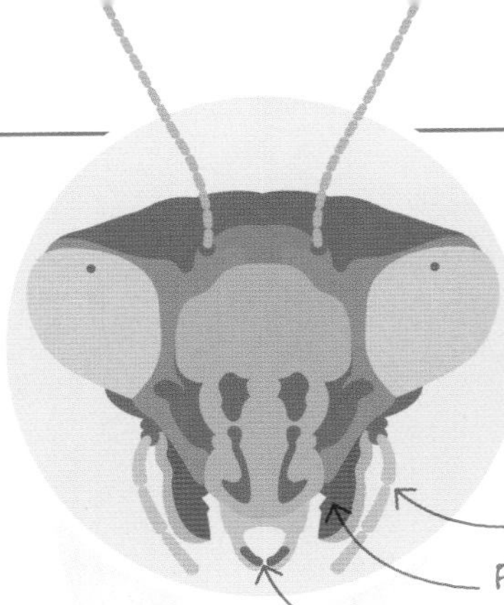

CHEWING MOUTHPARTS
The jaws of a mantis are small but very sharp. They can chew through an insect's tough exoskeleton as if it were a stick of celery.

For tasting
For chewing
For manipulating

A mantis has large, widely spaced eyes and can turn its head to look behind its body, giving it a wide field of vision.

The long wings work well but are rarely used.

The extended thorax gives the trapping forelimbs longer reach.

Powerful arm muscles help a mantis strike quickly.

Spines on the forelimbs help a mantis hold its prey in a tight grip.

EATING LARGE PREY
A praying mantis is not venomous, so it relies on power and size for hunting and usually targets prey smaller than itself. Big females regularly eat smaller males after or even during mating with them. However, some larger mantises will occasionally seize and eat something much bigger, such as a lizard or tree frog.

The victim's long legs will be discarded.

LIZARD

FROG

HOW PARASITES WORK

A parasite uses the live body of another animal, called its host, as a source of food. Parasites benefit from living in this way at the expense of their host. Some parasites live on the surface of their host, but others, such as intestinal worms, live deep inside their host's body.

▼ PARASITE TURNED PREDATOR

While many parasites keep their hosts alive, the larva of a jewel wasp eventually kills its host. A female jewel wasp paralyses a cockroach and lays an egg on its body. The larva eats its way through the live cockroach before emerging from the shrivelled body as an adult. Parasites like the jewel wasp that kill their hosts are also known as parasitoids.

Long antennae help the wasp to detect new hosts.

The wasp directs its sting into the brain of the cockroach.

Immobilized cockroach

LIFE CYCLE

The female jewel wasp uses gruesome tactics to feed her young. Laying an egg on a paralysed cockroach, she provides this large meal to help her larva develop into a mature wasp. As it eats its way through the cockroach's insides, the wasp larva saves the vital organs until last, so the cockroach stays alive and fresh for as long as possible.

1 THE ATTACK
The wasp stings the body of the cockroach to paralyse its front legs before climbing onto its head and injecting a sting into its brain.

2 THE TRANCE
The paralysed cockroach lets the wasp chew away half of its antennae, possibly as a way for the wasp to replace the vital fluids it lost when delivering the sting.

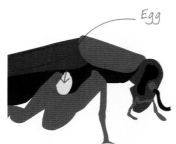

Egg

Husk of dead cockroach

3 THE ABDUCTION
The wasp leads the dazed cockroach away by its damaged antenna, like a dog on a lead. It drags the host into a burrow and lays its egg on the cockroach's body.

4 THE FEAST
Once hatched, the wasp larva eats its way through the body of the still-living cockroach. It forms a cocoon inside, and emerges as an adult wasp just over a week later.

OTHER PARASITES

Parasites that feed on the surface of their host are called ectoparasites. Bloodsucking ectoparasites, such as ticks and tsetse flies, make brief visits to hosts when hungry. Parasites that live inside their hosts are called endoparasites. They can survive for months or even years.

Blood

TSETSE FLY
This bloodsucking fly uses skin-piercing mouthparts to drink the blood of its host, and can infect the host with microbes that cause diseases such as sleeping sickness.

TAPEWORM
With no digestive system of its own, the tapeworm must live in the intestines of another animal. Here, it can absorb nutrients from the food eaten by its host.

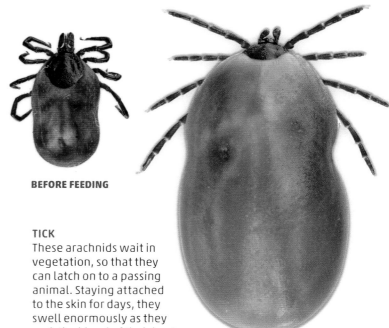

BEFORE FEEDING

TICK
These arachnids wait in vegetation, so that they can latch on to a passing animal. Staying attached to the skin for days, they swell enormously as they suck the blood of their host.

AFTER FEEDING

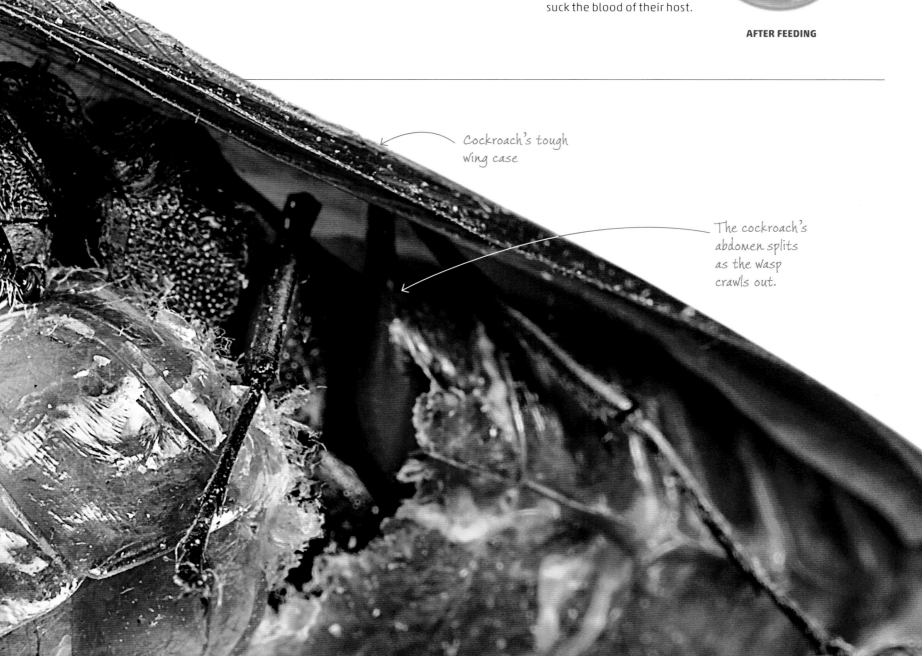

Cockroach's tough wing case

The cockroach's abdomen splits as the wasp crawls out.

HOW CHEMICAL DEFENCES WORK

To fend off hungry animals, many insects have developed chemical weapons as a primary method of defence. Some merely smell or taste unpleasant, but others can sting, injure, or even kill a predator. There are two types of chemical defence – poison, which is swallowed, and venom, which is injected into the skin.

▶ **WARNING COLOURS**
Coloured in blue, red, yellow, and green, this Australian wattle cup is an attractive moth caterpillar. However, its bright appearance is a warning to predators not to touch it. Its body is covered in venomous spines that can inflict a painful sting.

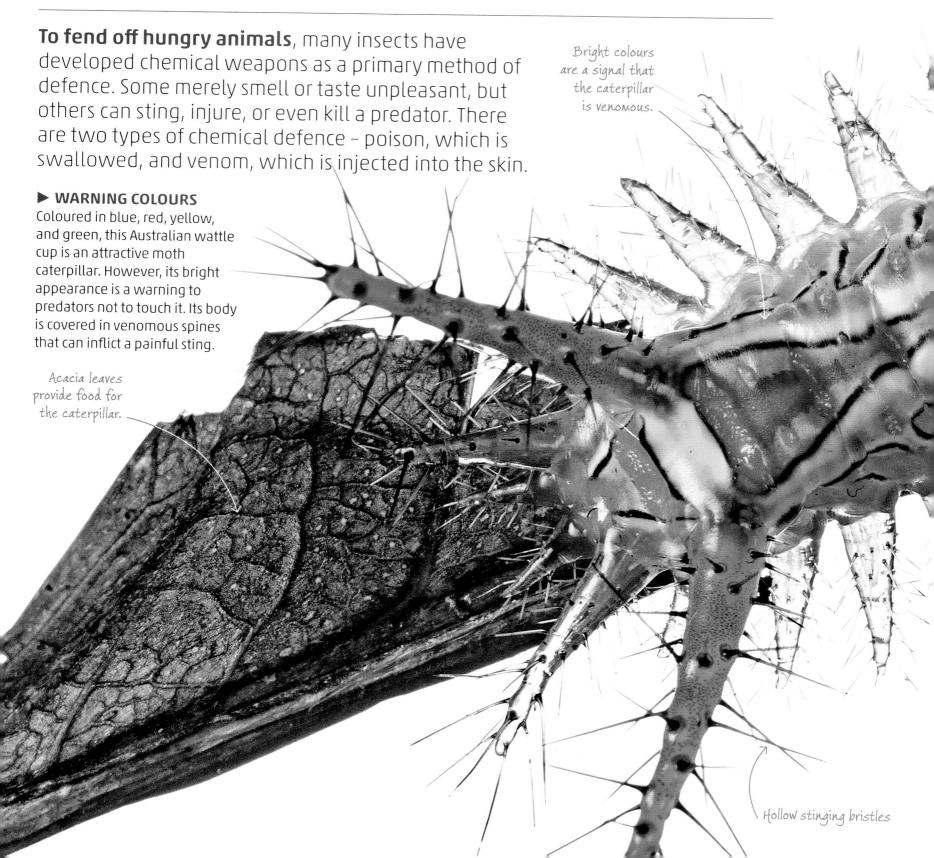

Bright colours are a signal that the caterpillar is venomous.

Acacia leaves provide food for the caterpillar.

Hollow stinging bristles

The front and rear ends look the same to confuse predators.

Each bristle has its own venom gland.

STINGING BRISTLES
Venom generated inside the tubercle is fed into the hollow bristles. These break off at their tip to release venom into the soft tissue of the mouths of predators such as birds.

Venom is made in swellings called tubercles.

The tip breaks off to release venom.

Venom-filled channel

POISONOUS DEFENCES
Some insects emit foul-smelling chemicals that can ward off a predator immediately. Others release poisonous substances or taste unpleasant to predators.

EXPLOSIVE VAPOUR
Bombardier beetles are small but armed with an explosive, bleach-like spray. They mix chemicals in their abdomen to generate a hot irritating vapour, which is squirted with a loud pop from their behind at predators.

TOXIC FOAM
Found across Africa, the koppie foam grasshopper produces toxic foam from glands in its thorax to deter predators. The poison comes from highly toxic plants that the grasshopper eats, such as milkweed.

EATING POISON
Caterpillars of the monarch butterfly eat milkweed, which is poisonous to many other creatures. The poison stays in the insect after it changes into a butterfly, and predatory birds learn to avoid it.

Bright colours warn
other animals to
stay away.

▼ **WASP STINGER**
Like all wasps, this hornet has a
stinger that is normally hidden
inside the abdomen but emerges
like a needle when the insect
attacks. Venom flows out
through an opening near the
sharp tip of the stinger.

Like many insects, this
hornet has a dense
layer of sensory hairs.

The segmented abdomen can
flex to manoeuvre the stinger.

HOW STINGERS WORK

Bees and wasps are armed with sharp, needle-like stingers that puncture skin and inject a painful venom. Bees use their stingers to defend their colonies, but wasps also sting to paralyse prey. The venom of social wasps contains an alarm chemical that alerts other members of the colony to join in the attack. Bees can only sting once because their stingers stick in skin, but wasps can sting repeatedly.

TYPES OF STING

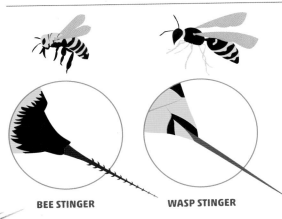

BEE STINGER   **WASP STINGER**

A wasp can withdraw its smooth stinger after piercing a victim, but a bee's sting has barbs that cause it to lodge in flesh. As the bee flies away, the tip of its abdomen tears off, fatally wounding the insect. A small muscle and a venom sac remain attached to the stinger, which saws its way deeper into the flesh, still injecting venom.

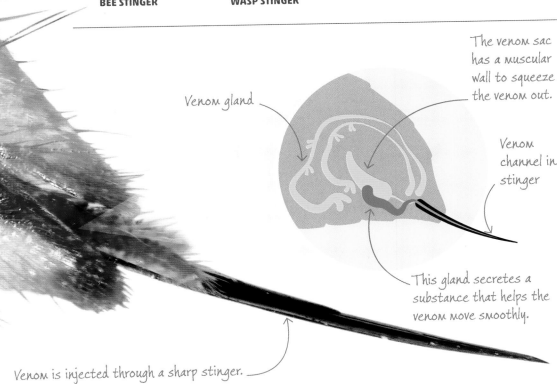

Venom gland

The venom sac has a muscular wall to squeeze the venom out.

Venom channel in stinger

This gland secretes a substance that helps the venom move smoothly.

Venom is injected through a sharp stinger.

HOW WASPS STING

Only female wasps have stingers. They strike quickly, aiming to escape before the victim senses pain.

1 LANDING
A wasp lands on a victim it perceives as a threat, and bends its abdomen into position.

2 STING
The wasp plunges its stinger into the victim's flesh, and injects venom into its skin.

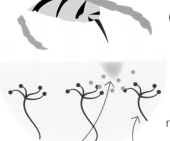

3 PAIN RECEPTORS
The wasp removes its stinger from the victim and flies away. The venom then starts to trigger pain receptors in the skin.

Venom   Pain receptors

4 INFLAMMATION
The venom makes cells in the skin release histamine – a chemical that causes redness and inflammation.

Histamine

5 SWELLING
A painful burning and itching sensation spreads around the site of the sting as the skin swells up.

HOW **CAMOUFLAGE** WORKS

In the struggle for survival, any animal that can avoid detection by its predators has a big advantage. This has led to the evolution of camouflage – body colours and shapes that imitate an animal's surroundings. Insects are masters of this form of defence, and their incredibly varied exoskeletons can mimic anything from a fresh green leaf to a broken twig.

Real leaves have damage that is imitated by the leaf insect.

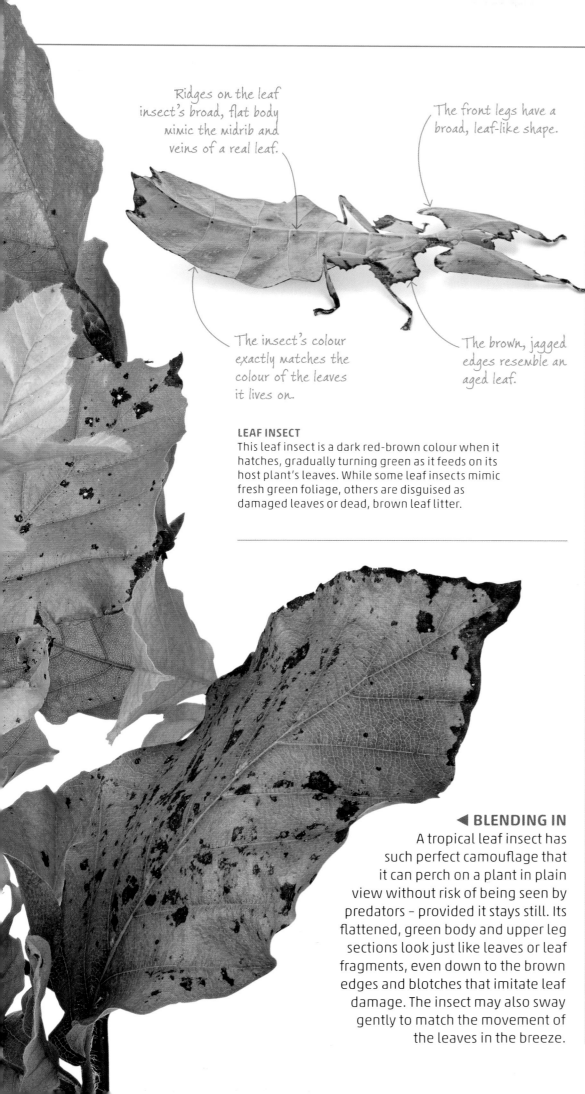

Ridges on the leaf insect's broad, flat body mimic the midrib and veins of a real leaf.

The front legs have a broad, leaf-like shape.

The insect's colour exactly matches the colour of the leaves it lives on.

The brown, jagged edges resemble an aged leaf.

LEAF INSECT

This leaf insect is a dark red-brown colour when it hatches, gradually turning green as it feeds on its host plant's leaves. While some leaf insects mimic fresh green foliage, others are disguised as damaged leaves or dead, brown leaf litter.

◀ BLENDING IN

A tropical leaf insect has such perfect camouflage that it can perch on a plant in plain view without risk of being seen by predators – provided it stays still. Its flattened, green body and upper leg sections look just like leaves or leaf fragments, even down to the brown edges and blotches that imitate leaf damage. The insect may also sway gently to match the movement of the leaves in the breeze.

VANISHING ACT

Many different types of insect rely on camouflage to make them invisible to predators, such as insect-eating lizards and birds. A few also use camouflage to conceal them from their prey, so they can ambush other insects that stray within range.

BUFF-TIP MOTH

Although very common, the buff-tip moth is rarely noticed. This is because it looks just like a broken birch twig when it is resting on a tree during the day. Like most moths, it flies only at night.

Thorn bug (also known as treehopper) in camouflage

THORN BUG

This relative of the greenfly sucks sap from plant stems, where its thorn-like shape provides a perfect disguise. Its prickly appearance may also deter big plant-eating animals from eating it by mistake.

ORCHID MANTIS

The beautiful but fiercely predatory orchid mantis imitates the colour and shape of a tropical orchid flower. When an unsuspecting insect lands on the orchid, the mantis seizes and eats it.

▶ FAKE SNAKE

When this tropical sphinx moth caterpillar is alarmed by a bird or other possible enemy, it pulls its head back into the front part of its soft body, making it swell up like a balloon. As the body skin stretches, two coloured spots expand to look like a snake's eyes. It even pretends to strike at its enemy like a snake. A real snake would be much bigger, but most birds still leave the caterpillar alone.

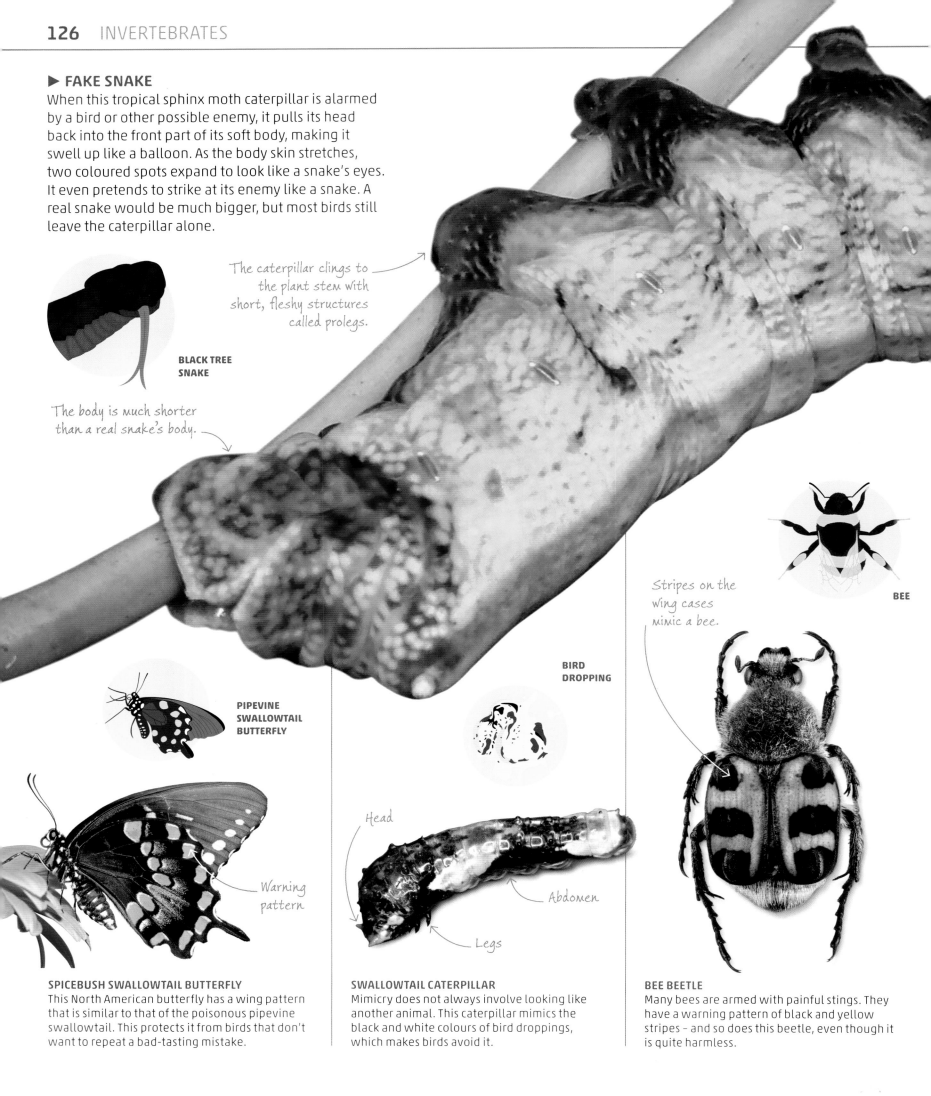

The caterpillar clings to the plant stem with short, fleshy structures called prolegs.

BLACK TREE SNAKE

The body is much shorter than a real snake's body.

BEE

Stripes on the wing cases mimic a bee.

PIPEVINE SWALLOWTAIL BUTTERFLY

BIRD DROPPING

Warning pattern

Head

Abdomen

Legs

SPICEBUSH SWALLOWTAIL BUTTERFLY
This North American butterfly has a wing pattern that is similar to that of the poisonous pipevine swallowtail. This protects it from birds that don't want to repeat a bad-tasting mistake.

SWALLOWTAIL CATERPILLAR
Mimicry does not always involve looking like another animal. This caterpillar mimics the black and white colours of bird droppings, which makes birds avoid it.

BEE BEETLE
Many bees are armed with painful stings. They have a warning pattern of black and yellow stripes – and so does this beetle, even though it is quite harmless.

HOW **MIMICRY** WORKS

Most animals are in constant danger of being killed and eaten by predators. Many rely on camouflage to conceal themselves from enemies, but some use a different strategy, mimicking the appearance of animals that are poisonous or venomous. The mimicry may not be perfect, but if it makes an attacker hesitate, the mimic gets a chance to escape. Mimicry is not just a form of defence: some predators confuse their prey by mimicking harmless animals.

The top of the "snake's head" is actually the underside of the caterpillar.

Stretched skin forms an eyespot.

The head retracts into the body.

WASP

The black and yellow stripes mimic a wasp.

The abdomen is shaped like an ant's.

ANT

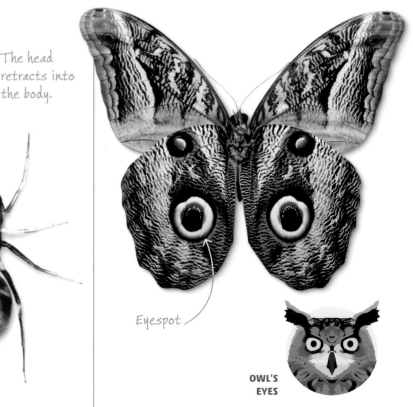

Eyespot

OWL'S EYES

HOVER FLY
Named for its ability to hover on the spot like a tiny helicopter, this nectar-feeding fly has black and yellow stripes like a wasp. It cannot sting, but the stripes fool predators.

ANT-MIMICKING SPIDER
The body shape of this spider makes it look like an ant, which deters predators as ants may sting. However, other spider species prey on ants and even mimic ants to access their colonies.

OWL BUTTERFLY
The huge eyespots on the underwings of American owl butterflies resemble the eyes of owls. The butterflies scare away lizards by opening their wings to flash the eyespots.

HOW BEES WORK

Some insects live together in large societies, cooperating to build homes, find food, and raise young. A honey bee colony can contain up to 80,000 bees. As with other social insects, the society is divided into different "castes", each of which does a different job.

THE BEE TEAM
There are three castes in a honey bee colony. While the majority of work is done by the thousands of worker bees, only one bee lays eggs: the queen.

Worker bees have a stinger at the tip of the abdomen.

WORKER
Workers clean the hive, build honeycomb, feed the larvae, and fly outside the hive foraging for nectar to make honey. Workers are all female, but they cannot reproduce.

Long, tubular mouthparts for sucking nectar.

Worker bee

Drones have no stinger.

DRONE
Drones are male honey bees. Their only job is to fly in search of new queens and mate with them so the queens can start new colonies.

Large abdomen for laying eggs.

Larva developing inside a cell.

QUEEN
The main task of the hive's queen bee is to lay eggs. During spring, she can lay up to 2,000 eggs every day, which is more than her own body weight.

HIVE OF ACTIVITY ▶
The centre of a honey bee's life is the nest, which is packed with hexagonal cells made of wax secreted by the workers. Sealed cells may contain stores of honey, pollen, or developing larvae.

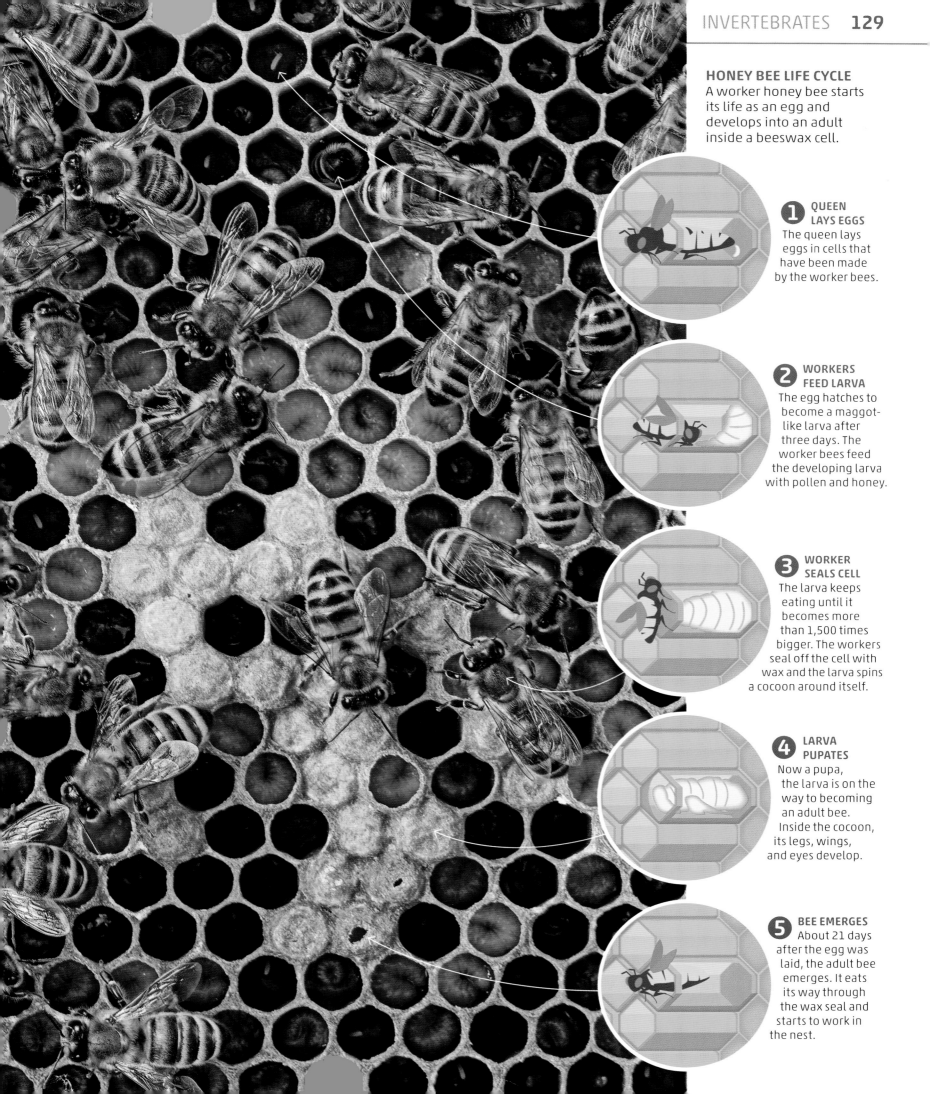

HONEY BEE LIFE CYCLE
A worker honey bee starts
its life as an egg and
develops into an adult
inside a beeswax cell.

1 QUEEN LAYS EGGS
The queen lays
eggs in cells that
have been made
by the worker bees.

2 WORKERS FEED LARVA
The egg hatches to
become a maggot-
like larva after
three days. The
worker bees feed
the developing larva
with pollen and honey.

3 WORKER SEALS CELL
The larva keeps
eating until it
becomes more
than 1,500 times
bigger. The workers
seal off the cell with
wax and the larva spins
a cocoon around itself.

4 LARVA PUPATES
Now a pupa,
the larva is on the
way to becoming
an adult bee.
Inside the cocoon,
its legs, wings,
and eyes develop.

5 BEE EMERGES
About 21 days
after the egg was
laid, the adult bee
emerges. It eats
its way through
the wax seal and
starts to work in
the nest.

HOW **ANTS** WORK

Ants are sociable insects that live in colonies that can contain millions of ants working together to keep the colony fed and protected. The workers are all females – daughters of the single large, egg-laying queen that stays protected at the nest's centre.

▶ FORAGING TEAM

Carpenter ants are named for their nesting habits. They use their jaws to cut channels in damp wood, where they tend the queen and raise their young. Using their strong, serrated jaws, a swarm of tiny rainforest carpenter ants can make short work of a dead spider. Working together, they separate its body into parts small enough to carry back to the nest.

DUTIES OF A WORKER

There are more than 12,000 different species of ant. Some are fearsome predators, but others are herbivores or scavengers. In some colonies, there are several types of worker, with specialized roles such as soldiers that fight off attackers and foragers that seek new sources of food for the colony.

FARMING FOR APHIDS
Aphids release a sweet substance called honeydew. Many kinds of ant collect droplets of this nutritious fluid and, in return, protect the aphids from predators.

GROWING FUNGI
Leafcutter ants store leaves in a "fungus garden". They infect the leaves with a fungus, which is later harvested for food.

BRIDGING GAPS
Some ants are able to link their bodies to make bridges, helping other ants to reach across gaps that would otherwise be impossible to cross.

sharp-edged **BITING MOUTHPARTS**

Jagged edges help the jaws grip.

The spider's abdomen is cut from the body and carried away to the nest.

DIVIDING A SPIDER

Carpenter ants don't typically hunt live prey, but instead scavenge at night for dead invertebrates. Teams of ants search the rainforest for food to share with the rest of their colony. They rip apart their prey before carrying it home to feed on the soft internal flesh and body fluids.

1 DISCOVERY
A small advance group of foraging workers finds the dead spider. As the worker ants travel between their nest and the spider, they leave a trail of chemicals called pheromones, which the other workers follow to reach the food.

The spider's body is still intact when the ants discover it.

New workers arrive, having followed the chemical trails left by others.

2 GATHERING
Having followed the pheromone trail, more worker ants arrive. They cooperate to break up the spider and then carry its severed head and legs back to the nest. Once the inner meat has been consumed, the outer husk of the spider will be discarded.

A hundred or more workers split the spider into fragments.

Workers attack limb joints, where the exoskeleton is easier to cut.

The queen begins life with wings, but loses them after she has established a nest.

Workers have no wings.

Male ants (drones) have wings.

ANT CASTES

The members of a colony are divided into different groups, called castes, which vary in their appearance and role within the colony. There is typically one queen in a colony, and she is responsible for laying eggs. Male drones are only produced when new colonies are being established, but female workers are permanent residents.

WORKER
Workers, which are all female, dominate in mature ant nests. They are wingless and don't breed. Instead, they spend their time hunting for food and defending the colony.

MALE
At the birth of a colony, winged male ants mate with queens in group displays called nuptial flights. The males play no further role in the colony and die.

QUEEN
A queen ant's sole function is to reproduce, so that she can build up a colony. Once she has mated with a male ant, the queen begins to lay the eggs that will hatch into new workers.

FIREFLIES

At the beginning of the rainy season, thousands of fireflies light up this forest on the island of Shikoku in Japan. Fireflies are winged beetles that use chemicals in their bodies to create light in their abdomens. This light, called bioluminescence, is used by fireflies in courtship displays to communicate with mates. Bioluminescence is found widely throughout nature and can also be used to ward off predators, lure prey, and attract mates.

HOW SPIDERS WORK

Unlike insects, spiders cannot fly, but they are superbly equipped to catch and kill. Some chase or ambush their victims, but many produce threads of silk to make webs and other traps. They detect vibrations of moving prey, which most spiders then immobilize with venom delivered through stabbing fangs.

SPIDERS VS INSECTS
In contrast to insects, spiders lack antennae and wings. And whereas insects have three body parts – head, thorax, and abdomen – spiders have just two: their head and thorax are fused to form a single unit. However, spiders have eight legs, while insects only have six.

Fused head and thorax

These appendages contain the fangs.

Silk glands

Abdomen

Sensitive hairs help spiders detect prey by sensing vibrations.

▶ AGGRESSIVE PREDATOR
This baboon spider is a large, fast-running tarantula found in African grassland. Baboon spiders are notoriously aggressive and will rear up, fangs ready to strike, if they feel threatened. They usually ambush prey from a burrow in the ground.

Each leg consists of seven segments.

HOW SPIDERS FEED
Spiders' guts are so narrow, they can only take in fluids. To feed, they regurgitate digestive juices to liquefy their prey, suck in the part-digested tissues, and discard hard tissues that can't be digested.

Spiders have front appendages called pedipalps, which they use to manipulate food.

Adhesive foot pads help spiders climb smooth surfaces, and some spiders can even walk upside down.

Although spiders have eight eyes, their vision is poor and they rely on their sense of touch to hunt.

Spiders have four pairs of legs.

The sharp, pointed fangs inject venom into prey.

VENOMOUS FANGS
A spider's fangs have a small hole in the tip and a venom-filled duct inside. The venom paralyses the spider's prey by disabling its muscles and nervous system.

HOW SPIDER SILK WORKS

All spiders produce silk – an extremely stretchy fibre that is even stronger and tougher than steel. Specialized silk glands in a spider's abdomen create different types of silk to suit a variety of purposes. Producing silk requires a lot of energy, which a spider will sometimes regain by eating its own silk.

USES OF SPIDER SILK

Silk is vital to the lives of spiders. The earliest spiders probably used it to line their burrows, and many still do this. But spiders also spin webs to trap prey, extra-strong silk for lifelines to escape predators, protective cases for their eggs, and scented silk to attract mates.

REELING IN PREY
A bolas spider spins a line of silk with a sticky blob at the end to snare moths. Each moth is reeled in like a hooked fish.

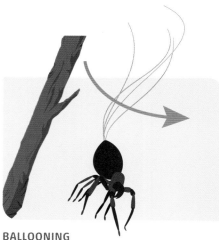

BALLOONING
To look for food, some small spiders travel at great heights by ballooning – spinning threads of silk to catch the wind.

MAKING A HOME
A purse-web spider lives in a silk-lined burrow. The lining extends above ground and the spider seizes insects through it.

SILKEN SHROUD ▶
Spider silk is amazingly versatile. This garden spider uses it to weave a circular web between plants to snare flying insects. When it catches one, it spins a different type of silk to wrap the insect up, binding it so tightly that it cannot defend itself or escape.

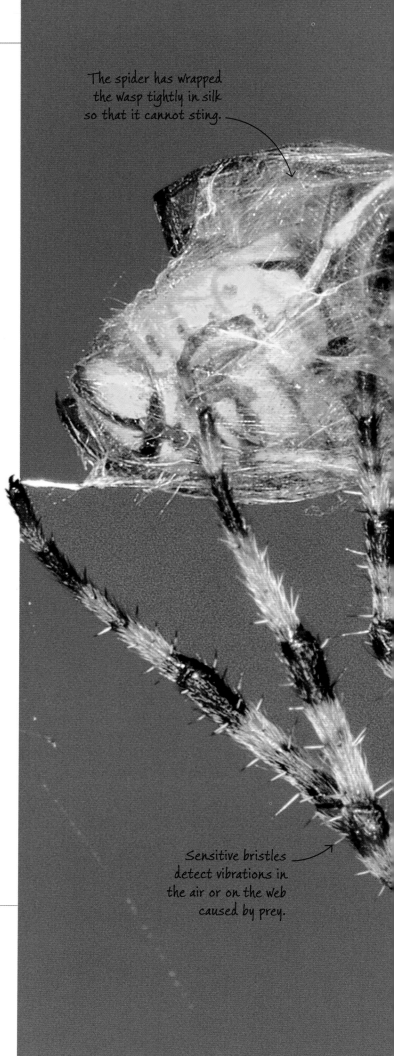

The spider has wrapped the wasp tightly in silk so that it cannot sting.

Sensitive bristles detect vibrations in the air or on the web caused by prey.

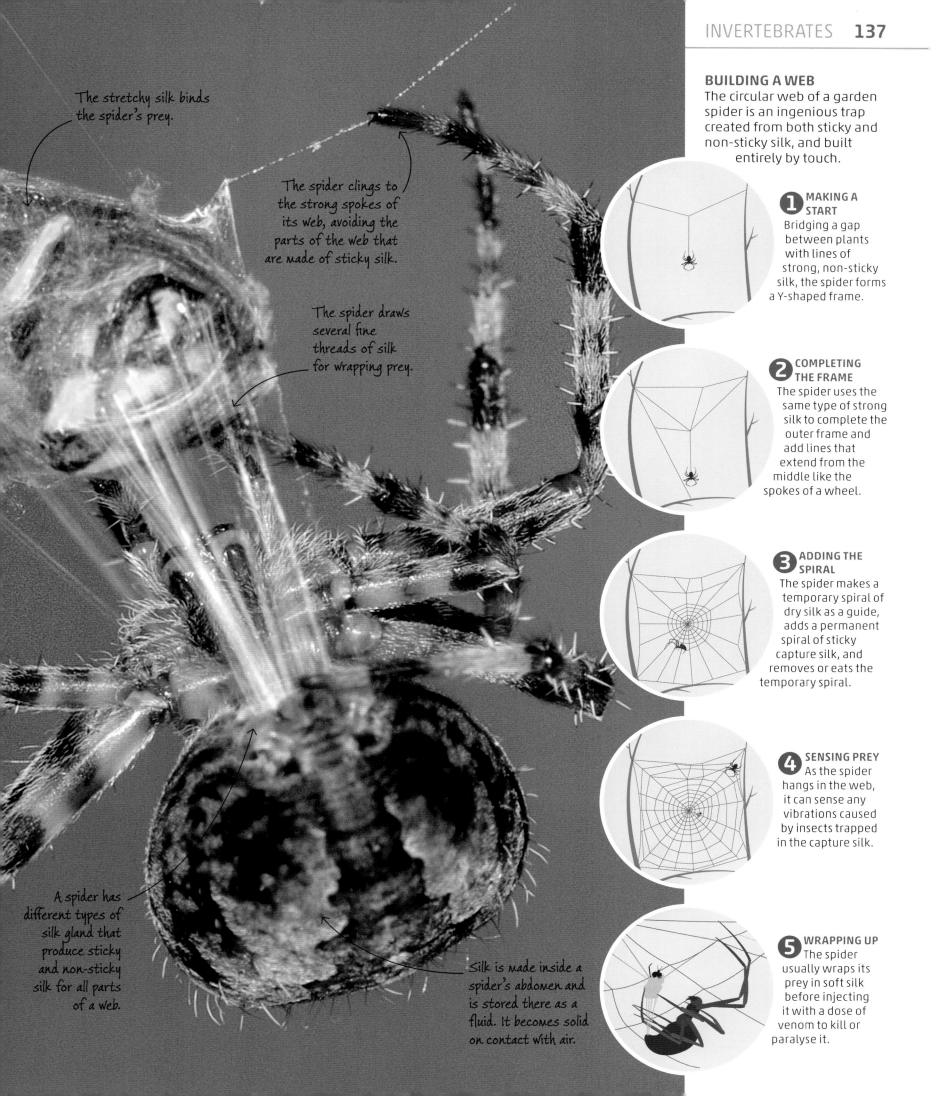

The stretchy silk binds the spider's prey.

The spider clings to the strong spokes of its web, avoiding the parts of the web that are made of sticky silk.

The spider draws several fine threads of silk for wrapping prey.

A spider has different types of silk gland that produce sticky and non-sticky silk for all parts of a web.

Silk is made inside a spider's abdomen and is stored there as a fluid. It becomes solid on contact with air.

BUILDING A WEB
The circular web of a garden spider is an ingenious trap created from both sticky and non-sticky silk, and built entirely by touch.

1 MAKING A START
Bridging a gap between plants with lines of strong, non-sticky silk, the spider forms a Y-shaped frame.

2 COMPLETING THE FRAME
The spider uses the same type of strong silk to complete the outer frame and add lines that extend from the middle like the spokes of a wheel.

3 ADDING THE SPIRAL
The spider makes a temporary spiral of dry silk as a guide, adds a permanent spiral of sticky capture silk, and removes or eats the temporary spiral.

4 SENSING PREY
As the spider hangs in the web, it can sense any vibrations caused by insects trapped in the capture silk.

5 WRAPPING UP
The spider usually wraps its prey in soft silk before injecting it with a dose of venom to kill or paralyse it.

The flexible tail is made of six segments.

Sensory hairs guide a scorpion's tail into place as it stings.

Venom is released through two channels in the stinger.

DEADLY DEATHSTALKER
One of the most deadly scorpion species, the deathstalker has a potent venom that can cause extreme pain, convulsions, and paralysis in humans, which can be fatal. It is found mainly in the arid desert regions of the Middle East and North Africa.

The deathstalker has small pincers because it can rely on its powerful sting to kill prey.

Nerve fibres control how the tail moves.

Venom is stored in two venom bulbs.

A scorpion's eyes detect changes in light but don't form detailed images.

Clawed feet help the scorpion climb over rocks, logs, and branches without losing its grip.

HOW SCORPIONS HUNT

Armed with powerful pincers and a venomous sting, scorpions are fearsome hunters that prey on a wide range of small animals, from insects to mice and lizards. Most species live in tropical deserts and rainforests, where many keep cool in rocky burrows during the day and hunt at night. They have poor eyesight and rely on their highly sensitive touch to find their prey.

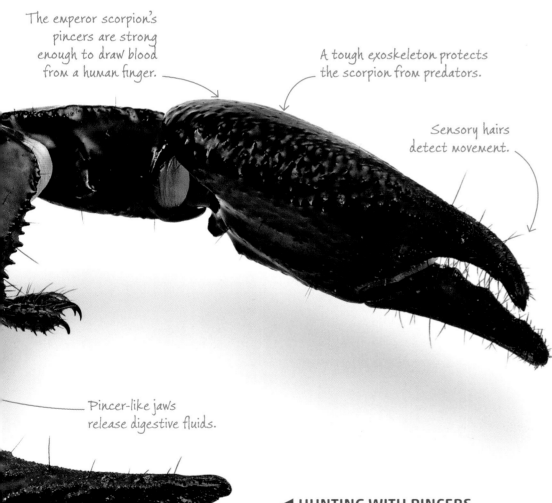

The emperor scorpion's pincers are strong enough to draw blood from a human finger.

A tough exoskeleton protects the scorpion from predators.

Sensory hairs detect movement.

Pincer-like jaws release digestive fluids.

◀ **HUNTING WITH PINCERS**
This emperor scorpion is one of the largest species of scorpion in the world. Young emperor scorpions use their stings to paralyse prey, but adults kill by tearing victims apart with their pincers.

HUNTING TECHNIQUE
Most scorpions are ambush hunters, waiting until a victim has moved to within striking distance before attacking.

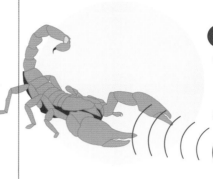

1 The sensitive hairs on a scorpion's legs detect tiny ground and air vibrations that determine the precise distance and direction of an approaching victim.

2 When prey is detected, the scorpion runs towards its victim and seizes it with its powerful claws. This can crush the prey to death.

3 If the prey is large or aggressive, the scorpion administers a sting from its tail. The venom from the sting paralyses the victim and stops it escaping.

4 As the scorpion tears its prey apart, it secretes digestive fluids from its jaws. These break down the victim's soft body parts into a liquid.

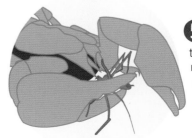

5 The scorpion sucks the liquid in through its small mouth, leaving behind any solid matter that it can't digest, such as an insect's exoskeleton.

HOW MILLIPEDES WORK

Millipedes and centipedes belong to a group of invertebrates called myriapods. Myriapods share many features with insects, such as an external skeleton (exoskeleton) and breathing tubes rather than lungs. However, they have many more legs and long, cylindrical bodies divided into multiple segments. Millipedes are slow-moving burrowers that eat dead leaves and rotting wood, whereas centipedes are fast-running predators.

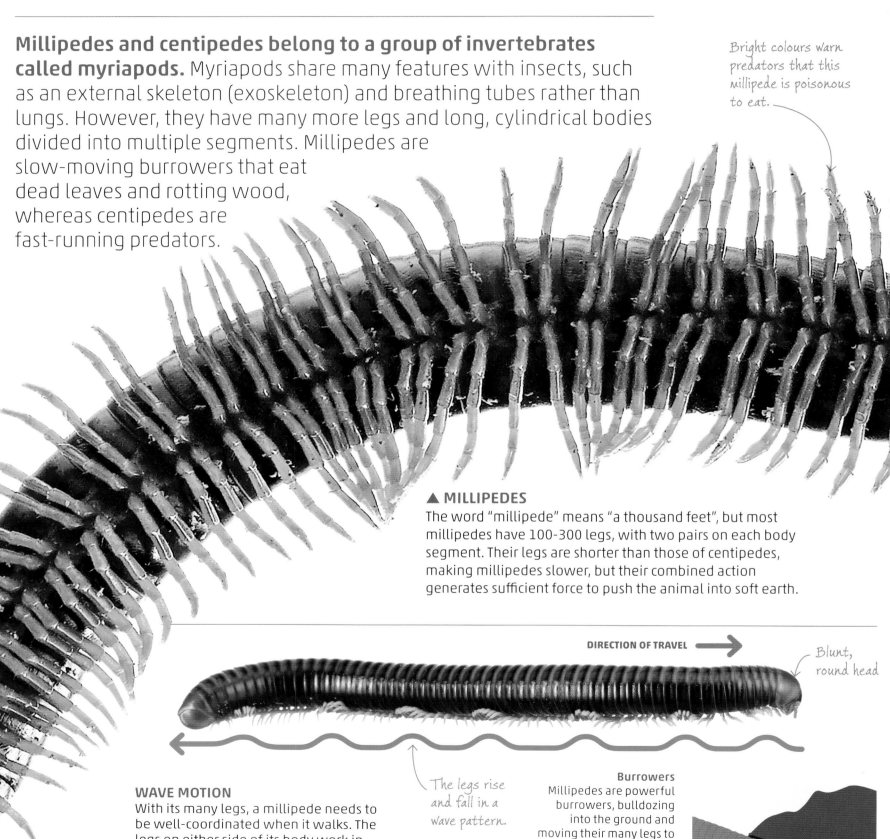

Bright colours warn predators that this millipede is poisonous to eat.

▲ **MILLIPEDES**
The word "millipede" means "a thousand feet", but most millipedes have 100-300 legs, with two pairs on each body segment. Their legs are shorter than those of centipedes, making millipedes slower, but their combined action generates sufficient force to push the animal into soft earth.

DIRECTION OF TRAVEL →

Blunt, round head

WAVE MOTION
With its many legs, a millipede needs to be well-coordinated when it walks. The legs on either side of its body work in sequence, moving up and down in waves that sweep from the head to the tail. A millipede can move between 10 and 20 legs at once in this way.

The legs rise and fall in a wave pattern.

Burrowers
Millipedes are powerful burrowers, bulldozing into the ground and moving their many legs to widen the hole and push themselves forwards.

MILLIPEDE SENSES
Millipedes have a round head with antennae, simple eyes, jaws, and sensory organs to detect humidity. Most millipedes have poor vision or are blind, but they can feel their way around by tapping their antennae on the ground in front of them.

Each segment has two pairs of jointed legs.

The hard exoskeleton protects the millipede from predators.

DEFENCE TACTICS
Millipedes are slow walkers, so will coil themselves into a tight ball to protect their legs and soft underside if threatened by a predator. Some millipedes, like this fire millipede, secrete a poisonous liquid that can burn an attacking insect.

HATCHLINGS
Like insects, millipedes must shed their exoskeleton in order to grow. They begin life with just six segments and three pairs of legs. Each time they moult, they emerge with a larger exoskeleton with more segments and legs.

1 STAGE 1
When it hatches, a millipede has just six segments and three pairs of legs.

2 STAGE 2
After its first moult, a young millipede has eight segments, one with two pairs of legs and four with just one pair of legs.

3 STAGE 3
After the second moult, a millipede has 11 segments, four with two pairs of legs and three with one pair of legs.

4 STAGE 4
The millipede will continue to add segments and legs after each moult until it reaches maturity.

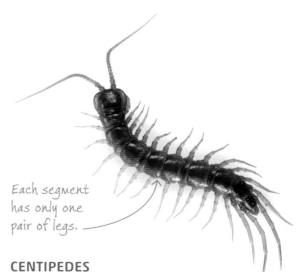

Each segment has only one pair of legs.

CENTIPEDES
Centipedes have fewer segments than millipedes and only one pair of legs per segment. They can grow to lengths of 30 cm (12 in). Their venomous, fang-like claws can be used to paralyse prey as large as frogs and mice.

HOW **CRABS** WORK

Crabs belong to a large and varied group of invertebrates called crustaceans, which also includes lobsters and shrimps. Most crabs live in the sea but many have adapted to live partly on land, using eight of their ten legs to walk with a distinctive sideways gait. Crabs find food by crawling over the sea floor or shore looking for algae, worms, detritus, and shelled animals, which they pick up and crush with their claws.

▶ ARMOURED BODY

Like other crustaceans, crabs have hard external coverings, or exoskeletons, that they must shed from time to time in order to grow. They have five pairs of jointed legs, the front pair of which are modified to form pincers. In some crabs, one claw is much larger than the other and is used for crushing prey or attracting mates. Most crabs breathe through gills under their shells, but this African rainbow crab has lungs to breathe air.

REPRODUCTION

After mating, a female crab uses her tail flap to protect and carry as many as 180,000 eggs, which look like small berries. She releases these into the ocean, where they hatch into swimming larvae that look very different from adult crabs. The larvae drift away and later settle on the seabed, where they take on their adult shape.

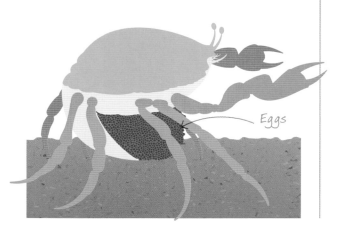

Eggs

The larger "crusher claw" is used for crushing prey.

Crabs have eyes on stalks.

VIEW FROM ABOVE

A broad shield called a carapace covers the main part of the body.

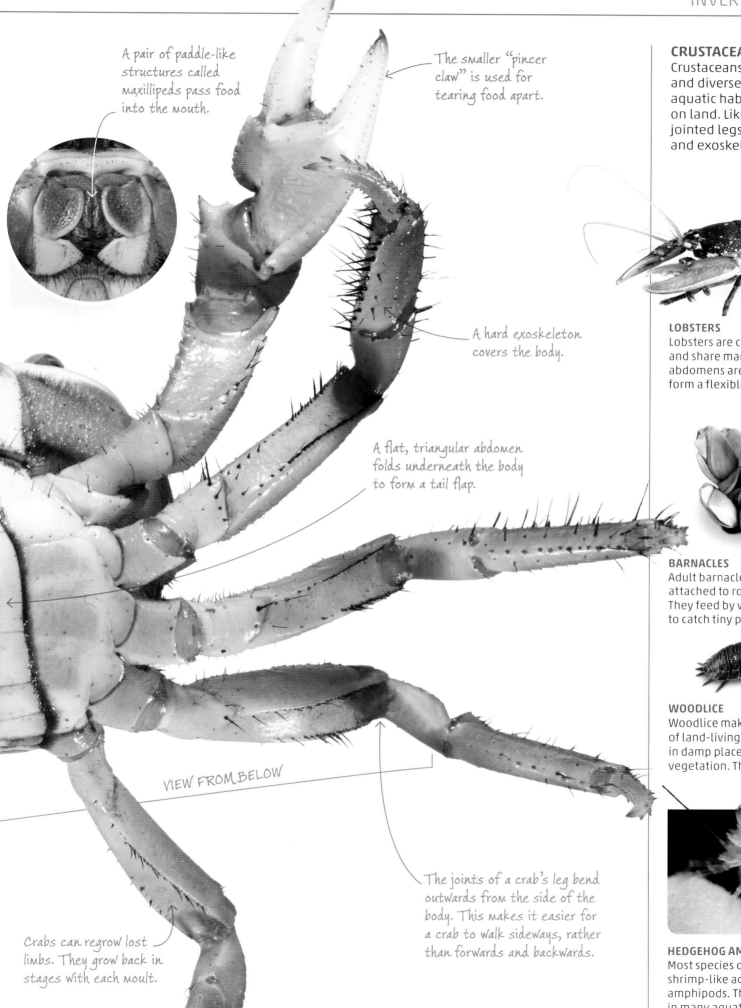

A pair of paddle-like structures called maxillipeds pass food into the mouth.

The smaller "pincer claw" is used for tearing food apart.

A hard exoskeleton covers the body.

A flat, triangular abdomen folds underneath the body to form a tail flap.

VIEW FROM BELOW

Crabs can regrow lost limbs. They grow back in stages with each moult.

The joints of a crab's leg bend outwards from the side of the body. This makes it easier for a crab to walk sideways, rather than forwards and backwards.

CRUSTACEANS

Crustaceans are as common and diverse in the sea and other aquatic habitats as insects are on land. Like insects, they have jointed legs, segmented bodies, and exoskeletons.

LOBSTERS

Lobsters are closely related to crabs and share many features, but their abdomens are not folded and instead form a flexible tail for swimming.

BARNACLES

Adult barnacles live permanently attached to rocks and other surfaces. They feed by waving feathery limbs to catch tiny particles of food.

WOODLICE

Woodlice make up the largest group of land-living crustaceans. They live in damp places and feed on rotting vegetation. They are active at night.

HEDGEHOG AMPHIPODS

Most species of crustacean are small, shrimp-like aquatic animals such as amphipods. They live in vast numbers in many aquatic habitats.

The first animals to evolve backbones were **fish**, which appeared on Earth almost 500 million years ago. Fish are **aquatic creatures** that are adapted to life in the world's oceans, lakes, and rivers. They can **breathe underwater**, and many have **streamlined** shapes that allow them to swim quickly through the water.

FISH

HOW FISH WORK

Half of the world's vertebrates are fish. Some species live in the salt water of oceans, and others, in the fresh water of rivers, ponds, and lakes, but all are adapted to a life spent swimming. Most have a streamlined, scaly body with fins to control their movement and gills for breathing underwater.

Dorsal fins keep fish upright by stopping them rolling sideways.

The fish's small brain controls its body and behaviour.

Human eyes have eyelids to keep them moist, but fish eyes are always wet, so they don't have any.

Gills absorb oxygen from water.

▶ LIVING UNDERWATER
Like most fish, a glassfish is tapered at the front and back to make it streamlined in the water. In most fish, the digestive and reproductive organs are clustered at the front of the body, while the rear is packed with muscles. These flex the body sideways to propel the fish through the water.

The digestive and reproductive organs are located near the front of the body.

The swim bladder is a gas-filled sac that lets the fish control its depth in the water.

PROTECTIVE SCALES
The skin of most fish is covered with scales that protect their soft bodies and allow them to glide through water without resistance. A slimy coating of mucus acts as a barrier against parasites and disease.

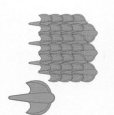

PLACOID
The hard, tooth-like, bony scales of sharks and rays make their skin feel rough, like sandpaper. These scales are as tough as leather.

GANOID
Some primitive types of bony fish, such as sturgeon and gar, have thick, diamond-shaped scales that interlock to form a suit of armour. This type of scale lacks flexibility.

LEPTOID
Most fish have small, flexible scales, which grow backwards and overlap like roof tiles. They make the fish streamlined.

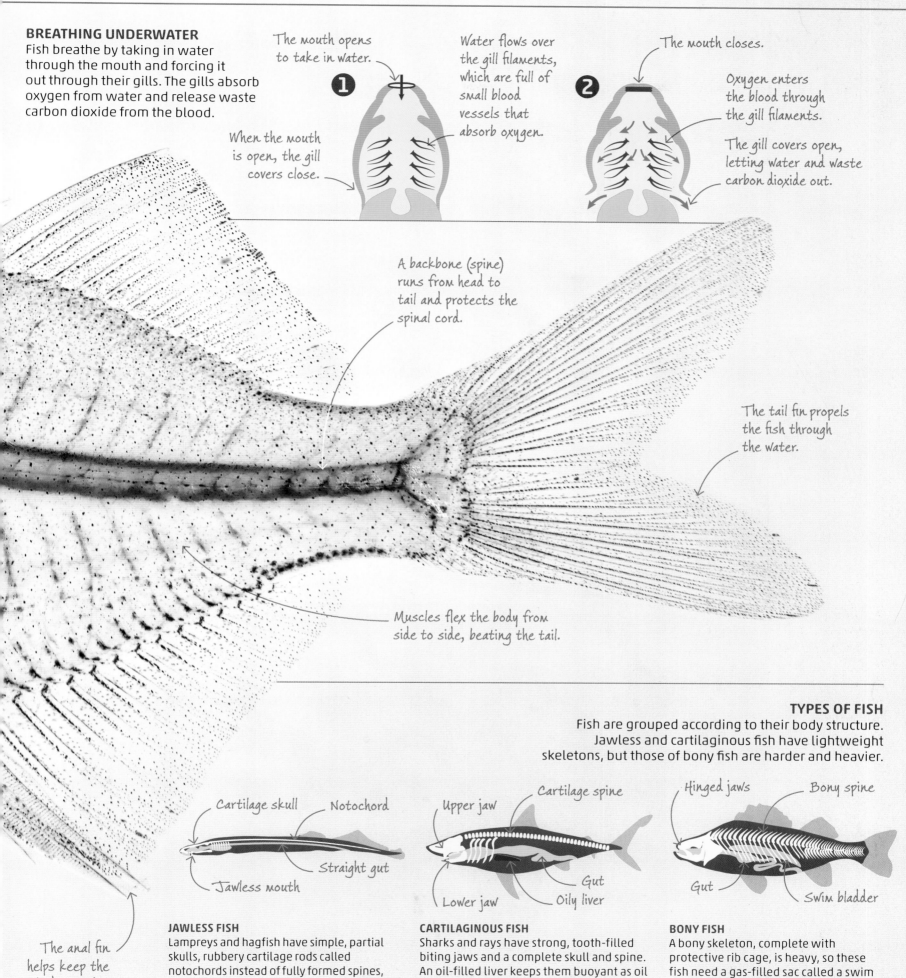

BREATHING UNDERWATER
Fish breathe by taking in water through the mouth and forcing it out through their gills. The gills absorb oxygen from water and release waste carbon dioxide from the blood.

The mouth opens to take in water. ❶

Water flows over the gill filaments, which are full of small blood vessels that absorb oxygen.

When the mouth is open, the gill covers close.

The mouth closes. ❷

Oxygen enters the blood through the gill filaments.

The gill covers open, letting water and waste carbon dioxide out.

A backbone (spine) runs from head to tail and protects the spinal cord.

The tail fin propels the fish through the water.

Muscles flex the body from side to side, beating the tail.

The anal fin helps keep the body upright.

TYPES OF FISH
Fish are grouped according to their body structure. Jawless and cartilaginous fish have lightweight skeletons, but those of bony fish are harder and heavier.

Cartilage skull   Notochord

Upper jaw   Cartilage spine

Hinged jaws   Bony spine

Straight gut

Jawless mouth

Lower jaw   Oily liver   Gut

Gut   Swim bladder

JAWLESS FISH
Lampreys and hagfish have simple, partial skulls, rubbery cartilage rods called notochords instead of fully formed spines, and circular gill openings. Instead of hinged, biting jaws, they have sucker-like mouths.

CARTILAGINOUS FISH
Sharks and rays have strong, tooth-filled biting jaws and a complete skull and spine. An oil-filled liver keeps them buoyant as oil is lighter than water. Uncovered gills open to the outside as a series of slits.

BONY FISH
A bony skeleton, complete with protective rib cage, is heavy, so these fish need a gas-filled sac called a swim bladder to keep them buoyant. Gill covers protect their gills.

HOW **FISH** SWIM

All fish swim using both body and fin movements, but they move in different ways depending on their environment. Many species have swim bladders to help their muscle-packed bodies stay buoyant in the water. They use their fins for steering and stabilization and propel themselves forwards with their tails.

The dorsal fin is used for stabilization.

▶ **SWIMMING IN STYLE**
The mandarin fish is a slow swimmer. Like most fish, the sweeping tail fin pushes it through the water. In contrast, the fastest swimmers have streamlined, rigid bodies that hardly bend, and stiff tails that beat rapidly to generate forward thrust.

BUOYANCY
Bony and cartilaginous fish are denser than water, so they have internal organs to improve their buoyancy.

As it moves up and down, the fish adjusts the amount of gas in its swim bladder.

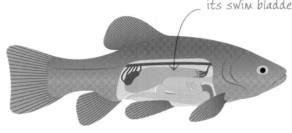

BONY FISH
Bony fish typically have a gas-filled sac called a swim bladder, which inflates and deflates using gas from the bloodstream. The swim bladder lets the fish control its position in the water without using energy for swimming.

Pectoral fins pulse, which provides some propulsion.

CARTILAGINOUS FISH
Sharks have large, oily livers. This organ helps to keep them buoyant because oil is lighter than water. However, most sharks also need to swim continuously to maintain their buoyancy.

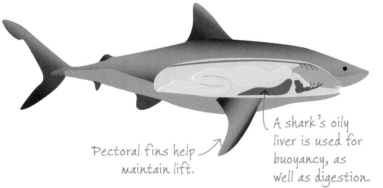

Pectoral fins help maintain lift.

A shark's oily liver is used for buoyancy, as well as digestion.

S-SHAPED CURVES
Fish swim using a series of S-shaped curves that start at the head and sweep along the body. When a curve reaches the tail, the tail moves from side to side, pushing the fish forwards.

 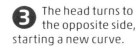

1 The head moves to one side and the rest of the body follows, creating a curve.

2 The curve moves down the body, reaching the tail, which pushes outwards, moving the fish forwards.

3 The head turns to the opposite side, starting a new curve.

4 The new curve causes the tail to push in the opposite direction. The next curve begins.

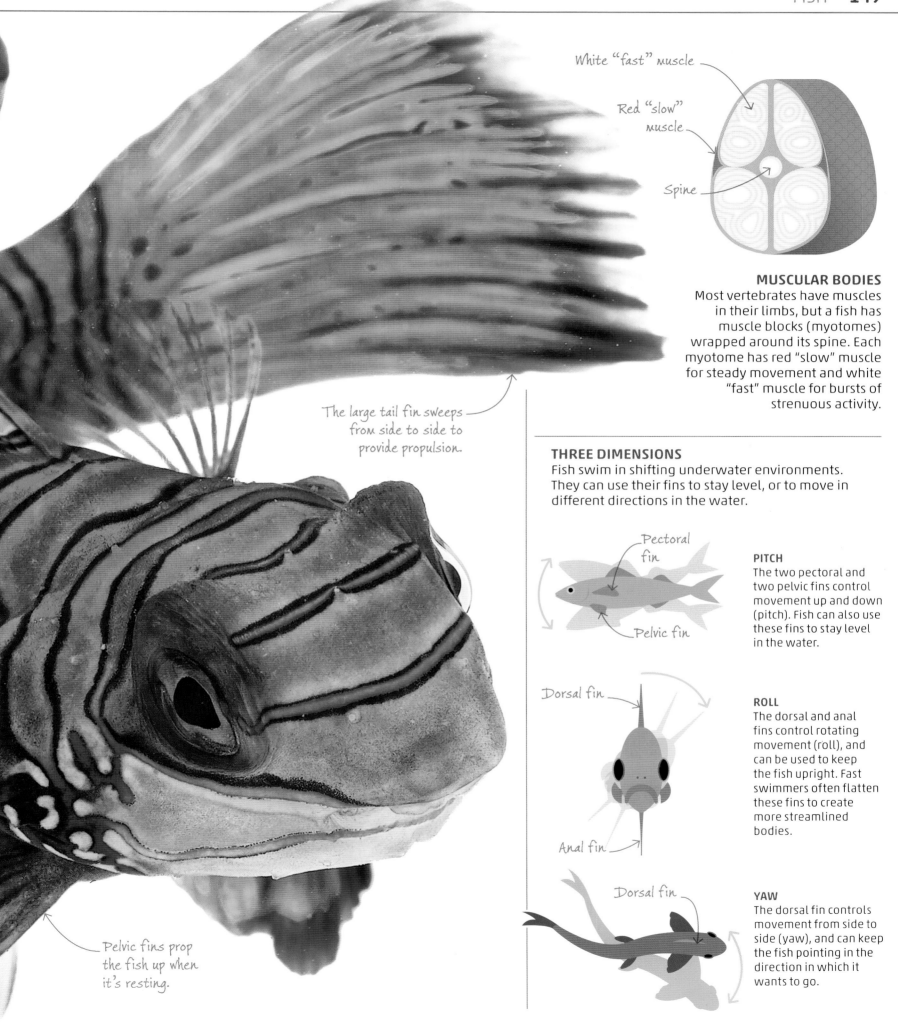

White "fast" muscle

Red "slow" muscle

Spine

MUSCULAR BODIES
Most vertebrates have muscles in their limbs, but a fish has muscle blocks (myotomes) wrapped around its spine. Each myotome has red "slow" muscle for steady movement and white "fast" muscle for bursts of strenuous activity.

The large tail fin sweeps from side to side to provide propulsion.

THREE DIMENSIONS
Fish swim in shifting underwater environments. They can use their fins to stay level, or to move in different directions in the water.

Pectoral fin

Pelvic fin

PITCH
The two pectoral and two pelvic fins control movement up and down (pitch). Fish can also use these fins to stay level in the water.

Dorsal fin

Anal fin

ROLL
The dorsal and anal fins control rotating movement (roll), and can be used to keep the fish upright. Fast swimmers often flatten these fins to create more streamlined bodies.

Dorsal fin

YAW
The dorsal fin controls movement from side to side (yaw), and can keep the fish pointing in the direction in which it wants to go.

Pelvic fins prop the fish up when it's resting.

HOW FISH SENSES WORK

Fish can hear, see, smell, touch, and taste, just like humans, but they have extra senses, too. Specially adapted organs sense tiny movements in water, and some species even detect electricity. As a fish explores its environment, its brain constantly receives sensory information, which it uses to avoid predators, seek out prey, and swim precisely.

SEEING UNDERWATER
Unlike the lenses inside human eyes, which change shape to focus on objects near and far, the shape of a fish's lens is fixed. Instead, the lens moves forwards and backwards to focus like a camera.

This ligament keeps the lens in place.

A muscle pulls the lens backwards.

The spherical lens inside a fish eye moves forwards and backwards to focus.

Inside the nostrils, folds of skin are covered in receptors, which detect chemicals produced by prey and predators.

Packed with taste buds, these barbels feel along the river bottom for food.

This catfish has good eyesight and sees in colour, but its vision is only helpful when hunting in clear water.

▼ HOW CATFISH SENSE

The channel catfish has a super-sensory body for finding food in muddy rivers. As well as excellent vision and a keen sense of smell, it's equipped with more than 100,000 taste buds. Thousands are concentrated not only on its whisker-like barbels, but also cover its scaleless body.

SPECIAL SENSES

Although fish often have good eyesight, it can be difficult for them to see because there isn't much sunlight underwater. Many fish rely on extra senses to find their way around.

Scales

The water-filled channel is open to the outside.

Water-filled channel

Tiny hairs detect any movement nearby.

LATERAL LINE SYSTEM

Most fish have water-filled channels on each side of their body between the gills and tail fin, known as the lateral line system. Each channel contains sensory hairs that detect small movements in the water, helping the fish to feel prey and predators swimming nearby.

The snout generates an electric field, which bounces off objects back at the fish.

INNER EAR

Bony fish typically use their gas-filled swim bladders to control their buoyancy. Some species, however, use their swim bladders to amplify sounds, too. These sounds reach the fish's inner ear through a vibrating chain of tiny bones.

Sound waves cause the swim bladder to vibrate.

Swim bladder

Tiny bones transmit the vibrations through the body.

The sound reaches the inner ear.

ELECTRORECEPTION

Some species can produce and detect faint electrical signals. An elephantfish's long snout generates electrical signals, that bounce off objects in the water. The elephantfish's head, back, and belly are covered in receptors which sense these signals as they return, allowing the fish to dodge obstacles and find food.

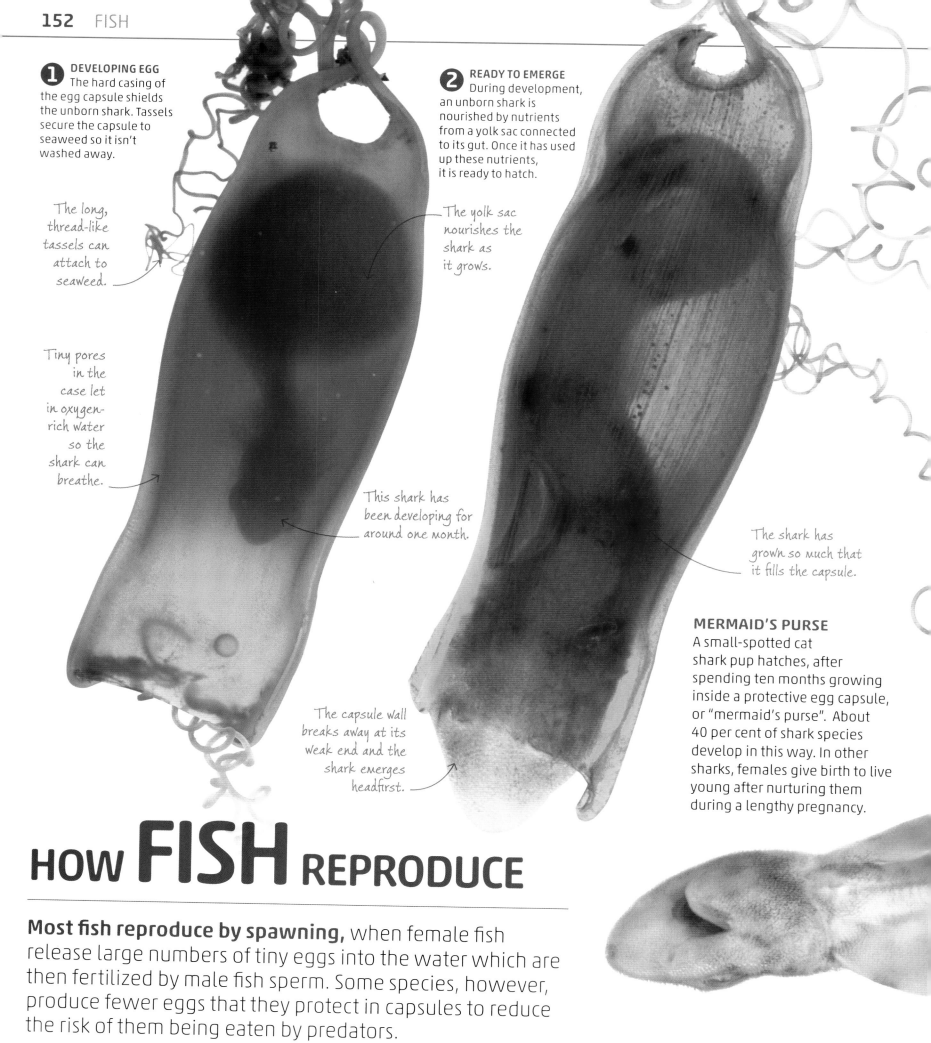

1 DEVELOPING EGG
The hard casing of the egg capsule shields the unborn shark. Tassels secure the capsule to seaweed so it isn't washed away.

2 READY TO EMERGE
During development, an unborn shark is nourished by nutrients from a yolk sac connected to its gut. Once it has used up these nutrients, it is ready to hatch.

The long, thread-like tassels can attach to seaweed.

Tiny pores in the case let in oxygen-rich water so the shark can breathe.

The yolk sac nourishes the shark as it grows.

This shark has been developing for around one month.

The shark has grown so much that it fills the capsule.

The capsule wall breaks away at its weak end and the shark emerges headfirst.

MERMAID'S PURSE
A small-spotted cat shark pup hatches, after spending ten months growing inside a protective egg capsule, or "mermaid's purse". About 40 per cent of shark species develop in this way. In other sharks, females give birth to live young after nurturing them during a lengthy pregnancy.

HOW **FISH** REPRODUCE

Most fish reproduce by spawning, when female fish release large numbers of tiny eggs into the water which are then fertilized by male fish sperm. Some species, however, produce fewer eggs that they protect in capsules to reduce the risk of them being eaten by predators.

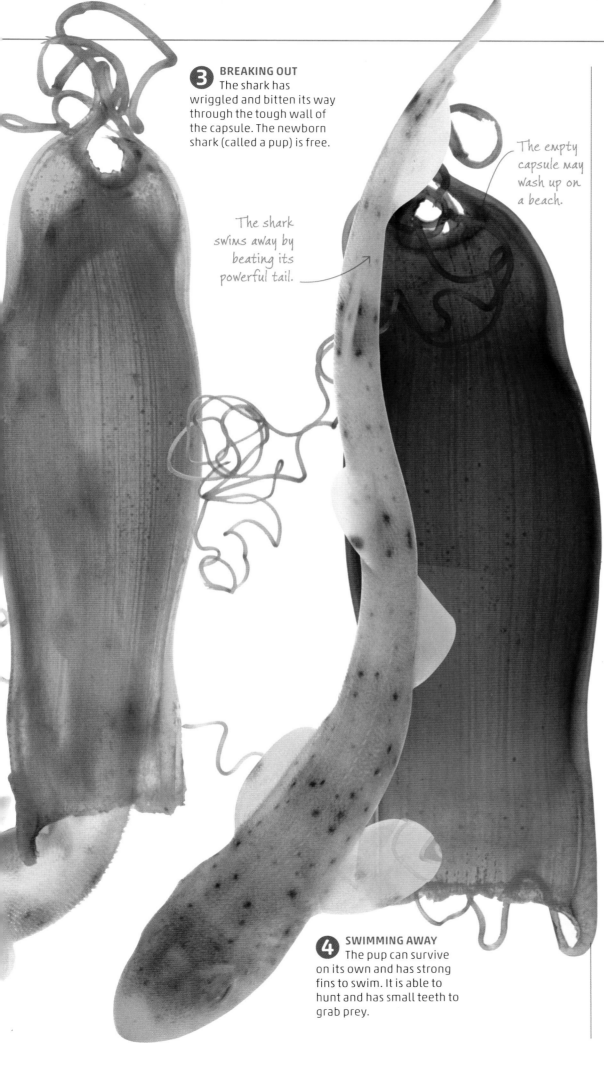

3 BREAKING OUT
The shark has wriggled and bitten its way through the tough wall of the capsule. The newborn shark (called a pup) is free.

The empty capsule may wash up on a beach.

The shark swims away by beating its powerful tail.

4 SWIMMING AWAY
The pup can survive on its own and has strong fins to swim. It is able to hunt and has small teeth to grab prey.

EGGS AND BABIES

Fish reproduce in many different ways. Some species release their eggs into the water, while others become pregnant and give birth.

MASS SPAWNING
Fish such as these twinspot snappers release sperm and eggs into the open water in a process called spawning. When large groups produce clouds of eggs, fertilization is more likely to happen.

GROWING UP
In most fish, the newly hatched babies – or larvae – are tiny and undeveloped. A nourishing yolk sac is attached to their bellies and shrinks as it is used up by the growing baby.

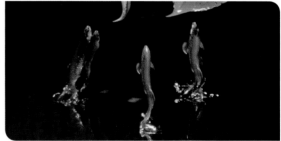

SPLASHING OUT
To hide their eggs from predators, splash tetras jump from the water to stick them to overhanging leaves. They flick water at the eggs with their tails to stop them drying out.

PREGNANCY AND BIRTH
Some fish, such as this swordtail, mate so that male sperm goes directly into the female's body. The female carries the fertilized eggs while they develop, then gives birth to live young.

HOW FISH CARE FOR THEIR YOUNG

After laying eggs, most fish abandon their offspring and leave them to their fate. About one in four fish species, however, take care of their vulnerable larvae (newly hatched fish), protecting them from danger, building nests, or even providing food to help them grow.

CARRYING BABIES
A male seahorse takes eggs from a female into a pouch in his belly, where he fertilizes them and supplies them with nutrients and oxygen. Once they have hatched, he lets them out of the pouch one by one.

BUBBLE NESTS
Gouramis keep their eggs from harm in bubble nests. The male blows saliva-lined bubbles that float at the water's surface, and then, using his mouth, he places the eggs in the mass of bubbles. He protects the young until they are independent.

FEEDING YOUNG
Few fish are as attentive when raising their young as the discus fish. Both parents produce a special mucus on the side of their bodies, and for three weeks after hatching, their babies nibble on this for nourishment.

◄ BABES IN THE MOUTH

For a week, this male yellowhead jawfish has been mouthbrooding – protecting the eggs inside his mouth and swirling water around them to provide oxygen. The male is unable to eat until the eggs hatch.

HIDING IN THE MOUTH

Some fish, such as the big-mouth hap, continue to mouthbrood after their babies have hatched. The young fish can hide from predators in their mother's mouth.

1 VENTURING OUT
The baby fish – called fry – are already old enough to swim and find food. The mother lets them out of her mouth, but they don't stray far from her.

2 DANGER ALERT
The mother has spotted danger: an approaching Malawi eyebiter, which preys on fry. Baby fish are extremely vulnerable to predators.

3 RETURNING TO SAFETY
A jolt of the mother's body calls the babies back. Her jaws open and they swarm inside, safe from harm.

SALMON MIGRATION

Ready to breed, millions of sockeye salmon congregate in their birthplace in Kurile Lake, Russia, after three years in the Pacific Ocean. They have swum almost 1,600 km (1,000 miles) on their journey to the lake, using Earth's magnetic field to navigate. Once home, they must run the gauntlet of hungry brown bears before laying eggs in shallow water and, finally, dying from exhaustion.

HOW SHARKS WORK

Sharks are the top predators of the underwater world.
They are intelligent and skilful hunters, with streamlined bodies that allow them to move at speed through water, and powerful muscles that help them to overwhelm prey.

▶ SPEEDY PREDATOR

Sharks rely on a variety of hunting techniques to catch prey. This shortfin mako is the fastest shark in the world, able to reach speeds of 74 kph (46 mph). It ambushes its prey from below, either seizing or tearing a chunk off it before the animal has time to react.

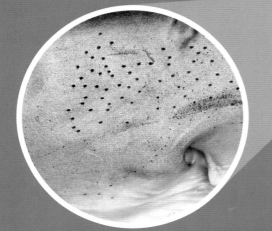

SENSORY ADVANTAGE

Tiny pores full of sensory cells dot the shark's skin. Called the ampullae of Lorenzini, these jelly-filled cells detect weak electrical signals given off by prey, which helps the shark to pinpoint where the prey is.

ROTATING TEETH

During their lifetime, sharks can use and lose thousands of teeth. New rows grow in the gum tissue behind the front rows, and then gradually move forwards and straighten before eventually dropping out.

The teeth move to the front before dropping off.

Like other fish, many sharks often swim with their mouth open to let water flow through their gills.

The powerful tail fin provides the majority of the forward thrust.

Seen from below, a shark's pale belly merges with the bright surface light.

COUNTERSHADING
Sharks are coloured in a way that makes them difficult to see, with a lighter underside and a darker topside. They can approach their prey or hide from larger predators from above or below without being spotted.

Seen from above, the dark colours of a shark's back match the dark water below.

Sharks have distinctive hard, spiky scales that give their skin a sandpaper-like texture.

HUNTING TECHNIQUES
Sharks find and catch food in many ways. Some filter plankton and small fish from the water, but most are active hunters.

PACK HUNTING
Blue sharks use speed and agility to catch fish and squid. They sometimes hunt in packs like wolves.

AMBUSH HUNTING
Well-camouflaged wobbegongs wait motionless on the sea bed, ready to ambush unsuspecting fish swimming by.

HUNTING BY ELECTRICITY
Hammerhead sharks swing their heads from side to side to sense tiny electrical fields made by their favourite prey, rays, hidden in the sand.

SHARK ANATOMY
Shark skeletons are made of flexible cartilage, which is lighter than bone. To breathe, they extract oxygen from the water through the gills, and most sharks need to keep moving as they lack the ability to pump water over their gills. Sharks don't have swim bladders, but have oily livers to improve their buoyancy. Sharks range in length from 20 cm (8 in) to more than 12 m (40 ft) long.

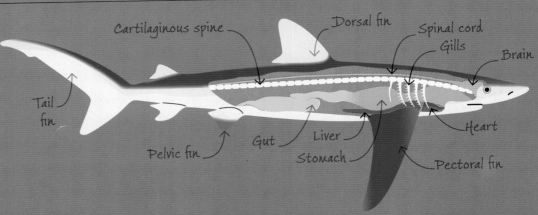

Cartilaginous spine
Dorsal fin
Spinal cord
Gills
Brain
Tail fin
Pelvic fin
Gut
Liver
Stomach
Heart
Pectoral fin

HOW FISH DEFENCES WORK

Fish are easy prey for bigger fish and animals such as seals and dolphins. Many small fish use speed to avoid predators – darting away from danger faster than a predator can catch them. However, some have evolved a variety of other defensive strategies, including grouping together, camouflage, hiding, or exaggerating their size.

Warning stripes may also act as camouflage by making the fish's outline blend in with its surroundings.

Pectoral fins are used to funnel prey towards the lionfish's mouth.

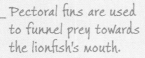

FRONT VIEW OF LIONFISH

▶ **WARNING STRIPES**
This spectacular lionfish lives on tropical coral reefs, where it ambushes and eats smaller fish. Its dazzling, striped appearance is a warning to bigger predators that it is defended by sharp spines laced with a powerful venom.

The broad pectoral fins are divided into fans of long, narrow finlets.

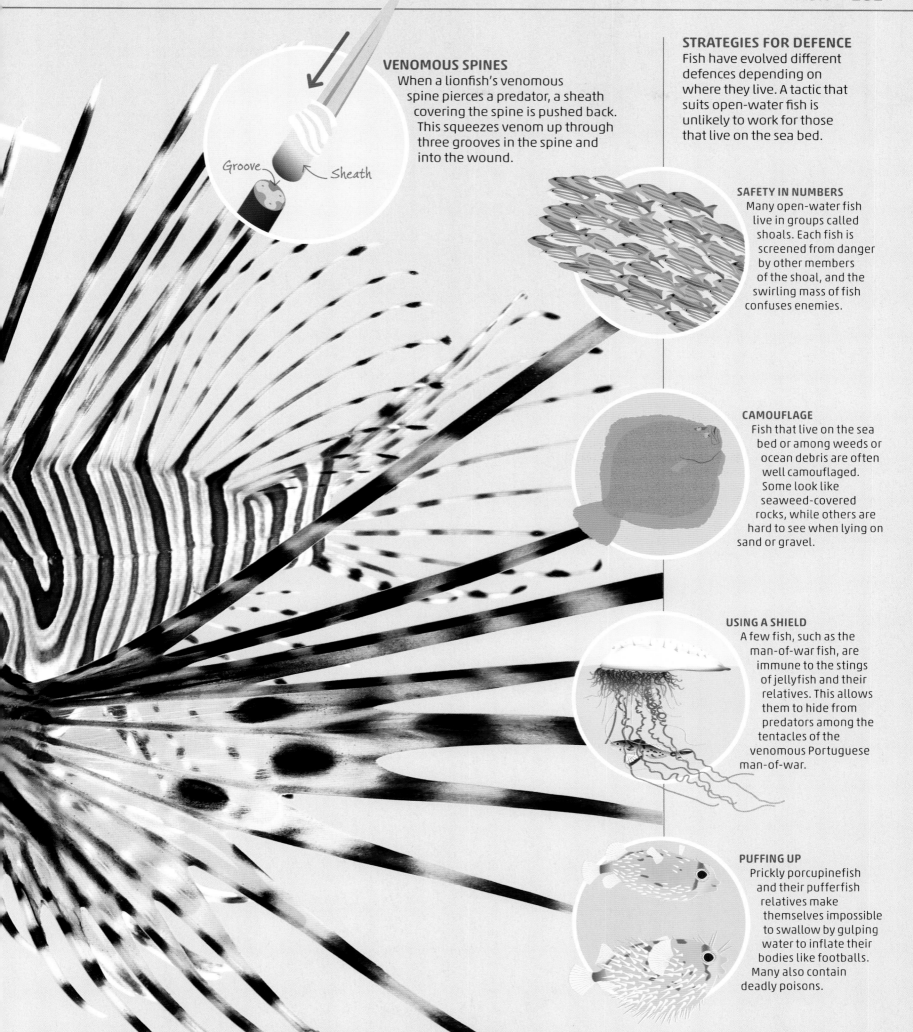

VENOMOUS SPINES
When a lionfish's venomous spine pierces a predator, a sheath covering the spine is pushed back. This squeezes venom up through three grooves in the spine and into the wound.

Groove   Sheath

STRATEGIES FOR DEFENCE
Fish have evolved different defences depending on where they live. A tactic that suits open-water fish is unlikely to work for those that live on the sea bed.

SAFETY IN NUMBERS
Many open-water fish live in groups called shoals. Each fish is screened from danger by other members of the shoal, and the swirling mass of fish confuses enemies.

CAMOUFLAGE
Fish that live on the sea bed or among weeds or ocean debris are often well camouflaged. Some look like seaweed-covered rocks, while others are hard to see when lying on sand or gravel.

USING A SHIELD
A few fish, such as the man-of-war fish, are immune to the stings of jellyfish and their relatives. This allows them to hide from predators among the tentacles of the venomous Portuguese man-of-war.

PUFFING UP
Prickly porcupinefish and their pufferfish relatives make themselves impossible to swallow by gulping water to inflate their bodies like footballs. Many also contain deadly poisons.

HOW CAMOUFLAGE WORKS

To evade predators, many fish are camouflaged – coloured or patterned to blend in with their surroundings so they are difficult to see. Some specialize in mimicking stones, coral, seaweed, or sand, but others can change their appearance to suit their location. Predators also use camouflage to conceal themselves while waiting to ambush prey.

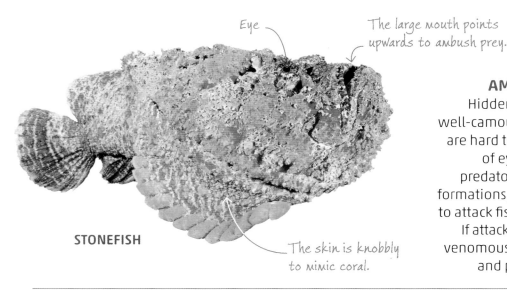

Eye

The large mouth points upwards to ambush prey.

STONEFISH

The skin is knobbly to mimic coral.

AMBUSH PREDATOR ▶
Hidden in the picture are two well-camouflaged stonefish. They are hard to see, so look for a pair of eyes and a mouth. These predators, which look like coral formations, lurk on the reef, ready to attack fish swimming overhead. If attacked or stepped on, their venomous spines inflict a painful and potentially lethal sting.

CHANGING COLOUR

Frogfish can change colour over time to match their surroundings. Their skin contains special cells called chromatophores, which are filled with particles of coloured chemicals (pigment). These particles can clump together or spread out, changing the animal's colour.

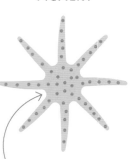

DISPERSED PIGMENT

When the pigment particles are dispersed, the colour of the cell is lighter.

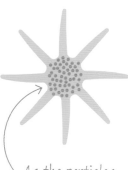

CONCENTRATED PIGMENT

As the particles clump together, the frogfish's skin darkens.

CAMOUFLAGE FOR ATTACK

Chasing prey takes a lot of energy, but camouflage allows a predator to get close to its prey before attacking. Many predatory fish blend into their surroundings by mimicking underwater objects.

TASSELLED DISGUISE

The tassels of this tasselled wobbegong shark's "beard" mimic the branches of coral on the bed of a reef. The body of the shark is also covered in blotches to match the sea bed, where it waits, completely motionless, ready to lunge at passing fish.

HIDDEN MENACE

The stargazer fish, named for its upward-facing eyes, buries its large, venomous-spined body by using its fins to dig a hole. It leaves just its sand-coloured face exposed and waits for smaller fish to swim by. It takes just a split second for the stargazer to snatch and swallow unwary prey.

CAMOUFLAGE FOR DEFENCE

Vulnerable animals use camouflage to protect themselves from predators. Some species are so well disguised that they can continue feeding while drifting in the water, even when danger is close by.

FLOATING SEAWEED

The leafy seadragon looks like a scrap of seaweed. It is covered in leaf-like flaps of skin, used purely for camouflage, that can change colour from brown to yellow or green. It is a poor swimmer and drifts slowly in the water, mimicking the movement of seaweed.

CORAL SEAHORSE

Just 2 cm (0.7 in) tall, the pygmy seahorse is almost impossible to spot clinging by its tail to a pink sea fan – a type of coral. The world's smallest seahorse, it is covered in pink bumps to match the tentacles of the coral polyps.

FISH SCHOOL

Thousands of oxeye scad have gathered together in this group, known as a school, in the Pacific Ocean near the Solomon Islands. Schooling fish swim in formation, with each fish watching its neighbours to ensure they swim together. Swimming in groups can make catching individual fish difficult for predators as they become confused by the large numbers.

HOW **SYMBIOSIS** WORKS

Sometimes, animals from different species live together in close relationships. This type of interaction is called symbiosis. In many cases, both partners benefit from the partnership, but often, one gains and the other is unaffected. In other cases, one animal may be exploited by its partner, which lives on its body as a parasite.

Large pectoral fins help the remora swim on its own when necessary.

The grooves are linked to strong muscles.

▼ CLINGING ON

The remora clings to sharks, whales, turtles, and even boats, all of which carry it through the water. The fish benefits from its host's protection, but it seems to have no effect on the animal it clings to.

SUCKER

The oval sucker of a remora has ridges and grooves that the fish moves to create suction. If the remora is pushed back by flowing water, its grip gets stronger, but it can release itself by swimming forwards.

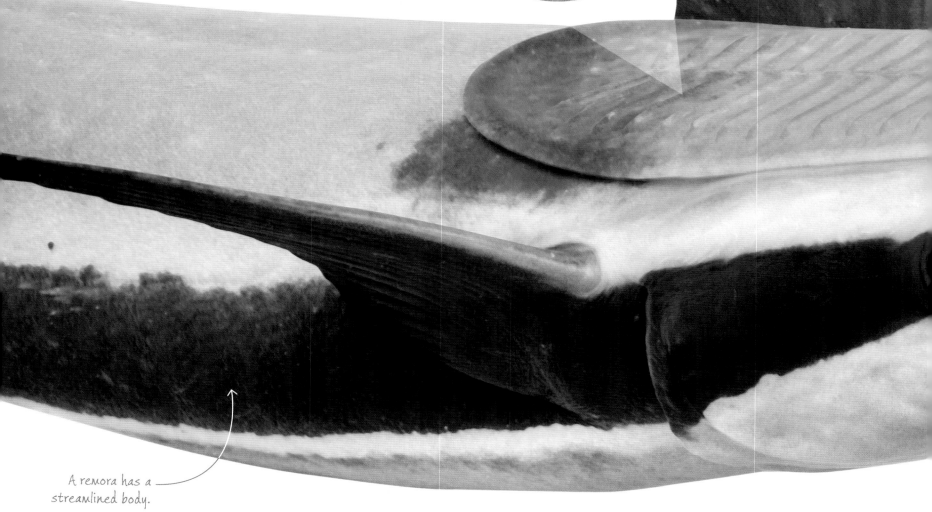

A remora has a streamlined body.

LIVING TOGETHER
A remora can travel vast distances attached to a big, fast fish like this shark. But travel is not its main concern. It clings to its host to pick up food, nibbling on leftover scraps and even eating the host fish's excrement.

A remora's sucker is a highly modified dorsal fin.

An upward-opening mouth allows the remora to pick food off the host's skin.

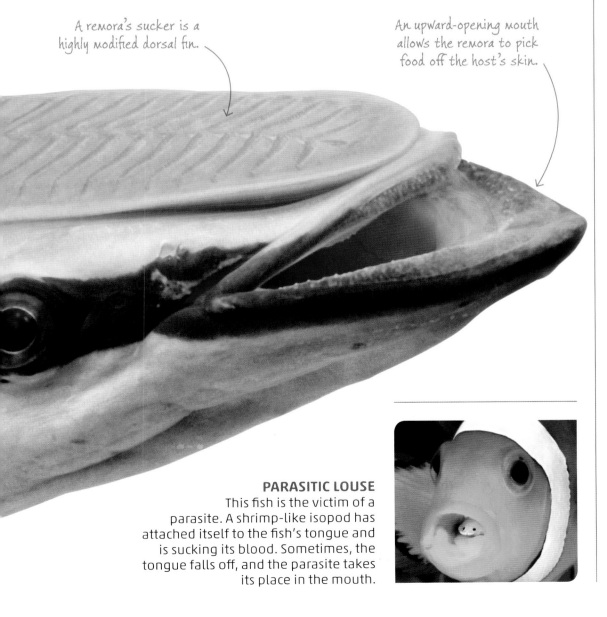

PARASITIC LOUSE
This fish is the victim of a parasite. A shrimp-like isopod has attached itself to the fish's tongue and is sucking its blood. Sometimes, the tongue falls off, and the parasite takes its place in the mouth.

MUTUAL BENEFIT
Some forms of symbiosis improve life for both animals, with each benefitting in different ways. Often, the relationship is temporary, but some species have become adapted to spend their lives together.

SHARING A BURROW
On the fringes of coral reefs, burrowing shrimps share their homes with small fish called gobies. The shrimp's burrow provides the goby with a refuge, and the fish repays the shrimp by watching for danger. If the fish senses a threat, they hide in the burrow together.

STINGING DEFENDER
Most fish avoid the stinging tentacles of sea anemones, but the clownfish is able to live among them because it is covered in an extra thick layer of mucus. Staying among the stinging tentacles protects it from bigger fish, while the excrement of the clownfish supplies the anemone with food.

FISH CLEANERS
The bluestreak cleaner wrasse specialize in picking parasites and dead skin off larger fish. It lives in certain parts of coral reefs that are known to other fish who visit to be treated. This harlequin sweetlips has even allowed the cleaner wrasse into its mouth.

HOW
DEEP-SEA FISH
WORK

Deep-sea fish live in the dark, cold ocean depths, from 1.8 km (1.1 miles) below the water's surface down to the sea floor. As a result, they are some of the strangest and least-understood animals of all. Some deep-sea fish are blind, but many have developed huge eyes and use light to find mates and attract prey.

Large eyes absorb as much light as possible in the dark.

The front teeth are so long that the fish cannot completely shut its mouth.

▶ DEEP-SEA HUNTER
Like many deep-sea fish, a Sloane's viperfish has a large mouth to catch prey and a large stomach to digest food of various sizes. It uses a lure that extends from its dorsal fin to attract prey, while its transparent fangs are nearly impossible to see in the dark. When an animal comes close, the viperfish lunges with its huge jaws and swallows it whole.

LIGHT IN THE DARK
Another fish that uses a lure is the deep-sea anglerfish. Its lure contains bacteria that produce and emit light in a chemical reaction called bioluminescence, causing the lure to glow in the dark. The anglerfish fishes for prey by wiggling the lure about, which makes it look like a small animal.

Scientists think that bacteria enter the lure from the water and multiply until they give off light.

Because of its poor vision, the anglerfish uses sensory organs along its skin to detect movement in the water.

DEEP-SEA ANGLERFISH

The viperfish attacks by swimming at high speed into the body of its prey. The bones behind its head are extra strong to withstand the force of the collision.

A lure is attached to the dorsal fin.

These large, silvery scales reflect the faint light, possibly to confuse larger predators.

Tiny light-producing organs called photophores line the viperfish's belly.

FEEDING STRATEGIES

The extreme environment of the deep ensures that fewer animals can live there than can live closer to the surface. However, those in deep-sea habitats come in a variety of bizarre shapes, and display survival techniques that make the most of the limited resources available to them.

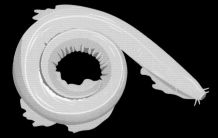

EXPANDING STOMACH

With food scarce, deep-sea creatures must eat whatever comes their way, even if it's bigger than them. The black follower fish can achieve this with its extremely stretchy stomach, which can accommodate prey twice as long and ten times heavier than the fish itself.

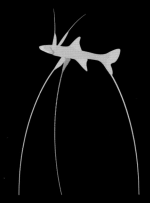

EATING FROM THE INSIDE

Slimy, blind hagfish are jawless, but they have strong, rasping teeth, which they use to burrow into dead and dying prey and rip off pieces of flesh from the inside.

SITTING AND WAITING

A tripod fish props itself up above the muddy sea bed to catch small fish. It balances on the tips of a very long lower tail lobe and two front fins, waiting for prey to drift by in the current.

The world's first **amphibians** appeared around 370 million years ago, and they were the first **animals with backbones** to live on land. The defining feature of amphibians is that they spend **part of their life in water and part on land** – the word "amphibian" means "double life". There are three main types of amphibian: frogs and toads, salamanders and newts, and the lesser-known caecilians.

AMPHIBIANS

HOW AMPHIBIANS WORK

Amphibians are animals with a backbone and soft skin. They lack the scales, feathers, or hairs of other vertebrate groups. Although largely terrestrial, their lives are connected to water in important ways. Most have an aquatic, gilled larval stage, but then develop by metamorphosis into land-living adults that use lungs to breathe air. Some, like this African bullfrog, have developed clever ways of staying alive in challenging circumstances.

▶ DROUGHT DEFENCE
Found across arid parts of Africa, the African bullfrog survives drought by spending most of the year cocooned underground, and only becomes active following summer rains. It develops an enormous appetite during its long fast and will attack any animal that can fit into its huge mouth.

ON LAND AND IN WATER
Most amphibians spend part of their life on land, and part of it in water. The eggs typically hatch into swimming larvae. In frogs and toads, these are called tadpoles, and they grow legs and reabsorb their tails as they metamorphose into adults, which move from water to land. But many amphibians complete their entire life cycle on land by laying their eggs on wet ground.

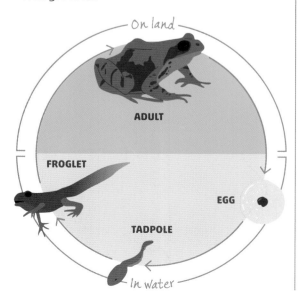

On land

ADULT

FROGLET

EGG

TADPOLE

In water

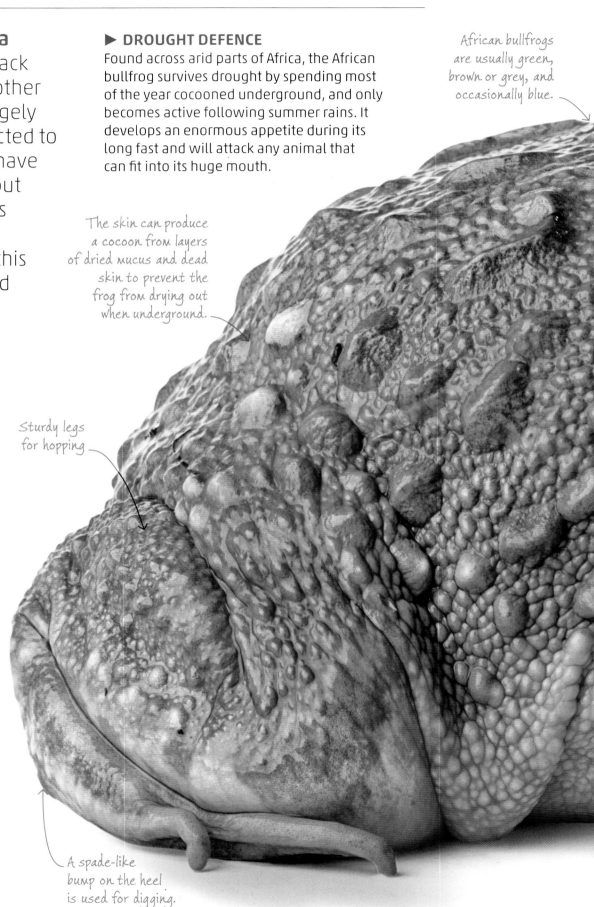

African bullfrogs are usually green, brown or grey, and occasionally blue.

The skin can produce a cocoon from layers of dried mucus and dead skin to prevent the frog from drying out when underground.

Sturdy legs for hopping

A spade-like bump on the heel is used for digging.

Many amphibians have two eyelids, one of which is clear and allows them to see when underwater.

The lower jaw has two tusks for grasping prey.

Large mouth for catching and swallowing prey whole

AMPHIBIAN FAMILY

There are three subgroups of amphibians. The first, which includes salamanders and newts, occurs in America and temperate Eurasia. Frogs and toads are found worldwide, except in Antarctica. Finally, the legless caecilians are confined to the tropics.

RED SALAMANDER

SALAMANDERS AND NEWTS

Both salamanders and newts have a tail and four limbs. Salamanders only return briefly to water to lay eggs, but breeding newts spend longer in water, developing showy tail fins for courtship.

BIG-EYED TREE FROG

FROGS AND TOADS

Accounting for nearly 90 per cent of all amphibian species, smooth-skinned frogs and warty-skinned toads have a short and squat body, with elongated hind legs for jumping.

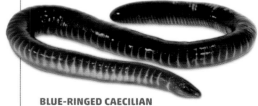

BLUE-RINGED CAECILIAN

CAECILIANS

The worm-like body of caecilians is perfect for burrowing through leaf litter and soil, although some caecilians are entirely aquatic. They are rarely seen above ground.

① FROGSPAWN
The common frog lays floating bundles of eggs called frogspawn in still water. The egg consists of a colourless but nutritious jelly that surrounds a tiny, black embryo that grows at the centre. The embryo will become a wriggling tadpole after a few days.

Growing embryo

DAY 1

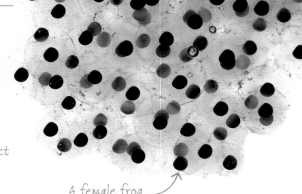

The jelly swells with water to protect the embryo inside.

DAY 3

A female frog usually lays 1,000–1,500 eggs at a time.

This tadpole is just about to hatch.

DAY 5

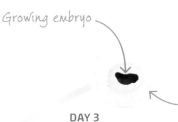

EXTERNAL GILLS

extract oxygen from the water.

External gills

DAY 7

HOW TADPOLES GROW

A frog goes through dramatic changes as it grows up. It starts off as a swimming larva called a tadpole. Over time it gradually develops into its adult form, with legs for moving about on land. This change is called metamorphosis.

Strong muscles move the tail from side to side when swimming.

DAY 12

Limb buds

② TADPOLE
A tadpole hatches by breaking through the jelly. It has feathery gills for breathing underwater and a long tail for swimming. It grazes on algae at first, but later adds worms, water fleas, and even smaller tadpoles to its diet to obtain the nutrients needed to grow.

COMMON FROG LIFE CYCLE
The common frog takes about 16 weeks to develop from an egg into a mature adult. Its metamorphosis is gradual, the legs and lungs developing first before the tail is absorbed and disappears.

The external gills become internal gills when skin grows over them.

WEEK 10

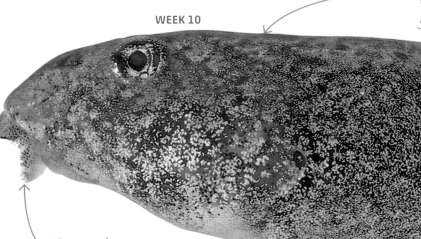

Tiny teeth mean the tadpole can eat vegetation and other animals.

The hind legs develop before the front legs.

WEEK 16

With long toes and strong legs, the adult frog is now able to walk and hop on land.

④ ADULT FROG
The first froglets to make landfall are tiny, but they soon grow into adults. They never move far from water and will return to a pond the following year to mate.

The tail shortens to a stump, and then is completely absorbed into the body.

❸ FROGLET
When it has developed all four legs, the tadpole is called a froglet. The froglet's body begins preparing it for life on land. Its swimming tail – which would be useless on land – is absorbed into the rest of the body, and its gills are replaced with lungs for breathing air.

WEEK 14

The eyes grow larger.

The froglet looks like a frog with a long tail.

WEEK 12

A broad fin surrounds the tail to help with propulsion through the water.

DIFFERENT LIFE CYCLES
About half of all frogs have a life cycle similar to that of the common frog. The rest develop in a variety of ways, such as on the back of a female, or out of water completely.

Each baby toad is less than 2 cm (0.8 in) long.

SURINAME TOAD
Most amphibians don't look after their offspring, but the female Suriname toad is an exception. After the male has fertilized her eggs, he embeds them into small pockets in her back. The eggs sink in, and begin developing. When ready, tiny baby toads "hatch out" from their mother's skin.

DIRECT-DEVELOPING FROGS
The rainforest habitat is so wet that some don't need to lay their eggs in water. Hundreds of species of direct-developing frogs lay their eggs on land, hidden in leaf litter. The eggs develop directly into miniature versions of the adults, skipping the aquatic stage of the life cycle.

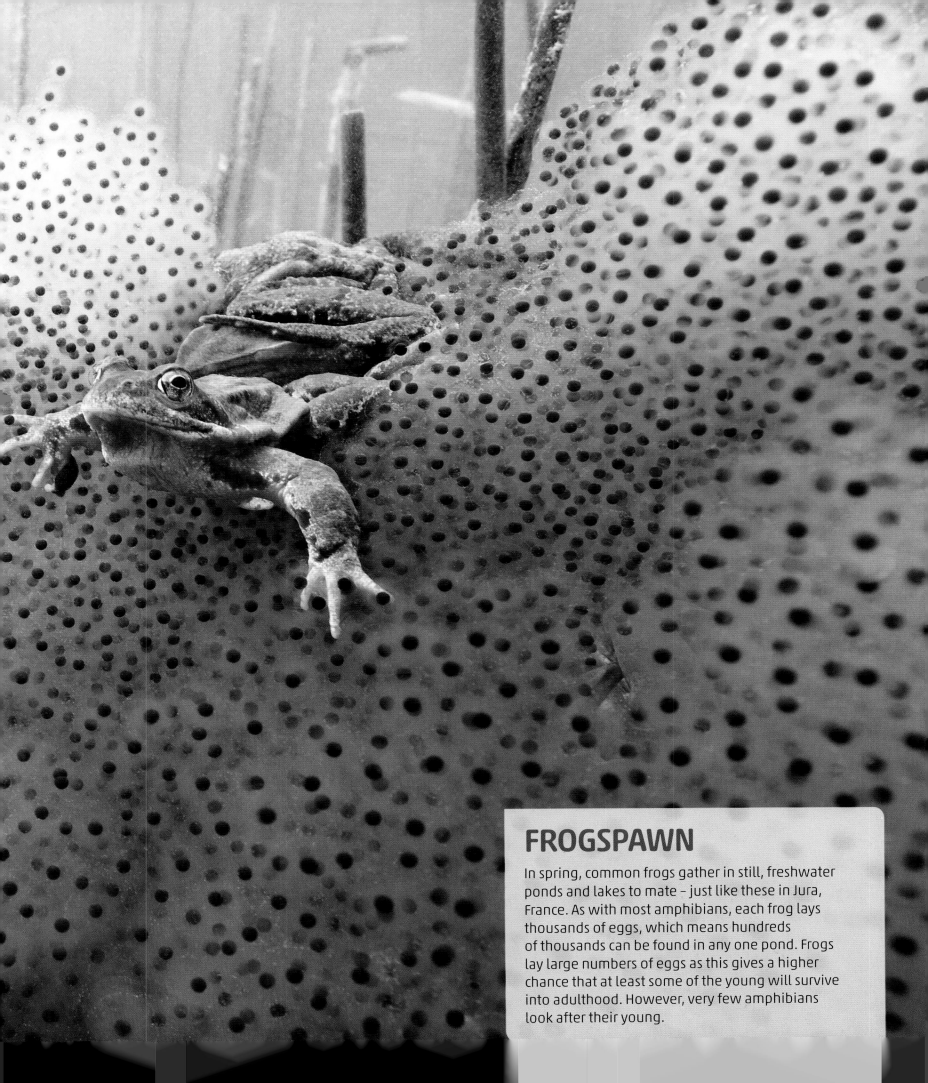

FROGSPAWN

In spring, common frogs gather in still, freshwater ponds and lakes to mate – just like these in Jura, France. As with most amphibians, each frog lays thousands of eggs, which means hundreds of thousands can be found in any one pond. Frogs lay large numbers of eggs as this gives a higher chance that at least some of the young will survive into adulthood. However, very few amphibians look after their young.

HOW FROGS MOVE

Frogs are adapted to live both in water and on land. Their webbed feet and large hind legs, packed with powerful muscles, make them strong swimmers. When on land, they can leap great distances – crucial when escaping predators. A frog's less powerful front limbs help it with swimming, and act as shock absorbers when landing from a hop.

HOW FROGS SWIM
All frogs can swim, and while most species spend all or much of their time on land, the few that spend all their lives in water have bigger feet with wider webbing. Because water is denser than air, it takes more effort for frogs to move in water than on dry land.

WEBBED FEET
Many frogs have a thin layer of skin between the toes on their hind limbs. This webbing allows them to use their limbs like paddles, helping them to swim.

1 STROKE
A frog's swimming stroke begins when the legs are brought forwards, bending the knees and ankles. The toes bunch up, closing the webbing so the feet can easily move through the water to prepare for the next power stroke.

2 FOLLOW THROUGH
The frog kicks back with both of its hind legs simultaneously. As the ankles extend, the toes spread out to open their webbing. This pushes against the water to move the frog forwards.

▼ LIVING IN AND OUT OF WATER
The green and golden bell frog is found in the swamps, streams, and ponds of Australia and New Zealand, where it spends much of its time underwater. When on land, the frog uses its strong leg muscles to move. It has remarkable strength and stamina, and often moves more than 1 km (0.6 miles) from its home pond to look for better living conditions.

The webbed hind feet kick back to propel the frog forwards.

The front legs are held back when swimming through water.

HOW FROGS JUMP

Relative to their size, many frogs jump further than any other vertebrate animal. Some can jump more than 20 times their body length.

The back feet stay on the ground for as long as possible, to provide push.

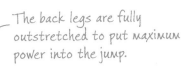

The back legs are fully outstretched to put maximum power into the jump.

1 LOADED TENDONS
Before jumping, a frog stretches its leg tendons so they are held taut by ankle bones, just like the string of a bow when it is pulled back.

2 TENDONS RELEASED
The frog uses its muscles to push on the ground with its feet, and starts to leap into the air. At the same time, it releases its tendons.

3 CATAPULTING JUMP
The freed tendons spring the frog up and forwards. The frog closes its eyes while jumping to protect them.

4 SAFE LANDING
The frog reaches with its outstretched front feet to prepare for landing, while the long hind legs trail behind.

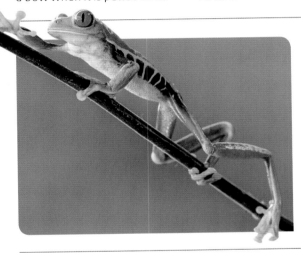

CLIMBING HIGH

This red-eyed tree frog has sticky pads on its toes that help it to cling to branches when climbing. The pads constantly clean themselves to help the frog stick to surfaces.

The frog has reasonably waterproof skin, which even lets it bask in sunshine without drying out.

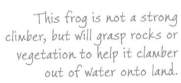

This frog is not a strong climber, but will grasp rocks or vegetation to help it clamber out of water onto land.

The toes have suckers to help grip when on land.

Nostril

Vocal sac

Vocal cords

Lung

Air moves from lungs to vocal sac and back again to produce sound in vocal cords.

MAKING NOISE

A frog's vocal sac is an inflatable pouch that connects to its mouth. Before calling, a frog fills its lungs with air. It then closes its nostrils and uses its muscles to push air over its vocal cords into the sac. This amplifies the vibration of the vocal cords.

HOW
FROGS
COMMUNICATE

Like most tree frogs, this frog has a single large vocal sac, but some species of frog have paired sacs that inflate either side of the mouth.

Many frogs are most active at night, so their main way of declaring their territory or communicating with mates is with sound. Each species croaks, chirps, or whistles in a distinctive way. A few kinds of frog – including those that lack voice boxes – communicate with visual signals or touch.

The long fingers and toes secrete a gluey substance, which helps the frog to stick to trees.

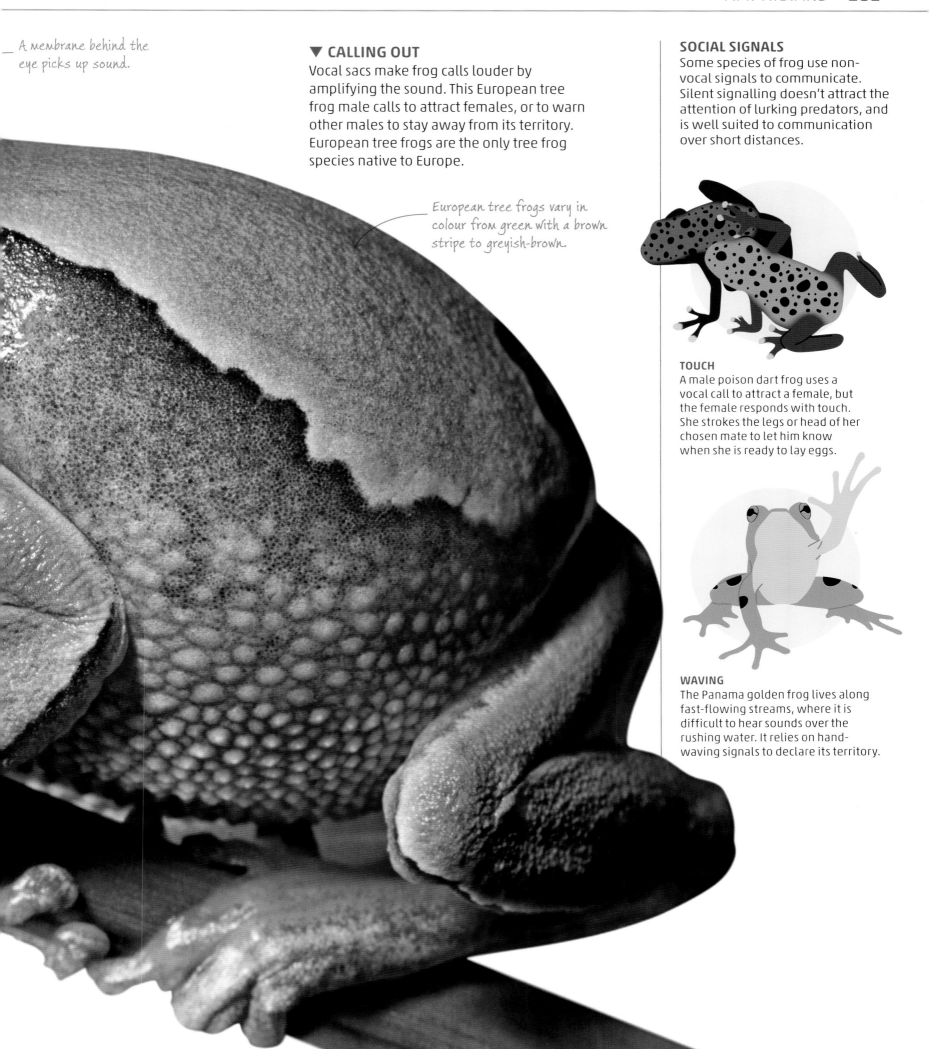

_ A membrane behind the eye picks up sound.

▼ **CALLING OUT**
Vocal sacs make frog calls louder by amplifying the sound. This European tree frog male calls to attract females, or to warn other males to stay away from its territory. European tree frogs are the only tree frog species native to Europe.

_ European tree frogs vary in colour from green with a brown stripe to greyish-brown.

SOCIAL SIGNALS
Some species of frog use non-vocal signals to communicate. Silent signalling doesn't attract the attention of lurking predators, and is well suited to communication over short distances.

TOUCH
A male poison dart frog uses a vocal call to attract a female, but the female responds with touch. She strokes the legs or head of her chosen mate to let him know when she is ready to lay eggs.

WAVING
The Panama golden frog lives along fast-flowing streams, where it is difficult to hear sounds over the rushing water. It relies on hand-waving signals to declare its territory.

DEFENSIVE STRATEGIES
Amphibians have evolved a diverse range of clever strategies to outfox their predators.

UNKEN REFLEX
Used by the oriental fire-bellied toad and many other amphibians, the unken reflex is a defensive display where an amphibian curls its body upwards to show a predator its bright underside, and releases toxins to the surface of its skin.

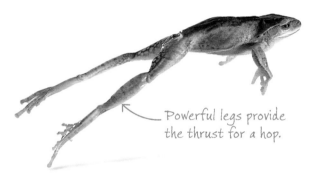

Powerful legs provide the thrust for a hop.

HOPPING
A frog's hopping motion can disorientate predators used to capturing prey that moves in a more predictable way. It is a great getaway strategy too: even from a sitting position, some frogs can jump more than 20 times their own body length.

Rearing up and inflating with air may frighten a predator.

BLUFFING
When cornered, some amphibians will try to bluff their way out of danger. Playing dead is one option; another is to swell in size to look more menacing.

HOW DEFENCE WORKS

Lacking both rigid body armour and sharp weaponry, amphibians must instead rely on cunning methods to ward off predators. Their main trick is camouflage – the best way to survive a fight is to avoid it completely. If this fails to work, many amphibians will try to frighten a predator away by revealing vibrant colours, playing dead, making themselves appear bigger, or by producing poisonous toxins.

Short, sharp barbs cover the toad's back.

▶ **WARNING SIGN**
When seen from above or the side, the oriental fire-bellied toad's mottled green skin helps it to blend in with its forest environment. If threatened, however, the toad reveals its vibrant orange and black markings on its underside. These markings are a warning sign, letting the predator know that the toad is poisonous and dangerous to eat.

Camouflaged upper surface

The pupils in the eyes are triangular.

The toad's back is covered with warty growths called tubercles.

SIDE VIEW OF ORIENTAL FIRE-BELLIED TOAD

Cross-section of oriental fire-bellied toad **TOAD SKIN**

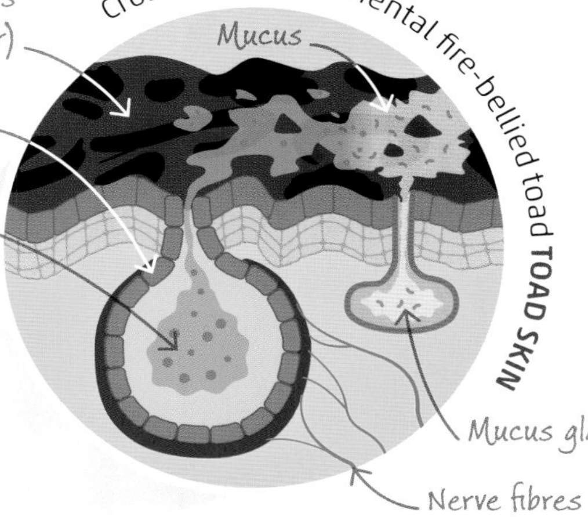

Epidermis (outer skin layer)

Mucus

Poison gland

Poison

Mucus gland

Nerve fibres

HOW THE POISON IS MADE
Poison is made in the cells lining the poison glands and stored in the glands before being released. Nerve fibres cause the poison cells to squeeze the poison out to the epidermis, where it mixes with mucus made in the mucus glands.

Its smooth, brightly coloured underside warns predators that the toad is poisonous.

DRASTIC DEFENCE
If attacked, some salamanders are able to snap off their tails at will as a last-gasp attempt to escape. The broken-off tail wriggles violently, distracting the attacker as the salamander flees. Its wound soon heals, and its tail may grow back.

Special muscles stop the wound from bleeding badly.

GREENHORN MOUNTAINS SLENDER SALAMANDER

A salamander crawls on its belly.

FIRE SALAMANDER FROM THE FRONT

▼ WARNING COLOURS
The dazzling colour scheme of this European fire salamander warns snakes, birds, and other predators that its skin is covered with a poisonous fluid. Most of the poison is produced by glands behind its eyes and on its back. Many other salamanders have similar defences and are just as colourful. They need such protection because they move too slowly to escape their predators easily.

The poison glands are concentrated in the yellow patches.

A fire salamander can spray poison at attackers through these pores.

HOW SALAMANDERS WORK

Salamanders and newts are relatives of frogs and toads, but they have long tails and four short legs. The majority of species are found in cool parts of the northern hemisphere, but many reach into tropical South America. Although a few species are totally aquatic, most salamanders spend all their lives on land. About 20 per cent of species lay eggs in water, which hatch into aquatic larvae; the rest breed on land.

Stubby toes give grip on soft, damp ground.

Big glands behind the eyes produce defensive toxins.

Poison oozes through these pores.

Indentations on the side called costal grooves mark the position of the ribs.

The big eyes are sensitive to dim light, helping the salamander hunt at night.

Short legs make it easy to slip through dense vegetation.

Oxygen (red arrows) and carbon dioxide (blue arrows) can be exchanged through the lining of the mouth, the lungs, and the skin.

BREATHING
Many salamanders breathe air using lungs, and some that live in the water have gills, like fish. But most have neither: instead, they absorb all the oxygen they need through their thin skins.

During the breeding season, the male European smooth newt has a tall crest and dark spots.

NEWT
A type of salamander, newts have a distinct aquatic stage as breeding adults. They develop fin-like fringes on their tails, and males often adopt bright colours in order to attract females. After the breeding season, most newts return to land and assume a more salamander-like appearance.

HOW AXOLOTLS WORK

The axolotl is a salamander that spends its whole life in water, and is found only in the waters around Lake Xochimilco in Mexico. Unlike most amphibians, axolotls reach adulthood without going through metamorphosis. In the event of injury, they have the ability to regrow limbs, and can even regenerate some internal organs.

▼ EXTERNAL GILLS
Axolotls rely on their six distinctive, feathery external gills to breathe. The gills filter water for oxygen and pass it into the bloodstream. Axolotls can also breathe through their skin, thanks to fine blood vessels close to the surface of the skin, through which oxygen can pass directly into their bloodstream.

AXOLOTL

Axolotls can reach up to 30 cm (12 in) in length.

The external gills absorb oxygen and get rid of carbon dioxide from the animal's body.

Unlike most salamanders, axolotls have eyes that do not protrude from their sockets.

Axolotls have simple limbs that feature long, thin digits.

When at the water's surface, axolotls sometimes breathe through the mouth as they have simple lungs.

FOREVER YOUNG

Unlike most salamanders, which go through metamorphosis from their juvenile stage to become adults, axolotls remain in their juvenile form for their whole life. Known as neoteny, this condition means axolotls retain features such as external gills, a dorsal fin, and short, undeveloped legs. It is thought that axolotl neoteny may be caused by a lack of the hormone thyroxine.

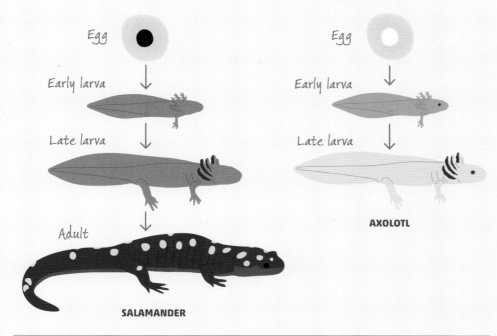

Egg

Early larva

Late larva

Adult

SALAMANDER

Egg

Early larva

Late larva

AXOLOTL

HOW AXOLOTLS REGROW LIMBS

Axolotls can regrow their limbs and organs, including their kidneys, lungs, and even parts of their brain. This regeneration results in a perfect duplicate every time – even if the axolotl has lost the same body part many times over.

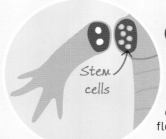

Stem cells

1 LIMB LOST
When an axolotl loses a limb, the blood, bone, and muscle cells at the wound turn into special stem cells that can change into other types of cell. First, they cover the open flesh to protect the wound.

2 REGROWTH
The cells at the wound site begin to form new bones, blood, and muscle. The limb regrows, bit by bit, starting as a bud and gradually developing as the cells multiply.

3 NEW LIMB
After a month or so, the new limb is complete. It is indistinguishable from the old one, with no signs of injury, such as scarring.

Blood vessels are visible through the skin, which can be pale pink, golden, grey, or black.

Like most salamanders, axolotls have four toes on the front feet and five on the back feet.

Axolotl skin is soft and rubbery.

The flat tail can be used like a fin for swimming.

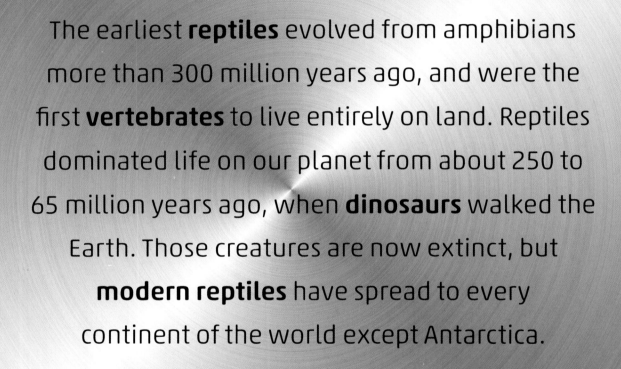

The earliest **reptiles** evolved from amphibians more than 300 million years ago, and were the first **vertebrates** to live entirely on land. Reptiles dominated life on our planet from about 250 to 65 million years ago, when **dinosaurs** walked the Earth. Those creatures are now extinct, but **modern reptiles** have spread to every continent of the world except Antarctica.

REPTILES

HOW REPTILES WORK

Reptiles were the first vertebrates to live entirely on dry land. They achieved this by evolving scaly, waterproof skins that stopped their bodies drying out, and by having tough-skinned eggs that they could lay in dry places. An amazing diversity of species evolved, including turtles, crocodiles, lizards, snakes, and the prehistoric ancestors of mammals and birds.

▼ SCALY LIZARD

The most notable feature of all reptiles is their scaly skin. Scales are made from keratin – the same material that makes human hair and nails – and they provide a strong but flexible covering for a reptile's body. Aside from this, all reptiles crawl on their bellies, many propelled by stubby legs. Some lizards – and all snakes – have no legs at all. Most reptiles prey on other animals, ranging from insects to the big mammals seized by crocodiles. But green iguanas – such as the one shown here – are unusual reptiles as they eat only plants.

A keen sense of smell helps reptiles locate food.

Many reptiles have excellent colour vision.

Although usually green, the iguana can also be blue or orange.

Tough scales protect a reptile's skin.

A flap of skin helps to control the green iguana's temperature, and is used to communicate with other iguanas.

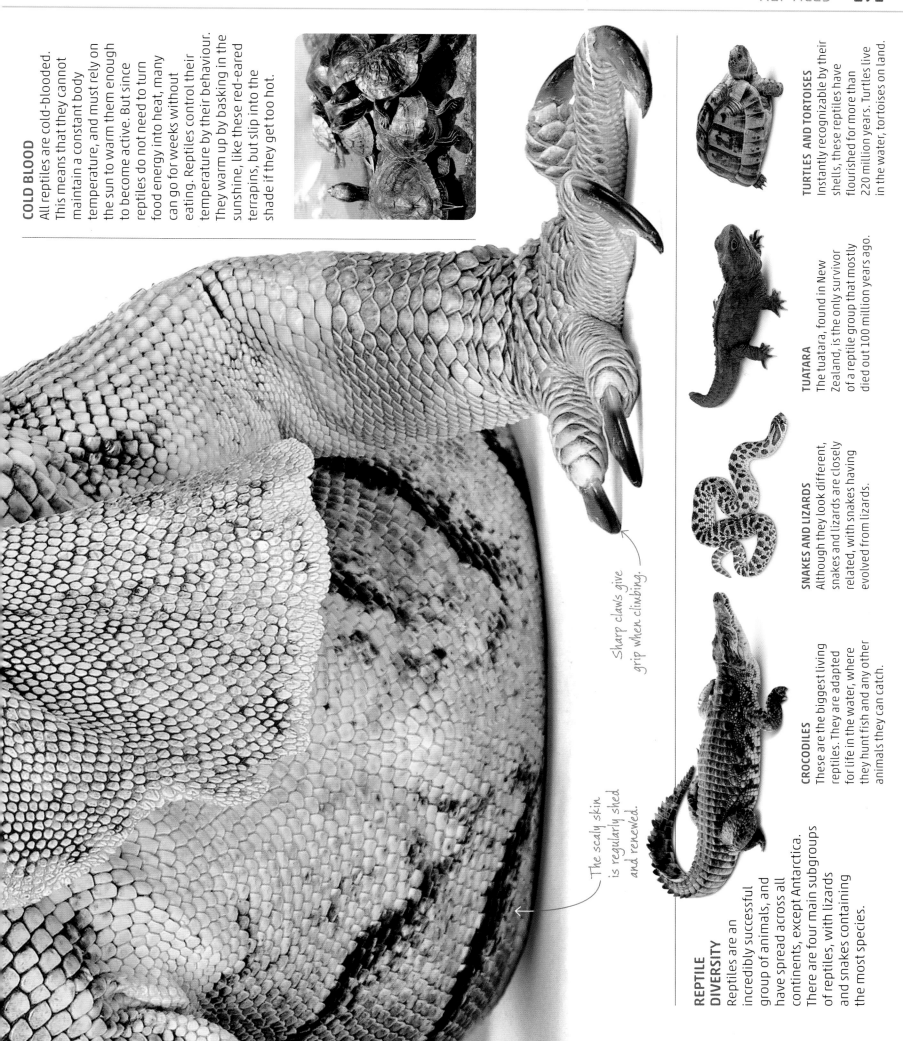

COLD BLOOD

All reptiles are cold-blooded. This means that they cannot maintain a constant body temperature, and must rely on the sun to warm them enough to become active. But since reptiles do not need to turn food energy into heat, many can go for weeks without eating. Reptiles control their temperature by their behaviour. They warm up by basking in the sunshine, like these red-eared terrapins, but slip into the shade if they get too hot.

TURTLES AND TORTOISES

Instantly recognizable by their shells, these reptiles have flourished for more than 220 million years. Turtles live in the water, tortoises on land.

TUATARA

The tuatara, found in New Zealand, is the only survivor of a reptile group that mostly died out 100 million years ago.

SNAKES AND LIZARDS

Although they look different, snakes and lizards are closely related, with snakes having evolved from lizards.

Sharp claws give grip when climbing.

CROCODILES

These are the biggest living reptiles. They are adapted for life in the water, where they hunt fish and any other animals they can catch.

The scaly skin is regularly shed and renewed.

REPTILE DIVERSITY

Reptiles are an incredibly successful group of animals, and have spread across all continents, except Antarctica. There are four main subgroups of reptiles, with lizards and snakes containing the most species.

The snake rubs its old upper lip scale away to start the shedding process.

SPECIALIZED SCALES

Reptile scales are often modified in various ways to do different jobs. Some form strong defensive armour, while others help the animal scare away its enemies.

Crocodiles have big scales called scutes on their backs that protect the animals and help to regulate their temperature. A bony core, called an osteoderm, is embedded in each scute.

Rattlesnakes have hollow segments of skin that knock against each other when shaken. The snakes use this rattling sound to ward off predators.

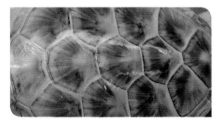

Turtles also have scutes made of keratin, but they are fused together to form a rigid protective shell. The scutes get steadily bigger as the animal grows.

Only the horny outer layer of the skin peels away.

New scales have formed under the old ones.

▲ PEELING AWAY

As new skin grows, it replaces old skin. In crocodiles, turtles, and most other vertebrates, this happens continuously. But in lizards and snakes, it is periodic. It takes two weeks to regrow all their skin, after which the old skin is shed. With enough food for growth, they can renew and shed their skins more frequently.

HOW SCALES WORK

The overlapping scales of this garter snake have central ridges, called keels, for strength.

All reptiles have scaly skin, which forms a tough barrier against damage and disease and stops vital body moisture escaping. The scales are made of keratin, the same substance as human fingernails, and sometimes have bony cores in the skin called osteoderms.

Belly scales form broad plates that grip the ground as the snake moves.

HOW SHEDDING HAPPENS
By shedding its skin, a snake gets rid of any tiny parasites living on it. The scales are replaced with new ones that form beneath the outer layer, giving the skin a fresher and healthier look. Snakes never stop growing, and younger ones shed more often.

1 ITCH AND SCRATCH
When the outer skin is ready to be shed, it separates from the layer beneath. The snake then scratches its upper lip against a rough surface to make the skin peel away.

2 PUSH AND PULL
The snake pushes through plants and stones to pull the old skin off its body. The skin often comes off in one piece – unlike the skin of lizards, which falls away in big flakes.

3 WRIGGLING FREE
When the snake has dragged the old skin down to its tail, it is able to wriggle free. It slips away, gleaming with new colour, and leaving the old, inside-out skin behind.

HOW SNAKE SENSES WORK

▼ **ADEPT HUNTER**
Despite hunting in the tangled trees of a rainforest at night, this Wagler's pit viper has no problems finding prey. It waits patiently to ambush any rodent that comes close. Heat-sensitive pits help the snake to pinpoint its prey's warm body, after which it waits patiently until the victim is within striking range.

Snakes are cold-blooded killers with incredibly sharp senses. Although their vision is poor and they have no external ears, their remaining senses, including those of smell and touch, are highly developed to track and pinpoint prey with deadly accuracy. Some snakes have evolved special sense organs that give them the remarkable ability to "see" heat, allowing them to track prey in darkness.

The pit organ senses prey's body heat.

The nostrils detect odours.

The forked tongue picks up odours, and can work out which direction an odour is coming from.

Muscles in the tongue work to flick it into and out of the mouth.

The small bumps on the scales are called tubercles and may be sensitive to touch.

SENSING HEAT

Boas, pythons, and pit vipers have special sense organs on their heads that can pick up the infrared (heat) radiation coming from a warm-blooded animal up to 1 m (3 ft) away. On the right, a special camera helps us to visualize how a pit viper views a target before striking. The body heat generated by a mouse glows against the colder blue background.

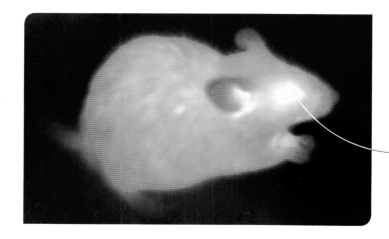

The pits can pick up changes in temperature as small as 0.2°C (0.4°F).

White patches show which parts of the mouse are warmest; pink is cooler than orange; and the blue areas at the tips of the ears are colder still.

JACOBSON'S ORGAN

The splayed tips of a forked tongue tell a snake the direction of its next meal. They collect any odour that hangs in the air, and when the tongue is brought back into the mouth, they dab it on a taste organ called a Jacobson's organ in the roof of the mouth. If it tastes like prey, the snake will get ready to strike.

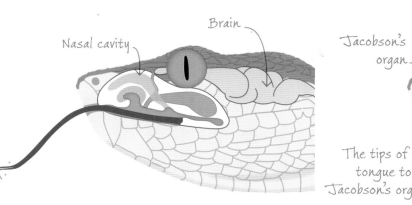

The tongue collects odour particles from the air.

Nasal cavity

Brain

Jacobson's organ

Nerves carry signals from Jacobson's organ to the brain.

The tips of the tongue touch Jacobson's organ.

Vertical, slit-like pupils control how much light enters the eyes, an adaptation for nocturnal hunting.

The green, white, and brown pattern provides daytime camouflage among foliage.

Scales have ridges called keels in the centre that give the snake a rough appearance.

HOW **REPTILE EGGS** WORK

Most reptiles reproduce by laying eggs. Inside each egg, special membranes help the baby to develop. A hard shell, which can be leathery or brittle, protects the baby inside, and stops it from drying out. Most reptile mothers abandon their eggs after burying them to keep them warm, but some parents stay and look after them until they hatch. The ability to lay eggs made it possible for vertebrates to live on land.

▼BREAKING OUT

After 15 weeks of development inside their eggs, these African spurred tortoises take their first steps outside. A bony spike on each baby's nose, called an egg tooth, helps it break through the shell. The egg's temperature during development affects a tortoise's sex: high temperatures produce females, while cooler conditions produce males.

The tortoise's powerful legs help it to crawl out of the shell.

Tortoise eggs have brittle shells, like birds' eggs.

INSIDE A REPTILE EGG

Before hatching, the baby reptile is called an embryo, and grows inside a membrane called an amnion, filled with amniotic fluid. A yolk sac provides essential nutrients, while a structure called the allantois removes wastes and supplies vital oxygen. The embryo, yolk, and allantois are protected by the chorion and outer shell.

The chorion allows oxygen and carbon dioxide to pass between the embryo and the outside world.

The yolk sac gets smaller as the embryo uses its food supplies.

The embryo is protected within the amnion.

The amnion contains amniotic fluid, which protects and nurtures the embryo.

The allantois gets rid of waste.

The shell stops the egg drying out.

CROCODILE EGG

LIVE BIRTH

Some lizards and snakes, such as this European sand viper, give birth to fully formed young instead of laying eggs. This is most common among reptiles that live in cooler climates, where the warmth needed to incubate eggs cannot be relied upon.

The strong shell gives the tortoise protection from enemies.

The tortoise's body is fully formed when it hatches.

A horny projection called an egg tooth is used to break the shell.

This baby has hatched with its yolk sac. It will absorb it in the first few days of its life.

MARINE IGUANAS

The world's only sea lizards, marine iguanas live on the Galapagos Islands. They dive into the chilly Pacific Ocean to eat the red and green algae that grows on the rocks underwater, holding their breath for ten minutes at a time. Like all reptiles, they cannot regulate their body temperature themselves, so they must soak up the Sun's rays between dives to be able to move.

HOW CROCODILES HUNT

Crocodiles are ambush hunters, which means that they wait for their prey to come to them before attacking them. A crocodile will often lie motionless in water for a long period of time, with just its eyes and nostrils above the water line. When prey comes close enough, the crocodile will burst into action and swiftly overwhelm its victim with its sharp teeth and powerful jaws.

▶ NILE CROCODILE

One of the largest and most dangerous crocodiles, the Nile crocodile is powerful enough to kill large mammals such as antelopes and zebras. They often lurk in rivers and pools to ambush thirsty animals wading into the water to drink. They may even drag them from the bank and into the water to drown.

Nostrils high on the snout allow the crocodile to breathe when half-submerged.

A bony plate separates the nasal cavities from the mouth.

VITAL VALVE

A fleshy flap at the back of the crocodile's tongue keeps its airway separate from its mouth when it is submerged. This allows it to keep a grip on prey underwater, without water entering its lungs or stomach. When diving, the crocodile seals its nostrils off.

The palatal valve seals the back of the throat when underwater.

Massive jaw muscles give colossal biting power and a vice-like grip.

Sharp conical teeth are adapted for gripping prey.

Tiny pressure sensors on the jaw help the crocodile to track its prey's movements.

Good vision allows crocodiles to hunt by night as well as day.

The ears are located just behind the eyes, and give the crocodile keen hearing.

Powerful legs give the crocodile immense speed when attacking prey.

ON THE HUNT

Crocodiles make use of their amazing sense of smell and great eyesight to hunt for prey. They often study their prey for days or even weeks before striking at the right moment.

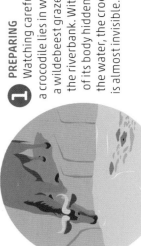

1 PREPARING
Watching carefully, a crocodile lies in wait as a wildebeest grazes on the riverbank. With most of its body hidden by the water, the crocodile is almost invisible.

2 STRIKING
Bursting from the water, the crocodile strikes, grabbing a leg with its immensely powerful jaws. It drags the struggling wildebeest off the bank and back towards the water.

Powerful muscles in the back, rear legs, and tail help the crocodile to ambush its prey.

3 DROWNING
With its prey in the water, the crocodile uses its weight and strength to hold the victim down until it drowns.

4 RIPPING
If the prey struggles, or if it is too big to swallow whole, the crocodile may spin rapidly in the water while gripping a body part to rip it off, a behaviour known as the "death roll".

The scaly skin is camouflaged to match murky water and conceal the crocodile from its prey.

The back is armoured with bone-reinforced scales, known as scutes.

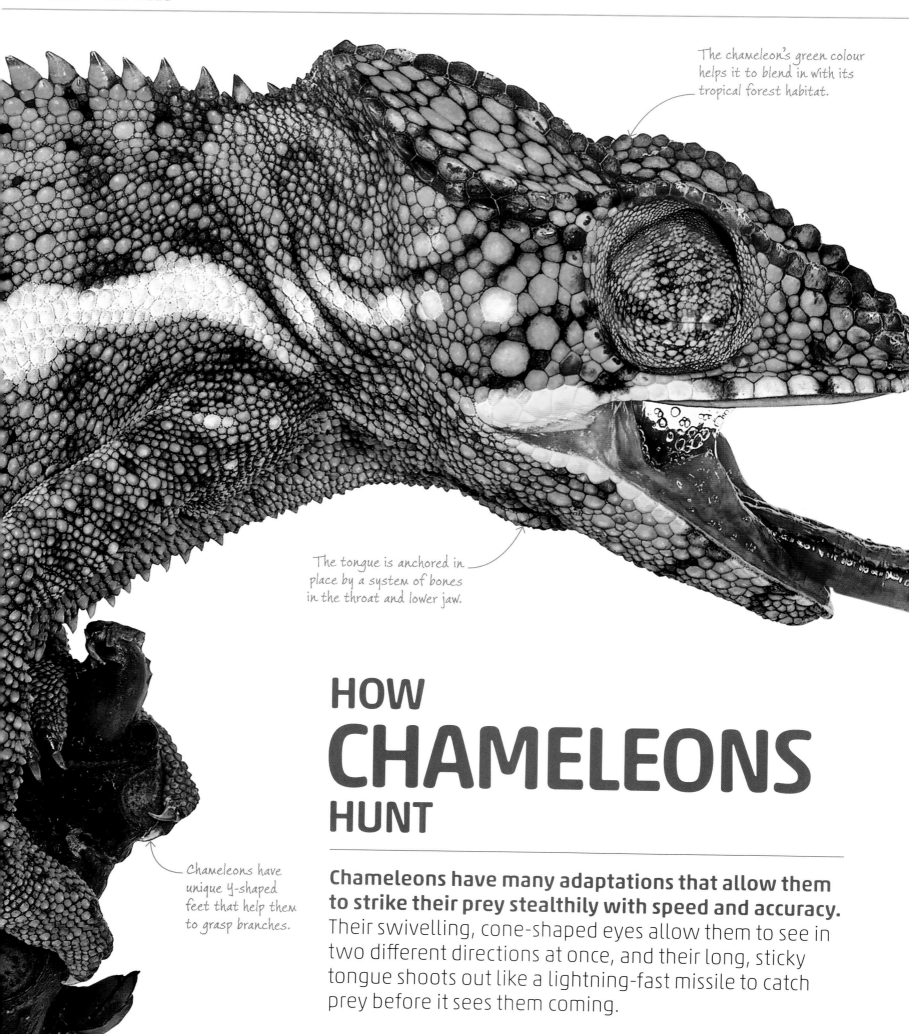

The chameleon's green colour helps it to blend in with its tropical forest habitat.

The tongue is anchored in place by a system of bones in the throat and lower jaw.

Chameleons have unique Y-shaped feet that help them to grasp branches.

HOW
CHAMELEONS
HUNT

Chameleons have many adaptations that allow them to strike their prey stealthily with speed and accuracy. Their swivelling, cone-shaped eyes allow them to see in two different directions at once, and their long, sticky tongue shoots out like a lightning-fast missile to catch prey before it sees them coming.

INSIDE THE HEAD

A chameleon's head houses its long tongue and the bones and muscles that are used to propel the tongue forwards. Of these, the accelerator and retractor muscles are responsible for the speed and power of the tongue.

A special bone runs through the centre of the tongue.

Hyoid bone

Retractor muscle

Elastic fibres

Accelerator muscle

The hyoid bone moves forwards, lifting the tongue up and pushing it out.

Once the prey has been hit, the retractor muscle reels the tongue back in.

The tongue pad engulfs the prey.

Accelerator muscle

1 READY AND WAITING
When not in use, the tongue is stored in the base of the mouth. Elastic fibres between the tongue bone and accelerator muscle hold the accelerator muscle in place, like a compressed spring.

2 TONGUE FIRED
When prey is located, the tongue is moved up and out of the mouth. Once the chameleon has judged the prey's exact position, the accelerator muscle contracts and detaches from the compressed elastic fibres. The energy stored in the tongue's fibres causes it to fly rapidly towards the prey.

▼ AS QUICK AS A FLASH

The panther chameleon is a native of Madagascar. It can launch its extensible tongue with pinpoint accuracy. Normally tucked inside the mouth, the chameleon's tongue can reach more than its body length and shoots out at a speed of up to 6 metres per second (20 ft per second). The sticky tip then makes the catch, before the tongue is reeled back into the wide mouth.

The tongue can reach prey in less than 0.07 seconds.

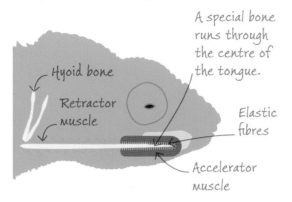

HOW CHAMELEON EYES WORK

Chameleon eyes are mounted on cone-shaped turrets and can rotate independently of each other, enabling a 360-degree view. When hunting, both eyes focus on the prey and lock on to it, enabling the chameleon to accurately judge the distance and position of its prey.

The club-shaped tip, covered with sticky saliva, partially wraps around the prey.

HOW CHAMELEONS CHANGE COLOUR

Some chameleons turn darker to help them absorb heat when cold.

Chameleons can't change their colour to match any background, but they can alter it a little to blend with their surroundings. Many chameleons also use colour changes to signal their mood, as posturing males rely on bright colours to impress the females or intimidate their rivals.

HOW THE SKIN CHANGES COLOUR

Just below a chameleon's skin are cells containing yellow pigments. Beneath these lie a layer of cells that contain crystals separated by fluid. When the crystals are close together, blue light is reflected – which can be altered to green by the yellow layer. If the crystals are apart, the chameleon can appear red, orange, or yellow. The yellow layer can change how much it alters the colour. A chameleon's colour depends upon how the different skin layers interact.

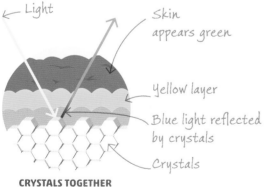

Light

Skin appears green

Yellow layer

Blue light reflected by crystals

Crystals

CRYSTALS TOGETHER

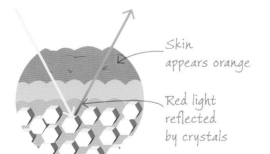

Skin appears orange

Red light reflected by crystals

CRYSTALS APART

The muscular tail can cling to branches.

The tall crest of the veiled chameleon gets bigger with age.

◄ LIGHT AND DARK

The veiled chameleon is native to Yemen and Saudi Arabia. When it feels threatened by a rival or danger, it turns a darker colour. Both sexes change colour according to their mood. Females turn brighter to signal to males that they are ready to mate, while males show off with multicoloured displays that warn other males to stay away, or that attract a mate.

LOCAL COLOURS

As well as changing colour with their mood, chameleons may also vary in colour depending on where they live. In Madagascar, the panther chameleon may be red, green, blue, yellow, or orange, though all these "morphs" belong to the same species.

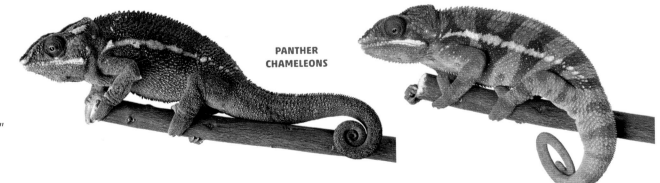

PANTHER CHAMELEONS

HOW GECKOS CLIMB

Geckos are small, insect-eating lizards that mainly hunt by night, using their large eyes to spot prey. Many are expert climbers, having feet that are adapted for gripping tree bark and leaves. Some can even climb glass and run across ceilings upside down.

Most geckos have no eyelids, and keep their eyes moist by licking them.

Skin is camouflaged to hide the gecko during the day.

A toothed crest along the neck gives this gecko its name.

The muscular tail has a sticky pad on the tip.

Lamallae

STICKY TOES
The gecko's feet are divided into broad pads called lamallae. Each pad is covered with millions of tiny, hair-like structures divided into many microscopic branches. These form a weak electric bond with the surface, helping the gecko to stick.

Small scales protect the skin and help stop the gecko from drying out.

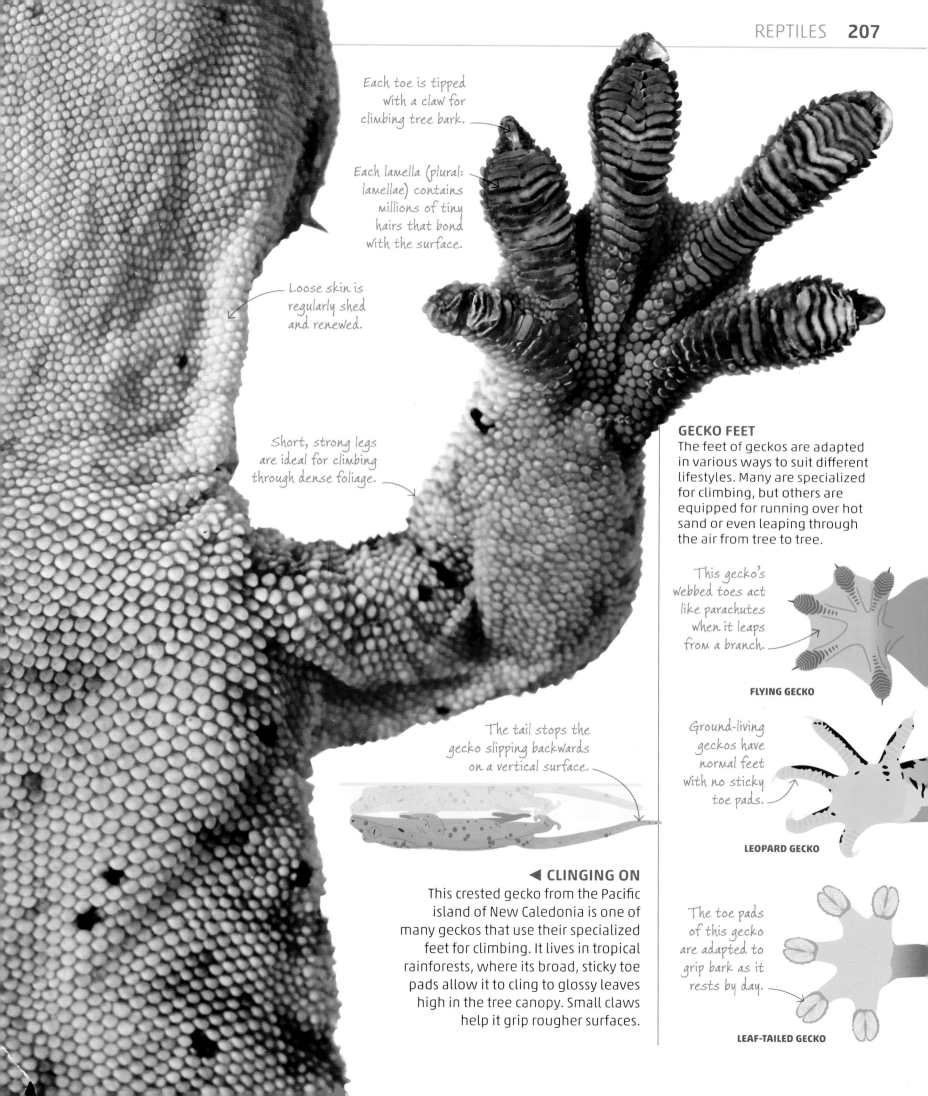

Each toe is tipped with a claw for climbing tree bark.

Each lamella (plural: lamellae) contains millions of tiny hairs that bond with the surface.

Loose skin is regularly shed and renewed.

Short, strong legs are ideal for climbing through dense foliage.

GECKO FEET
The feet of geckos are adapted in various ways to suit different lifestyles. Many are specialized for climbing, but others are equipped for running over hot sand or even leaping through the air from tree to tree.

This gecko's webbed toes act like parachutes when it leaps from a branch.

FLYING GECKO

The tail stops the gecko slipping backwards on a vertical surface.

Ground-living geckos have normal feet with no sticky toe pads.

LEOPARD GECKO

◄ CLINGING ON
This crested gecko from the Pacific island of New Caledonia is one of many geckos that use their specialized feet for climbing. It lives in tropical rainforests, where its broad, sticky toe pads allow it to cling to glossy leaves high in the tree canopy. Small claws help it grip rougher surfaces.

The toe pads of this gecko are adapted to grip bark as it rests by day.

LEAF-TAILED GECKO

HOW TUATARAS WORK

Though it looks like an ordinary lizard, the tuatara is actually the only survivor of a group of prehistoric reptiles that lived alongside the dinosaurs. Unusually for a reptile, the tuatara thrives in cool temperatures on rocky New Zealand islands. Because of the cold, it takes over a year for a tuatara to hatch from an egg – and more than ten until it is ready to breed. Many live to be 100 years old.

A tuatara's tail can break away if caught by a predator, and a replacement tail will grow.

▲ A UNIQUE REPTILE
Like many lizards, tuataras have small, overlapping scales, and catch prey with their projectile tongues. But there are other features that set them apart. They have a double row of teeth in their upper jaw that interlocks with a single row in the jaw below, and their primitive vertebrae (back bones) are more like those of amphibians.

Tuataras shed their skin 3–4 times a year as juveniles, and once a year as adults.

THIRD EYE
Many fish, amphibians, and reptiles have a "third eye" in the top of their head, but it is especially well developed in tuataras. Although it gets covered with scales as they grow older, it remains sensitive to light, helping the body respond to daily cycles of the Sun.

The lens focuses light into the retina.

The retina picks up the light signal.

A nerve carries information picked up by the third eye to the brain.

Its eyes are adapted for night vision, with a reflective layer that enhances vision in the dark.

Though they have no external ears, tuataras are not deaf. They are sensitive to low-pitched sounds, which they pick up as vibrations.

The throat and belly are covered in bumpy, round scales called tubercles.

The long claws and short, powerful legs are ideally suited to digging burrows.

Tuataras have brown or olive-green skin. Young tuataras have yellow or creamy coloured spots that fade with age.

SHARING A HOME
Tuataras spend the day in burrows, only emerging under the cover of darkness. Sometimes, they dig their own home, but they often share the burrows of breeding seabirds. They feed on invertebrates attracted to the seabird dung, but will occasionally eat a chick to get a richer meal.

HOW SNAKES MOVE

A snake's smooth belly scales grip surfaces like the grooves on a shoe's sole. Each rectangular belly scale has its own dedicated muscle and vertebra. As they work together, they allow the snake to move in a strong yet flexible way, pushing the snake forwards.

The female green tree python can grow as long as 2 m (6.6 ft).

▶ MOVING IN THE TREES
Some snakes, such as the green tree python from Indonesia and northern Australia, spend their whole lives in the trees, draped over branches by day and hunting for small mammals and reptiles at night. To help them move in this challenging environment, the snake's vertebrae can lock together to form a strong, rigid beam, which helps it to stretch out unsupported as it moves from branch to branch.

Its long, slender body helps the green tree python move in the trees.

The python's strong muscles allows it to hold branches tightly.

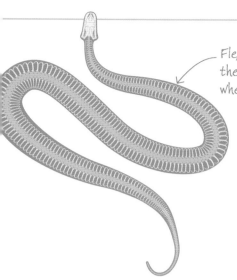

Flexible ribs allow the snake to expand when swallowing prey.

SNAKE ANATOMY
A human has 33 bones in his or her spine, but a snake may have between 200 and 400, with each one attached to a pair of ribs and to special muscles in its belly. Each bone makes the snake more flexible, and each muscle gives it strength.

CROSS-SECTION of a snake

Muscles beside the spine help the snake turn sideways.

Muscles between the ribs and skin help the snake move forwards.

A snake will often follow scents detected by its tongue.

Rib   Spine

Body cavity

The front of the body is slender and lightweight, allowing the head to reach from branch to branch.

STYLES OF MOTION
Snakes have developed four main ways to move, and some can switch between them to better suit the type of ground they are travelling over.

Snake adopts an "S" shape.

Rock

Tail is pressed to the ground.

Head is pressed to the ground

Snake moves diagonally.

STRAIGHT
To move in a straight line, a snake lifts and stretches some of its belly scales forwards, before touching down and pulling the scales behind forwards.

SERPENTINE
The most common type of movement happens when a snake pushes its sides against objects on the ground to help it to move forwards.

CONCERTINA
When moving across smooth surfaces, a snake may bunch up and launch itself forwards, before pulling its tail forwards.

SIDEWINDING
Used on shifting surfaces such as sand, sidewinding involves a snake throwing its head sideways through the air, with the body following.

SPITTING VENOM

A few species of African cobra, such as this Mozambique spitting cobra, spit venom into the eyes of predators. Each fang has a small opening, through which venom is forced at high pressure. The venom can reach 3 m (10 ft) away and can cause irritation or even blindness in its target.

▶ **AMAZON TREE BOA**

A nocturnal hunter, the Amazon tree boa catches birds, lizards, frogs, and small mammals in the treetops, and kills its prey with constriction. The snake coils around its prey and gradually increases the pressure until the victim's heart stops beating. The lifeless animal is then swallowed whole.

The snake feels for movement in the muscles, lungs, and heart of its prey and responds by tightening its coils.

The snake's strong muscles help it to hang from branches.

The snake's flexible lower jaw expands to swallow prey.

This bird gulps for air as it is squeezed.

Heat-sensitive pits detect warm-blooded prey.

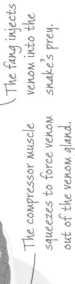

Venom flows down the venom canal inside the fang.

The fang injects venom into the snake's prey.

The venom gland produces venom.

The compressor muscle squeezes to force venom out of the venom gland.

HOW SNAKES KILL

Snakes are formidable, highly efficient predators. They detect prey by sensing smell, warmth, vibrations caused by movement, and sometimes also by sight. Snakes swallow their prey whole, but must subdue and kill them first. Constrictors squeeze their victims, but other snakes use venom – lethal toxins delivered by needle-sharp fangs – to kill.

VENOM AND FANGS

Some snakes have a pair of highly modified teeth in the upper jaw called fangs that deliver toxins called venom. In a lightning-quick strike, the fangs stab the victim and inject venom into it. In vipers (right), the venom causes swelling and blood loss, and can even destroy tissue. Other snakes use venom to paralyse their prey.

HOW SNAKES EAT

Although snakes don't have limbs and can't chew, they manage to eat by using some clever techniques. Their jaws are flexible enough to engulf food wider than their own bodies. Practically all snakes have sharp teeth to subdue struggling prey, but egg-eating snakes are toothless and have other adaptations for their diet.

▶ EATING AN EGG

An egg-eating snake can swallow an egg that is more than two times the diameter of its head and body. The egg is then crushed inside the snake, and its rich, nutritious contents digested.

The quadrate bone, which connects the top and bottom jaws, allows the jaws to open wider.

The lower jaw can separate at the front to allow it to expand sideways.

The snake may wedge the egg against firm objects like rocks or stones to help manoeuvre the egg into its throat.

Throat muscles push the egg down.

Flexible skin between the snake's scales stretches.

1 OPEN WIDE
The ligaments of the snake's jaws open wide enough to take the egg in, as the snake pushes down slightly to get its bottom jaw under the egg.

2 DOWN THE THROAT
Once swallowed, powerful throat muscles push the egg into the snake's throat. At this stage, the egg is still completely intact.

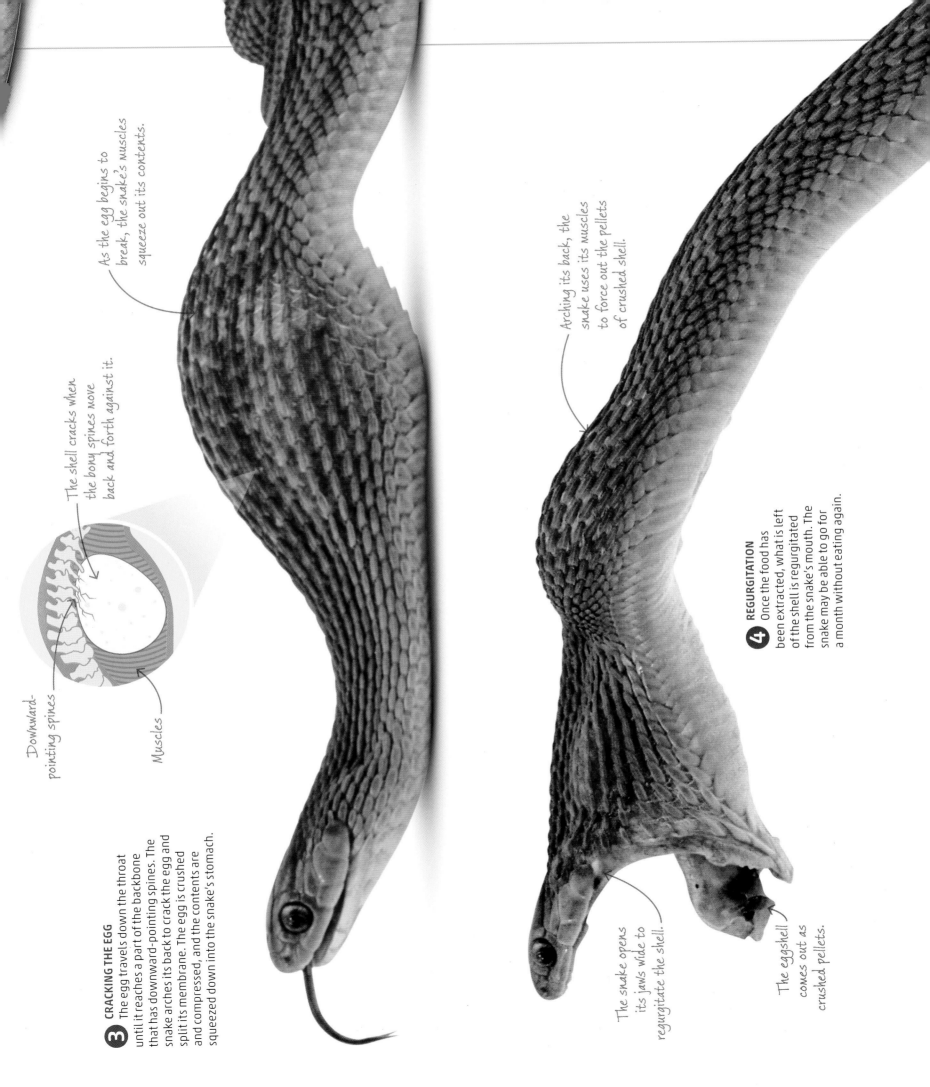

3 CRACKING THE EGG

The egg travels down the throat until it reaches a part of the backbone that has downward-pointing spines. The snake arches its back to crack the egg and split its membrane. The egg is crushed and compressed, and the contents are squeezed down into the snake's stomach.

Downward-pointing spines

Muscles

The shell cracks when the bony spines move back and forth against it.

As the egg begins to break, the snake's muscles squeeze out its contents.

Arching its back, the snake uses its muscles to force out the pellets of crushed shell.

4 REGURGITATION

Once the food has been extracted, what is left of the shell is regurgitated from the snake's mouth. The snake may be able to go for a month without eating again.

The snake opens its jaws wide to regurgitate the shell.

The eggshell comes out as crushed pellets.

HOW TORTOISES WORK

Tortoises and turtles have their own body armour: thick bony shells that cover their bodies, into which they can withdraw their vulnerable head and limbs. Tortoises live on land, and tend to have high-domed shells to protect them from predators. Turtles, which live in water, have smoother, streamlined shells that make swimming easier.

The big, jagged scutes will get smoother with age.

SIDE VIEW OF INDIAN ROOFED TURTLE

The bright orange and black pattern of the shell's underside may help scare off predators.

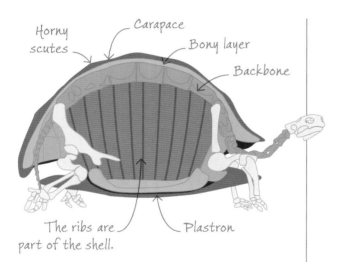

Horny scutes

Carapace

Bony layer

Backbone

The ribs are part of the shell.

Plastron

SHELL CONSTRUCTION
The hard plates that make up a tortoise's or turtle's outer shell are formed from big, specialized scales called scutes. Each forms a horny outer casing over a bony base under the skin. The upper shell – called the carapace – forms a dome over the back. The flatter lower shell – the plastron – covers the belly.

A side-necked turtle's neck is powerful enough to be able to flip the turtle upright if it is upside down.

TURNING HEADS
When danger threatens, a turtle or a tortoise can pull its head into its shell. Members of one group – called the side-necked turtles – bend their head sideways under the roof of the shell. Others, including all land tortoises, are called hidden-necked. They withdraw their neck back into the shell so the head stays facing forwards.

A high ridge called a keel is coloured red in baby Indian roofed turtles.

UNDER THE SEA
Many turtles have webbed feet for swimming, but only the larger ocean-going turtles have flippers. Marine turtles spend most of their life in water, but like all turtles, they lay hard-shelled eggs, so they must crawl onto a sandy beach to bury them on land.

◀ SAFE FROM HARM
With its head and feet safely retracted inside, this baby Indian roofed turtle is well protected. Like many other kinds of turtle, the shell changes shape as it matures, turning into a smoother dome. Indian roofed turtles live in rivers in south Asia.

Folds of skin around the neck encircle the head as it is retracted.

The limbs and feet can close in around the head to help protect the face.

Birds evolved from **dinosaurs** more than 150 million years ago, and are close relatives of modern **reptiles**. All birds are covered in **feathers** and have wings, which most species use to fly. This power of flight has allowed birds to spread all over the world and allows some birds to travel great **distances** each year to spend the winter months in warmer climates.

BIRDS

HOW BIRDS WORK

The defining feature of birds is their feathers, which no other living animals have. Feathers cover birds' bodies and fulfil many different functions, from enabling flight to providing insulation, camouflage, and bright coloration for displays that help birds find mates. Birds are also the only living vertebrates apart from bats to possess wings. Other key features include beaks, lightweight hollow bones, and massively powerful flight muscles.

Birds have large eyes and excellent colour vision for spotting predators or food.

This northern cardinal has a short, cone-shaped beak for crunching seeds.

The crown feathers can be raised into a crest when the bird is trying to attract a mate.

To save weight and make flight easier, the beak has no teeth. However, it is made of a hard material called keratin and is strong enough to crush food.

A bird's streamlined body shape makes flight possible.

The breast contains enormous flight muscles.

BREATHING

Birds' lungs are connected to nine air sacs, which keep air flowing through the lungs in one direction. This makes birds much better at extracting oxygen from the air than other animals, giving them enough energy for flight.

Air with less oxygen flows through the upper air sacs and out of the windpipe.

Air sac

Trachea, or windpipe

Lung

Oxygen-rich air flows through the lower air sacs and into the lungs.

This male bird's colourful feathers help him attract a mate. In many bird species, males have more colourful feathers than females.

▶ PERCHING BIRD

This northern cardinal belongs to the largest group of birds, called the perching birds, or passerines. All perching bird species have a long, strong hind toe adapted for gripping branches or other perches. This extremely varied group includes over half of all birds – around 5,800 species.

Long, clawed toes give grip for perching.

Streamlined flight feathers allow air to flow smoothly over the wing.

Long tail feathers help birds balance when perching and steer when flying.

Bands of tissue in a perching bird's leg make its toes automatically lock around a perch when it lands on one. This means the bird can stay perching even when asleep.

BIRDS OF PREY
These predators and scavengers have hooked beaks and talons for hunting, and very sharp eyesight for spotting prey. They include falcons, hawks, eagles, ospreys, and vultures.

WATERFOWL
Ducks, swans, and geese have webbed feet for swimming, and most have broad, flattened beaks to help them forage for food. They spend much of their lives on or near water.

FLIGHTLESS BIRDS
Five families of birds are known as the flightless birds, or ratites. They have powerful legs and feet for running.

TYPES OF BIRD
There are more than 10,000 species of bird in the world. These are divided into 36 major groups called orders, which are divided in turn into 236 families.

HOW BIRD SKELETONS WORK

Birds have strong, streamlined bodies

and highly specialized skeletons for efficient, aerodynamic flight. Their bones are hollow to save weight, but reinforced with internal struts for strength. Their breastbones anchor powerful wing muscles, and their compact body shape helps them perch upright on two legs.

▶ FALCON SKELETON

The peregrine falcon makes high-speed dives at prey and kills it on impact. To withstand this, it has a streamlined, rigid skeleton. Like all strong flying birds, the falcon has an enlarged keel, which allows for larger flight muscles and greater flapping power.

Eye orbit (opening) for large eyes

In some birds, the upper part of the beak can move independently of the rest of the skull. Birds have no teeth, possibly to save weight.

A ring of bone called the sclerotic ring holds the falcon's tubular eyeball in place. This means that it cannot swivel its eyes, but it has a highly flexible neck so can compensate by turning its head.

A strong bone called the coracoid holds each shoulder away from the body and helps lift the shoulders during flight.

Overlapping projections in the rib cage and fused trunk vertebrae give the skeleton extra rigidity.

The neck has many bones called vertebrae, which make it highly flexible.

The wishbone is springy enough to store energy with each wingbeat during flight.

The keel supports the falcon's powerful flight muscles.

There is a space between the bird's lower wing bones (the ulna and the radius) for the muscles that flex the end of the wing.

The hand bones are fused to withstand the impact of flight.

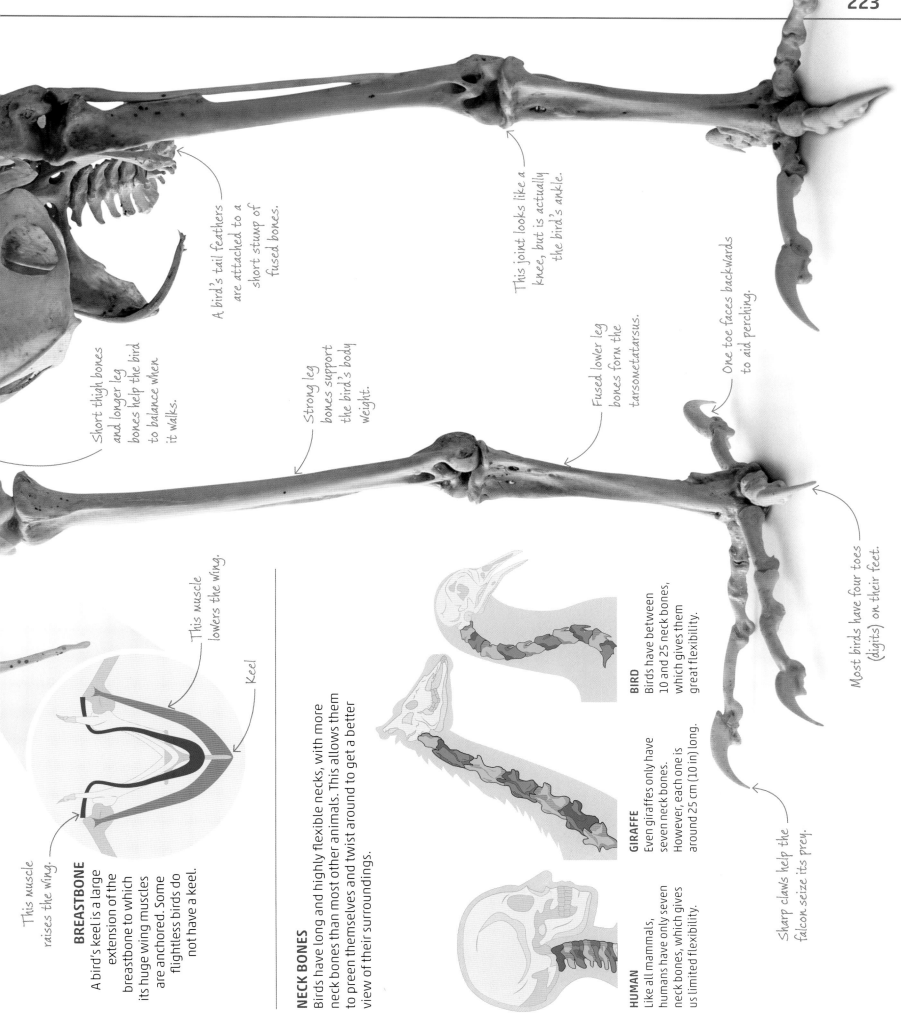

Short thigh bones and longer leg bones help the bird to balance when it walks.

A bird's tail feathers are attached to a short stump of fused bones.

This joint looks like a knee, but is actually the bird's ankle.

Strong leg bones support the bird's body weight.

Fused lower leg bones form the tarsometatarsus.

One toe faces backwards to aid perching.

Most birds have four toes (digits) on their feet.

Sharp claws help the falcon seize its prey.

This muscle raises the wing.

This muscle lowers the wing.

Keel

BREASTBONE
A bird's keel is a large extension of the breastbone to which its huge wing muscles are anchored. Some flightless birds do not have a keel.

NECK BONES
Birds have long and highly flexible necks, with more neck bones than most other animals. This allows them to preen themselves and twist around to get a better view of their surroundings.

HUMAN
Like all mammals, humans have only seven neck bones, which gives us limited flexibility.

GIRAFFE
Even giraffes only have seven neck bones. However, each one is around 25 cm (10 in) long.

BIRD
Birds have between 10 and 25 neck bones, which gives them great flexibility.

A patch of leathery skin called the cere surrounds the nostrils.

The beak is covered in a tough layer of skin.

Upper and lower jaw bones make up the beak.

The sharp hook at the tip of an eagle's beak can rip off fur and feathers, and tear flesh.

MEAT EATERS
Birds of prey, such as this golden eagle, use their sharply hooked beaks to tear meat. Most kill with their powerful talons, but some, such as falcons, use their beaks to inflict a fatal bite.

GREAT EGRET

GOLDEN EAGLE

FISH EATERS
Herons and many other fish eaters have long, dagger-like beaks for grabbing prey. They rarely stab their food. Instead, their beaks have serrated edges to grip slippery fish.

A dagger-shaped beak can spear a fish, but birds rarely do this.

This egret's long, flexible neck allows it to strike quickly.

TYPES OF BEAK

More than any other part of its body, a bird's beak, or bill, gives the best clue about what it eats. Over millions of years, beaks have evolved into a range of shapes and sizes. Predators have sharp beaks that work like weapons for hunting and fishing, while plant eaters need grasping beaks to pull at fruit, or strong ones to crush nuts and seeds.

A sword-billed hummingbird's beak is longer than the rest of its body.

NECTAR FEEDERS
Hummingbirds have long, pointed beaks to probe flowers for nectar, which they lap up with their long tongue. The sword-billed hummingbird's beak is especially long to reach into tubular flowers.

SWORD-BILLED HUMMINGBIRD

FILTER FEEDERS
Flamingos have uniquely shaped beaks that are lined with fringes like the bristles on a broom. A flamingo lowers its slightly open beak upside down into water and pumps with its tongue so the bristles trap particles of food.

LESSER FLAMINGO

BLACK-HEADED PARROT

FRUIT AND NUT EATERS
A parrot's beak has a flexible hinge in both its upper and lower halves. This means the parrot can use it to manipulate food and grasp and split fruit and nuts. The beak is so flexible that a parrot can also use it as a "third foot" for climbing.

SEED EATERS
Birds such as finches have stout, cone-shaped beaks that can deliver crushing force to split seeds open. There are countless variations on this basic shape according to the type of seed that a bird eats. Seeds are wedged in a special groove in the upper beak for cracking.

GOULDIAN FINCH

The thick, sturdy beak crushes a seed's tough casing.

The curved shape of a flamingo's beak helps it collect food.

A sharp hook is ideal for grasping fruit.

FLAPPING WINGS

Birds flap their wings to generate the two forces necessary for flight: thrust and lift. By flapping their wings, birds push themselves forwards and produce the thrust that counteracts drag, or air resistance. Once the bird is airborne, lift is created by the stream of air that pushes over the curved surfaces of the bird's outstretched wings.

Downstroke

Folded wings

1 DOWNSTROKE
As this eagle lowers its wings in what is called a downstroke, the air pressure underneath the wings pushes it forwards and upwards.

2 UPSTROKE
The eagle begins to raise its wings in an upstroke. It partially folds its wings to save energy and reduce forces that would drag it downwards.

▼ SOARING FLIGHT
To save energy and gain height for spotting prey, birds of prey such as this golden eagle favour soaring and gliding over flapping flight. With long wings that span 2.3 m (7.5 ft), the golden eagle is well suited to this gliding style of flight.

The outer tips of the main flight feathers are spread out for slow, gliding flight.

A group of feathers called the alula is held open in slow flight to stop the eagle stalling.

HOW **BIRDS** FLY

Birds are excellent fliers, with massive flight muscles that make up at least a quarter of their entire body weight. Their feathers provide a streamlined body covering and allow the position and shape of their wings and tail to be changed for precise control while flying. Their skeletons are extremely light so as not to impede flight, but strong enough to withstand the impact of flight.

The tail feathers are fanned out to create a force called lift that keeps the bird in the air.

3 **RAISED WINGS**
The eagle unfolds its wings once they are fully raised, ready for another downstroke or soaring flight.

Unfolded wings

4 **COMING IN TO LAND**
The eagle holds its wings in a shallow V for slow gliding flight, and starts to lower its legs as it prepares to land.

The legs are lowered to prepare for landing.

These feathers remain close together to divert air over the wing.

Gaps in the wing reduce air resistance.

These feathers are called coverts and create a smooth surface for air to flow over.

These feathers are called marginal coverts and protect the eagle's wing bones.

The lightweight beak contains no teeth.

The eagle's streamlined body shape aids flight.

The angle of the wing makes the air flow faster over it, so the downward pressure on the wing is lower.

Cross-section of the bird's wing

Flight is powered by enormous breast muscles.

The higher pressure below the wing creates lift.

Air under the wing flows more slowly, so the upward pressure on the wing is higher.

Powerful talons can kill prey on impact when the eagle swoops down on it.

AIR ON THE WING
As an eagle glides, the angle and shape of its wing diverts the flowing air. Airflow over the wing is faster and the pressure is lowered; under the wing, it is slower and the pressure is raised. This pressure difference creates an upwards force called lift.

HOW **WINGS** WORK

Birds' wings are light, strong, and flexible, and enable them to fly faster and further than any other animal. With a front edge that is thicker than the back, and feathers that narrow to a point and create a streamlined surface for air to flow over, wings are ideally shaped to keep birds in the air. The wings are anchored to the body by light, hollow bones and controlled by powerful chest muscles.

A group of feathers called the alula acts like a flap to control the bird's lift at slow speeds.

Covert feathers cover the other feathers to make the wing streamlined and aerodynamic.

Secondary flight feathers keep the bird in the air and give it lift.

Tertiary flight feathers cover the space between the body and the wing.

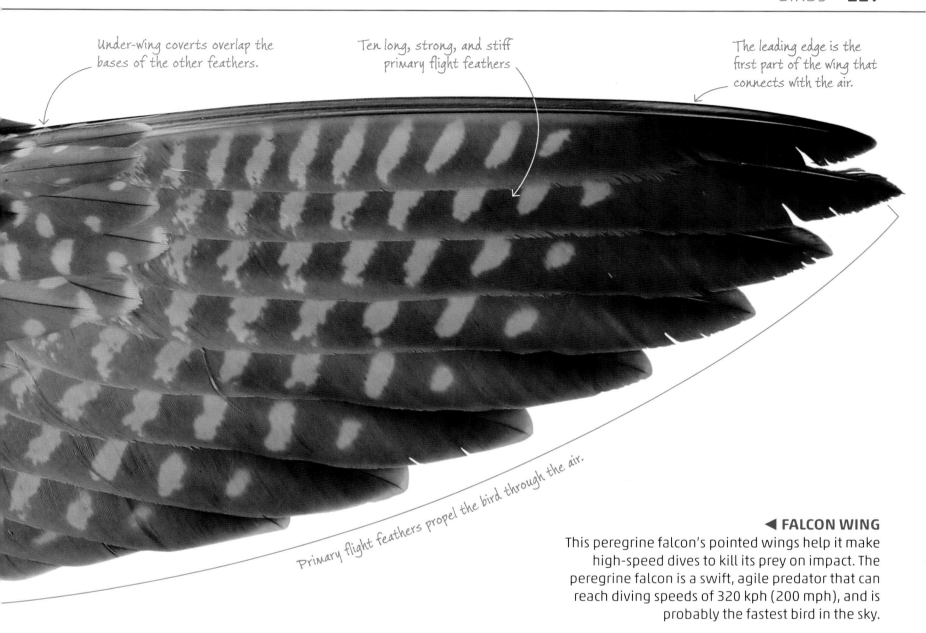

Under-wing coverts overlap the bases of the other feathers.

Ten long, strong, and stiff primary flight feathers

The leading edge is the first part of the wing that connects with the air.

Primary flight feathers propel the bird through the air.

◀ FALCON WING
This peregrine falcon's pointed wings help it make high-speed dives to kill its prey on impact. The peregrine falcon is a swift, agile predator that can reach diving speeds of 320 kph (200 mph), and is probably the fastest bird in the sky.

WING SHAPES
Although they are all constructed in the same basic way, bird wings have developed into a variety of different shapes and sizes to allow them to flap, glide, hover, and swoop through the sky. The shape of a bird's wings is directly related to its flight needs. For example, some birds have short wings for manoeuvrability, while others have long wings for soaring for hours.

FALCON

ALBATROSS

COOPER'S HAWK

GOLDEN EAGLE

HIGH-SPEED WINGS
Fast-flying birds have slender wings that end in a narrow point. These wings can be flapped in rapid bursts to reach high speeds quickly.

GLIDING
Most gliding birds' wings are longer than they are wide. Instead of being continually flapped, these wings are often held out to catch the wind.

MANOEUVRING
Many forest birds have short, rounded wings that enable tight manoeuvring in confined spaces and fast take-offs to evade predators.

SOARING
Many birds of prey have long, broad wings that help them soar on rising currents of warm air. Slotted feathers at the wing tips help keep the bird in the air.

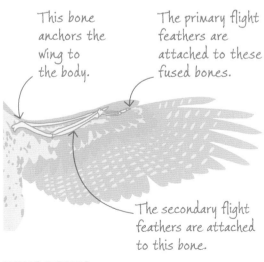

This bone anchors the wing to the body.

The primary flight feathers are attached to these fused bones.

The secondary flight feathers are attached to this bone.

WING BONES
Apart from the shoulder, bird wings have two main joints that are equivalent to a human elbow and wrist. These are the joints that make the wing open, shut, and swivel, which are the crucial elements for flight.

HOW FEATHERS WORK

Feathers are extremely tough, yet light and flexible, and make up just 5–10 per cent of a bird's weight. They grow from the skin and are made of keratin, like human fingernails and hair. Each feather is anchored in a small pit called a follicle and grows within a tube called a feather sheath. Once a feather is fully grown, it unfolds and the feather sheath falls away.

PHEASANT PLUMAGE
Like that of most birds, the ring-necked pheasant's plumage consists of several different kinds of feather. Contour feathers cover all of its body apart from the beak, legs, and bare patches on the face. Down feathers under the contour feathers provide insulation.

Contour feathers

Secondary flight feathers

Tail feathers

Down feathers under the contour feathers

Primary flight feathers

STREAMLINED SURFACE
The central shaft of a feather has many side branches (barbs), all of which in turn have many smaller branches (barbules). Some barbules have tiny hooks (barbicels) that lock onto the barbules underneath them, creating a sleek surface for flight.

Barbules

Parallel barbs

The barbicels are hooks that lock the barbules together.

The lower section of the feather shaft is called the quill. It sprouts from a follicle in the skin. Unlike the rest of the shaft, it is hollow.

The downy base of this tail feather insulates the bird's skin.

The exposed parts of feathers can be colourful, but hidden parts are usually dull.

The solid part of the feather shaft is called the rachis. It provides support for the barbs.

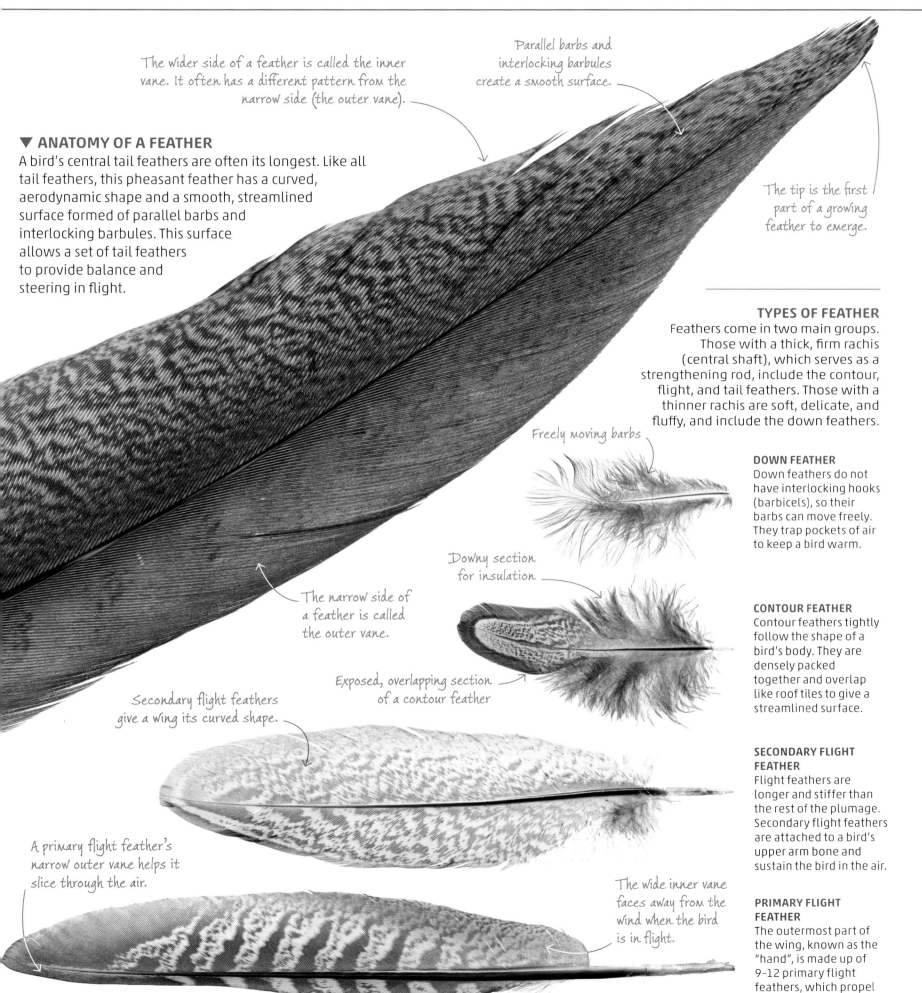

The wider side of a feather is called the inner vane. It often has a different pattern from the narrow side (the outer vane).

Parallel barbs and interlocking barbules create a smooth surface.

The tip is the first part of a growing feather to emerge.

▼ ANATOMY OF A FEATHER
A bird's central tail feathers are often its longest. Like all tail feathers, this pheasant feather has a curved, aerodynamic shape and a smooth, streamlined surface formed of parallel barbs and interlocking barbules. This surface allows a set of tail feathers to provide balance and steering in flight.

TYPES OF FEATHER
Feathers come in two main groups. Those with a thick, firm rachis (central shaft), which serves as a strengthening rod, include the contour, flight, and tail feathers. Those with a thinner rachis are soft, delicate, and fluffy, and include the down feathers.

Freely moving barbs

DOWN FEATHER
Down feathers do not have interlocking hooks (barbicels), so their barbs can move freely. They trap pockets of air to keep a bird warm.

Downy section for insulation

The narrow side of a feather is called the outer vane.

Exposed, overlapping section of a contour feather

CONTOUR FEATHER
Contour feathers tightly follow the shape of a bird's body. They are densely packed together and overlap like roof tiles to give a streamlined surface.

Secondary flight feathers give a wing its curved shape.

SECONDARY FLIGHT FEATHER
Flight feathers are longer and stiffer than the rest of the plumage. Secondary flight feathers are attached to a bird's upper arm bone and sustain the bird in the air.

A primary flight feather's narrow outer vane helps it slice through the air.

The wide inner vane faces away from the wind when the bird is in flight.

PRIMARY FLIGHT FEATHER
The outermost part of the wing, known as the "hand", is made up of 9-12 primary flight feathers, which propel a bird through the air.

HOW HUMMINGBIRDS HOVER

Strong muscles, a rapid wing beat, and flexible joints are the keys to a hummingbird's flight technique. Unlike other birds, which mainly use the downstroke of their wings to keep them in the air, hummingbirds have a powerful upstroke, too.

1 DOWNSTROKE
The downstroke provides lift, which keeps the bird in the air, and thrust, which causes it to go forwards. On this stroke, the wings are brought rapidly forwards and down.

The wings twist back around and down.

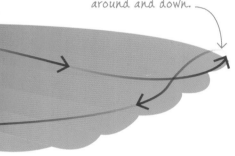

2 FIGURE OF EIGHT
At the end of the downstroke, flexible shoulder joints allow the wings to trace a smooth figure-of-eight shape, which minimizes loss of energy as the wings change direction.

3 UPSTROKE
As the wings sweep back, the upstroke provides an equal thrust to that of the downstroke. These forces cancel each other out, which means the bird stays in a fixed position in the air.

A hummingbird's wings move horizontally backwards and forwards, which helps it to feed from flowers.

Wings move too fast for the human eye to track, making them appear as a blur.

The beating wings produce a deep humming sound, which gives the bird its name.

The feathers have a metallic sheen and appear to change colour when the bird moves.

TIRELESS WINGS

Hummingbird wings typically beat about 80 times per second, but during the excitement of its courtship flight, this rufous hummingbird can exceed 200 beats per second. Their small but powerful wings allow some hummingbirds to reach speeds of 100 kph (62 mph).

HOW HUMMINGBIRDS HOVER

No birds live quite as frantically as hummingbirds.
They are so skilled in flight that they can hover and even fly backwards, their wings beating with such speed that they appear as a blur. Such a busy body requires a heart that beats more than ten times faster than ours, and a diet that consists almost entirely of energy-rich nectar.

▼ FUELLING STATION

The sugar in nectar supplies hummingbirds with energy. They need to hover to keep their position in front of flowers while they lap up the sweet liquid with their long flicking tongue. Like other kinds of hummingbird, this chestnut-breasted coronet gets 90 per cent of its food from nectar. The rest of its diet consists of small insects, which provide the protein it needs for growth.

Highly mobile shoulder joints allow the wing to rotate 180 degrees, as they pivot back and forth.

The head stays still while the bird hovers and feeds.

Hummingbirds' bills vary in length to feed from different kinds of flower.

Large breast muscles make up 30 per cent of the bird's body weight and help power the wings.

The tiny, light feet are useful for perching only.

The pollen of the rainbow heliconia flower sticks to the hummingbird and may pollinate the next flower the bird visits.

The tail feathers hang vertically, helping the bird to balance during flight.

LIFE ON THE MOVE

A dense flock of wild budgerigars descends from the Australian sky. These small, seed-eating parrots often fly large distances in search of food and water. When they breed, their numbers can grow rapidly, creating huge flocks of several thousand birds. Flying in large flocks has many benefits – it helps birds save energy, and gives them a much better chance of spotting or deterring predators.

HOW BIRDS MIGRATE

In birds, migration involves flight from one region to another as the seasons change. This means they can breed in one place and spend the winter elsewhere, to find food and escape harsh weather. Changes in day length and temperature alert birds that it is time to move on. Migration takes a great deal of energy, so birds eat a lot before setting off and along the way. Many also fly in large flocks for safety, or in a V-shape to save energy.

FINDING THE WAY

Migrating birds can sense the approximate time of day. By comparing this with the angle of the Sun's rays, they know which way is north, south, east, and west. Other navigational aids include the stars, landmarks such as mountains and coasts, smells, and Earth's magnetic field, which birds may be able to detect using their eyes.

Birds see the setting Sun in the evening and know that it is in the west.

Birds in the northern hemisphere see the Sun at its highest point and know that it is south of them.

Birds see the rising Sun in the morning and know that it is in the east.

Birds in the southern hemisphere see the Sun at its highest point and know that it is north of them.

The Sun is at its highest point in the middle of the day.

Huge, broad wings allow whooper swans to glide on the wind.

This young whooper swan is strong enough to make its first migration journey.

▼ EFFICIENT FLIGHT

Whooper swans breed in Scandinavia and Siberia and migrate southwards to countries including the UK and Japan. Like many birds, they migrate in flocks. Before setting off, they feed intensively to lay down fat to fuel the journey. Once airborne, they can maintain a steady 75 kph (47 mph). They can fly over 300 km (185 miles) in a single day but may stop en route to rest and refuel. They may also change course to avoid bad weather.

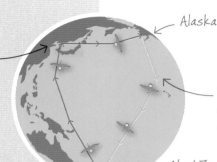

The return journey includes a stopover in China, so the birds are in good condition for breeding on their arrival in Alaska.

Alaska

Non-stop route over Pacific Ocean

New Zealand

LONG VOYAGES

Bar-tailed godwits migrate from Alaska to New Zealand in a fast, non-stop flight of eight days – a record among birds. Before setting off, their bodies turn non-essential tissue into fat and muscle.

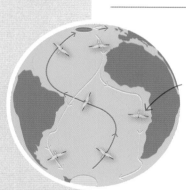

The birds fly south along the coast of Africa or South America.

Fat reserves power huge breast muscles for several hours of non-stop flight.

POLE TO POLE

Arctic terns breed in the Arctic and migrate to spend October to March in Antarctica, avoiding the Arctic winter. Their round trip is nearly 100,000 km (60,000 miles) long. This means some terns fly the distance of three return trips to the Moon in their lifetime.

Long, flexible flight feathers at the tip of the wing help to reduce drag, making flight more efficient.

The streamlined neck and body shape reduce air resistance to make flight easier.

V-FORMATION

Migrating geese fly in a V-shape and take turns to lead the flock. Apart from the leader, each bird flies in air currents created by the bird in front, saving energy.

The leader sets the pace.

Following birds save energy.

COURTSHIP IN OTHER BIRDS

In some birds, males display in groups called leks, so a female can compare and choose. These males mate with many females and play no part in raising offspring. But many birds form more stable partnerships and even share parental duties.

GREATER BIRD OF PARADISE

With heads bowed and up-ended tail plumes, two male greater birds of paradise combine colour with acrobatics as they display to watching females at the top of rainforest trees.

RED-CROWNED CRANE

The courtship ritual of the red-crowned crane involves both sexes. Their elegant leaping dance and loud honking duet seal a bond that pairs them in parenthood, and for life.

BOWERBIRD

Male bowerbirds build areas known as bowers of sticks, and then add blue decorations, such as flowers. The green-coloured female judges the results and chooses the best architect.

HOW COURTSHIP WORKS

In the contest to get a mate, some male birds use song, dance, and vivid colours to grab the attention of females. This behaviour is called courtship. Because females tend to prefer males with the biggest and brightest feathers, many male birds have evolved spectacular plumage and extravagant rituals.

The peacock's train grows from the base of his back, just above his tail.

MALE INDIAN PEAFOWL (PEACOCK)

▶ DAZZLED WITH COLOUR

A peacock fans his colourful feathers to impress a female. The spots of blue and gold, which look like eyes, are thought to improve his chances – but he must parade them at just the right angle. The female peafowl – called a peahen – is sombre in comparison, but her drab feathers help her to avoid attracting predators when she raises her family alone.

Each eyespot is called an OCELLUS.

The colours are iridescent, which means they change hue as they move in the light.

Each of the 100-150 feathers can reach up to 2 m (6.5 ft) in length.

The length of the male's train feathers increases with age.

Both male and female have a head crest.

Muscles at the base of each feather contract to raise the train.

The male gets his eyespots in his third year.

FEMALE PEAFOWL (PEAHEN)

HOW NESTS WORK

A bird's nest provides a safe place to incubate eggs and raise chicks, keeping them warm and hidden from predators. Most birds build one at the start of the breeding season and abandon it when the young fledge, but many storks, herons, and birds of prey use theirs year after year. Some birds' nests are highly complex, but others can be as simple as a cliff ledge, a hole in a tree, a or hollow in the ground.

▼ HANGING OUT

Many species in the weaver family, such as this southern masked weaver from Africa, construct intricate nests suspended from a branch. Only the male builds the main structure; the female helps to line it with feathers for warmth. For added security, the birds often breed in small colonies and choose spots over a river or water hole to deter predators. If a weaver does build a nest alone, he may build it near a wasp nest or beneath an eagle nest for extra protection.

BUILDING A NEST
A male southern masked weaver often builds several nests at a time in an attempt to find a mate. If the nest doesn't win a female bird's approval, the male has to dismantle it and start again.

1 WEAVING A SPIRAL
The male winds strands of grass around the branch that will support the nest.

2 MAKING STIRRUPS
More grass is added to make stirrups that support the weight of the bird.

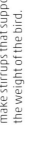

3 FORMING A RING
The two stirrups are joined to form a ring, which is thickened to make the scaffold of the nest.

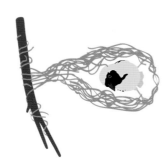

4 CREATING A CHAMBER
The ring is extended to form a chamber with an entrance at the bottom. The male and female then line the inside of the nest.

The nest hangs from the end of a thin, sagging branch, making it harder for predators to reach.

The nest is neatly woven from fresh grass, occasionally with a few extra leaves.

The weaver's sharp, conical beak is ideal for cutting strips of grass.

Strong feet with long claws make hanging upside down easier.

TYPES OF NEST

In general, nests reflect a bird's size and habitat. A wealth of materials may be used, from sticks and twigs to leaves, moss, fur, mud, pebbles, and pieces of plastic or other refuse.

CUP NESTS

A cup is one of the most common nest shapes, especially among small birds – and hummingbirds build some of the smallest of all. They bind the structure together with silk from spiders' webs.

ADHERENT NESTS

Swifts fasten their nests to cliffs, caves, and walls. Some use mud or plant material mixed with saliva, but this edible swiftlet nest is made entirely from saliva.

CAVITY NESTS

Tree hollows are occupied by a wide range of birds, from woodpeckers and owls to tits and parrots. Wood shavings and feathers are often the only lining.

PLATFORM NESTS

The bald eagle, like many big birds of prey, builds a huge treetop stick nest. Pairs mate for life, and their nest grows every year as the male and female add new material.

FLOATING NESTS

Some waterbirds, such as this great crested grebe, construct raft-like nests from aquatic vegetation. The nests are safe from predators on land, and rise and fall with the water level.

① GROWING EMBRYO
At first, the egg is one huge cell. While the parent bird sits on it to keep it warm, the cell begins to divide many times, forming the different organs and tissues. This is sustained by the nutrients and water stored in the egg. Shining a light through the egg allows us to see what is happening inside.

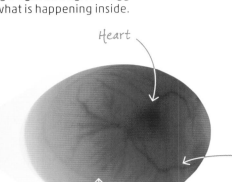

Heart

The shell has tiny holes that allow air to pass through it.

DAY 1: FRESHLY LAID EGG

An air sac at the blunt end of the egg will provide oxygen once the chick can breathe on its own.

WEEK 1

The yolk and other fluids in the egg nourish the embryo.

INSIDE AN EGG
The shell and protective membranes enclose the nourishing yolk, albumen (egg white) that cushions the embryo, and an air sac. Rope-like strands called chalazae secure the yolk.

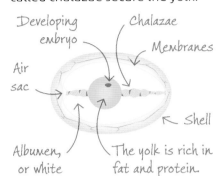

Developing embryo

Chalazae

Membranes

Air sac

Shell

Albumen, or white

The yolk is rich in fat and protein.

The embryo's eyes are developing.

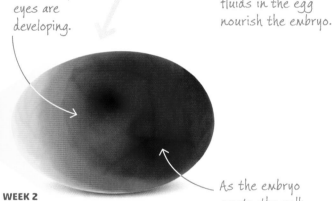

WEEK 2

As the embryo grows, the yolk is used up.

HOW **EGGS** DEVELOP

Unlike baby mammals, which develop inside the mother's body, baby birds develop inside eggs. An egg is packed with the nutrients that the embryo – the unhatched bird – needs to grow. The time from laying to hatching varies between species, from just ten days for woodpeckers to 80 days for large albatrosses.

GROWING AND HATCHING
A duck embryo takes four weeks to develop fully. By this time, it is squashed inside the egg with its head tucked in over its belly. Once the duckling is ready to hatch, it breaks through the shell of the egg with its beak, cuts a circle around the shell, and pushes the end away to emerge into the outside world.

Egg tooth on beak

The chick wriggles in the shell, which weakens it.

DAY 28

The chick gradually chips away at the shell to widen the hole.

② BREAKING THE SHELL
The chick is ready to hatch after 28 days. It breaks the air sac inside the egg and breathes oxygen for the first time. It then repeatedly strikes the shell with its egg tooth – a sharp projection on its beak. Eventually, it breaks through the shell and widens the hole to allow more air in.

DAY 28

The chick cuts a circle around the shell.

Pushing with its feet, the chick emerges rear end first.

DAY 28

The feathers are wet and untidy at first, but will dry out and fluff up within a few hours of hatching.

The small, stumpy wings are weak and lack flight feathers.

The duckling must also break through the shell membranes that protected it from bacteria.

BLOOD VESSELS
A network of blood vessels, seen here inside an empty egg after hatching, supplies the embryo with oxygen and takes away waste carbon dioxide.

❸ HATCHING OUT
The chick extends the hole to cut a circle around the egg and pushes the blunt end of the shell away with its feet. During the final push, it rotates its body and wriggles out of the membranes that have surrounded it.

The duckling hatches fully alert, with its eyes open.

A fully developed chick has a muscle along the back of its head and neck to help it strike and break the shell as it hatches.

1 EARLY STAGES
Although the duckling needs a rest after breaking out of its egg, it already has open eyes and a full covering of warm down. Soon, it is able to run, swim, and eat, though for safety it stays near its mother.

The legs and feet are too weak to lift the chick up.

NEWLY HATCHED

The feathers are still damp from being in the egg.

Wing bud

The downy feathers have dried out.

ONE DAY OLD

EGG TOOTH
A chick's beak is relatively soft – too soft to break through an eggshell. However, chicks have a small, hard projection called an egg tooth on their beaks to help them hatch. Newly hatched chicks still have their egg tooth, but it falls off 2–4 days after hatching.

The beak has developed fine, tooth-like projections along its edges.

The duckling can now walk upright.

The wing buds remain small but are growing fast.

The beak has hardened and started to lengthen.

Fluffy down still covers the body.

Longer neck

Growing wing bud

The tail is just visible.

18 DAYS OLD

FOUR WEEKS OLD

2 GROWING UP
As its skeleton grows, the once-plump duckling develops a longer neck and the beginnings of a tail. Its beak and wing buds grow and the webbing on its feet expands. But the duckling is still fluffy – it lacks any adult feathers.

HOW **BIRDS** GROW

The development of baby birds varies enormously.
Some, such as waterfowl, gamebirds, and shorebirds, can walk within hours of hatching and soon learn to fend for themselves. In contrast, most songbirds start life weak, naked, and sightless, so depend completely on their parents for food, warmth, and shelter. Some large seabirds and birds of prey take months to become independent.

▼ DEVELOPING DUCK
Waterfowl such as this Pekin duck are known as precocial birds, which means their young are relatively independent on hatching and can soon walk and swim. After just 16 weeks, the duck has developed all the features that make it so well suited to living on or near water, such as waterproofed feathers and fully expanded webbing on its feet.

FLIGHT FEATHERS
This duck's flight feathers can be seen growing inside tubes called feather sheaths. The feathers start growing as pulp inside the sheaths, and the tips gradually emerge to form blades. Once a feather is fully grown, the sheath falls away.

The beak and legs have the orange colour of an adult duck.

The duck's wings are fully grown, so it is able to fly.

Adult feathers replace the fluffy down.

Complete set of white adult feathers

Growing flight feathers

SIX WEEKS OLD

16 WEEKS OLD

3 FULL SIZE
By now, the duck looks just like its parents. Its plumage is made up of several different types of feather, and its enormous breast muscles are fully formed, enabling the young adult duck to fly for the first time.

HOW CUCKOOS WORK

Most birds raise their own young, but some get others to do the job for them. Female cuckoos lay their eggs in the nests of small songbirds, one in each nest. When a baby cuckoo hatches, it gets rid of any other eggs or young in the nest. Despite this, its foster parents never realize that the bird is an impostor, and instinctively keep feeding it until it is old enough to fly away.

The orange mouth lining may warn predators not to approach the nest.

The adult reed warbler must work hard to satisfy the appetite of the huge cuckoo chick.

▲ **IMPOSTOR**
By the time they are ready to fly, young cuckoos are nearly always far bigger than the adult birds that look after them. Here, a reed warbler struggles to feed an insect to a young Eurasian cuckoo, dwarfed by the outsized imposter it has raised.

This cuckoo's wing feathers are fully grown, so it will soon be able to fly away.

When fully developed, the cuckoo leaves the nest, but still may be fed by its foster parents.

The pin-tailed whydah chick's mouth mimics that of a common waxbill chick.

Common waxbill chick

MOUTH MIMICS

Unlike cuckoos, young African whydahs do not destroy the other eggs in the nest. They let them hatch, but claim a share of food by imitating their nest-mates, gaping for food to reveal similar markings inside the mouth.

TAKEOVER BID

An adult male cuckoo will sometimes lure a host bird away from its nest so that the female cuckoo can slip in. She pushes one of the eggs out of the nest, and then lays her own egg. The cuckoo egg resembles the eggs already in the nest. When the young cuckoo hatches, it ejects all the other eggs – and even any hatched chicks.

1 EGG DECEPTION
Cuckoos lay eggs with patterns that match the eggs of their victims. Each female targets a species that offers the best match, although the cuckoo egg is usually bigger.

2 FIRST OUT
The cuckoo egg develops faster than the other eggs and usually hatches before them. The young cuckoo is naked and blind.

3 KILLER INSTINCT
Within hours, the young cuckoo works each of the other eggs (or hatched chicks) onto its back and pushes them out of the nest. It does this to stop other chicks competing with it for food.

HOW OWLS SENSE PREY

A great grey owl does not have ear tufts, unlike many owls.

Owls are stealth hunters that use their keen senses, sharp claws, and soft feathers to swoop silently from their perch and snatch unsuspecting prey. Armed with super-sensitive hearing and vision, some owls can pinpoint the exact location of a moth in the dark or a mouse scampering under snow or fallen leaves. Most owls are nocturnal but some species, such as the great grey owl, also hunt by day.

▶ FACIAL DISC

The great grey owl's most striking feature is its large facial disc made from a concave ring of feathers. Each side of the face acts as one half of the disc, focusing sound towards each ear. The owl can adjust its facial feathers to focus sound even more precisely. The disc is especially big in this species to help it detect prey under snow.

HUNTING BY EAR

The great grey owl's right ear opens slightly lower than its left ear, which means sound from below arrives at the right ear fractionally sooner than it does at the left ear. The owl can use this time difference to work out the exact location of its prey, even when the prey is hidden under leaves or snow.

The facial disc collects sound energy and funnels it towards the ears.

The left ear opens slightly higher than the right ear, so sound reaches it later.

Prey's sound waves

The feathers form a disc shape, which directs sound towards the owl's ears.

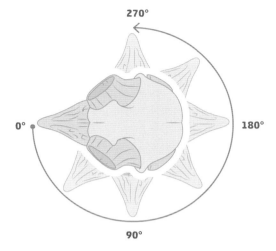

270°

180°

0°

90°

HEAD ROTATION
Owls have large, tubular-shaped eyes that cannot move in their sockets. However, owls can rotate their heads 270 degrees in each direction, allowing them to look behind themselves without moving their bodies.

Its forward-facing eyes give 3D vision, helping the owl to judge distance.

This tawny owl feather has a serrated edge.

SILENT FLIGHT
Some species of owl, including the great grey owl and the tawny owl, have a serrated, comb-like edge on their outer primary flight feathers. This muffles the sound of the owl's beating wings and enables its flight to be almost silent, so it can swoop down on its prey without being heard.

The beak is short enough not to interfere with the owl's vision.

The feathers fan out for landing.

Lightweight, overlapping feathers

SOARING ON THERMALS
Eagles save energy by soaring on thermals – rising columns of warm air. They circle upwards before gliding to the next thermal and soaring again. This means they can keep at great heights to scan for prey without flapping their wings.

Circling

HUNTING TECHNIQUE
Bald eagles swoop down onto water, drop their feet below the surface to catch a fish, and fly off with it. They sometimes steal fish from other birds, such as ospreys, and also scavenge on dead fish left by bears or leftovers from human picnics.

Each foot has four large claws called talons.

Human-eye, long-distance view

EAGLE VISION

HIGH-RESOLUTION VISION
Compared with humans, eagles have five times as many light receptors in the part of the eye that resolves images most sharply. They can see prey clearly at distances of 3 km (1.9 miles).

The broad wings can catch rising air currents, helping the eagle soar.

Ridges on the eagle's feet help it grip prey.

HOW **EAGLES** HUNT

With their enormous wingspans, hooked beaks, and keen eyesight, eagles are formidable hunters. They belong to a group known as raptors (birds of prey) and kill with their lethal talons. The largest of the raptors, eagles use their talons to grab animals from the ground or water. They then fly up to a perch and tear their catch apart, using a sharp hook at the tip of the powerful beak to butcher the carcass.

▲ **POWERFUL TALONS**

The force of this bald eagle's talons is usually strong enough to kill a fish outright when the eagle seizes it from the water. However, the eagle also has ridges on its feet that help it grip a slippery, struggling fish. The powerful talons can carry prey weighing up to a third of the eagle's weight.

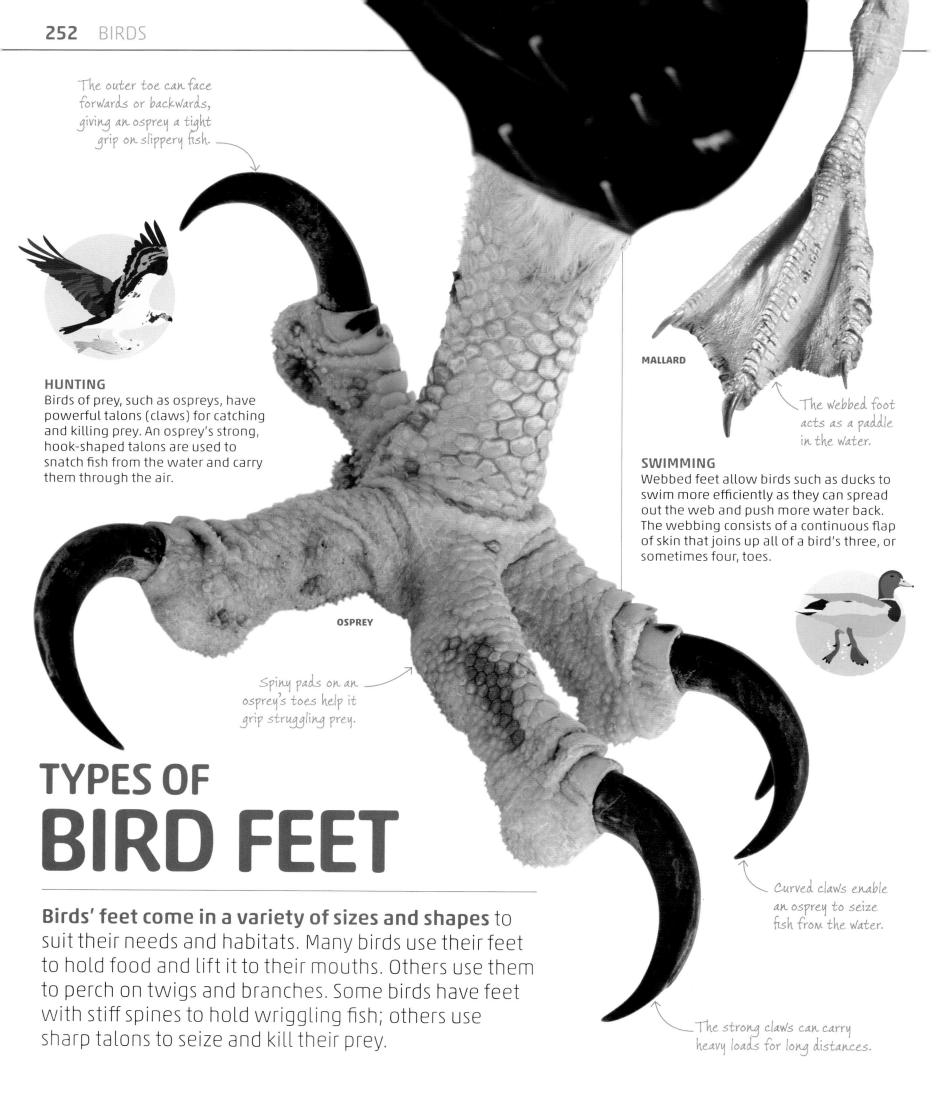

The outer toe can face forwards or backwards, giving an osprey a tight grip on slippery fish.

HUNTING
Birds of prey, such as ospreys, have powerful talons (claws) for catching and killing prey. An osprey's strong, hook-shaped talons are used to snatch fish from the water and carry them through the air.

MALLARD

The webbed foot acts as a paddle in the water.

SWIMMING
Webbed feet allow birds such as ducks to swim more efficiently as they can spread out the web and push more water back. The webbing consists of a continuous flap of skin that joins up all of a bird's three, or sometimes four, toes.

OSPREY

Spiny pads on an osprey's toes help it grip struggling prey.

TYPES OF BIRD FEET

Birds' feet come in a variety of sizes and shapes to suit their needs and habitats. Many birds use their feet to hold food and lift it to their mouths. Others use them to perch on twigs and branches. Some birds have feet with stiff spines to hold wriggling fish; others use sharp talons to seize and kill their prey.

Curved claws enable an osprey to seize fish from the water.

The strong claws can carry heavy loads for long distances.

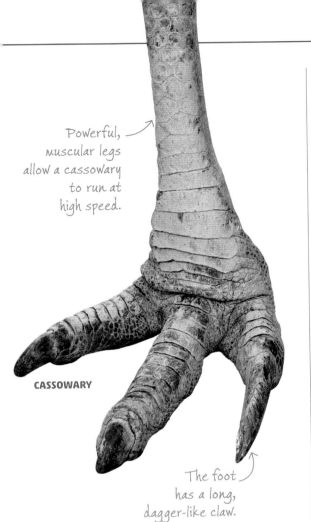

Powerful, muscular legs allow a cassowary to run at high speed.

CASSOWARY

The foot has a long, dagger-like claw.

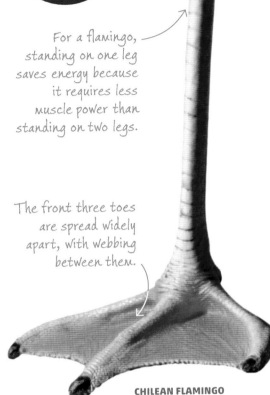

For a flamingo, standing on one leg saves energy because it requires less muscle power than standing on two legs.

The front three toes are spread widely apart, with webbing between them.

CHILEAN FLAMINGO

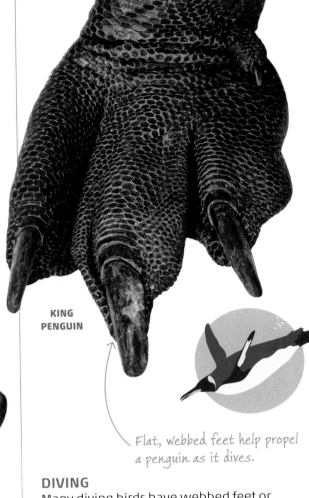

KING PENGUIN

Flat, webbed feet help propel a penguin as it dives.

RUNNING

Flightless birds, such as cassowaries, have muscular legs and sturdy feet. A cassowary can run at up to 50 kph (31 mph) and jump up to 1.5 m (4.9 ft) high. Cassowaries have a dagger-like claw that they use when they kick animals in defence.

WADING

Birds that wade in shallow water to feed have long toes, often with webbing between them. This spreads their weight to stop them sinking into sand or mud, and helps them maintain their balance. Their long legs enable them to walk through water without getting their feathers wet.

DIVING

Many diving birds have webbed feet or stiff, scaly flaps on their toes to propel themselves in water. The king penguin can reach depths of 300 m (1,000 ft) and has specially adapted feet to withstand freezing temperatures on the ice.

GRIPPING

Owls have very powerful feet, with curved, razor-sharp talons for perching or grasping prey. On each foot, two toes face forwards and two backwards. This allows the toes to splay out as far as possible, making the grip even stronger.

OWL

The talons have sharp tips for piercing flesh.

PREEN OIL prevents a duck's feathers from absorbing water.

The preen gland near the tail contains waterproofing oil that makes water slide off the duck's back.

▶ STRONG SWIMMER

Ducks such as this mallard swim by pushing and pulling their webbed feet through the water, which propels the duck forwards. Ducks can swim more efficiently by spreading out the webbing of a foot as it pushes back against the water and folding up the web when pulling a foot forwards.

PREENING

Ducks and other waterfowl have very effective preen glands. They spread preening oil over their feathers to waterproof themselves, keeping their feathers dry and helping them to stay buoyant and warm.

Strong, muscular legs provide swimming power.

Webbing between a duck's front three toes helps it swim, paddle, steer, and walk on mud.

The feathers are waterproofed.

The webbing of a duck's foot can be spread out to increase the power of each leg stroke as it swims.

Preening oil is smeared around.

TAKING OFF ON WATER

Ducks such as mallards have relatively large wings in relation to their body weight and can take off by making a single thrust with their feet. Heavier waterfowl, such as swans, must run on the water to gain momentum before taking off.

HOW DUCKS SWIM

With waterproofed feathers, webbed feet, and streamlined bodies that make them excellent swimmers, ducks are well adapted to their aquatic habitats. They have beaks that can filter out food from water. Most ducklings can swim as soon as their feathers have dried after hatching. As well as being strong swimmers, most duck species are fast and powerful fliers, capable of migrating long distances.

A duck's long body helps it float on water, but makes it walk awkwardly on land.

A layer of down feathers beneath the waterproof feathers keeps the duck warm in cold water and helps it to float by trapping air.

Mallards are dabbling ducks, which means they dip their heads under the surface of the water to feed, rather than diving.

The inside of a duck's beak is lined with comblike structures called lamellae, which filter out food from water when the duck eats.

A sensitive, flattened beak allows ducks to forage for food using touch.

The eyes have strong muscles to help the lenses focus underwater.

In this side view of a duck, six of its nine inflated air sacs are visible. The air sacs hide the lungs and most of the duck's internal organs.

The duck inflates its air sacs to stay afloat.

AIR SACS

Like all birds, ducks have nine air sacs that surround their lungs. These sacs pump air through the lungs and ensure a steady flow of oxygen into the blood. Ducks inflate their air sacs when they are swimming, and some ducks partially deflate them when they dive.

LANDING ON WATER

By landing on water, ducks are able to come in at speed and have a softer touchdown than on land. Ducks lower their legs and spread the webbing between their toes to take the impact of the landing and slow them down.

HOW KINGFISHERS DIVE
A kingfisher dive is over in seconds. Each dive is impressive in its precision, as the kingfisher aims its streamlined body like a missile to catch a fish.

1 **TARGET SPOTTED**
After spotting a fish just below the water's surface, the kingfisher begins to judge its angle of attack – and even factors in the bending of light at the water's surface.

The kingfisher perches on a branch above the water.

2 **DIVE BEGINS**
The kingfisher drops off its perch, and dives towards the surface of the water. It may flap its wings to adjust its dive as it goes.

The head and body are straightened, ready for the plunge.

3 **THE APPROACH**
As it gets close to the surface, the kingfisher pulls its wings towards its body until they are about half closed. They are also moved back to make a more streamlined shape.

By slightly changing its wing position, the bird can alter its speed and direction.

4 **INTO THE WATER**
The sharply pointed bill cuts through the water first. At this point the kingfisher has closed its "third eyelid" as protection against hitting the water.

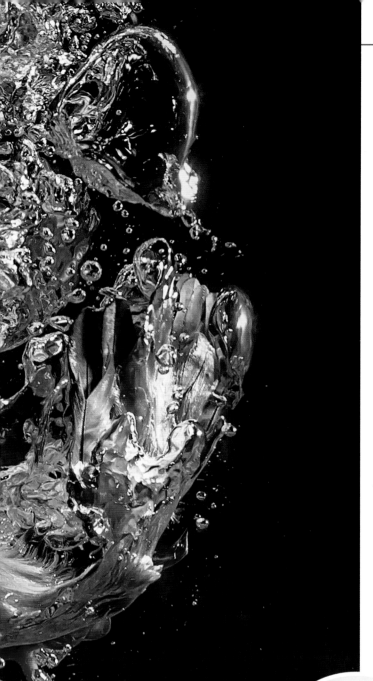

HOW **BIRDS** DIVE

Diving birds use very dramatic tactics to hunt. Some birds can hurtle into water from above at speeds exceeding 80 kph (50 mph), to take their prey by surprise. Other birds dive from the surface, and are adept swimmers. Diving birds must work hard to stay underwater, as their light bodies are inclined to float.

◄ COMMON KINGFISHER

Diving to a depth of 1 m (3.3 ft), the common kingfisher feeds primarily on small fish, but may also eat amphibians, crustaceans, and insects. Kingfishers dive so fast that they can even penetrate a layer of ice to make a catch. When diving, a "third eyelid" – called a nictitating membrane – closes over each eye to protect it underwater.

DIVING BIRDS

Many diving birds can plunge to great depths and hunt underwater for minutes at a time. Powerful muscles that work the legs or wings help to propel them when underwater.

FOOT-PROPELLED DIVERS

Grebes have strong legs and feet with toe flaps that work like paddles. They dive to hunt, but also to avoid danger.

WING-PROPELLED DIVERS

Guillemots can reach 210 m (690 ft) underwater, the deepest of any diving bird. They flap their wings to swim.

WETSUIT DIVERS

Cormorants must dry their soaked wings after diving as they lack the waterproofing of other birds.

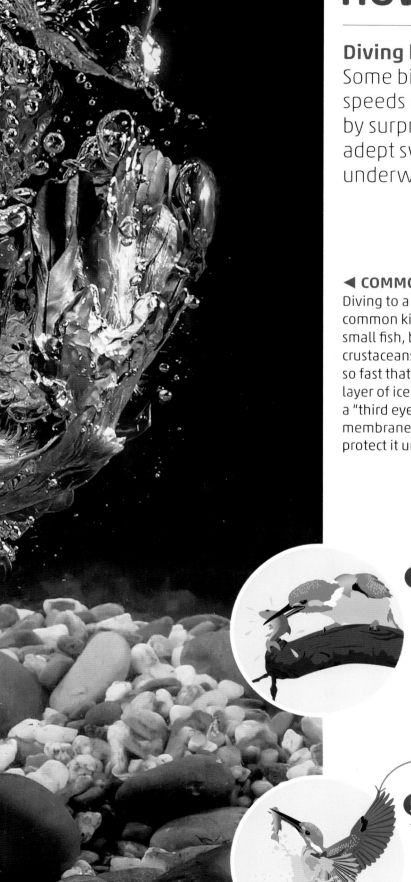

6 THE KILL

Holding the fish by its tail, the kingfisher strikes it on a branch to stun it. This also shatters the fish's spine, so it will pass more easily through the kingfisher's digestive system when eaten.

Water rolls off the kingfisher's waterproof plumage.

5 THE RETURN

After catching a small fish, the kingfisher's natural buoyancy and a couple of wing flaps brings it back to the surface. As it flies upwards, it holds the fish cross-wise in its bill.

HOW PENGUINS MOVE

As flightless birds, penguins have all the skill in the water that they lack in the air. With super-sleek bodies, dense plumage, flippers for wings, and powerful legs set far back on the body to propel them through the water, they swim faster and deeper than any other birds. Gentoo penguins, the fastest, reach 35 kph (22 mph) in short bursts underwater. Penguins can't breathe underwater, but emperor penguins can hold their breath for up to ten minutes.

▼ **LIVING AT SEA**
These king penguins spend far longer at sea than on land, even in icy winter temperatures. A thick layer of fat, or blubber, under their plumage offers superb insulation. They hunt fish and squid, and parents with a hungry chick to feed may dive 100 times a day. King penguins can dive over 300 m (1,000 ft) deep.

Jets of bubbles surround the penguin as it dives, reducing water resistance and helping it gain speed.

The flippers have evolved from wings and are suited to swimming rather than flight.

A penguin's streamlined body shape makes it an extremely agile swimmer and diver.

Short, oily feathers on the body and flippers trap air to keep a penguin warm and help it float.

Strong breast muscles power a penguin's flippers.

A long beak with barbs inside helps a penguin catch fish.

The webbed feet aid swimming and act as a rudder, helping to steer the penguin in the water.

MOVING ON ICE

When out of the water, penguins move awkwardly and slowly with some effort, so most stay as close to the sea as possible. To cope with the limitations of a heavy, plump body and stumpy legs, they leap, slide, and dive whenever they can. At other times, an unsteady waddle is the best they can manage.

LEAPING
Emperor penguins return to the ice by darting out of the water. Speed is of the essence, as predatory leopard seals lurk nearby.

TOBOGGANING
To save time and energy, penguins such as this chinstrap flop onto their round bellies to slide down icy slopes.

WADDLING
Rear-set legs give penguins an upright posture, forcing them to shuffle clumsily. They stick their flippers out for balance.

DIVING
At their breeding colonies, Adélie penguins line up to make impressive leaps between ice floes or to enter the water.

FLIPPER BONES

A penguin's flipper is stiff, narrow, and curves gently backwards – the optimum shape for a paddle. It has solid, tightly packed bones and bends only at the shoulder, unlike a normal bird's wing, which also moves at the wrist and elbow joints.

Penguins have a dark back to camouflage them from above when swimming. Large birds such as eagles prey on penguins from the air.

The eyes are adapted for underwater vision

A penguin's white belly gives it camouflage because, seen from below, it is difficult to distinguish from the bright surface of the water. This protects the penguin from predators such as seals.

A gland just above the penguin's eye helps it filter salt out of sea water as it catches and swallows fish. The salt – which is bad for a penguin's health in large quantities – is secreted through the penguin's beak.

The flipper sweeps up and down in a similar motion to the wing of a flying bird, but only the downstroke propels the penguin forwards.

SURVIVING THE STORM

On the remote island of South Georgia, between South America and the icy Antarctic, these king penguins huddle tightly together to keep warm in a blizzard. Breeding penguins shelter their eggs and chicks, ensuring that all the birds survive the bitter cold. Keeping warm and staying still for long periods of time helps penguins save energy. This is particularly important in the winter, when feeding is difficult.

HOW OSTRICHES WORK

The ostrich is the largest living bird and the fastest animal on two legs. It lives on open plains in Africa, where being big and speedy is an excellent way to avoid predators. Ostriches are flightless birds as they don't have the strong breast muscles needed to power wings. They are closely related to rheas, emus, and kiwis.

Muscles for running are concentrated in the thighs, keeping the legs lightweight.

Strong cords called tendons run down the leg, connecting thigh muscles to the foot bones.

The smaller toe scarcely touches the ground and plays little role in walking and running.

▶ **GIGANTIC FOOT**
The ostrich is the only bird with just two toes. The much bigger toe clips the ground like a hoof, helping the bird pick up speeds of up to 70 kph (44 mph). Ostriches and their relatives evolved from flying ancestors. In grasslands and deserts, they came to rely more on running, and gradually lost their ability to fly.

Large scales called scutes cover the tops of the toes.

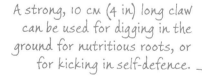
A strong, 10 cm (4 in) long claw can be used for digging in the ground for nutritious roots, or for kicking in self-defence.

CLOSE RELATIVES

Ostriches belong to a group of flightless birds called ratites. It is believed that ratites gained and lost the ability to fly many times in their evolution. Each continent has its own native species of ratite.

CASSOWARY

Living in New Guinea rainforests, cassowaries are related to the emu of the Australian outback.

RHEA

South American rheas share the floppy wings of African ostriches, but are smaller in size.

KIWI

The smallest ratites, forest-living kiwis from New Zealand have short legs, and a long probing bill.

Tiny, bead-like scales cover the sides of the foot.

The weight of the ostrich is supported by the larger of the two toes on each foot.

RUNNING

An ostrich's long legs give long strides. Like other birds, their muscles are concentrated high up in the thighs, leaving the lower part of the leg lightweight and worked by tendons. This gives the ostrich an extra-fast swing to each giant stride.

The wings are used for balance when running.

The extensor thigh muscle swings the leg forwards.

The calf muscles pull the tendons to straighten the leg.

The flexor thigh muscle pulls the leg back.

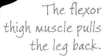

Mammals evolved from reptiles about 220 million years ago. **The first mammals** were small, shrew-like insect eaters living in the shadows of dinosaurs. But once the dinosaurs died out around 65 million years ago, mammals became more **diverse** and spread over the Earth. **Humans** are mammals, so we share many similarities with other animals in this group.

MAMMALS

MAMMAL DIVERSITY

From small beginnings as rat-sized insect eaters, mammals have evolved into an amazing variety of forms. Today they dominate life on land, but they have also adapted to life in the sea and in the air.

PRIMATES
Monkeys, apes, and their relatives are some of the most intelligent mammals.

UNGULATES
These hoofed mammals are mainly plant eaters, and many live in herds.

RODENTS
About 40 per cent of mammal species are rodents, such as rats, mice, and chinchillas.

BATS
The only mammals that can fly using flapping wings, bats are mainly active at night.

MONOTREMES
Some mammals, including this echidna, reproduce by laying eggs, as reptiles do.

MARSUPIALS
These mammals are born as tiny young that usually develop in a pouch.

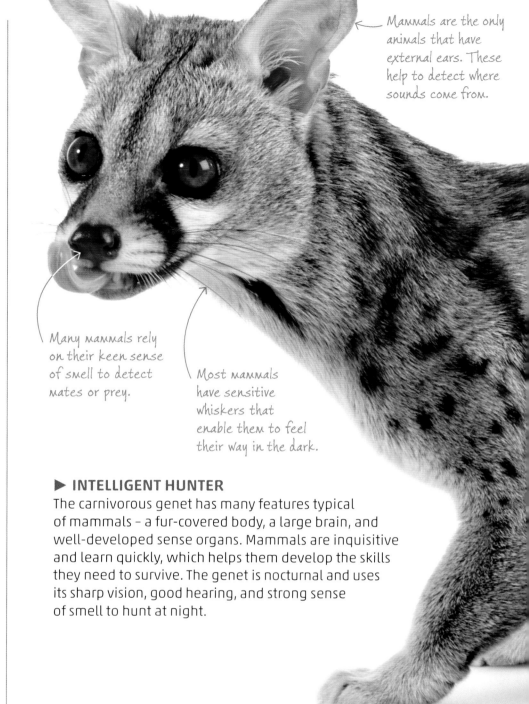

Mammals are the only animals that have external ears. These help to detect where sounds come from.

Many mammals rely on their keen sense of smell to detect mates or prey.

Most mammals have sensitive whiskers that enable them to feel their way in the dark.

▶ INTELLIGENT HUNTER

The carnivorous genet has many features typical of mammals – a fur-covered body, a large brain, and well-developed sense organs. Mammals are inquisitive and learn quickly, which helps them develop the skills they need to survive. The genet is nocturnal and uses its sharp vision, good hearing, and strong sense of smell to hunt at night.

WARM BLOOD

Mammals are warm-blooded, meaning they maintain a constant body temperature. To cool down in hot weather, elephants flap their enormous ears. On this thermal image the ears have a different colour from the rest of the body because they are cooler.

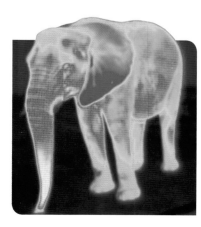

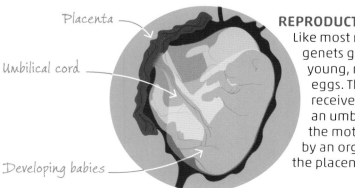

Placenta

Umbilical cord

Developing babies

REPRODUCTION

Like most mammals, genets give birth to live young, rather than laying eggs. The growing babies receive nutrients through an umbilical cord linked to the mother's bloodstream by an organ called the placenta.

HOW **MAMMALS** WORK

Unlike their cold-blooded reptile ancestors, which had scaly skin and laid eggs, mammals are warm-blooded, have coats of hair or fur, and give birth to live young. All mammals feed their babies with milk and care for them until they are strong enough to look after themselves. There are more than 5,000 species of mammal, including the largest animal that has ever lived on Earth – the blue whale – and our own species.

A thick coat of fur stops a mammal's body heat escaping during cold weather.

Most mammals have a tail for balance when climbing and jumping, or for grabbing objects like an extra arm.

Most mammals walk on all fours. Genets walk on their toes, like cats.

FUR LAYERS
Like most mammals, the polar bear has two layers of fur. The outer fur consists of long guard hairs. These protect the underfur from getting too wet and give the coat its colour. The inner layer is made up of more densely packed finer hairs that trap warm air like a quilted jacket. A polar bear also has a thick layer of insulating fat under its skin.

Long guard hairs protect the dense underfur.

Fat under the skin can be up to 10 cm (4 in) thick.

Beneath its white coat, the polar bear's skin is black.

Short, woolly underfur keeps the bear warm.

BARBED SPINES
Also known as quills, the spines of porcupines are highly modified hairs coated in thick layers of keratin, a tough protein. They have barbed tips and are loosely rooted in the porcupine's skin, so if stabbed into an enemy they detach and stay embedded in the wound.

Each spine is tipped with tiny backward-facing barbs that act like hooks, making it difficult to remove the spine.

HOW **HAIR** WORKS

Up to 90 per cent of the food that a mammal eats is turned into the energy it uses to keep its body warm.
The less heat it loses, the less it has to eat, so good insulation can be vital, especially in cold climates. This is why mammals have hair. It's a unique feature of mammals, and often grows densely to form thick fur that traps layers of warm air.

▶ DIFFERENT COATS
Some mammals have virtually naked skin, but most have furry coats that help to keep them warm. Tiny muscles attached to every hair can make them bristle up for extra insulation. Hair colour can vary, forming patterns. These can provide camouflage, either for defence from predators or to conceal hunters from their prey. In some mammals, hair has evolved to form defensive spines, or even scales.

ARCTIC INSULATION

A polar bear has a very dense fur coat that, combined with a thick layer of fat under the skin, keeps it warm throughout the polar winter. It lives on Arctic Ocean sea ice, and often swims in near-freezing water, so good insulation is essential to its survival.

Each hair of the outer fur is hollow and transparent, but looks white.

SPIKY DEFENCE

Porcupines have a coat of sharp spines. These are thickened hairs, which grow from the skin in the same way. The spines of the North American porcupine lie flat against its body. When the animal feels threatened, muscles in the skin raise the spines and make them fan out, ready to deter an attacker.

About 30,000 spines cover a porcupine's body.

CAMOUFLAGE COLOURS

Black and orange hair growing from the skin of a tiger is arranged in bands to create a pattern of vertical stripes. In the tiger's native forests, the stripes disguise the hunter's shape as it stalks its prey through the trees and long grass.

Stripes hide the tiger in a forest's shady undergrowth.

ARMOUR PLATING

The hair of a pangolin is combined with a flexible armour of overlapping scales. Like the pangolin's hair and claws, these are made of tough keratin. If attacked, the pangolin rolls into a prickly ball, with the edge of each scale acting as a sharp, protective blade.

Scales cover the pangolin from head to tail.

HOW MAMMAL SENSES WORK

Like other animals, mammals rely on an array of senses, both to keep them safe and help them to find food. Most mammals have the same five senses as us, but many rely more heavily on scent and sound, especially if they are active at night. Some mammals also have extra senses that we can barely imagine.

▶ SHARP SENSES

Many mammal species have evolved senses to suit their environments. Hunters like this nocturnal red fox rely heavily on smell and hearing to track their prey, including voles and mice.

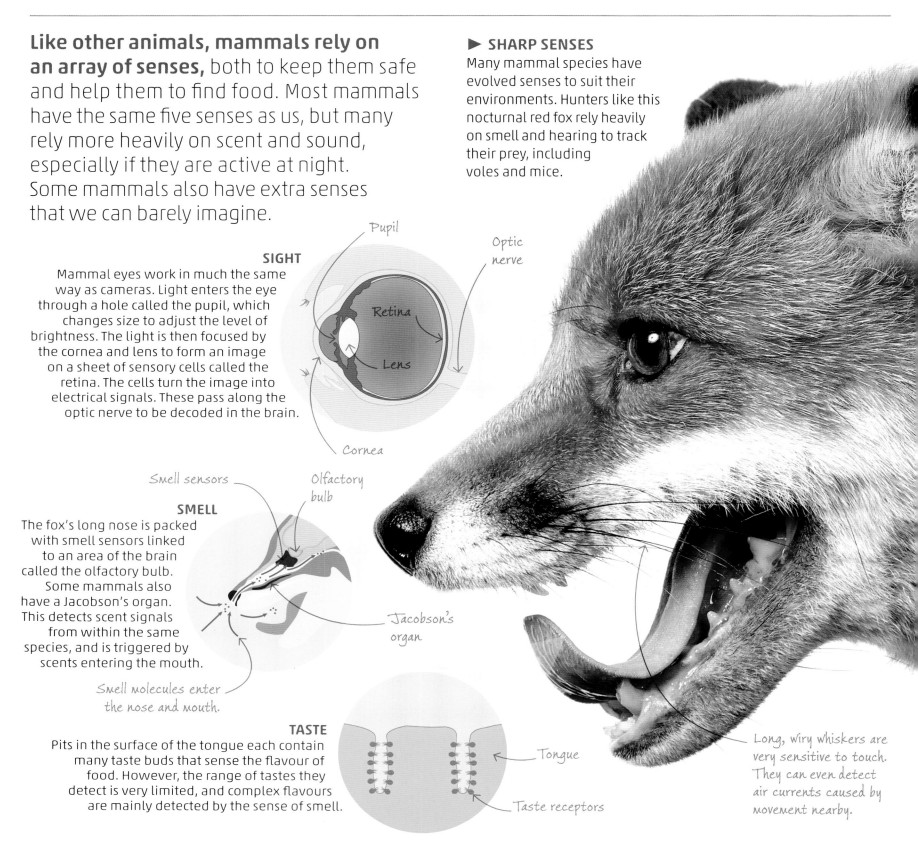

SIGHT

Mammal eyes work in much the same way as cameras. Light enters the eye through a hole called the pupil, which changes size to adjust the level of brightness. The light is then focused by the cornea and lens to form an image on a sheet of sensory cells called the retina. The cells turn the image into electrical signals. These pass along the optic nerve to be decoded in the brain.

Pupil

Optic nerve

Retina

Lens

Cornea

SMELL

The fox's long nose is packed with smell sensors linked to an area of the brain called the olfactory bulb. Some mammals also have a Jacobson's organ. This detects scent signals from within the same species, and is triggered by scents entering the mouth.

Smell sensors

Olfactory bulb

Jacobson's organ

Smell molecules enter the nose and mouth.

TASTE

Pits in the surface of the tongue each contain many taste buds that sense the flavour of food. However, the range of tastes they detect is very limited, and complex flavours are mainly detected by the sense of smell.

Tongue

Taste receptors

Long, wiry whiskers are very sensitive to touch. They can even detect air currents caused by movement nearby.

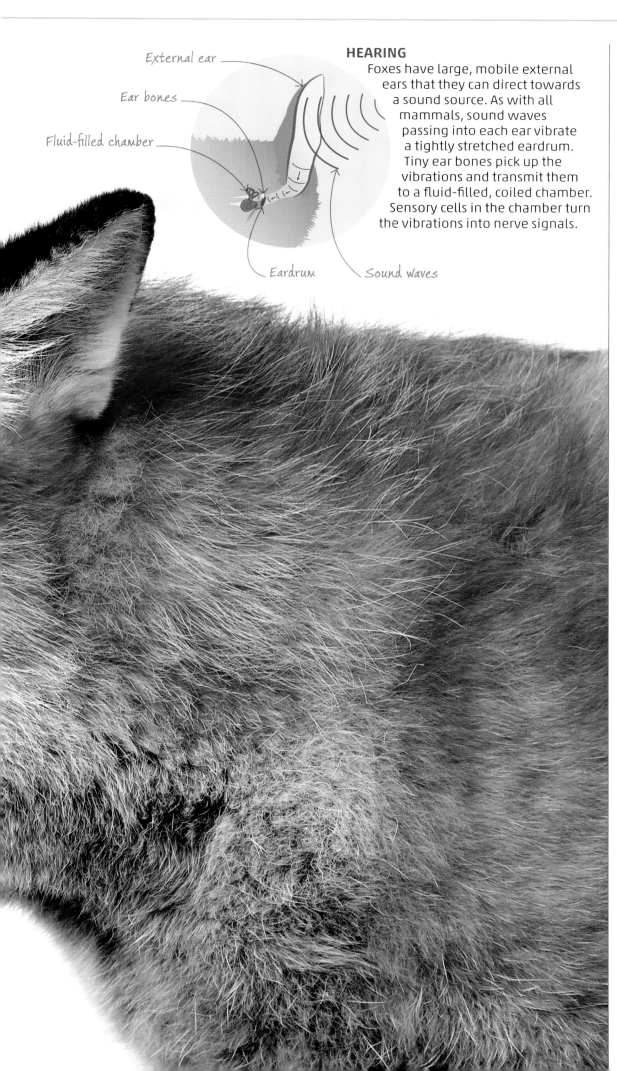

HEARING

External ear

Ear bones

Fluid-filled chamber

Foxes have large, mobile external ears that they can direct towards a sound source. As with all mammals, sound waves passing into each ear vibrate a tightly stretched eardrum. Tiny ear bones pick up the vibrations and transmit them to a fluid-filled, coiled chamber. Sensory cells in the chamber turn the vibrations into nerve signals.

Eardrum

Sound waves

SPECIAL SENSES

The senses of many mammals have become specialized for life in particular environments. Some have lost certain senses – for example, burrowing mammals that live in total darkness are often blind. But others have extra senses that allow them to live in places where normal perception is not good enough.

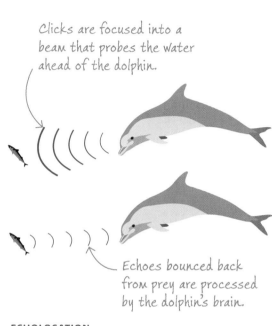

Clicks are focused into a beam that probes the water ahead of the dolphin.

Echoes bounced back from prey are processed by the dolphin's brain.

ECHOLOCATION

A dolphin senses its surroundings by sound, but not in the way we do. By emitting a rapid series of clicks and detecting the echoes bounced back from objects in the water, a dolphin can build up an image of its environment without using its eyes. This is vital for hunting in cloudy water. Bats use a similar echolocation system.

The bill picks up electrical signals from prey.

About 40,000 tiny sensors are located on the tip of the bill.

ELECTRORECEPTION

The rubbery, duck-like bill of the Australian platypus is equipped with a sense that is virtually unique in mammals. It can detect the electrical nerve signals that control the muscles of small animal prey. The platypus uses this extra sense to locate animals in the murky depths of muddy pools, where vision is useless.

HOW MAMMALS ARE BORN

Most mammals spend a long time growing inside their mother's body, where they are nourished by an organ called a placenta. This supplies the baby with food and oxygen from the mother's blood via a tube called an umbilical cord. When the young are old enough to survive outside the mother's body, she gives birth – but the babies are still vulnerable and will need caring for until they can look after themselves.

▶ **NEWLY EMERGED**
Like many newborn mammals, kittens are highly dependent on their mother in the first weeks of life. They huddle close to her for warmth and feed on her nutrient-rich milk, which helps them to grow quickly. Mammal mothers and babies learn to recognize each other by their distinctive scents.

Newborn kittens are damp because they develop surrounded by fluid inside the mother's body.

Born blind, newborn kittens do not open their eyes for at least a week.

The blind kittens rely on their sense of smell to identify their mother.

LITTERS
Cats usually produce litters of two to five kittens. Many other mammals also have litters of multiple young. In wild mammals, not all the babies will survive natural dangers to reach maturity.

The kittens each grow in their own separate sac.

Each kitten is wrapped in its own placenta.

Uterus

Birth canal

GIVING BIRTH
Baby mammals develop in an organ called a uterus, each with their own separate placenta. Each kitten grows inside a protective sac, which is filled with fluid. When they are ready to be born, muscles in the wall of the uterus contract, pushing the babies down the birth canal one at a time.

SIZE AT BIRTH
Many large mammals, such as elephants and whales, give birth to big babies after long pregnancies. Their young can get around on their own soon after birth. However, other mammals are born tiny, blind, and helpless after a shorter time in the uterus.

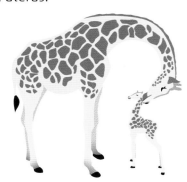

Giraffes are born after a year and a half in the uterus, weighing a tenth of their mother's weight. They can walk soon after they are born.

Orcas (killer whales) spend around 550 days in the uterus before being born in the water. A baby orca is a fiftieth of an adult's weight.

Panda babies are born tiny and helpless.

Giant pandas are born after 160 days and weigh one-thousandth of an adult's weight. They need more care than most newborns.

An adult kangaroo weighs 100,000 times more than a baby.

Kangaroos are marsupials – mammals that lack a placenta. Born tiny and undeveloped, they crawl into their mother's pouch to develop fully.

HOW MAMMALS
FEED THEIR YOUNG

**VIEW FROM SIDE OF BABY GUINEA PIG
SUCKLING FROM MOTHER**

Unlike others in the animal kingdom, female mammals produce milk from unique organs called mammary glands. Infants feed on this milk for weeks or even years until they can be introduced to adult food in a process called weaning.

▶ PLACENTAL MAMMALS
Most mammals, such as this guinea pig, give birth to live young rather than laying eggs. Before birth, young are nourished in the mother's uterus by an organ called the placenta. After birth, they feed on milk from teats linked to the mother's mammary glands.

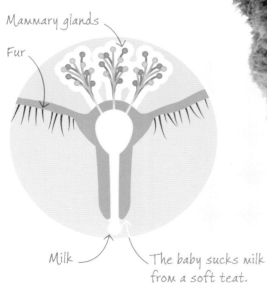

Mammary glands

Fur

Milk

The baby sucks milk from a soft teat.

SPECIAL BLEND
Milk is a concoction of fats, proteins, and sugars, which are essential for a baby's development. Light reflected by its many fat molecules causes milk to appear white.

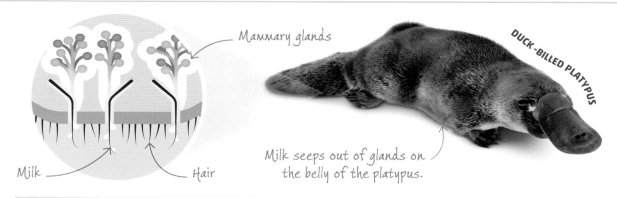

Mammary glands

Milk

Hair

DUCK-BILLED PLATYPUS

Milk seeps out of glands on the belly of the platypus.

MONOTREMES
Some mammals, known as monotremes, lay eggs instead of giving birth to live young. These include echidnas and platypuses. When the young hatch, their mother feeds them on milk, but she does not have teats; instead, her milk seeps into her fur from mammary glands and pools on her belly for her babies to lick.

VIEW FROM BELOW

This baby, like many placental mammals, is well developed at birth.

GREY KANGAROO

Pouch

MARSUPIALS
Unlike placental mammals, marsupials such as kangaroos produce tiny, half-formed babies after short pregnancies. Helpless and undeveloped, these babies crawl up their mother's body, usually into a pouch, and cling to a teat supplying the nutrients they need. They may stay in the pouch for weeks or even months.

The mother's ears are pricked for any hint of danger to her cub.

HOW
MAMMALS
CARE FOR THEIR YOUNG

Mammals care for their young in a variety of ways, including providing protection, food, warmth, and shelter. They invest a lot of time and energy in raising their offspring, in order to maximize their chance of survival. They also produce fewer young than most other animals, allowing them to focus their full attention on their offspring.

PROTECTION
Young mammals are easy prey, and depend on their parents to protect them from predators. This donkey must stand her ground to protect her foal as running away will leave it vulnerable to attack.

▼ TRANSPORT AND SHELTER

Like most mammals, tigers have just a few young, caring for each one to ensure its survival. When the cubs are old enough to venture outside the den, their mother will carry them in her mouth to guard them from dangerous situations, such as encounters with venomous snakes. If another predator discovers their den, the entire family may need to move home.

The cub is carried out of dangerous situations.

This cub is old enough to explore outside its den with its mother.

Camouflage stripes help the cub hide from predators that it is too small to fight.

The tiger's sharp claws are poised to defend against any threat to its young.

Soft, padded feet allow the tiger to tread quietly as it travels with its baby.

FOOD

Before they learn to hunt for themselves, carnivorous mammals rely on their parents to bring them food. Cats often bring live prey back to their cubs so the young can practise their hunting techniques.

WARMTH

Warmth is essential to young mammals, which are small and so lose heat easily. Parents ensure they don't get cold, sometimes by huddling as a family, like these Japanese macaques in their snowy mountain habitat.

1 NEWBORN FOX
At birth, a red fox is blind, deaf, toothless, and almost helpless. Its only instinct is to drink its mother's milk, which contains three times more fat than cow's milk. The baby grows rapidly, tripling its weight in ten days.

Fluffy, dark fur

Kits' eyes stay closed for the first two weeks.

NEWBORN FOX

A fox's eyes are blue at first.

HOW MAMMALS GROW UP

2 FIRST STEPS
The kit's eyes and ears open when it is two weeks old, and it becomes aware of its surroundings. By four weeks, it has taken its first unsteady steps. It starts to eat partially digested food regurgitated by its parents, as well as its mother's milk.

4 WEEKS OLD

Mammals take longer to become independent than other animals. Unlike baby reptiles, which fend for themselves as soon as they hatch, young mammals must be cared for by their parents while they gradually acquire the skills they need to survive on their own.

HOW FOXES GROW UP ▶
Foxes undergo many physical and mental changes as they grow from kits (young foxes) to adults that can produce kits of their own. These include growing larger and stronger, becoming able to see, and learning to walk, hunt, and look after young.

The ears grow larger to stand fully alert.

The blue eyes turn golden.

3 LEARNING FAST
At eight weeks old, the kit is eating solid food brought back to the den by its parents. It cannot hunt for itself, but it starts experimenting by chasing, and sometimes catching, insects and other small animals.

8 WEEKS OLD

EARLY LEARNING
Recognizing its parents is one of the first things a mammal learns. This involves a process called imprinting, where babies form an attachment to their first carer. This is important as they need their parents to look after them as they grow up.

WATCH AND LEARN
Mammals acquire some of their skills by watching others and copying their behaviour. At first, baby elephants awkwardly lie down to drink through their lips. Only by watching adults do they learn to use their trunks to squirt water into their mouths instead.

Although still young, these foxes have their bright adult coats.

4 YOUNG ADULTS
By 12 weeks, a hierarchy has been established among kits, and they play together, stalking, pouncing, and chasing each other, both for fun and to learn the hunting and fighting skills they will need in later life.

12 WEEKS OLD

HOW HIERARCHY WORKS

Many mammals live in social groups of several adults and their young. Within these groups, one animal or a pair dominates all the others in the group, who may all have similar rank, or who may form a hierarchy in which each animal has its own place.

▶ IN CHARGE

Gorillas live in troops led by a single mature male, known as the silverback because of the silvery fur on his back. He decides where the troop feeds and sleeps, and defends it from predators and rival males that may try to take over the troop.

THE TROOP

The rest of the gorilla troop consists of adult females and their young, and sometimes a few immature, dark-furred males called blackbacks. They all have similar importance within the troop.

As part of their threat display, silverbacks hoot.

A silverback beats his chest in a threat display to ward off a rival male.

All the baby gorillas in the troop are the offspring of the silverback.

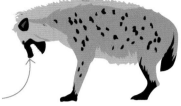

DOMINANT

A lowered head, flattened ears, and bared teeth indicate submission.

SUBORDINATE

A dominant female displays her importance by raising her head.

PECKING ORDER

Most mammal hierarchies are ruled by dominant males, but spotted hyena clans are dominated by females. Unlike gorillas, they form a pecking order. Each member of the clan submits to higher-ranking animals, but dominates any that are lower in the hierarchy. Their dominance or submission is expressed by their body language.

RULING QUEEN

East African naked mole rats are burrowing rodents that live in complex societies like those of honey bees. Each colony is controlled by a queen who is mother to all the young. She is attended by two or three breeding males. All the other mole rats – up to 300 of them – are workers that dig burrows, find food, and defend their queen.

Smaller workers forage, look after the offspring, and maintain tunnels.

Larger workers also defend the burrow.

Breeding males

Queen with offspring

▶ UNDERWATER TACTICS

Some of the most sophisticated pack-hunting techniques have been developed by marine mammals, especially dolphins and orcas (killer whales). These intelligent mammals live in family groups that are in constant communication to help organize their hunt.

Dolphins swim round the bait ball to prevent prey from escaping.

Fish squeeze together in a swirling ball.

Each dolphin gets a chance to share the feast.

HERDING FISH

One tactic used by dolphins is to herd fish into a tight ball. The dolphins swoop around the fish, scaring them together, while they take turns to dart through the shoal and snap up as many fish as possible.

HOW PACK HUNTING WORKS

Most meat-eating mammals hunt alone, but a few hunt in groups and share the prey they catch. This tactic has several advantages. A group can overpower and kill an animal that is bigger and stronger than any individual hunter. It can also surround animals, or split up to drive them into an ambush. Only the most intelligent, highly social mammals are capable of such teamwork.

Dolphins work as a team to catch their prey.

DEADLY WAVE

Orcas are giant dolphins that often prey on other mammals, including seals. In Antarctic waters, they have perfected a way of catching seals resting on drifting ice floes. Swimming in formation, several orcas surge towards the ice floe and dive under it. This creates a wave that sweeps over the floe, washing the seal into the water. The orcas drag it below the surface to drown it, and then share it between them.

The wave pushes the seal off the ice.

The orcas' speed pushes up a deadly wave.

THE LONG CHASE

African wild dogs have a simple hunting strategy – they chase their prey until it is exhausted. At that point, one dog races ahead of the animal to stop it in its tracks. Another flings itself at the victim's tail, while the most agile hunter seizes its upper lip. The end is quick.

Lionesses drive the impalas towards the trap.

The impalas run from the predators.

Lionesses hide, ready to ambush the impalas.

AMBUSH HUNTERS

In a pride of lions, the females do most of the hunting. They use teamwork, dividing into groups with different jobs. Some slip around the far side of the prey to lie in ambush. Others stalk the prey, then break cover to make them run. Meanwhile, lionesses on each side scare the prey straight into the trap.

OCEAN GIANTS

Found throughout the world's oceans, sperm whales live in groups called pods. They are the largest living predators on Earth, and dive to depths of more than 2 km (1.2 miles) in search of their favourite prey – deepwater squid. When a mother dives for food, members of the pod keep watch over the young, protecting them from sharks and other predators. Between dives, sperm whales like to float beneath the sunlit ocean surface.

THREAT TACTICS

Most conflicts between mammals end with one animal scaring the other away before any fighting happens. The scarier the animal can look, the more successful it will be. This has led to the evolution of some alarming threat displays.

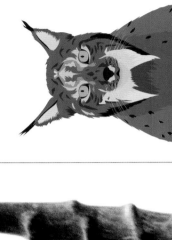

CANINE FRIGHT

Male olive baboons have long, sharp canine teeth. To avoid a fight, they intimidate each other by yawning as wide as they can, displaying their long canine teeth.

TWICE AS BIG

When a lynx is relaxed, its fur falls sleekly around its face. But if it feels threatened, its fur stands on end, making the lynx look much bigger than it is, so its enemy backs off.

DANGEROUS BATTLE

When different species come into conflict, the risks are higher. This dispute between spotted hyenas and lions is over food, and if threats do not work, the resulting fight could be lethal.

HOW CONFLICT WORKS

As mammals compete to survive and breed, they come into conflict. Some disputes flare up between different species squabbling over food, but most involve members of the same species, usually males, competing for territory and mates. These conflicts often begin with aggressive threat displays, but may end in a fight.

HEAD-TO-HEAD

On the plains of Africa, rival male Thomson's gazelles come into conflict over territory. Fighting can be risky, so each gazelle tries to discourage the other by using displays of strength. Only if this fails will they have a head-to-head fight.

1 GRAZING DUEL

A territorial challenge often involves competitive feeding. Each gazelle tries to edge the other back, away from its personal space.

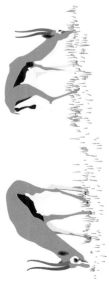

2 HEAD-DUCKING

If neither gazelle backs off, the rivals begin head-ducking displays of their horns, demonstrating their readiness to fight.

3 FULL-ON FIGHT

As a last resort, the gazelles fight. Usually, the battle is a trial of strength, with locked horns, and serious injuries are rare.

Only males have thick, ridged horns like these. The horns of females are much slimmer and shorter.

Males mark the borders of their territories with scent released from these glands under their eyes.

Thick horn bases protect the skull during the battle.

▲ **FACE-TO-FACE**
The ridged, gently curved horns of male Thomson's gazelles have evolved to catch and hold an opponent's horns in a head-to-head conflict. But the horns have sharp tips, so when the loser turns and runs, it must move away quickly to avoid being stabbed.

HOW **DEFENCE** WORKS

Most mammals have predators. If attacked, some mammals run or hide, while others stand their ground and rely on defensive adaptations to protect them. These can be physical, like the armour of an armadillo, or behavioural, like the defence tactics of meerkats.

The shoulder and hip shields are connected by hoops of bony armour linked by flexible skin.

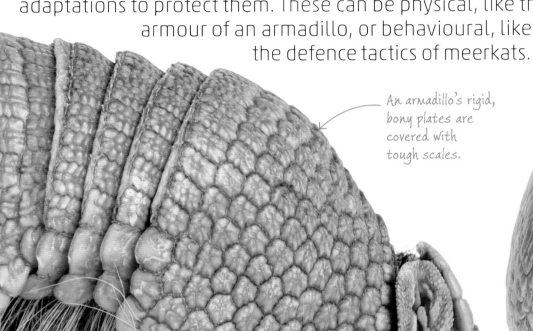

An armadillo's rigid, bony plates are covered with tough scales.

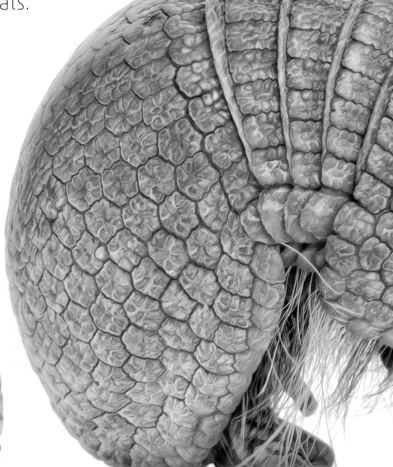

Its soft underside is not protected by armour.

LIVING TOGETHER
Many mammals have evolved defensive patterns of behaviour. One of the most common is to live in groups, like these meerkats. Group living provides many eyes to watch for danger. When meerkats are out in the open, one acts as a lookout. If it sees a predator, it gives an alarm call to identify the predator.

Meerkats take turns to stand guard.

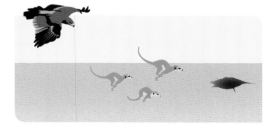

AERIAL ATTACK
If a bird of prey is approaching, the guard's alarm call sends the meerkats scurrying for a bolt hole. These are special tunnels that hold a large number of meerkats.

GROUND ATTACK
A snake like this cobra may well be attacked by the meerkats. At first, they will stand together to scare off the predator. If this fails, they may try to bite the snake.

▶ ARMOURED BALL

South American three-banded armadillos have body armour consisting of big, bony, shell-like plates over their shoulders and hips. These are linked by three narrow bands that allow movement. The connecting armour is so flexible that a three-banded armadillo is able to roll itself into an armoured ball. This makes it almost impossible for a predator to get at the armadillo's soft underparts.

INSIDE VIEW

The armadillo's bony armour develops from its skin, and, unlike the shell of a tortoise, it is not attached to the animal's skeleton.

The armoured ball is complete.

The head and legs tuck in.

DEFENSIVE WALL

Prey animals that live in herds may join forces to deter their predators. In the Arctic, musk oxen can fend off an attacking wolf pack by forming a defensive ring around their calves. Faced by a wall of lowered heads armed with long, curved horns, the wolves often have no option but to give up.

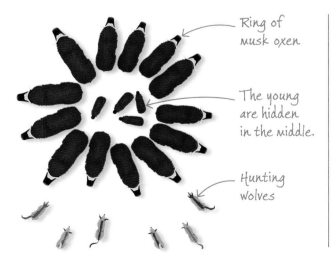

Ring of musk oxen

The young are hidden in the middle.

Hunting wolves

CHEMICAL DEFENCE

Many mammals have scent glands that they use for defence. The most powerful belong to skunks. They defend themselves by spraying a foul-smelling fluid into the face of their predator. The black and white pattern of a skunk's fur acts as a warning – predators learn to leave it well alone.

A direct hit into the eyes can cause temporary blindness.

HOW **CARNIVORES** WORK

Carnivores are animals that feed on the flesh of other animals. Carnivorous mammals, such as cats, dogs, and bears, are equipped with special weapons to capture, kill, and butcher their prey, including sharp claws and flesh-piercing teeth. They also rely on cunning to outwit wary prey and physical strength to overpower them.

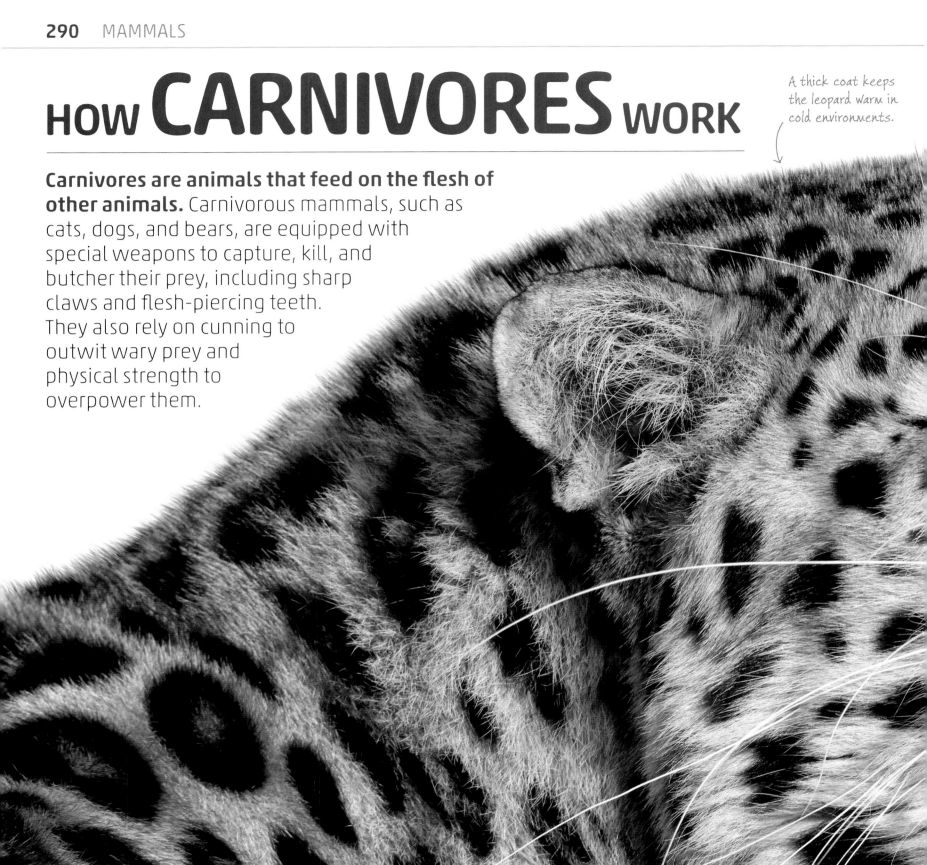

A thick coat keeps the leopard warm in cold environments.

A leopard's hearing is five times better than that of a human.

Camouflage enables the animal to sneak up on prey.

Whiskers help nocturnal animals feel their way in the dark.

Powerful neck and shoulder muscles

A long tail helps the leopard balance.

AMUR LEOPARD

Silent padded feet

◀ BUILT FOR STEALTH

Amur leopards, like most cats, are stealth hunters, either lying in ambush until a victim comes close, or stalking prey silently until close enough to make a sudden dash. They use their strong limbs and pointed claws to grasp prey, and their large canine teeth to grip the neck and inflict a deadly, suffocating bite.

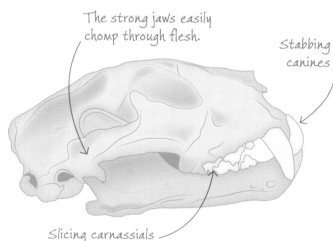

The strong jaws easily chomp through flesh.

Stabbing canines

Slicing carnassials

TEETH

Many carnivorous mammals have two types of teeth to cope with their meaty diet. Long canine teeth at the front of the mouth impale and grip prey. Knife-like carnassial teeth at the back shear through flesh.

The tongue is covered in tiny, razor-sharp ridges for scraping meat off bones.

Sharp canine teeth for stabbing

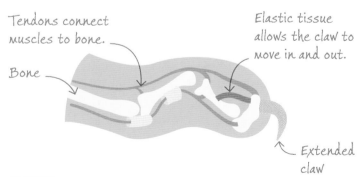

Tendons connect muscles to bone.

Elastic tissue allows the claw to move in and out.

Bone

Extended claw

CLAWS

Carnivorous mammals have claws to hunt, climb, dig, and fight. Cats' retractable claws fold into their feet when not in use, so their tips don't wear down. When extended, the claws turn the paw into a formidable weapon.

HOW **INSECT EATERS** WORK

Some mammals hunt small creatures such as insects, snails, and other invertebrates. Called insectivores, they typically have a long snout and sensitive nose to seek their prey, clawed feet to dig them up, and sharp teeth to crunch their exoskeletons. Most are active by night. With small eyes and often poor vision, they rely on smell, hearing, and touch to find their way.

▼ **HUNTING HEDGEHOG**
Most hedgehogs sleep in a den by day and emerge after dark to forage for food. Their diet includes not only invertebrates but also frogs, reptiles, berries, mushrooms, and rotting meat (known as carrion). Their strong jaws can easily crack the shells of snails or birds' eggs.

Muscles in the hedgehog's back can raise or lower its spines to defend itself.

Hedgehogs have excellent hearing, to make up for their limited sight.

Sharp incisors

Strong molars

HEDGEHOG SKULL
Like most insectivores, hedgehogs have a long skull with a small chamber for the brain. They have 36 teeth, including strong molars for crunching hard objects and fang-like incisors for impaling soft flesh.

Hedgehogs' small eyes offer limited vision.

The long snout is packed with smell receptors.

Beetle grub

Pointed incisor teeth are used to grasp and pierce.

HUNTING TECHNIQUES

Many different kinds of mammal eat invertebrates, and they have a variety of strategies by which they capture prey. Many ant-eating mammals have no teeth at all, but have other adaptations.

MOLES
Spending almost their whole life underground, moles use their spade-like forelimbs to dig long networks of tunnels, in which they live and catch worms and other invertebrates to eat.

SHREWS
These tiny but highly active mammals rely on speed and ferocity to satisfy a huge appetite. Shrews need to eat their entire body weight in food each day to survive.

ANTEATERS
The long tongue of an anteater darts out of its toothless mouth and deep into ants' nests. It is covered in tiny hooks and sticky saliva to catch prey.

CLOSE-UP VIEW of hooks on anteater's tongue

The protective spines are special hairs made stiff with extra proteins.

The sharp claws are used for digging through soil.

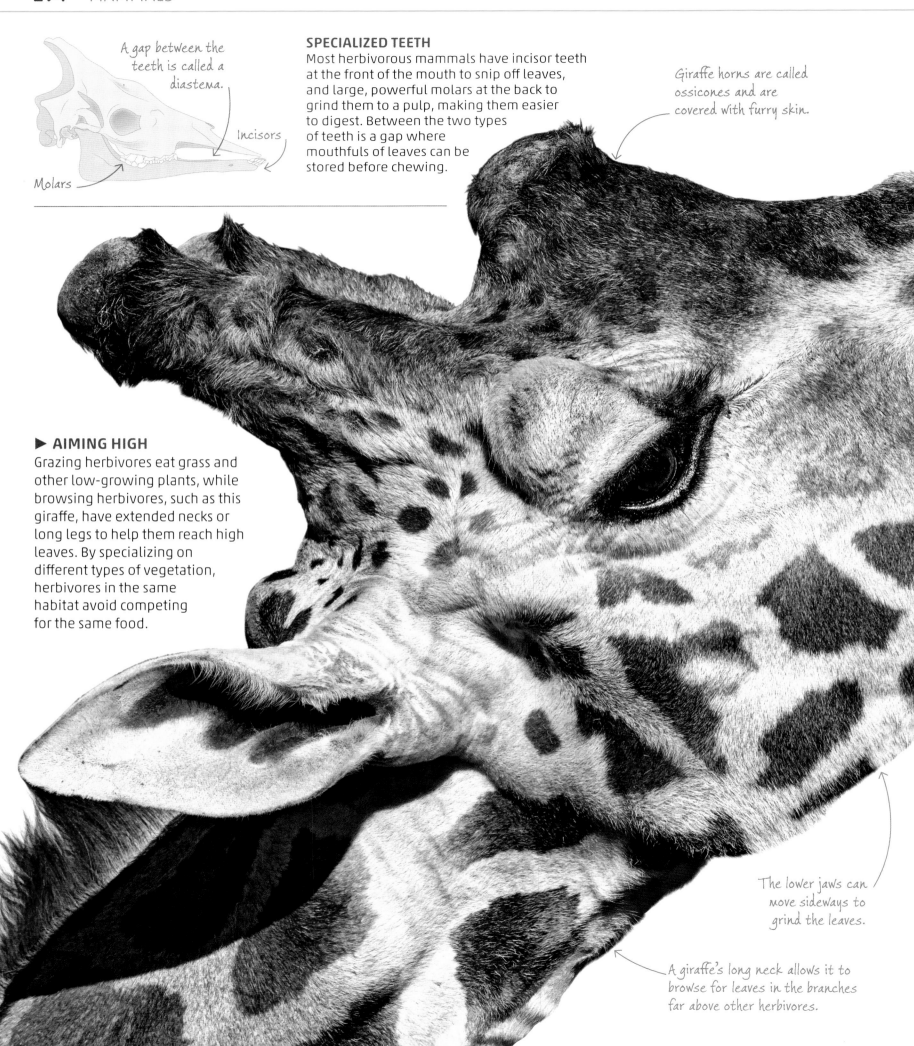

A gap between the teeth is called a diastema.

Incisors

Molars

SPECIALIZED TEETH
Most herbivorous mammals have incisor teeth at the front of the mouth to snip off leaves, and large, powerful molars at the back to grind them to a pulp, making them easier to digest. Between the two types of teeth is a gap where mouthfuls of leaves can be stored before chewing.

Giraffe horns are called ossicones and are covered with furry skin.

▶ AIMING HIGH
Grazing herbivores eat grass and other low-growing plants, while browsing herbivores, such as this giraffe, have extended necks or long legs to help them reach high leaves. By specializing on different types of vegetation, herbivores in the same habitat avoid competing for the same food.

The lower jaws can move sideways to grind the leaves.

A giraffe's long neck allows it to browse for leaves in the branches far above other herbivores.

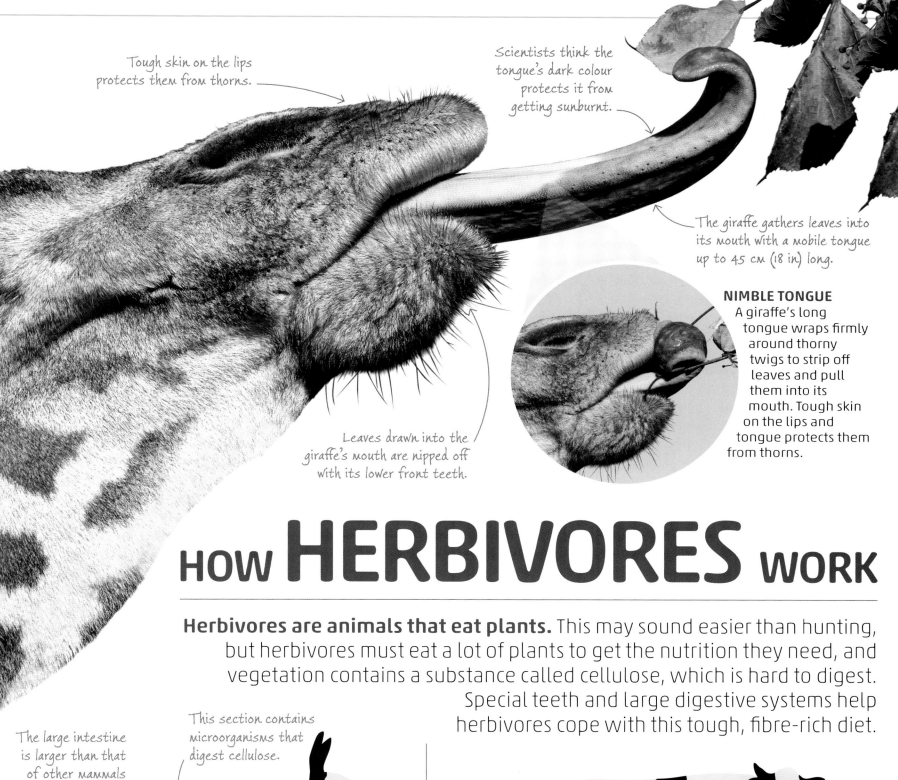

Tough skin on the lips protects them from thorns.

Scientists think the tongue's dark colour protects it from getting sunburnt.

The giraffe gathers leaves into its mouth with a mobile tongue up to 45 cm (18 in) long.

NIMBLE TONGUE
A giraffe's long tongue wraps firmly around thorny twigs to strip off leaves and pull them into its mouth. Tough skin on the lips and tongue protects them from thorns.

Leaves drawn into the giraffe's mouth are nipped off with its lower front teeth.

HOW HERBIVORES WORK

Herbivores are animals that eat plants. This may sound easier than hunting, but herbivores must eat a lot of plants to get the nutrition they need, and vegetation contains a substance called cellulose, which is hard to digest. Special teeth and large digestive systems help herbivores cope with this tough, fibre-rich diet.

The large intestine is larger than that of other mammals to help digestion.

This section contains microorganisms that digest cellulose.

Stomach

Small intestine

Regular large intestine

Most nutrients are absorbed by the small intestine.

The stomach chambers process food.

HIND GUT FERMENTERS
These mammals have cellulose-digesting microorganisms in the large intestine. Rabbits even swallow their droppings, to ensure that maximum nutrients are absorbed.

RUMINANTS
These mammals have four stomach chambers containing microorganisms to break down cellulose. Swallowed food is regurgitated to be chewed again, making it easier to digest.

▼ **SILVERY MOLE RAT**
Mole rats spend most of their time underground, using their huge incisor teeth to dig tunnels in which to live and search for roots to eat. These burrows can be up to 1 km (0.6 miles) long. Mole rats' lips close behind their teeth, preventing them from swallowing dirt as they dig.

Mole rats have small eyes and poor vision but excellent hearing.

Folds of skin guard the nostrils to keep out soil when digging.

The roots of the incisors extend into the skull.

The lips can close behind the teeth.

Incisor teeth

The mole rat has an exceptional sense of touch to feel its way in the dark.

HOW RODENTS WORK

Rodents form the largest group of mammals, and include rats, gerbils, and moles. They use their large front teeth to dig burrows, gnaw tough foods, or defend against attack. They can find food and shelter in most environments, allowing them to survive almost everywhere, from the Arctic tundra to hot, dry deserts.

The cheeks stretch all the way to the shoulders.

Cheeks filled with nuts

Food such as nuts is carried in the cheek pouches.

CHEEK POUCHES
As well as sharp front teeth, many rodents also have cheek pouches to transport food to safe locations. Hamsters can store food weighing up to half their body weight in their pouches, and can also carry their newborn young like this. Hamsters have no saliva, so their cargo is always dry.

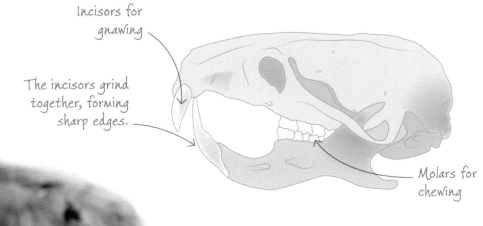

Incisors for gnawing

The incisors grind together, forming sharp edges.

Molars for chewing

RODENT TEETH
Rodents' front teeth grow continuously to prevent them wearing down from gnawing. They are made from a hard material called enamel at the front, and a softer material called dentine at the back. As the top and bottom teeth slide over each other, the dentine wears down, causing the teeth to form sharp edges.

HOW RODENTS USE THEIR TEETH
Most rodents use their gnawing teeth to feed on nuts, seeds, and other tough foods, using the sharp incisor edges to nibble and crack through hard cases and shells. Some rodents also use them for digging tunnels, felling trees, and for capturing live animals to eat.

GRASSHOPPER MICE
These carnivores bite through the skeletons of grasshoppers, scorpions, and snakes, severing their nerves and paralysing them before eating them.

BEAVERS
To form dams across rivers, beavers cut down trees by gnawing through them. The dams block water, creating ponds in which the beavers build homes called lodges.

SQUIRRELS
So that they have enough food to survive the cold winter months, squirrels bury nuts in the ground. They use their front teeth to break through the nuts' hard shells.

HOW BEAVERS LIVE

No wild mammal does more to shape its habitat than the beaver. This large, semi-aquatic rodent, a distant relative of rats and squirrels, is a natural engineer that cuts down trees with its teeth. It then uses the logs to build a fortified home surrounded by water to defend itself from predators.

▶ GNAWING TEETH

Beavers live in Earth's northern forests, where the cool, damp climate creates large areas of swampy ground drained by streams. The beavers turn the streams into pools by creating dams that stop the flow, so that they can build their homes. They do most of the work with their large front teeth, which have self-sharpening chisel tips and never stop growing.

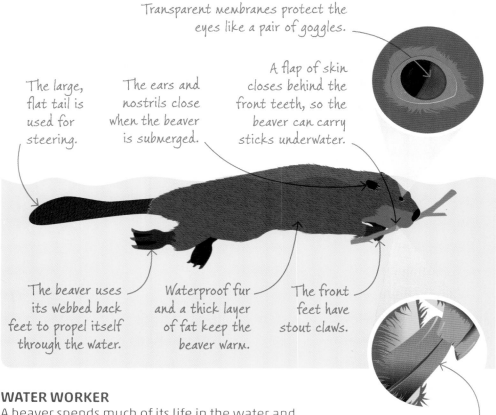

Transparent membranes protect the eyes like a pair of goggles.

The large, flat tail is used for steering.

The ears and nostrils close when the beaver is submerged.

A flap of skin closes behind the front teeth, so the beaver can carry sticks underwater.

The beaver uses its webbed back feet to propel itself through the water.

Waterproof fur and a thick layer of fat keep the beaver warm.

The front feet have stout claws.

WATER WORKER

A beaver spends much of its life in the water and can stay submerged for up to 15 minutes. It swims using its webbed hind feet and paddle-shaped tail. Other aquatic adaptations also allow it to work easily underwater. But a beaver's heavyweight build and short legs make it less agile on land.

The teeth wear down at the back, leaving hard enamel at the front to form a sharp blade.

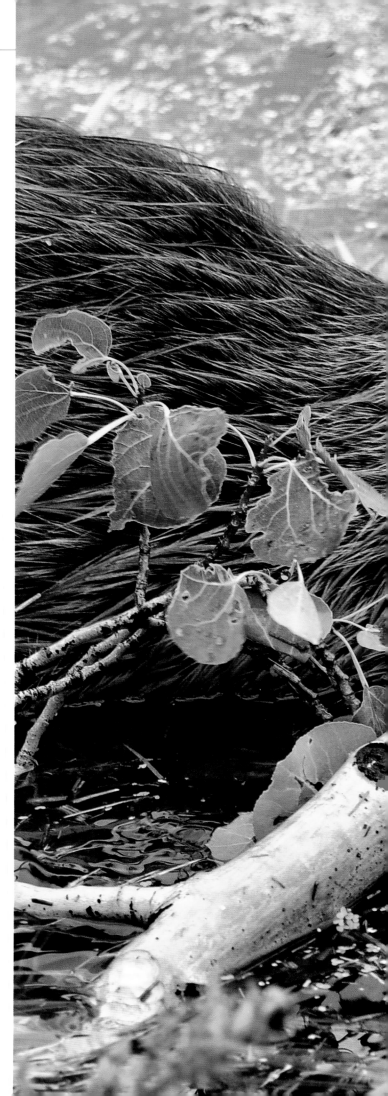

BUILDING A HOME

Beavers work hard to build a barrier called a dam across a river, so that they can create a pool of water. Their homes, known as lodges, are built in the middle of this pool. Underwater entrances enable the beavers to come and go.

1 FELLING TREES
A beaver selects a tree by a river and gnaws through its trunk so it falls into the water. It cuts down more trees and uses them to build a barrier.

A beaver can gnaw trees up to 60 cm (24 in) wide.

2 THE DAM
To build a dam, beavers strengthen the barrier by pushing branches vertically into the river bed. They then add branches horizontally and fill all the gaps with stones, weeds, and mud.

The dam can be more than 4 m (13 ft) high.

3 THE LODGE
Once the dam is built, beavers use sticks and mud to build a lodge. The floor is raised above water level to provide a dry living area. A lower platform is used for drying off.

Beavers store food under the water, ready for the cold winter months.

4 SAFE REFUGE
Surrounded by water in summer, the beavers are safe in their lodge. In winter, if the lake surface freezes, so does the mud plastered over the lodge, and this gives protection against predators.

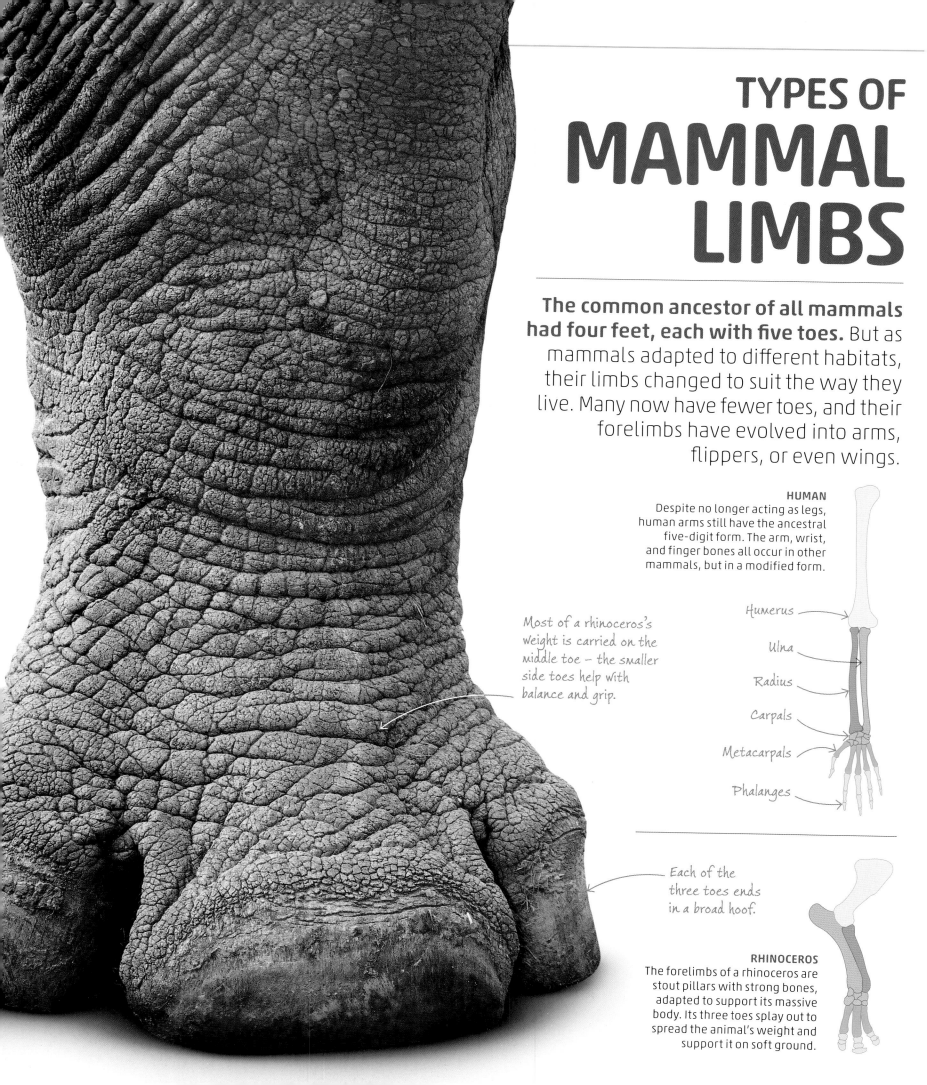

TYPES OF MAMMAL LIMBS

The common ancestor of all mammals had four feet, each with five toes. But as mammals adapted to different habitats, their limbs changed to suit the way they live. Many now have fewer toes, and their forelimbs have evolved into arms, flippers, or even wings.

HUMAN
Despite no longer acting as legs, human arms still have the ancestral five-digit form. The arm, wrist, and finger bones all occur in other mammals, but in a modified form.

Humerus

Ulna

Radius

Carpals

Metacarpals

Phalanges

Most of a rhinoceros's weight is carried on the middle toe – the smaller side toes help with balance and grip.

Each of the three toes ends in a broad hoof.

RHINOCEROS
The forelimbs of a rhinoceros are stout pillars with strong bones, adapted to support its massive body. Its three toes splay out to spread the animal's weight and support it on soft ground.

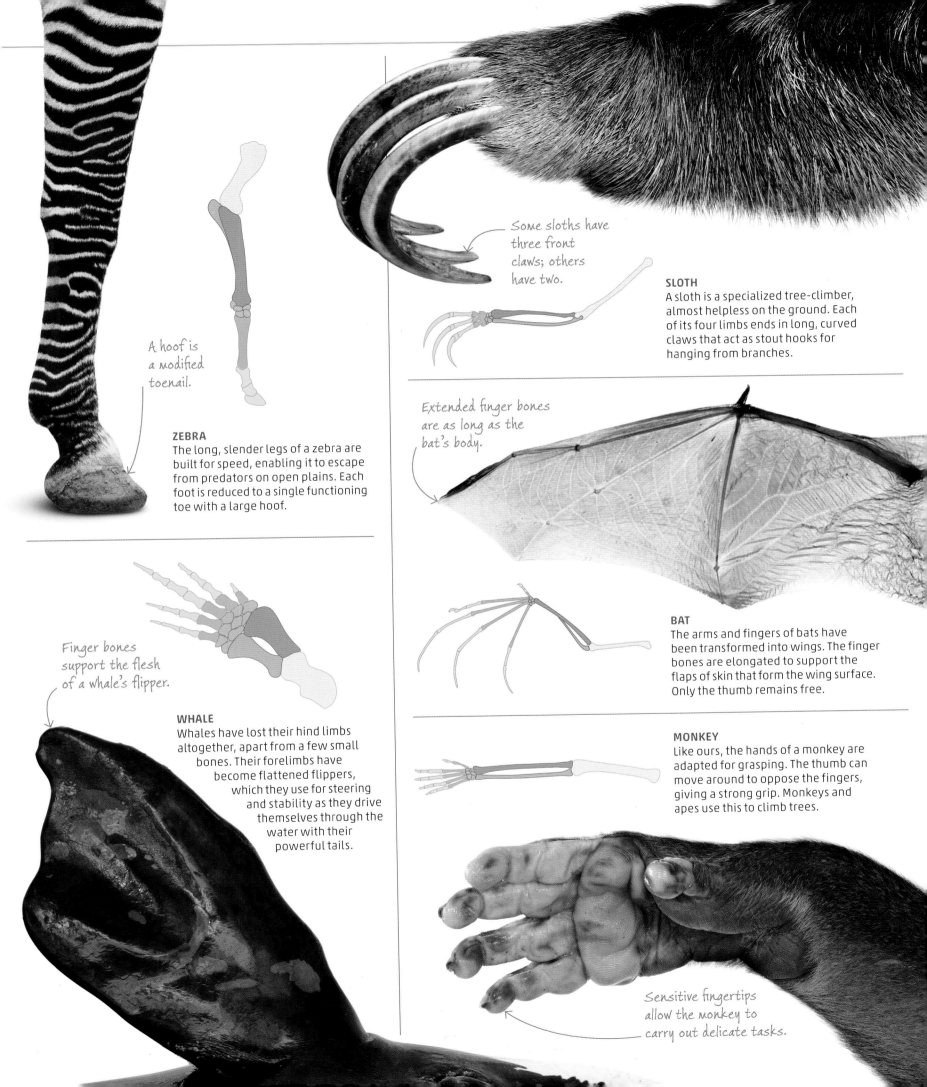

A hoof is a modified toenail.

ZEBRA
The long, slender legs of a zebra are built for speed, enabling it to escape from predators on open plains. Each foot is reduced to a single functioning toe with a large hoof.

Some sloths have three front claws; others have two.

SLOTH
A sloth is a specialized tree-climber, almost helpless on the ground. Each of its four limbs ends in long, curved claws that act as stout hooks for hanging from branches.

Extended finger bones are as long as the bat's body.

BAT
The arms and fingers of bats have been transformed into wings. The finger bones are elongated to support the flaps of skin that form the wing surface. Only the thumb remains free.

Finger bones support the flesh of a whale's flipper.

WHALE
Whales have lost their hind limbs altogether, apart from a few small bones. Their forelimbs have become flattened flippers, which they use for steering and stability as they drive themselves through the water with their powerful tails.

MONKEY
Like ours, the hands of a monkey are adapted for grasping. The thumb can move around to oppose the fingers, giving a strong grip. Monkeys and apes use this to climb trees.

Sensitive fingertips allow the monkey to carry out delicate tasks.

HOW **BATS** WORK

Bats are the only mammals capable of flight. Their wings consist of elastic skin stretched between hugely elongated finger bones, connected by many joints. These flexible, manoeuvrable limbs are very different from the feathery wings of birds. Bats are nocturnal and have evolved to be skilled at navigating and hunting in the dark.

▼ NIGHT FLIGHT

Unlike most birds, bats fly by night. Big fruit-eating bats have large, sensitive eyes to see in the dark, but smaller insect-eating bats like this little brown bat detect obstacles or identify prey by sending out sound waves and listening to the echoes. They also use this technique, called echolocation, to find their way in the dark caves where they roost.

The bat's wing has many joints, enabling it to change shape as it manoeuvres through the air.

High-pitched noises made by the bat help it search for obstacles or prey.

A flap of skin stretches between the tail and the legs.

Bats are able to move the "fingers" in their wings much like humans move the fingers in their hands.

HANGING UPSIDE DOWN

A bat spends its day roosting. It hangs upside down from a high perch so it can easily get airborne. The weight of its body pulls tendons attached to its claws, causing them to clench. The bat only has to exert energy to release its grip, so if it dies while roosting, it will not fall from its perch.

Claw

Tendon

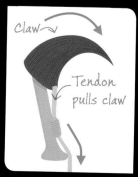

Claw

Tendon pulls claw

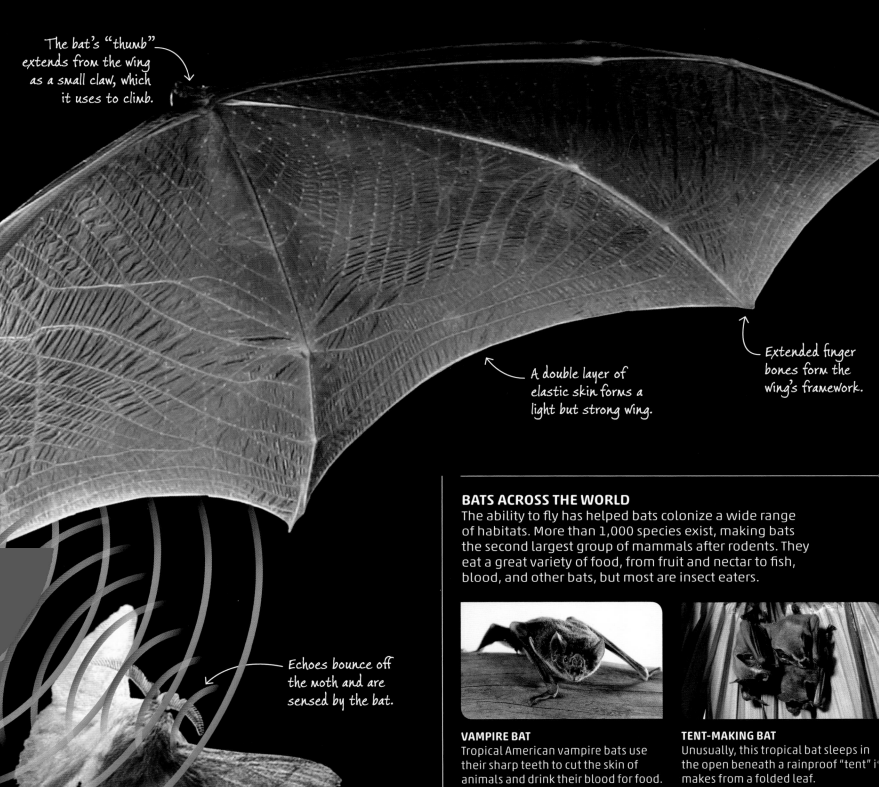

The bat's "thumb" extends from the wing as a small claw, which it uses to climb.

A double layer of elastic skin forms a light but strong wing.

Extended finger bones form the wing's framework.

Echoes bounce off the moth and are sensed by the bat.

Forest moths are typical prey.

HOW ECHOLOCATION WORKS
Some bats navigate by emitting a rapid series of high-pitched clicks, and then listening for echoes bouncing off objects like this moth. Their brains can convert these echoes into detailed images, so the

BATS ACROSS THE WORLD
The ability to fly has helped bats colonize a wide range of habitats. More than 1,000 species exist, making bats the second largest group of mammals after rodents. They eat a great variety of food, from fruit and nectar to fish, blood, and other bats, but most are insect eaters.

VAMPIRE BAT
Tropical American vampire bats use their sharp teeth to cut the skin of animals and drink their blood for food.

TENT-MAKING BAT
Unusually, this tropical bat sleeps in the open beneath a rainproof "tent" i makes from a folded leaf.

FRUIT BAT
These big bats live in tropical forests where they fly in search of fruit. They also roost in trees.

HORSESHOE BAT
The U-shaped flap of skin on a horseshoe bat's nose focuses the sound of its echolocation clicks.

CEILING SLEEPERS

Bats form larger colonies than any other mammal. Around two million Geoffroy's rousettes, a species of fruit bat, roost on the ceiling of this cave in the Philippines. They rest here in the daytime before flying outside to find food when night falls. As bats feast on fruit and nectar from the forests around their cave, they carry pollen on their fur. This helps tens of millions of plants to reproduce.

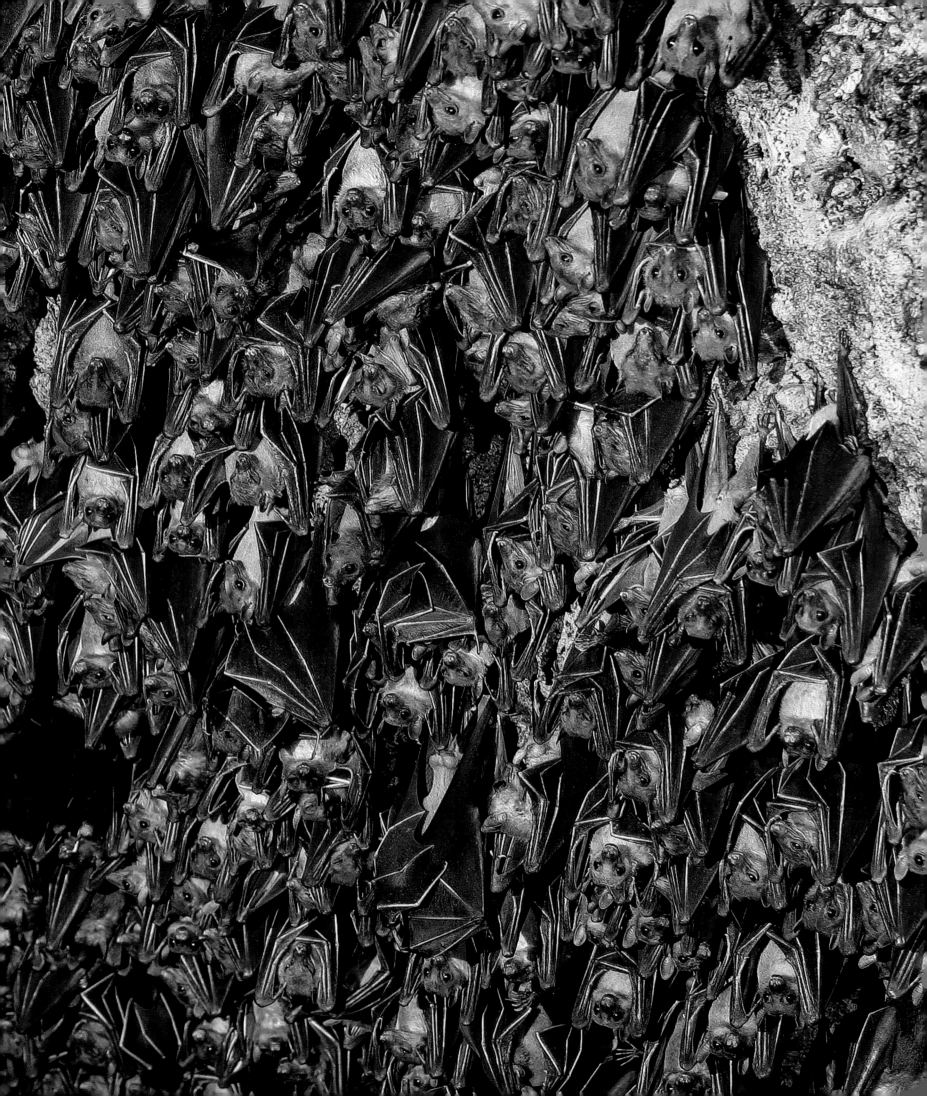

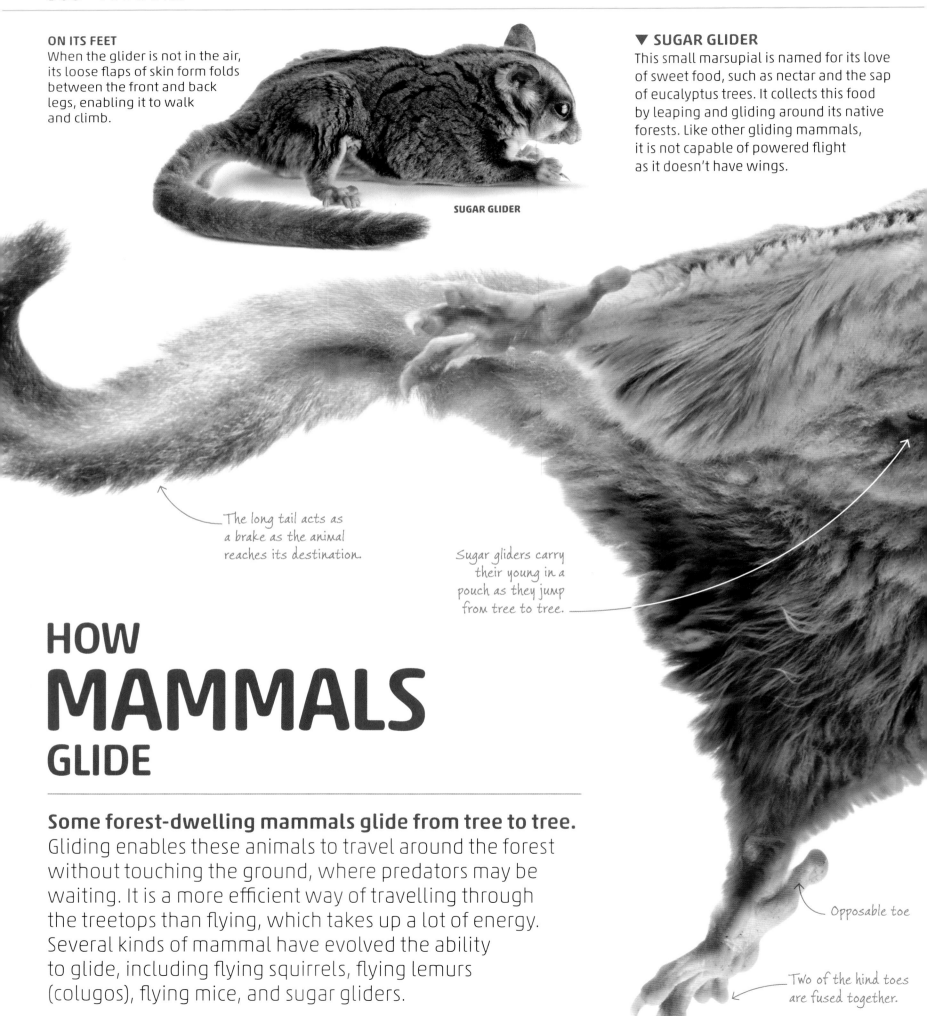

ON ITS FEET
When the glider is not in the air, its loose flaps of skin form folds between the front and back legs, enabling it to walk and climb.

SUGAR GLIDER

▼ **SUGAR GLIDER**
This small marsupial is named for its love of sweet food, such as nectar and the sap of eucalyptus trees. It collects this food by leaping and gliding around its native forests. Like other gliding mammals, it is not capable of powered flight as it doesn't have wings.

The long tail acts as a brake as the animal reaches its destination.

Sugar gliders carry their young in a pouch as they jump from tree to tree.

HOW
MAMMALS
GLIDE

Some forest-dwelling mammals glide from tree to tree.
Gliding enables these animals to travel around the forest without touching the ground, where predators may be waiting. It is a more efficient way of travelling through the treetops than flying, which takes up a lot of energy. Several kinds of mammal have evolved the ability to glide, including flying squirrels, flying lemurs (colugos), flying mice, and sugar gliders.

Opposable toe

Two of the hind toes are fused together.

The furry flap of skin that stretches from foot to foot on each side is called a patagium.

The sensitive ears can swivel.

Whiskers help the animal to feel its way through the trees.

GRIPPING FEET
Gliders' strong feet allow them to grasp branches as they clamber through the trees. Sharp claws help them grip surfaces when they land after a glide. The sugar gliders' hind feet have opposable toes. These are toes that can be moved independently to grip more easily.

Sugar gliders have five toes on each foot.

HOW GLIDING WORKS
Flaps of skin stretching between the forelimbs and hind limbs of gliding mammals form a parachute. The flaps slow their descent, allowing them to travel further. The greatest distance travelled by a gliding mammal ever to be recorded was 150 m (490 ft) – the length of one and a half football pitches.

Body tilts upwards

Limbs extend

Air catches underneath

Sharp claws ready to grip tree

TAKING OFF
The glider jumps into the air, leaping upwards to gain height.

STRETCHING OUT
It stretches its limbs to open out the flaps of skin between them.

CATCHING AIR
The flaps catch the air, slowing the animal's fall.

READY TO LAND
Nearing its target, the glider brings its feet forward, ready to land.

HOW GIBBONS SWING

The most acrobatic of all climbing mammals, gibbons move through the trees with a speed and agility no other animal can match. Their elongated hands serve as hooks as they swing from branch to branch, reaching speeds of 56 kph (35 mph) and making breathtaking leaps. Smaller and more slender than other apes, they can hang safely from the thinnest branches and swing to grab fruit that other animals can't reach.

Strong, muscular arms can support the gibbon's weight for long periods of time.

The bare skin on a gibbon's palm helps it grip branches without slipping.

Like all apes, gibbons have fingernails rather than claws.

Gibbons can carry objects such as this leaf in their mouths while swinging.

GRASPING HANDS
Gibbons are related to humans and their hands resemble ours. However, their palms and fingers are longer – to form a hook for swinging – while their thumbs are short and are easily tucked out of the way. Like human thumbs, gibbons' thumbs are opposable, which means they can move the opposite way to the fingers to grasp objects. Unlike humans, gibbons also have opposable big toes on their feet

Flexible wrist joints can swivel round, much like a human hip.

Hook-like hand

The forelimbs are extremely long.

Gibbons' arms are longer than their legs.

The long toe bones can grasp like fingers.

Flexible shoulder joints allow the arms to reach overhead.

Mobile hip joints allow the gibbon's legs to move in many directions.

FLEXIBLE SKELETON

The skeletons of gibbons show many adaptations to life in the trees. Their unique wrist joints swivel, reducing the amount of energy the arms need and allowing a gibbon to rotate its arm through 360 degrees without letting go. Gibbons have an upright stance, like us, and can even walk on two feet, throwing their hands up into the air for balance.

SPEEDY SWINGING

Gibbons swing their bodies like pendulums when they move during brachiation, working with both their arms and their legs. Their legs pump up and down with each swing to help them build up speed, much as humans work playground swings with their legs. As a result, they gain enough momentum to leap across gaps as wide as 15 m (50 ft).

▶ GRACEFUL GIBBON

Gibbons live in the canopies high up in rainforests, rarely descending to the ground. Instead, they use their immense upper body strength to swing gracefully through the treetops in search of fruit, insects, and leaves to eat. This distinctive mode of travel is called brachiation.

Opposable toes for gripping

HOW MAMMALS BURROW

Burrows are holes or tunnels that animals dig to live, sleep, or hide in. Some mammals use them to escape searing heat, whereas others dig them to shelter from the cold. Burrows can also be used as nurseries or places to hide from predators. Some mammals spend their whole lives underground.

Thick toe pads cushion the paw.

The blunt shape of the claws prevents them from breaking.

▶ DIGGING CLAWS
Eurasian badgers have large, shovel-like front feet, with long claws for digging their complex burrow systems, called setts. A badger's compact shape and short but muscular legs allow it to move easily underground. Badgers normally sleep in their burrows by day, emerging after dark to look for food.

Dirt doesn't cling to the bristly fur.

EURASIAN BADGER

The long claws are strong enough to shift large amounts of soil.

Stocky, powerful legs allow badgers to run as fast as 30 kph (19 mph), but only for short periods.

UNDERGROUND HOME
Eurasian badgers' setts are dug in soft soil and can extend for hundreds of metres, with many entrances, tunnels, and chambers. Large chambers lined with soft grass or other bedding are used for sleeping, or as nurseries where mothers raise their young. Badgers are very clean and regularly clear out old bedding, replacing it with fresh material.

Nursery chamber

Straw-lined sleeping chamber

Entrance hole

The tunnels are made smooth by constant use.

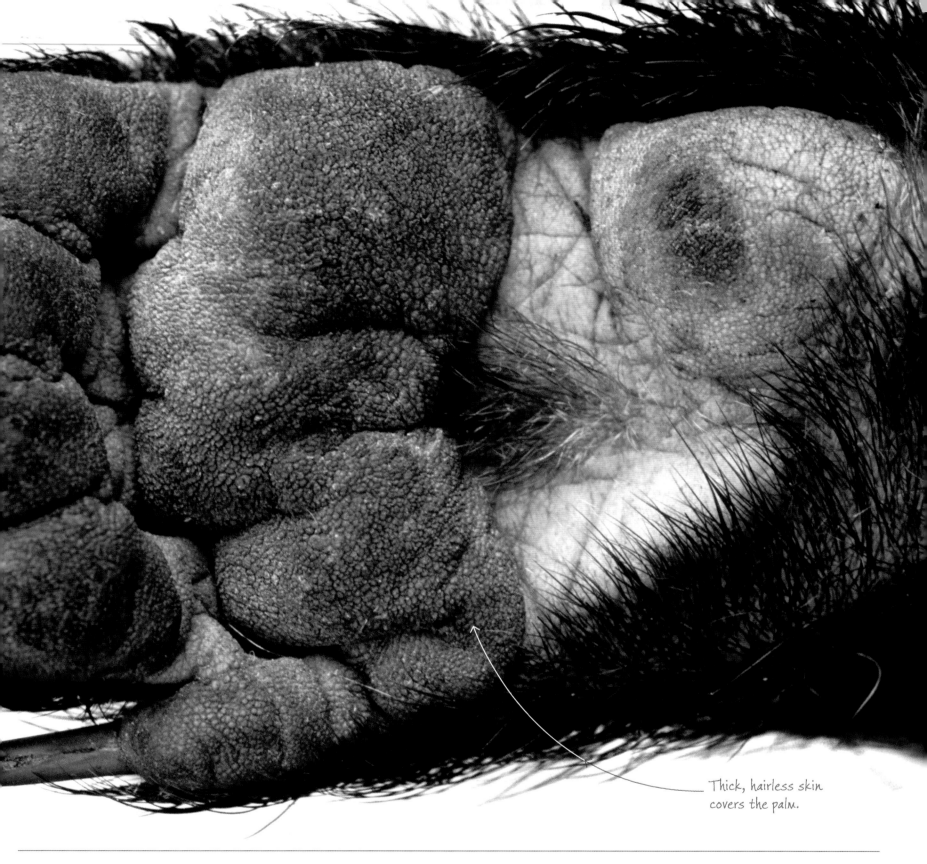

Thick, hairless skin covers the palm.

HIGH-SPEED DIGGER
The honey badger, or ratel, lives alone in a simple burrow that usually has just one nesting chamber. A strong digger, it can dig one of these burrows in ten minutes, using its powerful, long-clawed feet.

SNOW DEN
Pregnant polar bears dig dens in snow. They enter a hibernation-like state, in which they do not eat, and remain in the den to give birth. They do not emerge until the cubs grow large enough to venture outside.

HOW ELEPHANTS WORK

The biggest living land mammals, elephants are survivors from a prehistoric age of giant herbivores. Apart from their bulk and weight, their most prominent feature is a long, mobile, sensitive trunk – a unique organ that they use like a hand.

LIGHTWEIGHT SKULL

An elephant's massive, dome-shaped skull has air cavities to reduce its weight, but it is still strong enough to withstand considerable force. Its huge molar teeth, which are used for grinding tough fibrous food, are replaced six times during its life.

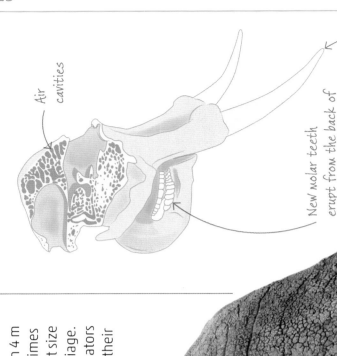

Air cavities

New molar teeth erupt from the back of the jaw and move forwards when the worn teeth fall out.

Tusks are extended incisor teeth, and are used for stripping bark, digging, and for defence.

The trunk is the elephant's primary tool for eating, drinking, and exploring its world.

▼ LAND GIANT

A fully grown African bull elephant can reach 4 m (13 ft) tall and weigh 7 tonnes – about five times the weight of a car. Elephants use their great size and strength to uproot trees and feed on foliage. Their size ensures they have no natural predators as an adult, but their ivory tusks have led to their near-extinction by human hunters.

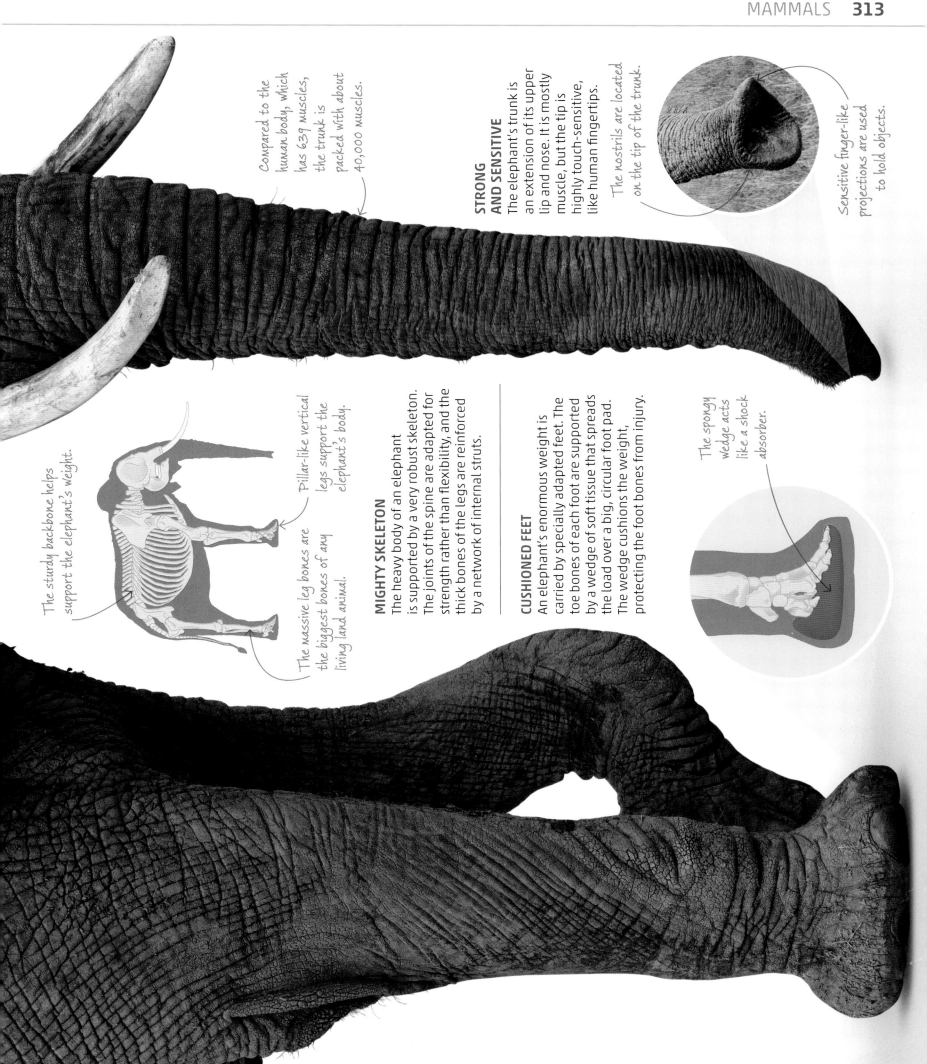

Compared to the human body, which has 639 muscles, the trunk is packed with about 40,000 muscles.

STRONG AND SENSITIVE
The elephant's trunk is an extension of its upper lip and nose. It is mostly muscle, but the tip is highly touch-sensitive, like human fingertips.

The nostrils are located on the tip of the trunk.

Sensitive finger-like projections are used to hold objects.

The sturdy backbone helps support the elephant's weight.

Pillar-like vertical legs support the elephant's body.

The massive leg bones are the biggest bones of any living land animal.

MIGHTY SKELETON
The heavy body of an elephant is supported by a very robust skeleton. The joints of the spine are adapted for strength rather than flexibility, and the thick bones of the legs are reinforced by a network of internal struts.

CUSHIONED FEET
An elephant's enormous weight is carried by specially adapted feet. The toe bones of each foot are supported by a wedge of soft tissue that spreads the load over a big, circular foot pad. The wedge cushions the weight, protecting the foot bones from injury.

The spongy wedge acts like a shock absorber.

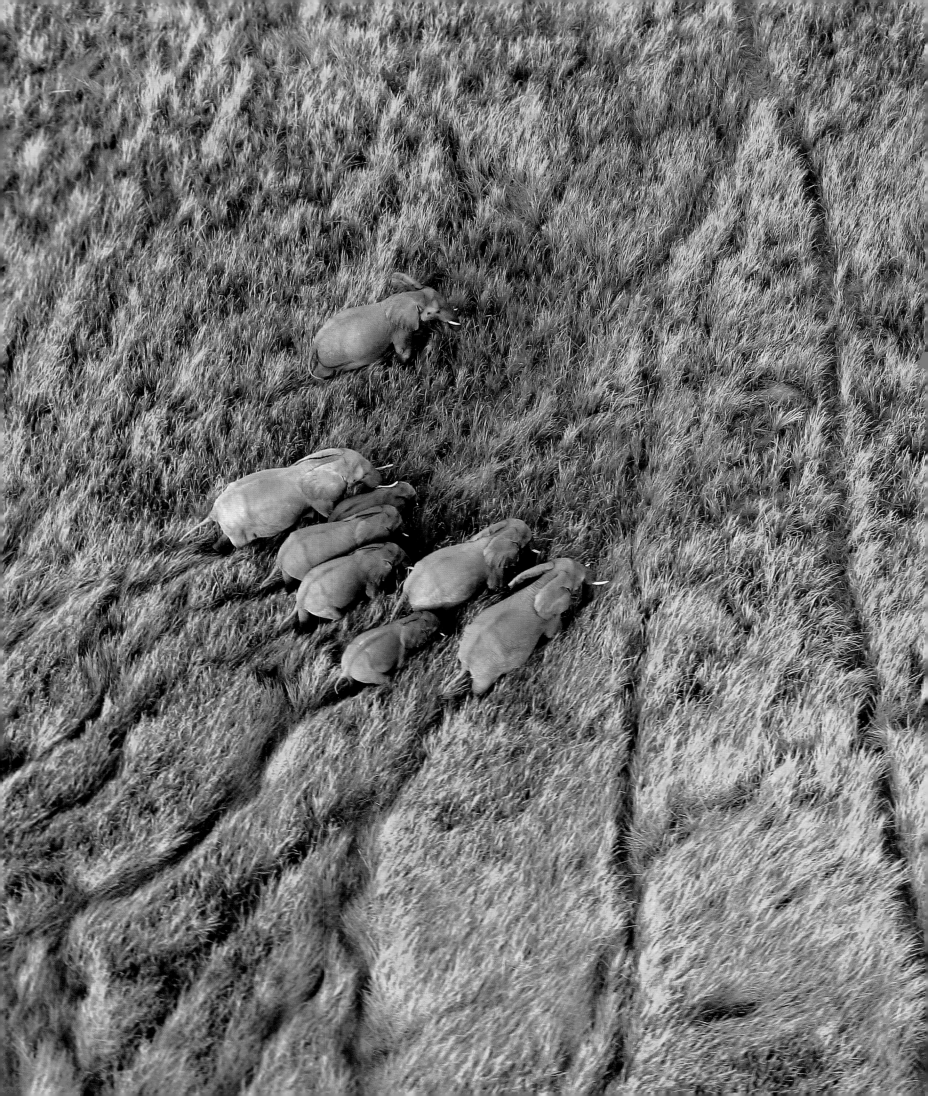

LAND GIANTS

Forging a path through the grasslands of Africa, this herd of elephants is led by its matriarch - the oldest and wisest female in the group. She remembers where to find food and water, and in times of crisis, the herd is guided by her. Elephants live in close-knit groups made up of about ten females and their calves. When males reach their teens, they leave the family and live alone, or join an all-male group – but their bonds are never as strong as those of the females.

A humpback has up to **400** bristly plates.

Muscles open a baleen whale's twin blowholes when it needs to breathe.

SURFACE BREATHERS
Like all mammals, whales must breathe air. They have nostrils in the tops of their heads called blowholes. Each time a whale surfaces, it breathes out, blasting a spray of air and water droplets from its blowhole.

FILTER-FEEDERS
The big filter-feeders are called baleen whales, because instead of having teeth, their mouths are fringed by rows of bristly plates known as baleen. Water drawn into the whale's huge mouth is forced out through the baleen, which trap any small animals.

This whale calf stays close to its mother for up to a year.

Baleen hanging from the upper jaw strain small fish and shrimp-like krill from the water.

Huge lumps on the humpback's head contain hair follicles.

▶ MARINE GIANTS
There are two types of whale. Some have teeth, and prey mainly on fish and squid, catching them one at a time. Others, such as this humpback whale and her calf, are equipped for filtering small prey from the water, scooping up hundreds with each mouthful. These filter-feeders are much bigger than toothed whales, and include the gigantic blue whale, the biggest animal on Earth.

Remoras – fish with suckers on their heads – cling to the whale's skin as it swims.

Large skin folds in the throat expand when the whale gulps a huge volume of water to sieve for prey.

HOW WHALES WORK

Of all marine mammals, whales are the most highly adapted to life in the water. Seals must return to land to breed, but whales – and their smaller relatives, dolphins and porpoises – spend their entire lives in the water. Their bodies have evolved to resemble those of fish, and they swim and dive with fish-like speed and efficiency as they travel the oceans in search of food.

INSIDE VIEW

A whale can grow to a gigantic size because its immense weight is supported by the water, instead of its bones. This has enabled a whale's skeleton to be reduced to the essentials needed for feeding and swimming – strong bones support its flippers and jaws, while the muscles that drive its powerful tail are anchored to a stout backbone. But although its land-walking ancestors had four legs, a whale does not need hind limbs, so only traces of those bones survive.

The rib cage stops water pressure collapsing the whale's organs when it dives.

A strong, but flexible spine anchors the tail muscles.

Extended jaw bones support the baleen plates.

The arm and finger bones support the long, flat flippers.

The pelvic and hind limb bones have almost disappeared.

The tail flukes have no bones – they are supported by fibrous gristle.

The small dorsal fin helps stabilize the whale as it swims through the water.

Using vertical strokes, the whale's powerful tail propels the animal through the water.

A human diver would be dwarfed by the colossal size of a humpback whale, which can grow to 19 m (52 ft) long.

The humpback has the biggest flippers of any whale, which it uses for steering.

Many sperm whales are scarred by the toothed suckers of giant squid.

Unlike baleen whales, toothed whales have a single blowhole.

A sperm whale's teeth are up to 20 cm (8 in) long.

TOOTHED HUNTERS

Most species of whale have conical, pointed teeth adapted for seizing slippery fish – although orcas (killer whales) regularly attack and eat seals, and even other whales. The largest species is the massively built sperm whale, which preys mainly on squid in the deep-ocean twilight zone.

Eye

Mouth

The long, narrow lower jaw has up to 52 teeth, but there are no upper teeth.

The **environment** in which an organism lives is known as its habitat. A habitat can be as small as the underside of a leaf or as large as an entire rainforest. **Communities of organisms** that live in major habitats – from forests and oceans to deserts and frozen wastes – often share similar **challenges**, but each species has **adapted** to tackle these problems in a unique way.

HABITATS

HOW BIOMES WORK

From the tropics to the poles, from the deepest ocean to the highest mountain, life is found everywhere on planet Earth. The community of plants and animals that live in a major habitat, such as a rainforest or a desert, is called a biome. Most biomes are shaped by a particular climate. Rainforests, for instance, occur wherever it is warm and rainy all year round.

▶ BIOME MAP

Scientists have identified at least 16 major biomes. Dividing the planet into biomes is useful as it helps us to understand how plants and animals have evolved to cope with similiar conditions in different parts of the world. Deserts as far apart as Africa and Australia, for example, have similar drought-adapted plants.

- Tropical rainforest
- Tropical grassland
- Dry woodland
- Temperate rainforest
- Temperate grassland
- Hot desert
- Cold desert
- Ocean
- Mediterranean
- Temperate forest
- Boreal forest
- Tundra
- Polar
- Mountain
- Wetland
- Lakes and rivers

ARCTIC CIRCLE

TROPIC OF CANCER

EQUATOR

TROPIC OF CAPRICORN

ANTARCTIC CIRCLE

TEMPERATE GRASSLAND
The prairies of North America, the Pampas of South America, and the steppes of Eurasia are grasslands that experience mild summers and cold winters.

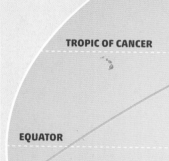

OCEANS
Oceans cover more than 70 per cent of Earth's surface and make up the largest biome of all. It includes many marine habitats, from tropical coral reefs to the deep sea.

WETLAND
Where land is often or permanently flooded with water – such as in bogs, swamps, and marshes – plants and animals have evolved to cope the semi-aquatic environment.

TEMPERATE FOREST
Between the tropics and the poles is the temperate zone, where forests experience big seasonal changes, from mild summers to cold winters.

DESERT
Places with very little rainfall are covered with sand or rock. Desert plants and animals have evolved ways to survive during long, dry periods.

BOREAL FOREST
The northernmost forests grow on ground that is often wet or icy. They are dominated by conifers: trees that don't shed their needle-like leaves and can survive the cold.

TUNDRA
Regions close to the poles are so cold that the ground is frozen all year round and trees are sparse. Summer days and winter nights are very long.

MOUNTAIN
At the highest peaks, temperatures fall and the air is thin. Forests give way to alpine grassland, bare rock, and glaciers. It snows regularly on mountaintops, even in the tropics.

LAKES AND RIVERS
Water that evaporates from the oceans falls onto the land as rainfall. It creates ponds, lakes, streams, and rivers – habitats for freshwater plants and animals.

TROPICAL GRASSLAND
Where land is too dry to support forest but not dry enough to be desert, grass flourishes. Tropical grasslands are home to herds of large mammals.

POLAR
The extreme north and south of Earth are covered in ice caps. The partly frozen Arctic Ocean is in the north, and the snowy Antarctic continent is in the south.

TROPICAL RAINFOREST
Boasting more species than any other land habitat, tropical rainforest is humid, dense, and wet all year.

HOW TROPICAL RAINFORESTS WORK

Far more species live in tropical rainforests than in any other land habitat. These fantastically diverse forests are lush and dense, with towering trees covered in vines and creepers. They have distinct layers, from the leaf-covered ground to the soaring treetops, each with different plants and animals. The great diversity of tropical rainforests leads to fierce competition for food and shelter.

▲ FOREST FLOOR

On the ground, fungi play a vital role by breaking down fallen leaves and other plant material. The nutrients they release are quickly absorbed by the roots of trees, making the soil poor. Shady and humid, the forest floor is home to many moisture-loving animals such as amphibians.

▲ UNDERSTOREY

New saplings form the understorey, or shrub layer. They grow slowly, waiting for light-filled gaps to open when trees fall so they can shoot upwards. Ferns and flowering plants sprout from tree trunks. Strangler figs grow from seeds in bird droppings on high branches. Their roots grow downwards around the host tree to reach the soil. As the fig plant grows, it smothers the host tree, eventually killing it.

BEARDED PIG

Wild pigs scour the forest floor for everything from fallen fruit and nuts to fungi, roots, and carrion (decaying dead animals). They find food by smell, and help to spread tree seeds in their dung.

WESTERN TARSIER

Weighing a mere 110 g (3.9 oz), this tiny nocturnal primate has larger eyes, relative to its size, than any other mammal. It climbs and leaps around the understorey to hunt insects such as beetles and cicadas.

AROUND THE WORLD

Tropical rainforests occur where it is always warm and damp. They cover 6–7 per cent of Earth's land surface but contain more than 50 per cent of Earth's plant and animal species. Rainforests around the world are under threat from human expansion.

CLIMATE FACTS

Daytime temperatures can hit 35 °C (95 °F) and never dip below 20 °C (68 °F) at night.

Rainfall may exceed 200 cm (79 in) a year. It rains nearly every day in many rainforests.

Two-thirds of the world's plant species grow in rainforests.

▲ CANOPY

Spreading treetops create an almost continuous layer, like a thick green blanket. About 75 per cent of the light that hits the canopy is absorbed by the billions of leaves at the top. Most rainforest animals – from monkeys to insects, frogs, and parrots – live up here, sustained by the fruits, seeds, and flowers of the many different trees.

▲ EMERGENT LAYER

Some massive trees have leafy crowns that soar above the canopy. In Borneo's rainforest, they include the tualang tree, which can reach up to 88 m (289 ft) tall. A tualang tree is supported by enormous, flared roots, known as buttress roots. They spread out from the base and provide stability in strong winds and heavy rain.

BORNEAN ORANG-UTAN

This endangered ape spends most of its time living in the trees, travelling by swinging on branches. It makes a new sleeping nest from leafy branches each evening. About 60 per cent of its diet consists of large fruits, especially figs.

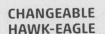

CHANGEABLE HAWK-EAGLE

Tall trees provide this rainforest bird of prey with an ideal perch from which to spot snakes, birds, lizards, and other prey. It builds huge nests in forks where a thick branch joins the main tree trunk.

HOW TEMPERATE FORESTS WORK

Until a few thousand years ago, forests covered great swathes of Earth's surface, including the area roughly midway between the equator and the poles – the mild temperate zone. Most temperate forests have been cut down or cleared, but large areas still survive. The majority of trees in these forests have broad leaves that are shed in winter. Temperate forests undergo dramatic changes as the seasons change.

▲ SPRING

As temperatures rise and snow melts, the days begin to lengthen, and the forest floor fills with colourful spring flowers. Hibernating animals wake up from their winter dormancy, and many birds and mammals begin forming pairs for the breeding season.

▲ SUMMER

By summer the trees have fully opened their broad leaves, capturing sunlight to make their food by photosynthesis. These leaves are eaten by vast numbers of insects, such as caterpillars, which in turn feed many songbirds. Below the canopy, enough light reaches the ground to sustain an understorey of shrubs, small trees, and saplings. Most animals are now rearing young.

AMERICAN REDSTART
This warbler spends winter in Central and South America, but returns to North America's temperate forests in May to breed. It darts through the branches, picking insects off the leaves.

NORTH AMERICAN PORCUPINE
Summer is a time of plenty for the North American porcupine. Its diet widens to include virtually any edible plant material in the forest, from fruit to roots and shoots.

AROUND THE WORLD

Temperate forests are found where summers may be pleasant and warm but winters are cold and often long, with temperatures below freezing. Rainfall is spread evenly through the year, falling as snow in winter.

CLIMATE FACTS

Temperate forests typically receive 75–150 cm (30–60 in) of rain per year.

The average yearly temperature is 10 °C (50 °F), and the summers average 21 °C (70 °F)

The tallest trees in this biome are 18–30 m (60–100 ft) tall.

▲ AUTUMN

As days shorten, the declining light makes it harder for the trees to photosynthesize, and they lose their leaves. The fallen leaves build up in a thick, moist carpet of leaf litter, which teems with invertebrate life, small rodents, and amphibians. Many trees produce nuts and seeds, which animals eat, and from which new trees can grow.

▲ WINTER

In winter the trees are bare, most plants have stopped growing, and food is scarce. Many animals, from squirrels to jays, survive this tough time by eating food stored in autumn. Others, such as bats and bears, enter a form of deep sleep called hibernation. The majority of birds that rely on insects for food migrate long distances, and return in spring.

EASTERN CHIPMUNK

Chipmunks forage on the ground, scurrying to and fro among the leaf litter to gather seeds and nuts. Large cheek pouches enable them to carry the food back to their burrows to store for the winter.

WOOD FROG

The wood frog from North America hibernates under leaf litter and can survive more than half of its body freezing. It is one of the first hibernating species to re-awaken, emerging as early as January to breed in small pools.

HOW BOREAL FOREST WORKS

Stretching like a green belt around the northern continents, the boreal forest is the largest land biome on Earth. Also known as the taiga, the boreal forest is dominated by conifer trees and covers much of northern Eurasia and North America. It has short, moist summers, and long, snowy winters that provide a serious challenge for the animals that live there.

▲ WINTER
Winter in the boreal forest is long and harsh. It can last up to eight months, with temperatures falling as low as –70°C (–93.6 °F). Many animals hibernate or migrate south to warmer places. There is no rain during winter, only snow, so water is scarce and animals and plants must endure a freezing drought.

SPRUCE
Northern conifers, such as the spruce, have waxy, needle-like leaves that help them to retain moisture and so cope with the absence of water during the long freeze. Their conical shape and drooping branches also help them shed snow.

BEAVER
Beavers build waterside lodges in ponds and rivers, which freeze over in winter. The underwater entrance to the lodge remains open, allowing beavers to continue foraging under the ice for food.

PINE MARTEN
Pine martens are well insulated by silky coats that grow longer for the cold winter. They rely more on carrion for food during the freezing winter months, when food is scarce.

AROUND THE WORLD
The boreal forest biome covers 17 per cent of Earth's land surface and encircles the Arctic region, covering much of Canada, Scandinavia, and Russia.

▲ SUMMER
Summer in the boreal forest is warm, wet, and short, lasting just three months. During this season, the forest springs back to life. Plants blossom, hibernating animals emerge from their dens, and winter migrants return from the south. Large, shallow bogs form as ice melts, attracting flies and mosquitoes.

CROSSBILL
The unusual beak of the crossbill has crossed tips to help it to extract seeds from conifer cones, which are abundant during the short summer.

BLACK BEAR
Black bears emerge from hibernation in spring, often with cubs in tow. They spend summer eating as much food as possible to gain weight before the next winter hibernation.

SPHAGNUM MOSS
Few flowering plants can survive in the cold, wet soil of the forest floor, but mosses flourish. Sphagnum moss forms a thick mat that can hold 20 times its dry weight in water.

HOW TROPICAL GRASSLANDS WORK

Many tropical regions have long dry seasons that alternate with seasons of heavy rain. Few trees can survive the months of drought, so the vegetation is dominated by grasses. During the dry season, the grasses dry out and may even catch fire, but revive when the rain falls. In Africa the grass provides food for herds of grazing animals, which are hunted by powerful predators.

▲ DRY SEASON

When the rains stops and the grass dries out, many grazing animals migrate north to regions where the grass is still growing. Other plant eaters stay in damp areas of the Serengeti, near rivers and water holes. Here they make easy targets for carnivores such as lions and spotted hyenas.

GIRAFFE
Long-necked giraffes use their leathery tongues to gather the foliage of spiny acacia shrubs. They can feed high in the crowns of tall trees, giving them access to food that other animals cannot reach.

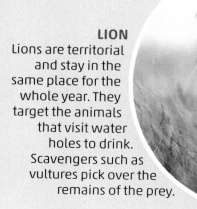

LION
Lions are territorial and stay in the same place for the whole year. They target the animals that visit water holes to drink. Scavengers such as vultures pick over the remains of the prey.

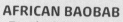

AFRICAN BAOBAB
Tropical grasslands are dotted with trees that are adapted to cope with months of drought. The African baobab survives by soaking up water in the rainy season and storing it in its swollen trunk.

AROUND THE WORLD

The most extensive tropical grasslands are south of the Sahara desert in Africa, where they are known as savannah. Others occur in India, South America, parts of Southeast Asia, and northern Australia.

CLIMATE FACTS

The temperature rarely drops below 17 °C (63 °F).

Annual rainfall is 50–130 cm (20–50 in).

Almost half of the African continent is covered in tropical grassland.

▲ WET SEASON

In the rainy season, lush grass grows on the Serengeti plains of east Africa. It is well adapted to being cropped by hungry zebras, antelopes, and gazelles because it grows from the base and not the tip like most plants. Grass also supports huge numbers of insects such as termites and swarming locusts.

SPEKE'S WEAVER

Weaver birds breed in the rainy season, when they can gather long blades of green grass for weaving their nests. They suspend these from the branches of trees, with the weaver birds building up to 200 nests in each tree.

COMMON WILDEBEEST

Wildebeest bear their calves at the start of the wet season, when there is plenty of grass for the mothers, which helps them to produce nutrient-rich milk. The calves can walk as soon as they are born.

DUNG BEETLES

Hordes of dung beetles recycle the waste produced by the grazing herds. They gather it into balls, bury it, and lay their eggs on it. When the eggs hatch, the beetle grubs eat the dung.

HOW TEMPERATE GRASSLANDS WORK

Some cool parts of North America, Eurasia, and southern South America are too dry to support forest, but not dry enough to become desert. In such areas, grasses fluorish. Temperate grasslands typically have snowy yet dry winters and hot, dry summers with occasional violent storms. They may support big herds of grazing animals.

▲ WINTER
On the North American prairies, winter temperatures plunge well below freezing. The grass stops growing, and grazing animals often have to dig beneath the snow to find food. Many birds migrate to warmer regions, and most small mammals retreat underground to spend the winter in hibernation.

COYOTE
A relative of the wolf, the coyote is an adaptable hunter. In winter it scavenges meat from the carcasses of big animals, such as deer, that have been killed by the harsh weather.

BISON
Bison survive the cold winters in small herds that migrate over the wild grasslands in search of food. Their size and thick coats protect them from the winter chill.

PRAIRIE DOG
These ground squirrels live in very big, complex burrow systems. On warmer winter days they emerge to nibble grasses and seeds with their sharp teeth, but they stay underground when it's cold.

AROUND THE WORLD

The main areas of temperate grassland are the American and Canadian prairies, the steppes of Eurasia, and the South American Pampas, which occurs mainly in Argentina.

CLIMATE FACTS

Summer temperatures can reach well over 38°C (100°F), and winter temperatures can be as low as –40°C (–40°F).

The snow that falls on grasslands in winter often acts as a reservoir of water when the grass begins to grow in spring.

Many grasslands are windy because there are few natural wind breaks, such as trees

▲ SUMMER

The Eurasian steppes burst into life in spring – the season when the grass grows most strongly. The hot, dry summer makes the grass dry out, and lightning strikes can make it catch fire. The flames destroy many competing plants, but the grasses survive and spring up again after it rains.

GRASSES

Blades of grass grow from the base of the plant, rather than from their tip, so they can continue to grow when they are bitten off at the top. Long roots grow deep into the ground to find water during droughts.

SAIGA ANTELOPE

The trunk-like nose of the saiga antelope helps it to cool its body during the summer. Its sensitive nose also help the saiga to locate areas where fresh new grass has grown after rain.

STEPPE EAGLE

Soaring tirelessly over the grasslands on outspread wings, the steppe eagle is able to target prey over a huge area, and easily spot it amongst the low-lying grasses.

HOW WETLANDS WORK

Most plants can't survive where the ground is waterlogged, especially if the water is salty. Such places develop into bogs, marshes, and swamps, with distinctive plants and wildlife that have adapted to live in flooded soil.

▲ FRESHWATER SWAMP
A swamp is a wetland full of trees. Some of the world's largest swamps are in the Amazon rainforest in South America, where the tropical heat encourages the growth of lush vegetation. In the rainy season, the rivers overflow and flood the surrounding forest, creating seasonal swamps, too.

▲ MARSH
A wetland dominated by low-growing plants is called a marsh. A vast expanse of marsh dominates the Everglades wetlands of southern Florida, USA. A tough, grass-like plant called sawgrass flourishes in the slow-moving water. Like many wetland plants, it has swollen roots that can survive dry periods when the water level falls.

GIANT WATER LILY
This plant roots in the muddy bed of shallow pools of water and has floating leaves and flowers. The tray-shaped leaves reach 3 m (10 ft) wide and can support the weight of a small child.

AMERICAN ALLIGATOR
The top predators in both freshwater and saltwater marshes of the American south are alligators. When parts of the Everglades dry out during the dry season, alligators dig out their own swamps, known locally as gator holes.

AMAZON RIVER DOLPHIN
In the rainy season, Amazon river dolphins leave their rivers to explore the seasonally flooded forest, swimming through the canopy of submerged trees in search of fish, turtles, and crabs. They use echolocation to find prey in the murky water.

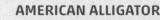

AROUND THE WORLD
Wetlands occur all over the world. Freshwater wetlands occur wherever there is enough rain. Salt marshes form in the mouths of rivers in cool regions. Mangrove swamps develop on most tropical seashores.

CLIMATE FACTS

Many freshwater wetlands dry out in summer, but their plants revive when the water returns.

In the last 100 years, roughly 50 per cent of the world's wetlands have been lost to farming and development.

Tangled mangrove roots form a barrier that helps protect the land from tropical storms.

 **MANGROVE SWAMP**
In tropical regions, such as Thailand in Southeast Asia, salt marshes are replaced by mangrove swamps – coastal forests flooded by seawater at high tide. Mangrove trees have specially adapted roots that absorb oxygen from the air, allowing the trees to grow in salty, waterlogged mud.

MANGROVE SNAKE
The venomous mangrove snake lives in the trees above the wet mud. It hunts lizards, tree frogs, birds, and small mammals among the branches at night.

ROSEATE SPOONBILL
The roseate spoonbill is one of many wading birds that feeds in wetlands. It feeds by swinging its bill through the water as it walks, sifting the mud for shrimp, insects, and amphibians.

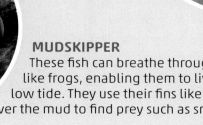

MUDSKIPPER
These fish can breathe through their wet skin, like frogs, enabling them to live on the mud at low tide. They use their fins like legs, skipping over the mud to find prey such as small crabs.

HOW MOUNTAINS WORK

Mountains are challenging habitats for wildlife. As height above sea level increases, the temperature drops, so a mountain peak in the tropics can be as cold as the Arctic tundra. Mountain animals have to cope with bitter cold, treacherous terrain, and a lower level of oxygen in the thin air.

▲ MONTANE FOREST

The lower slopes of mountains are often cloaked in forest known as montane forest, which provides food and shelter for animals. In Jiuzhaigou in China, the needle-shaped leaves of the conifer trees help them conserve water in winter, when it is difficult to absorb from the frozen ground.

▲ ALPINE GRASSLAND

Above the mountain forests, trees give way to low-growing shrubs and flower-rich meadows. In winter the alpine grasslands of Europe's Alps are snowbound, but in summer they provide rich pasture for grazing animals. Alpine flowers also attract butterflies and other nectar-feeding insects.

GIANT PANDA

Pandas are found only in the mountains of southwest China, where they feed on the bamboo plants that flourish in the cold, humid climate. Unlike other bears, they don't hibernate and instead rely on their dense, slightly oily fur to protect them from the rain and cold.

BAMBOO

Forests of bamboo – giant, fast-growing grasses – dominate the slopes of mountains in subtropical parts of China. Although not as hardy as conifer trees, some bamboo species can endure temperatures as low as –29 °C (–20°F).

LAMMERGEIER

Harsh mountain habitats take a heavy toll on animals but ensure there is plenty of food for scavengers, such as the lammergeier. A type of vulture, it drops bones onto rocks to expose the nutritious marrow inside.

AROUND THE WORLD

Mountain habitats occur worldwide, but some of the biggest are the American Rocky Mountains, the Andes of South America, the Himalayas of Asia and the Alps of Europe.

CLIMATE FACTS

The temperature falls as height above sea level increases, at the rate of 6.5°C per 1,000 m (3.56°F per 1,000 ft).

Mount Kilimanjaro in Africa lies close to the equator but its peak is so cold that it has permanent snow.

Mountains tend to have much wetter climates than the surrounding flatter land.

▲ ROCKY PEAKS

Few animals inhabit the peaks of mountains, where in ranges such as the Himalayas there is little but rock, rubble, and snow. Some insects and spiders survive on the snow fields, and predators use the high crags as vantage points for targeting prey below.

ALPINE IBEX

On European mountains, Alpine ibex climb the most rugged terrain to reach high pastures. They are amazingly agile, leaping between ledges and crags with sure-footed confidence.

SNOW LEOPARD

Camouflaged to hide in bare, rocky terrain, the snow leopard uses the rocks for cover as it hunts. It stalks prey silently to get close before rushing downhill to take its victims by surprise.

MOUNT EVEREST JUMPING SPIDER

This small spider lives in rock crevices on the high, barren slopes of Everest, where it preys on insects blown there by the wind. It lives permanently at a higher altitude than any other known animal.

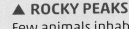

HOW DESERTS WORK

Deserts can be either hot or cold but all have an annual rainfall of less than 25 cm (10 in), making them very dry places. They may look like empty wastelands, but scattered among the rocks and sand dunes are many animals and plants that have adapted to cope with the hostile climate and lack of water.

▲ HOT DESERT

In hot deserts, such as the Sonoran Desert in North America, temperatures can soar to 50°C (122°F) by day but plummet at night and may even fall below zero. Most of the rain in the Sonoran falls in distinct seasons, turning the desert green and causing plants such as cacti to flower. Animals shelter from the sun during the day and are more active during the cooler nights.

DESERT POCKET MOUSE

Food in the desert is scarce. Pocket mice forage for seeds and store them in burrows to eat later. Their sand-coloured fur provides camouflage and hides them from predators.

SAGUARO CACTUS

Cacti soak up water after rainstorms and store it in their swollen stems. The saguaro is world's tallest cactus and can store enough water to survive for a year without rain.

DESERT TORTOISE

To conserve moisture, desert tortoises hide in burrows during the hottest part of the day. They are most active in the rainy season, when they forage for cactus flowers and other plants.

AROUND THE WORLD
Deserts cover more than a fifth of Earth's land and are found on every continent. Hot deserts (orange on map) are close to Earth's tropical zones, whereas cold deserts (yellow) exist further north or south. Polar regions (page 340–341) receive so little rain that they also count as deserts.

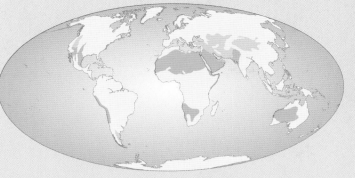

CLIMATE FACTS
The driest deserts get less than 1 cm (0.5 in) of rain a year.

Rain is so rare in some deserts that plants may go without it for years at a time.

The hottest temperature recorded on Earth was 70.7°C (159°F) in the Lut Desert in Iran.

▲ COLD DESERT
Cold deserts, such as the Gobi Desert in Asia, are found not only further north or south than hot deserts but also at higher altitudes, resulting in bitterly cold winters when frost and snow may cover much of the ground. In the Gobi Desert, winter temperatures fall as low as –40°C (–40°F). Plant life consists mostly of shrubs and grass, and many of the animals burrow in the ground to escape the cold.

ONAGER
This member of the horse family lives in Asia. It gets much of the water it needs from plants, but also digs holes in dry riverbeds to reach groundwater and eats snow during winter. Its sandy colour helps hide it from predators.

SALTWORT
Deep roots allow saltwort to take up moisture from the dry ground and stabilize itself in rocky or sandy soils. Saltwort has a high salt content that protects it from grazing animals.

BACTRIAN CAMEL
This camel can survive without water for months and can drink over 50 litres (100 pints) at once. Fat stored in the humps provides nourishment when food is scarce.

HOW TUNDRAS WORK

On the fringes of the icy polar regions is the tundra – a region where the ground below the surface is always frozen. Winters are dark, cold, and snowy, but in spring the snow melts and the upper ground layers thaw out. In the Arctic this turns large areas into waterlogged swamps, teeming with insect life that attracts vast flocks of birds.

▲ WINTER

The Arctic tundra is plunged into darkness for much of the winter. The land freezes and is covered by snow. Plants stop growing, and the insects disappear. Most of the birds leave, but snowy owls and other hunters remain, preying on small mammals that carry on their lives under the snow.

MUSK OX

Herds of shaggy-coated musk oxen – heavyweight relatives of wild goats – roam the tundra and dig through the snow to feed on grasses and moss. They are hunted by packs of Arctic wolves.

TUNDRA VOLE

Throughout the winter, small voles and lemmings stay active beneath the snow, insulated from the freezing winds above. They feed on grasses and juicy roots, and eat seeds they have stored in their burrows.

ERMINE

Voles and lemmings are hunted by slender weasels and ermines that can chase them through their burrows. In winter an ermine's fur turns pure white, but the tip of its tail stays black.

AROUND THE WORLD

Most of the world's tundra is on the northern continents, between the taiga forests and the Arctic Ocean. Tundra is also found on the Antarctic coast and on nearby islands in the Southern Ocean.

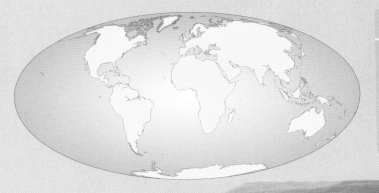

CLIMATE FACTS

Winter temperatures on the tundra can fall as low as −50 °C (−58 °F).

The permanently frozen ground below the surface is called permafrost.

The permafrost stops water draining away in summer, turning the tundra to swamp.

▲ SUMMER

In summer there is almost 24-hour daylight on the Arctic tundra. The surface thaws and becomes boggy, and tough, low-growing plants burst into flower. Millions of mosquitoes and other insects hatch, providing a feast for birds that migrate here to nest and raise their young before flying south again.

REINDEER

Big herds of reindeer trek north to feed on the plants that spring up when the snow melts. The calves are born near the beginning of summer, when there is plenty of food for their mothers.

RUDDY TURNSTONE

This shorebird flies north to breed on the Arctic tundra, where its young can be sure of plentiful insect food. It nests on the ground, where its colourful summer plumage provides excellent camouflage.

PURPLE SAXIFRAGE

Most tundra plants grow close to the ground, often forming dense cushions of foliage that protect them from icy winds. Purple saxifrage is typical, and one of the first to flower in summer.

HOW POLAR REGIONS WORK

Polar regions are among the least hospitable places on Earth, with bitterly cold winds and extremely low temperatures. In the short summers there are 24 hours of sunlight each day, while long, unforgiving winters go by in total darkness. Conditions are too hostile for trees, and only a few low-lying plant species and a variety of wildlife can survive. Most of the animals in polar regions depend on the sea for food.

▲ ARCTIC SEA ICE
The Arctic is a frozen ocean, centred on the North Pole, and is almost completely surrounded by land. Plant life is limited to algae, which cling to the underside of the ice and flourish on the ocean surface. Seals use the pack ice to rest or give birth to their young, and polar bears use it to travel.

GREENLAND SHARK
The Greenland shark lives about 1.2 km (0.7 miles) deep in the icy Arctic waters. It has the longest lifespan of any vertebrate animal, perhaps living for more than 500 years.

HARP SEAL
Harp seals can stay underwater for 15 minutes at a time as they search for fish and crustaceans. They are insulated from the chilly water by an extra-thick layer of fat called blubber.

POLAR BEAR
Polar bears depend on the sea ice as a hunting ground for seals. They have short, sharp claws to grip the ice and a thick layer of body fat for protection against the cold.

AROUND THE WORLD

The polar biome is found at the extreme north and south of Earth. As there is very little rain in Antarctica, it is also Earth's largest desert. Many scientists believe that the polar biome is under threat as a result of global warming – the rise in temperature caused by human activity.

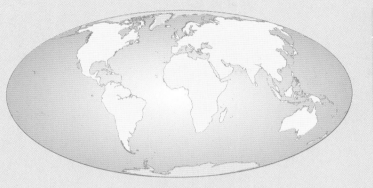

CLIMATE FACTS

The coldest recorded temperature on Earth is –89.2 °C (–128.6 °F), recorded in Antarctica in 1983.

Ice in the Arctic Ocean can be 50 m (165 ft) thick during the coldest part of winter.

▲ ANTARCTIC CONTINENT

The Antarctic continent lies over the South Pole and is almost entirely covered in ice. Vegetation is mostly limited to algae, lichens, and mosses that grow on ice or rock, and there are just two species of flowering plant. It is, however, home to many animals, such as penguins, seals, and the snow petrel – one of the only birds that breeds almost exclusively in Antarctica.

EMPEROR PENGUIN

These penguins live on the ice but dive into freezing waters to catch fish. Their streamlined bodies allow them to dive deep into the water, and they can remain submerged for almost 20 minutes at a time.

ANTARCTIC HAIR GRASS

A species of Antarctic flowering plant, Antarctic hair grass is self-pollinating as an adaptation to living in a harsh environment. Its flowers remain closed to prevent damage from the cold.

ANTARCTIC KRILL

Krill – shrimp-like crustaceans – reach such numbers in Antarctic waters that they are among the most numerous animals on Earth. Whales, seals, penguins, and other animals depend on them for food.

HOW RIVERS AND LAKES WORK

Only about one per cent of Earth's water is fresh water found in ponds, lakes and rivers. These habitats are home to 40 per cent of all the world's fish species and many aquatic plants and animals. Rainfall fills lakes and rivers, and all around the world living things depend upon them for survival.

▲ PONDS AND LAKES

Loch Lomond is the largest area of fresh water in Great Britain. Like other lakes, it contains still water that fills a depression in the ground. Lakes are bigger and deeper than ponds. Aquatic plants grow thickly along their shallow edges. Some old and remote lakes contain species found nowhere else.

QUILLWORT

Growing to depths of more than 4 m, the lake quillwort is named for its long, quill-like leaves, which emerge as clumps in cold, clear still water.

COMMON FROG

Never far from ponds and lakes, during springtime common frogs gather in fresh water to spawn. Many adults will return to the water in winter to hibernate in mud at the bottom of a pond or lake.

NORTHERN PIKE

An ambush predator, this sharp-toothed fish lurks among water weeds near the shallow edges of lakes, ready to shoot out and grab other fish and frogs.

AROUND THE WORLD

The world's largest freshwater habitats are the Great Lakes of North America, and the giant river basins of the Amazon and the Congo. Tropical habitats contains the most species: there are more fish species in the Amazon basin than in the entire Atlantic Ocean.

CLIMATE FACTS

Rivers and lakes are found throughout the world and so these freshwater habitats include many different climate conditions.

In winter, many temperate lakes and rivers freeze over but animals remain active under the icy surface.

▲ RIVERS AND STREAMS

The Mekong River runs from the Tibetan highlands to the South China Sea. Along the way, streams join it, adding to the flowing water. In some places, the current moves quickly, and animals need special adaptations so they are not washed away. At the river's mouth, the water gets saltier as it mixes with seawater.

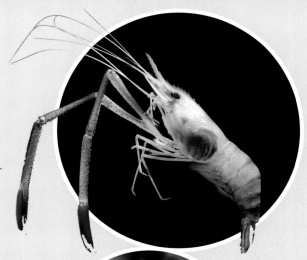

GIANT RIVER PRAWN

Young stages of this crustacean live in the salty estuary, but as they mature into adult prawns, they move upriver to spend all their time in fresh water.

BUTTERFLY LOACH

A fish of fast-flowing mountain streams, the butterfly loach has wide, sucker-like fins that can be used to grip rocks and so withstand the force of strong currents.

EURASIAN OTTER

River otters are semi-aquatic, which means they spend part of their time on land and part in water. There they hunt for fish, crustaceans, and frogs.

HOW OCEANS WORK

Oceans cover more than three-fifths of Earth's surface. Every part of an ocean – from the beaches and rock pools along its coast to its deepest, darkest depths – is home to organisms that have adapted to survive in their aquatic habitat. Some ocean habitats, such as coral reefs, have an especially rich divesity of wildlife.

▲ COASTAL ZONE

Where ocean meets land, the movement of the tides has a powerful influence. Animals and seaweeds that live here have to cling to the wave-washed shore and survive being periodically exposed to the air. Further offshore, many more kinds of animal live in the sunlit coastal waters.

▲ OPEN OCEAN

Out in the open ocean, far from land, life ranges from microscopic plankton to massive whales – the biggest animals on Earth. Most animals that live in the open ocean stay near the surface, where conditions are warmer and brighter, but some live on or close to the ocean floor.

KELP

Seaweeds such as kelp use their sucker-like structures called holdfasts attach themselves to rocks. The leafy fronds of these giant algae work like the leaves of plants to turn sunlight into food.

CORAL

Corals are tiny animals whose stony skeletons build up over time to form reefs in shallow tropical seas. Coral reefs support complex communities of ocean life. They grow best in the warm, brightly-lit waters near the coast.

PLANKTON

Ocean water teems with tiny drifting organisms called plankton. Many are algae that live near the surface and use the energy of sunlight to make food.

AROUND THE WORLD

More than 95 per cent of ocean species live in the shallow seas that surround Earth's continents. Beyond these seas, the ocean floor plunges to depths of 4,000 m (13,100 ft) or more.

OCEAN FACTS

The deepest part of the ocean is 10,994 m (36,070 ft) below the surface.

Coral reefs contain a quarter of all the species that live in the ocean.

The biggest animal alive is the blue whale, which can grow to 25 m (82 ft) long.

▲ DEEP SEA

Light from the Sun only reaches down to about 250 m (820 ft), and below this the ocean is dark. In the deep sea zone – below 1,800 m (5,900 ft) – animals must rely on food drifting down from above, or use special tactics to lure prey.

DEEP SEA ANGLERFISH

This fish possesses an organ filled with light-producing bacteria to attract small fish, which it then gulps into its enormous mouth.

HUMPBACK WHALE

This mammal strains water through a set of giant bristles (baleen plates) in its mouth to trap small animals. Like all mammals, a humpback whale must breathe air – but it can hold its breath for up to 30 minutes when diving.

DUMBO OCTOPUS

The dumbo octopus swims by flapping its ear-like fins. It hovers above the sea floor 3,000 m (9,850 ft) below the surface, searching for worms and other invertebrates to eat.

GLOSSARY

ABDOMEN
The hind part of an animal's body. The abdomen of a mammal is also called a belly.

ADAPTATION
A special feature of an organism that makes it better suited to its environment or way of life. The streamlined shape of a dolphin, for instance, is an adaptation to living in water.

ALBUMEN
The white of an egg, consisting of water and proteins to nourish the embryo developing inside the egg.

ALGAE
Simple, plant-like organisms that live in water and make their food by photosynthesis.

AMPHIBIAN
A cold-blooded, backboned animal, such as a frog or newt, that spends part of its life in water and part on land.

ANTENNAE
Sensitive feelers on the heads of insects or other invertebrates.

ARTHROPOD
An invertebrate that has an external skeleton and jointed legs. Insects, spiders, scorpions, and millipedes and are all types of arthropod.

AQUATIC
An aquatic animal or plant lives in water.

ARACHNID
An arthropod with eight legs, such as a spider or scorpion.

BACTERIA
Microscopic single-celled organisms that make up one of the main kingdoms of life on Earth. Many bacteria are helpful but some cause diseases.

BILL
The jaws of a bird, also called a beak.

BIOME
A major division of the living world, such as rainforest, desert, or temperate grassland. Each biome has its own distinctive climate, vegetation, and animal life.

BLOWHOLE
A hole or pair of holes on the top of a whale or dolphin's head, used to breathe air .

CAMOUFLAGED
Coloured, patterned, or shaped to match the surroundings. Animals use camouflage to hide.

CARBOHYDRATE
An energy-rich substance found in food. Sugar and starch are types of carbohydrate.

CARBON DIOXIDE
A gas found in air. Animals breathe out carbon dioxide as a waste product, but plants absorb it

CARNIVORE
A meat-eating animal with teeth especially shaped for tearing flesh.

CARRION
Dead or rotting animal flesh.

CARTILAGE
A tough but flexible tissue found on the bones of vertebrates. Cartilaginous fish have skeletons made almost entirely of cartilage.

CELL
A tiny unit of living matter. Cells are the building blocks of all living things.

CELLULOSE
A substance found in plant cell walls that gives plants their structure.

CETACEAN
An aquatic mammal with fins, such as a whale or dolphin.

CHLOROPHYLL
A bright green substance in plants that absorbs energy from sunlight, allowing plants to make food by photosynthesis.

CHLOROPLASTS
Tiny structures that are found inside plant cells and contain the green pigment chlorophyll. Photosynthesis takes place in chloroplasts.

COCOON
The silk case that a moth caterpillar spins around itself before turning into a pupa.

COLD-BLOODED
Cold-blooded animals, such as reptiles, allow their body temperature to rise and fall with the temperature of their surroundings.

COMPOUND EYE
An eye made up of many tiny light-detecting units, each with its own lens. Insects have compound eyes.

CORAL
A small marine animal that catches food with stinging tentacles. Coral reefs form from the hard skeletons of corals that live in large colonies.

CORNEA
A transparent layer covering the front of the eye

COURTSHIP
Behaviour that forms a bond between a male and a female animal before mating.

CRUSTACEAN
An invertebrate with a hard exoskeleton, gills, and usually more than 10 pairs of limbs, such as a shrimp or lobster. Most crustaceans live in water.

CYTOPLASM
The jelly-like interior of a cell.

DECOMPOSE
Break down into simpler chemicals. Dead organisms decompose (decay) because smaller organisms feed on their remains, digesting their tissue.

DIVERSITY
A term to describe the variety of different species.

DROUGHT
A long period of low rainfall resulting in a lack of water and very dry conditions.

ECHOLOCATION
A way of sensing objects by

producing sound and listening for echoes. Bats and dolphins use echolocation to "see" in the dark or in murky water.

ECOSYSTEM
A community of living things and their environment. An ecosystem may be as small as a pond or as large as a rainforest.

EGG
The protective capsule that contains a developing baby bird, reptile, or other animal. The word egg can also mean a female sex cell.

EGG TOOTH
A hard lump on the beak or jaw of a baby bird or reptile, used to break the shell when it hatches.

ELECTRORECEPTION
The detection of electric fields. Sharks use electroreception to precisely locate prey during an attack.

EMBRYO
The earliest stage in the development of an animal or plant.

ENZYME
A substance that an organism produces to speed up a particular chemical reaction. Animals produce digestive enzymes to speed up the reactions that break down food in their intestines.

EPIPHYTE
A plant that grows on another plant as a means of support.

EVOLUTION
The gradual change of a species, usually over many generations.

EXOSKELETON
A hard outer skeleton, such as that of an insect.

EXTINCT
Permanently gone. An extinct species no longer has any living member.

FERTILIZATION
The joining of male and female sex cells to produce a new living thing.

FRUIT
The ripened ovary of a flower, containing one or more seeds. Some fruits are sweet and juicy to attract animals.

FUNGUS
A living thing that absorbs food from living or dead matter around it. Mushrooms and toadstools are fungi.

GENE
An instruction encoded in the molecule DNA and stored inside a living cell. Genes are passed from parents to their offspring and determine each living thing's characteristics.

GERMINATION
The start of growth in a seed or spore.

GILL
An organ used to breathe underwater.

GLAND
An organ in an animal's body that makes and releases a particular substance. Human sweat glands, for instance, release sweat onto the skin.

HABITAT
The place where an organism lives.

HERBIVORE
An animal that eats plants.

HIBERNATION
A resting state like very deep sleep that occurs in some animals in winter.

HOOF
The hard tip of the foot of an animal such as a horse or deer. Hooves help animals to run quickly.

HOST
A living organism that a parasite feeds on.

INCUBATE
Keep eggs warm, for instance by sitting on them.

INSECTIVORE
An animal that mainly eats insects or other invertebrates.

INSULATION
Reduction of heat loss by a body layer such as fur, blubber, or feathers.

INTESTINE
A tube-like organ through which food passes while it is being digested. The intestine connects the stomach to the anus.

INVERTEBRATE
An animal without a backbone, such as an insect or worm.

IRIDESCENT
An iridescent object has bright, shiny colours that change when viewed from different angles.

IRIS
A coloured ring of muscle around the pupil of an animal's eye. The iris controls the size of the pupil and therefore how much light enters the eye

JACOBSON'S ORGAN
A scent-detecting organ in the roof of an animal's mouth.

KEEL
The enlarged breastbone of a bird. The large flight muscles of birds are anchored to the keel.

KERATIN
The tough protein that fur, hair, feathers, nails, horns, and hooves are made of. The outer layer of an animal's skin is toughened by keratin.

LARVA
The early stage in the life cycle of an animal that undergoes a major change when it develops into an adult.

LENS
The part of an eye that focuses light rays, creating a sharp image.

LIGAMENT
A band of tough, fibrous tissue that holds bones together in a joint.

MAMMAL
A warm-blooded vertebrate (animal with a backbone) that feeds its young on milk and usually has a covering of fur.

MARSUPIAL
A mammal that gives birth to very undeveloped young and that usually carries babies in a pouch.

MATING
Close physical contact between male and female animals that allows their sex cells to fuse and form an embryo.

MEMBRANE
A thin lining or barrier that stops some substances from passing through it, but allows others to cross.

METAMORPHOSIS
A dramatic change in the body of an animal as it matures. Caterpillars turn into butterflies by metamorphosis.

MICROORGANISM
An organism too small to be seen with the naked eye, such as a bacterium.

MIGRATION
A long journey undertaken by an animal to reach a new habitat. Many birds migrate every year between their summer and winter homes.

MIMICRY
Imitation of another, often more dangerous, animal. Many insects mimic venomous species in order to deter predators.

MOLECULE
A chemical unit made of two or more atoms bonded together. Nearly all matter is made of molecules.

MOLLUSC
A soft-bodied invertebrate that is often protected by a hard shell. Snails, clams, and octopuses are molluscs.

MONOTREME
An egg-laying mammal. Platypuses and echidnas are the only types of monotreme.

MOULT
Shed skin, hair, or feathers. Animals with exoskeletons must moult occasionally in order to grow larger.

MUCUS
A thick, slippery liquid produced by animals for various purposes. Mucus lines the intestines, helping food move through them.

MUSCLE
A type of animal tissue that contracts to cause movement.

NECTAR
A sugary liquid produced by flowers. Bees collect nectar in order to make honey.

NERVE
A bundle of specialized cells that carries electrical signals around an animal's body.

NOCTURNAL
Active at night but inactive during the day.

NUCLEUS
The control centre of cell, where the cells genes are stored in DNA molecules.

NUTRIENTS
Substances that animals and plants take in and that are essential for life and growth.

OMMATIDIUM
One of the many units that make up the compound eye of an insect.

ORGAN
A specialized part of an animal or plant that carries out a particular task, such as a stomach or a brain.

ORGANISM
A living thing.

OVARY
An organ in a female animal that produces egg cells, or the part of a flower that contains developing seeds.

OXYGEN
A gas that makes up 21 per cent of Earth's atmosphere. Most living things take in oxygen from the air and use it to release energy from food in a process called respiration.

PARALYSE
Stop an animal from moving, for instance by blocking the signals transmitted to muscles by nerves.

PARASITE
An organism that lives on or inside another organism (a host) and feeds on its flesh for an extended period. Parasites are harmful to their hosts.

PERMAFROST
Permanently frozen ground below the upper surface of the soil.

PHEROMONE
A chemical produced by an animal that affects another member of the same species. Many animals produce pheromones to attract mates.

PHOTOSYNTHESIS
The process by which plants use the Sun's energy to make food molecules from water and carbon dioxide.

PLACENTA
An organ in mammals that allows substances to pass between the bloodstream of an unborn baby and that of its mother.

PLUMAGE
A bird's feathers.

POISON
A substance that is toxic (harmful) when touched or eaten.

POLLEN
A powdery substance made by flowers that contains male sex cells. Insects unwittingly carry pollen from one flower to another, helping plants reproduce.

POLLINATION
The transfer of pollen from the male part of a flower to the female part of a flower. Pollination is essential for sexual reproduction in flowering plants.

POLYP
A form taken by some marine animals, such as jellyfish, sea anemones, and corals. Polyps have a mouth at one end, and are attached firmly at the base to a rock or the seabed.

PORE
A small opening an the outside of an organism that allows substances such as gases and liquids to pass through it.

PREDATOR
An animal that hunts other animals for food.

PREY
An animal hunted by other animals for food.

PROTEIN
A substance found in food that is essential for growth and is used for constructing many different types of tissue. Hair, spider silk, and muscle all consist mostly of protein.

PUPA
The resting stage in the life cycle of an insect that undergoes metamorphosis.

QUILL
The sharp spine of a porcupine or hedgehog, or the shaft of a bird's feather.

RECEPTOR
A molecule, cell, or organ that detects a stimulus. Light receptor cells in animals' eyes, for example, detect light and so create the sense of vision.

REGURGITATE
Bring swallowed food back up into the mouth. Many birds regurgitate food to feed their young.

REPRODUCTION
Production of new offspring.

REPTILE
A cold-blooded, scaly-skinned vertebrate (animal with a backbone); reptiles include snakes and lizards.

RESPIRATION
The process by which living cells use oxygen to release chemical energy from food molecules.

RETINA
A layer of light-sensitive cells lining the inside of an eye.

ROOT
The part of a plant that anchors it to the ground and obtains water and nutrients from the soil.

RUMINANT
A plant-eating mammal with a four-chambered stomach. Deer and cattle are ruminants.

SCAVENGER
An animal that feeds on the remains of dead animals or plants, such as a vulture.

SECRETION
A substance made and released (secreted) by cells.

SEED
A reproductive structure containing a plant embryo and a food store.

SERRATED
With a jagged edge. Serrated teeth cut through flesh like a steak knife.

SHOAL
A group of fish.

SPECIES
A type of organism, such as a cheetah or a giraffe. Members of the same species can breed together in the wild.

SPERM CELL
A male sex cell. When a male sex cell fuses with a female sex cell, they form a new organism.

SPORE
A microscopic package of cells, produced by a fungus or plant, that can grow into a new individual.

STREAMLINED
Smoothly shaped to move easily through air or water. Seals are streamlined to help them swim faster.

SYMBIOSIS
A close relationship between two different species that live together.

TENDON
A tough, fibrous band of tissue that anchors a muscle to a bone. Tendons pull bones when muscles contract, making an animal's body move.

TERRESTRIAL
Living on the ground.

THORAX
The central part of an insect's body or the chest of a vertebrate.

TISSUE
A group of similar cells that make up part of an organism. Skin is a type of tissue.

UMBILICAL CORD
A cord-like structure that carries food, oxygen, and other vital substances between an unborn baby mammal and its mother's body.

UTERUS
In female mammals, the part of the body that contains and nourishes developing babies.

VENOM
Any toxic fluid produced by an animal that is actively transferred into the body of another, usually via fangs, stings, or similar structures.

VERTEBRA
One of many small bones that form the backbone of a vertebrate.

VERTEBRATE
An animal with a backbone.

WARM-BLOODED
Warm-blooded animals, such as birds and mammals, maintain a constant internal body temperature. They typically have fur or feathers to stay warm.

WOMB
See uterus.

YOLK
The inner part of an egg, which is rich in protein and fat to nourish the developing embryo.

INDEX

Page numbers in **BOLD**
type refer to main entries

A

acorns 63
Africa 328–9, 335
  amphibians 172
  birds 237, 240, 247, 262
  invertebrates 79, 121, 134,
    138, 142
  mammals 19, 281, 283,
    286, 312, 315
  plants 71
  reptiles 196, 212
African wild dogs 283
air 32, 54
air sacs 255
Alaska 237
albatrosses 229, 242
albinos 16, 17
algae 24, 26, **30–3**, 89, 341
  and oxygen 27, 32
  and lichen 40, 41
alligators 332
Alps 334
Amazon 332
Amazon tree boa 212–3
amber 67
amoebas 26
amphibians **170–87**
  defences 182–3
  life cycles 174–5
  metamorphosis 172, **174–5**
  movement 178–9
amphipods 143
ampullae of Lorenzini 158
anglerfish 168

animals **10–11**, 15
  classification 20–21
  cold-blooded 191
  communication 132
  carnivores 276, 282–3,
    290–1
  evolution 18–19
  herbivores 190, **294–5**, 312
  prehistoric 19, 21, 188, 208
  reproduction 12–13
  species 20
  underground 96, 293, 296,
    310
  warm-blooded 266, 267
  see also individual animals
  and animal groups
Antarctica 237, **341**
anteaters 293
antennae 11, 76, 77, **110–11**,
  113, 141
antlions 102
ants 67, 102, 111, **130–1**
apes 266, 301, **308–9**
aphids 13, 130
arachnids 77, 119
archaea 11
Arctic 237, **340**
Arctic terns 237
armadillos 288–9
Asia 217, 333, 337
atmosphere 27, 32
Australia 88, 90–1, 210, 271
axolotls 186–7

B

babies
  birds 242–5
  fish 152–5

mammals 266, 267,
  272–9, 280
  reptiles 196–7
  see also larvae
baboons 286
bacteria 10, 11, 13, 27
  fish 168
  human body 28–9
badgers 310, 311
baleen 316
bamboo 334
banana plants 59
barbels 150
barbs 63, 123, 182, 158, 268
  feathers 230, 231
barnacles 89, 143
bar-tailed godwits 237
basking 191
bats 59, 266, 301, 302–5, 325
beaks
  birds 220, **224–5**, 233
  octopuses 84, 85
bears 325
  black 327
  brown 157
  polar 268, 311, 340
beavers 297, **298–9**, 326
bees 102, 109, 111, **128–9**
  as pollinators 12, 56, 58
  stings 123
beetles 59, 102, 126, 329
  chemicals 121, 132
  exoskeletons 104–5
  eyes 108–9
  flying 114
bigeye trevalies 164–5
bioluminescence 32, 132,
  168
biomes **320–321**
  see also individual biomes
birds 218–63
  classification 20

courtship 232, **238–9**
diving **256–7**, 259
eggs 242–3
flightless 221, 253, **262–3**
flying 226–9
nests **240–1**, 247, 329, 323
and plants 58, 63
of prey 221, 224, **226–9**,
  248–51, 323, 334
senses 220, 248, 251
skeletons 222–3
see also individual birds
birds of paradise 238
birds of prey 221, **226–9**,
  323, 334
  eagles 224, **226–7**, 229,
    241, 250–1
  owls **248–9**, 253, 338
bivalves **80–1**, 82
black bears 327
black follower fish 169
bloodsuckers 119
blowholes 316
blubber 258
bluestreak cleaner wrasses
  167
bobbit worms 99
bogs 320, 327
bombardier beetles 121
bones
  birds 220, **222–3**, 229, 259
  fish 147, 151, 160, 169
  human 223, 300
  mammals 223, 271, **300–1**,
    309, 312, 313, 317
  reptiles 211
Borneo 323
bowerbirds 238
brains
  axolotls 187
  fish 146, 150, 159
  mammals 266, 270, 303

snails 79
snakes 195
worms 97
breathing
amphibians 185, 186
insects 100
mammals 316
in water 80, 147, 152
worms 96
bristles 97, 98, 99, 120, 121
microorganisms 24, 25
bristleworms 99
brown bears 157
bubbles 154, 258
budgerigars 235
bugs 10, 102, 125
bullfrogs 172
buoyancy 148
burrows 139, 140
reptiles 209
mammals 281, 296, 310, 311, 336
spiders 136
butterflies 58, 104, 126, 127
caterpillars 103, 121, 126
migration 111
butterfly loahces 343

C

cacti 67, **70-1**, 336
caecilians 173
camels 337
camouflage
amphibians 182
birds 220, 259, 339
crabs 86
fish 159, 161, **162-3**
insects 102, 116, **124-7**
mammals 269, 277, 291
mimicry 58, 85, 125, 126-7, 162, 163, 247
molluscs 83, 85
reptiles 194, 201, 206

spiders 127
carapace 142, 216
carbohydrates 54
carbon dioxide
bees 111
breathing 100, 147, 185, 197, 243
photosynthesis 45, 54
yeast 27
carnivores 276, 282-3, **290-1**
carpels 56, 57
carrion flowers 59
cartilage 147, 159
cassowaries 253, 263
caterpillars 76-7, 103
defences 120-1, 126-7
metamorphosis 106-7
catfish 150-1
catkins 59
cats 272-3, 276, **290-1**
cells **14-15**
algae 30
chromatophores 162
division 13, 24
DNA 16
plant 55, 57
and regeneration 187
respiration 11
sensory 158, 270
centipedes 140, 141
cephalopods 82, 84-5
chameleons 202-5
chemicals
defences 67, **120-1**, 289
insects 110, **120-1**, 132
pheromones 110, 111, 131
pigments 17, 30, 65, 162
trails 131
China 334
chipmunks 325
chitin 104, 115
chitons 82
chlorophyll 30, 55
chloroplasts 15, 27, 30
chromatophores 162
cicadas 113
ciliates 26

clams 81, 82
claws
birds 221, 223, 224, 251, 252
burrowers 310, 209
centipedes 141
crabs 142
mammals 277, 291, 301
reptiles 191, 209
scorpions 139
climates
boreal forests 327
deserts 337
grassland, tropical 329
mountains 335
oceans 345
polar 241
rivers and lakes 343
temperat forests 325
tundra 339
climbing 179, 206-7, 301
clownfish 167
cnidarians 77, 86-93
cobras 212
cockroaches 118-9
coconuts 62
cocoons 106, 107
cold-blooded animals 191
colonies
corals 88
insects 102, 111, 123, **128-9**, 130, 131
mole rats 281
communication
amphibians 180-1
insects 111, 112, 113, 132
reptiles 190
conifers 45, 326, 334
constrictors 212-3
corals **88-9**, 90-1
reefs 88, 89, **90-1**, 160, 162, 163, 167
cormorants 257
cotyledons 46, 49
countershading 159
courtship
amphibians 173

birds 232, **238-9**
insects 113, 132
reptiles 205
crabs 82, 86, 142-3
craneflies 115
cranes 238
crests 185, 205, 206
crickets 102, 110, 113
crocodiles 191, **200-1**
scales 192
crossbills 327
crustaceans 77, 142-3
cuckoos 246-7
cytoplasm 24, 30

D

damselflies 102
deathstalkers 138
decomposition 39
defences
amphibians **182-3**, 184
birds 262
chemical **120-1**, 289
fish **160-1**, 163
insects 120-1, 124-7
mammals 28, 269, **288-9**
microorganisms 32
molluscs 78, 85, 87
myriapods 141
plants **66-7**
deserts 321, **336-7**
animals 139
plants 70-1
diatoms 27
dicotyledons 48
digestion
herbivores 295
dinosaurs 218, 264
diving birds 256-7, 259
DNA 15, 16-17
dogs, African wild 283
dolphins 271, **282-3**
river 332

dragonflies 102, 115
dry season 328
ducks 242-5, 252, **254-5**
dung beetles 329

E

eagles 224, **226-7**, 229, 241
  hunting 250-1
ears
  birds 248
  fish 151
  insects 112
  mammals 266, 271, 307
earthworms 96
earwigs 103
echidnas 275
echinoderms 76, 94-5
echolocation 271, 302, 303
eggs
  amphibians 174, 175, 177
  birds 220, **242-3**, 247,
    255
  crabs 142
  fish 152, 153, 157
  insects 100, 106, 107, 128,
    129
  mammals 266, 275
  reptiles **196-7**, 217
egg teeth 197, 242, 244
egrets 224
electrical signals 151, 158,
  159, 271
electroreception 151, 271
elephantfish 151
elephants 12, **312-13**, 266,
  315
  babies 279
  evolution 18-19
elytra 105
embryos
  birds 242
  amphibians 174
  plant 48, 57

reptiles 197
energy
  in cells 15
  and migration 236, 237
  from the Sun 14, 30, 31, 51
ermine 338
Europe 181, 184, 334
Everest, Mount 335
Everglades 332
evolution 18-19, 20, 218,
  264
excretion 11
exoskeletons 77, 100, **104-5**,
  113, 124
  moulting 105, 141, 142
eyelids 146, 173
eyes
  amphibians 183, 185
  birds 249, 250, 259
  compound 108, 109
  crabs 142
  fish 150, 168
  human 109
  insects 108-9
  mammals 270
  molluscs 79, 80
  reptiles 195, 203, 208, 209
  scorpions 138
  spiders 135
eyespots 103, 127

F

falcons 222, 224, 228-9
fangs 135, 168, 212, 213
feathers 220, **226-31**, 245,
  249
  and courtship 238-9
  waterproofing 254
feeding
  birds 224-5
  crabs 143
  fish 154, 169
  mammals 274-5

reptiles 191, **214-5**
scorpions 139
young 154, 274-5
feet
  birds 221, 223, 224, 244,
    251**252-3**, 262
  amphibians 178, 179,
    187
  insects 101
  mammals 277, 307, 310,
    313
  reptiles 217
  scorpions 138
  spiders 135
  webbed 178, 217, 244,
    252, 253, 254
ferns 45
fighting 286
filter feeders 89, 159, 225,
  255, 316
finches 225
fingernails 308
fins 146, 148, 149, 160, 163,
  166, 167, 317
  amphibians 175
fire-bellied toads 182-3
fireflies 132
fire salamanders 184
fish **144-69**, 316, 333, 343
  bony 146, 147, 148, 151
  camouflage 161, 162-3
  cartilaginous 147, 148
  classification 21
  deep sea 168-9
  defences 160-1
  jawless 147
  muscles 146, 147, 149
  reproduction 152-3
  senses **150-1**, 158, 168
  schools 164
  skeletons 147
  swimming 148-9
flagellates 27
flamingos 225, 253
flatworms 99
flies 59, 102, 109
  bloodsucking flies 119

mimicry 127
  and mushrooms 37
  wings 15
flightless birds 221, 253,
  262-3
flippers 217, 259, 301, 317
flocks 235, 338
flowers 44, **46-7**, 56-9, 60,
  72
  seeds 46-7, 57, 62-3
food chains
  marine 32
food poisoning 28
forests
  boreal 321
  montane 334
  temerate 320, **324-5**
  see also rainforests
fossils 11, 19, 67
foxes 270-1, **278-9**
frogfish 162
frogs 12, **172-3**, 177
  communication 180-1
  hibernation **325**, 342
  life cycle 174-5
  movement **178-9**, 182
frogspawn 174, 177
fruits 44, 60-1
fungi 10, 28, 34-9, 130, 322
  and lichen 40
fur 267, **268-9**, 338

G

Galapagos Islands 18, 189
garter snakes 192-3
gastropods 82
gazelles 286-7
geckos 206-7
geese 237
genes 17
genets 266-7
germination 46, 48
germs 28-9

gibbons 308-9
gills 80, 142, 147, 174
    external 186
giraffes 223, 273, **294-5**, 328
glassfish 146-7
gliding
    birds 225, 229
    mammals 306-7
global warming 89
Gobi Desert 337
gobies 167
gorillas 280-1
gouramis 154
grasshoppers 103, 104, 112,
    121
grasslands 18, 134, 262, 315,
    320, **328-9**
    Alpine 334
Great Barrier Reef 88, **90-1**
Great Britain 342
grebes 241, 257
guillemots 257
guinea pigs 274-5

H

habitats 318-345
hagfish 169
hair
    mammals 267, **268-9**
    sensory 101, 105, 111, 122,
        139
haltares 115
hammerhead sharks 159
hamsters 297
hawks 229
hearing
    birds 248
    fish 151
    insects 112-3
    mammals 271, 291
    reptiles 209
hearts
    worms 97

heat-sensitive pits 194
hedgehogs 16-17
herbivores **294-5**, 312
herds 289
hermaphrodites 13
herons 224
hibernation 324, **325**, 326,
    327, 342
hierarchy 279, **280-1**
Himalayas 335
hives 111, **128-9**
honey 128, 129
honey bees 111, **128-9**
honeydew 130
hoofed animals 266, 300,
    301
hormones, and plants 49
horns 286, 287
horses 276
hoverflies 127
humans 264
    bones 222, 300
    illness 28, 138
hummingbirds 225, **232-3**
    nests 241
hunters
    amphibians 185
    birds 248-9
    fish 163
    insects 115, 116, 139, 283
    reptiles 200-1, **212-3**
    underwater 158-9, 282-3,
        317
husks 46
hyenas 281, 286

I

ibex 335
ice 18, 30, 253, 259, 269,
    283, 340, 341
iguanas **190-1**, 198-9
illness 28, 138
imprinting 279

indonesia 210
insectivores 292-3
insects 10-11, 76, **100-33**
    growth 10, 105
    mouthparts 104-5
    and plants 11, 56, 57, 58,
        67, 68-9
    reproduction 10, 13
    senses 11, 108-13
    wings 101, 105, **114-15**,
        131
    see also individual insects
invertebrates 74-143
    arachnids 77
    classification 21
    cnidarians 77, **86-93**
    crustaceans 77
    echinoderms 76, 94-5
    insects 76, **100-17**
    molluscs 77, **78-85**
    worms 96-7
iridescence 238
isopods 167

J

Jacobson's organ 195, 270
Japan 132
Japanese macaques 277
jawfish 155
jaws
    fish 147, 168
    insects 100, 102, 117, 130,
        139
    reptiles 200, 214
    worms 98, 99
jellyfish 92-3
jet propulsion 92
Johnston's organs 113
jumping 179

K

kangaroos 273, 275
katydids 113
keels 195
kelp 30
keratin 190, 220, 268, 269
killer whales see orcas
kingdoms of life 10-11,
    20-21
kingfishers 256-7
kiwis 263
krill 341

L

lacewings 102
lakes **342-3**
    life in 27
lamallae 206
lammergeiers 334
larvae 102, 103, 104, 106,
    118, 129
    amphibians 174
    crabs 142
    fish 153
lateral line system 151
leaf insects 125
leaves 14-15, 46, 49, 51,
    54-5, 66
    aquatic plants 72
    carnivorous plants 69
    desert plants 71
    photosynthesis 45, 54, 55
    trees 52, 65
leopards 290-1
lichens **40-1**, 341
life cycles
    frogs 174-5
    honey bees 129
    jellyfish 93
    jewel wasps 118

moths 106-7
sunflower 46-7
lilies 58, 332
limbs
  octopus 84
  regeneration 84, 94, 143,
    184, **187**
limestone 88
lionfish 160-1
lions 283, 286, 328
litters 273
livers 148
lizards **190-1**, 206-7
  sea lizards 199
  shedding skin 193
lobsters 77, 143
Loch Lomond 342
lungs 175, 186, 220
lures 168
lynxes 286

M

Madagascar 203, 205
magnetic field 157
mammals 20, 264-317
  babies 266, 267, **272-9**,
    280
  carnivores 282-3
  defences 288-9
  egg-laying 275
  flying 302
  herbivores 294-5, 312
  insectivores 292-3
  milk 274
  ocean 282-3, 316-17
  reproduction 266
  rodents 296-7
  senses 266, **270-1**, 291
mammoths 18
mangroves 72, 333
mantises 116-17, 125
marine iguanas 198-9
marshes 332-3

marsupials 266, 273,
  275
maxillipeds 143
meerkats 288
Mekong River 343
melanin 17
metamorphosis 76, **106-7**,
  172, **174-5**
mermaid's purses 152-3
Mexico 186
mice 12, 297, 336
microorganisms 24-7
  germs 28-9
Middle East 138
migration 111, 157, **236-7**,
  326
milk 274
millipedes 140-1
mimicry 58, 85, 125, **126-7**,
  162, 163, 247
mitochondria 15
molecules
  DNA 17
mole rats 281, 296
moles 293
molluscs 77, 78-85
monkeys 266, 301
monocotyledons 48
monotremes 266, 275
mosquitoes 104, 113, 339
mosses 45, 327, 341
moths 103, 106-7, 113, 125
  antennae 110-11
  caterpillars 103, **106-7**,
    120-1, 126-7
moulds 38-9
moulting 105, 141, 142
mountains 277, 321,
  334-5
mouthbrooding 155
mucus 28, 78, 98
  amphibians 172, 183
  fish 146, 154, 167
mudskippers 333
muscles
  birds 220, 222, 226, 239,
    262

insects 105, 114
  mammals 268, 313
  reptiles 211, 212, 214
  worms 97
mushrooms 34-7
musk oxen 289, 338
mutations 17
myriapods 140

N

nacre 81
nautliuses 82
nectar 56, 58, 59, 128, 225,
  233
nerves 138, 183
nervous system 84
nests
  bees 128-9
  birds **240-1**, 247, 329
  fish 154
newts 173, **185**
New Zealand 191, 237, 263
Nile crocodiles 200-1
nocturnal animals 59
  amphibians 180, 185
  birds 248
  crustaceans 143
  insects 103, 125, 131
  mammals 266, 291, 293,
    302
  reptiles 195, 206, 210, 212
  scorpions 139
North America 126, 269, 324,
  326, 336
northern cardinals 220-1
nostrils 200
notochords 147
nucleus (cell) 15, 30
nuts 60

O

oceans 320, **344-5**
  global warming 89
  life 13
    birds 258-9
    crustaceans 142-3
    fish 146, 152-5, 158-69
    invertebrates 80-95, 98-9
    mammals 282-5, 316-17
    microorganisms 27,
      30, 32
    plants 72
    reptiles **198-9**, 217
  pollution 91
octopuses **84-5**, 345
olfactory bulbs 270
onagers 337
orang-utans 323
orcas 273, 282, 283
orchids 58
ospreys 252
osteoderms 192, 193
ostriches 262-3
otters 343
ovaries (plants) 57, 60
ovules 57
oxygen 10, 27, 32, 48, 54
  breathing 82, 100, 147,
    185, 220, 243, 255
owls **248-9**, 253, 338
oysters 81

P

Pacific Ocean 157, 164, 199,
  237
pack hunting 159
Panama golden frogs 181
pandas 273, 334
pangolins 269
parasites **118-19**, 167
parrots 225, 235

passerines 221

pathogens see germs

peacocks 238-9

peanut worms 99

pearls 81

penguins 253, **258-61**, 341

perching 221, 233

peregrine falcons 222, 228-9

permafrost

pheasants 230

pheromones 110, 111, 131

photophores 169

photosynthesis

  algae 26, 41, 89

  plants 45, 54, 55

pigments 17, 30, 65, 162

pigs, bearded 322

pike 342

pincers 139, 143

pine martens 326

pitcher plants 68

pit vipers 194-5

placenta 272, 273

plankton 88, 159, 344

plants **42-73**

  aquatic plants **72-3**, 342

  carnivorous plants 68-9

  classification 20-1

  defences 66-7

  desert plants 70-1

  evolution 19

  flowers 44, **56-9**, 60, 72

  fruits 44, **60-1**

  germination 46

  leaves 14-15, 46, 49, 51, **54-5**, 66

    aquatic plants 72

    carnivorous plants 69

    desert plants 71

    photosynthesis 45, 54, 55

    trees 52, 65

  mountain 334

  polar regions 341

  reproduction 12, 13, **56-7**

  roots 45, 46, 48, **50-1**

    aquatic plants 72

    desert plants 70, 71

trees 52

  seeds 44, **46-8**, 57, 61, 62-3

  stems 45, 51, 70

  tundra 339

platypuses 271, 275

pods 284

poison dart frogs 181

poisons 120

  amphibians 183, 184

  fish 161

  fungi 34

  insects 121

  millipedes 140, 141

  plants 67

polar bears 268, 311, 340

polar regions 321, 337, **340-1**

  migration 237

pollen 56, 57, 58, 59, 129, 304

pollinators 56, 57, 58, 59, 304

pollution 91

polyps

  coral 88

  jellyfish 93

porcupinefish 161

porcupines **268-9**, 324

pouches 266, 275, 306

prawns 343

pregnancies

  fish 152, 153

  mammals 273, 275

prehistoric animals 19, 21, 188, 208

primates 266, 322

proteins 17, 233, 274

protozoans 11

pupae 106, 129

pupils 183, 195, 270

pythons 210

queens

  ants 131

  bees 128, 129

  mole rats 281

quills 268

quillwort 342

rabbits 295

radiolarians 27

rainforests

  tropical 131, 139, 175, 194, 207, 238, 263, 309, 321, **322-3**

ratites 221

rattlesnakes 192

rays 146, 159

reefs 88, 89, **90-1**, 160, 162, 163, 167

regeneration 84, 94, 143, 184, **187**

regurgitation 215

reindeer 339

remoras **166-7**, 316

reproduction 10, **12-13**, 17

  birds 242-5

  crabs 142

  fish 152-3

  insects 10, 13

  jellyfish 93

  mammals 266

  microorganisms 13, 24

  molluscs 86

  plants 12, 13, **56-7**

  reptiles **196-7**, 208

  viruses 28

reptiles **188-217**, 264

  classification 21

  defence 192

  plant-eaters 190

  reproduction **196-7**, 208

  scales 190, **192-3**

  senses 190, **194-5**, 208

  temperature regulation 190, 192

resin 67

rheas 263

rhinoceroses 300

rivers **342-3**

  animals 200-1, 298-9, 332

  plants 72

rodents 266, 281, **296-9**

roots 46, 48, **50-1**, 70, 72

  buttress 323

ruddy turnstones 339

ruminants 295

Russia 157, 327

salamanders 173, **184-5**

  axolotls 186-7

saliva 28, 107

salmon 157

Saudi Arabia 205

savannah 329

scales

  fish 146, 169

  mammals 269

  reptiles 190, **192-3**

scallops 80

Scandinavia 237, 327

scavengers 131, 250, 328, 334

schools (fish) 164

scorpions 138-9

scutes 192, 216

sea anemones 13, **86-7**, 167

seadragons 163

seahorses 154, 163

seals 283, 340

seasons
  autumn 64–5, 325
  spring 324
  summer 325, 327, 334, 338
  tropical 328–9
  winter 325, 326, 334, 337, 338, 341, 343
seaweeds 30, 244
seeds 44, **46–9**, 57
  dispersal of 61, **62–3**
senses
  birds 220, 248
  fish 150–1, 158, 168
  invertebrates 11, 79, 84, 85, 108–13, 134
  mammals 266, **270–1**
  reptiles 190, **194–5**
sensory hairs 101, 105, 111, 122, 134, 139
sepals 56
Serengeti 328, 329
sharks **158–9**, 340
  buoyancy 148
  reproduction 152–3
  scales 146
  skeletons 147
  symbiosis 167
shedding skin 190, **192–3**
shells
  molluscs 78, 80, 82–3
  tortoises 197, 216
shoals 161
shrews 293
shrimps 167
Siberia 237
sight 108–9
  birds 249, 250
  fish 150
  mammals 270
  reptiles 190
  spiders 135
silica 27
silk 106, 136–7
silverbacks 280
single-celled organisms 10, 11, **24–7**, 30

reproduction 24
skeletons
  birds 222–3
  corals 88
  fish 147
  mammals 309
  whales 317
skin 24
  amphibians 172, 185, 186
  birds 224
  colour 17, 204
  fish 150
  gliders 306, 307
  reptiles 190, **102–3**, 204
  shedding 190, **192–3**
skulls
  birds 222
  fish 147
  mammals 292, 312
skunks 289
sloths 31, 301
slugs 13, 78
smell 110, 151
  mammals 270
  reptiles 190
snails **78–9**, 83
snakes 191, **192–3**, 288, 333
  catching prey 212–3
  eating 214–5
  movement 210–211
  senses 194–5
snow leopards 335
soaring 229, 250
soil 96
  bacteria in 28
  creation of 40
Sonoran Desert 336
South America 67, 184, 237, 263, 289
spawning 153
species 20
spiders 77, 127, **134–7**, 335
spines
  birds 252
  fish 147, 159, 161, 162, 163

insects 15, 113, 117, 120
  mammals 16, 17, 268, 269, 292, 293
  plants 67, 71
  shells 83
  snakes 211
Spirogyra 30–1
spitting 212
sponges 13
spoonbills 333
squirrels 297
stamens 56, 57
starfish 76, **94–5**
stargazer fish 163
stems 51, 70
stick insects 100
stigmas 56, 57
stings
  coral polyps 88
  fish 162
  insects 118, 120, **122–3**
  jellyfish 92, 93
  plants 66
  scorpions 138, 139
  sea anemones 86
stomachs
  acid 28
stonefish 162
streamlining
  in air 220, 237
  in water 146, 148, 149, 258
stromatolites 11
suckers 84, 95, 166, 179
sugar gliders 306–7
sundews 68–9
sunflowers 46–7
sunlight (and photosynthesis)
  algae 26, 41, 89
  plants 45, 54, 55
Suriname toads 175
swamps 332, 333
swans 236–7
swifts 241
swim bladders 146, 148, 151
swimming
  amphibians 178
  fish 146, **148–9**

jellyfish 92
whales 317
swinging through trees **308–9**, 323
swordtails 153
symbiosis 41, 67, 86, **166–7**

T

tadpoles 174–5
taiga 326–7
tails 317
  amphibians 173, 184, 185
  fish 148
  mammals 267, 306
  reptiles 207
  scorpions 138
talons 224, 251
tapeworms 119
tarsiers 322
taste 84, 151, 195, 270
tears 28
teats 274, 275
teeth
  fish 158, 168, 169
  invertebrates 79
  mammals 286, 291, 294, 296, 297, 312, 313, 317
  reptiles 208, 213
temperature regulation 190, 192, 266
tendons 179, 262, 263, 291, 302
tentacles 77, 79, 81
  jellyfish 92, 93
  octopuses 84
  polyps 88
  sea anemones 86
  worms 98, 99
terrapins 191
Thailand 333
third eye 208
thistles 58
thoraxes 100, 115, 134

thorn bugs 125
threat displays 286
thumbs 301, 308
ticks 119
tigers 269, **276-7**
toads 173, 175
  defences 182-3
toe pads 179, 207, 310
tongues 59, 295
  birds 225
  fish 167
  mammals 59, 270, 291,
    293, 295
  molluscs 77, 79
  reptiles 194, 195, 200,
    203-4, 208
tortoises 191, 196-7,
216-17, 336
  evolution 18
touch 110, 139, 181, 267
transport systems 94
tree frogs 179, 181
trees **52-3**, 59, 323
  autumn 52, 65
  defences 67
  desert 71
  grasslands 328
  mangroves 72, 333
  mountains 334
  nests 240-1
  seeds from 62, 63
  see also forests
tripod fish 169
tsetse flies 119
tuataras 191, **208-9**
tube feet 94, 95
tubercles 183, 194
tube worms 98
tundra 321, **338-9**
turtles 191, **216-17**
  scales 192
tusks 18, 19, 173, 312
tusk shells 82

U

umbilical cords 272
underground 96, 293, 296,
  310
ungulates 266
unken reflex 182
USA 332
uterus 273

V

vacuoles 15, 24, 25, 26, 30
vegetables 19
venom
  centipedes 141
  fish 161, 162, 163
  insects 120, 121, 122, 123
  jellyfish 92, 93
  Portuguese man-of-war
    161
  scorpions 138, 139
  snakes 212, 213
  spiders 134, 135, 137
  worms 99
Venus flytrap 68
vertebrates
  classification 21
viperfish 168-9
vipers 194-5, 197, 213
viruses 28
vocal cords 180
voles 338
vultures 334

W

warm-blooded animals 266,
  267
warning colours
  amphibians 182, 184
  birds 246
  fish 160
  fungi 34
  insects 120, 122, 126, 140
  mammals 289, 310
  reptiles 205
wasps 102, **122-3**
  parasitic 118
water
  and life 11, 27, 48
  frshwater habitat 321,
342-3
  plants 70, 71, 72-3
waterfowl 221, 241, **254-5**
  growing up 242-5
waterproofing oil 254
weather 91, 237
weaver birds **240-1**, 329
webs 136-7
wet season 329
whales 10, 284, 301,
  316-17, 345
whiskers 266, 270, 307
whydas 247
wildebeest 329
wind
  and plants 59, 62, 63
wings
  bats 301, 302
  birds 226-9, 232
  insects 101, 105, **114-15**,
    131
wobbegongs 159, 163
wolves 289
woodlice 143
woodpeckers 241, 242
worms **96-9**, 119

XY

Yemen 205
yok sacs 152, 153, 196, 242

Z

zebras 301

ACKNOWLEDGMENTS

DK would like to thank consultant Derek Harvey for his support and dedication throughout the making of this book.

In addition, DK would like to extend thanks to the following people for their help with making the book: Jemma Westing for design assistance; Steve Crozier at Butterfly Creative Solutions and Phil Fitzgerald for picture retouching; Victoria Pyke for proofreading; Carron Brown for indexing.

The publisher would also like to thank the following institutions, companies, and individuals for their generosity in allowing DK to photograph their plants and animals or use their images:

Leopold Aichinger

Animal Magic
Eastbourne, East Sussex, UK
www.animal-magic.co.uk

Animals Work
28 Greaves Road, High Wycombe Bucks, HP13 7JU, UK
www.animalswork.co.uk

Alexander Berg

Charles Ash
touchwoodcrafts.co.uk

Colchester Zoo
Maldon Road, Stanway, Essex, CO3 0SL, UK
www.colchester-zoo.com

Cotswold Wildlife Park Bradwell Grove, Burford, Oxfordshire, OX18 4JP, UK
www.cotswoldwildlifepark.co.uk

Crocodiles of the World
Burford Road, Brize Norton, Oxfordshire, OX18 3NX, UK
www.crocodilesoftheworld.co.uk
With special thanks to Shaun Foggett and Colin Stevenson.

Norman and Susan Davis

Stefan Diller
www.stefan-diller.com

Eagle Heights
Lullingstone Lane, Eynsford, Dartford, DA4 0JB, UK
www.eagleheights.co.uk

The Goldfish Bowl
118-122 Magdalen Road, Oxford, OX4 1RQ, UK
www.thegoldfishbowl.co.uk

Incredible Eggs South East Ltd
www.incredibleeggs.co.uk

Thomas Marent
www.thomasmarent.com

Waldo Nell

Oxford Museum of Natural History
Parks Road, Oxford, OX1 3PW, UK
www.oum.ox.ac.uk

Lorenzo Possenti

School of Biological Sciences, University of Reading
With special thanks to Dr Geraldine Mulley, Dr Sheila MacIntyre and Agnieszka Kowalik.

Scubazoo
www.scubazoo.com

Snakes Alive Ltd
Barleylands Road, Barleylands Farm Park, Billericay, CM11 2UD, UK
www.snakesalive.co.uk
With special thanks to Daniel and Peter Hepplewhite.

Sally-Ann Spence
www.minibeastmayhem.com

Triffid Nursery
Great Hallows, Church Lane, Stoke Ash, Suffolk IP23 7ET, UK
www.triffidnurseries.co.uk
With special thanks to Andrew Wilkinson.

Wexham Park Hospital, Slough
With special thanks to the Microbiology department for assistance with identification of selected bacterial isolates.

Explanatorium of Nature Picture Credits

The publisher would like to thank the following for their kind permission to reproduce their photographs:

(Key: a-above; b-below/bottom; c-centre; f-far; l-left; r-right; t-top)

1 123RF.com: cobalt (circle). **Dreamstime.com:** Christos Georghiou (screws); Mario Lopes. **naturepl.com:** SCOTLAND: The Big Picture (c). **2-3 Dreamstime.com:** Mario Lopes. **2 DK:** Courtesy of Colchester Zoo. **3 123RF.com:** cobalt (circle). **Alamy Stock Photo:** Fernando Quevedo de Oliveira (c). **Dreamstime.com:** Christos Georghiou (screws). **4-5 123RF.com:** cobalt (circles). **Dreamstime.com:** Mario Lopes. **4 123RF.com:** Serg_v (sky). **5 123RF.com:** Serg_v (sky). **6-7 123RF.com:** cobalt (circles); Serg_v (sky). **Dreamstime.com:** Mario Lopes. **6 DK:** Courtesy of The Goldfish Bowl (tl); Courtesy of Snakes Alive Ltd (tr). **7 DK:** Courtesy of Eagle Heights (tl); Courtesy of Cotswold Wildlife Park (tc); Courtesy of Scubazoo (tr). **8-9 Dreamstime.com:** Mario Lopes. **8 Dreamstime.com:** Christos Georghiou (screws). **9 123RF.com:** cobalt (circle); Serg_v (sky). **10-11 Dreamstime.com:** Wong Hock Weng John. **10 123RF.com:** Morley Read (bc). **naturepl.com:** Alex Mustard (br). **11 DK:** Wolfgang Bettighofer / DK (bl). **Dreamstime.com:** Robert Bayer (tr). **Science Photo Library:** Wolfgang Baumeister (bc). **12-13 Warren Photographic Limited. 13 Alexander Hyde. Dreamstime.com:** Dennis Sabo (cr). **Science Photo Library:** David Wrobel, Visuals Unlimited (br). **14 Science Photo Library:** Michael Abbey (br). **16-17 Alamy Stock Photo:** Erich Schmidt / IMAGEbroker. **18 DK:** Dave King / Natural History Museum, London (bl, bc). **18-19 DK:** Jon Hughes (c). **20 123RF.com:** Cathy Keifer (cra/two frogs); Eduardo Rivero (br/toucan). **DK:** Fotolia: fotojagodka (cla/dog); Jerry Young (ftl/red fox, tl/arctic fox, cra/echidna); Fotolia: anyaivanova (cr); Fotolia: Eric Isselee (ca). **21 123RF.com:** Ermolaev Alexander

Alexandrovich (fbl/snake); Morley Read (cb); Richard Whitcombe (fcla); smileus (fclb). **DK:** Wolfgang Bettighofer (cra/protozoa); David Peart (ftl/shark); Liberty's Owl, Raptor and Reptile Centre, Hampshire, UK (t); Jerry Young (clb, fbl/crocodile); Chris Hornbecker / Ryan Neil (bl). **naturepl.com:** Alex Mustard (br). **Science Photo Library:** Eye of Science (cra); Dorit Hackmann (tl). **22-23 Dreamstime.com:** Mario Lopes. **22 Dreamstime.com:** Christos Georghiou (screws). **23 123RF.com:** cobalt (circle); Serg_v (sky). **Dreamstime.com:** Christos Georghiou (screws). **24-25 Waldo Nell. 26 iStockphoto.com:** micro_photo (tc). **Science Photo Library:** Gerd Guenther (crb). **27 Getty Images:** Thomas Deerinck, NCMIR (tr); Wim van Egmond / Visuals Unlimited (c); Dr. Stanley Flegler / Visuals Unlimited (cra). **Science Photo Library:** Eye of Science (crb); Frank Fox (cl); Steve Gschmeissner (cb). **28 Science Photo Library:** Eye of Science (tr); Scimat (br). **29 DK:** Courtesy of the School of Biological Sciences, University of Reading (c). **Science Photo Library:** Dennis Kunkel Microscopy (tr); Dennis Kunkel Microscopy (br). **30 Alamy Stock Photo:** Jean Evans (tc). **naturepl.com:** Alex Mustard (tr). **31 Alamy Stock Photo:** Joe Blossom (bl). **naturepl.com:** Visuals Unlimited (tl). **32-33 Joanne Paquette. 35 Science Photo Library:** AMI Images (clb). **37 Dreamstime.com:** smikeymickey (cr). **39 Alexander Hyde:** (bl). **40 Science Photo Library:** Ashley Cooper (bl). **42-43 Dreamstime.com:** Mario Lopes. **42 Dreamstime.com:** Christos Georghiou (screws). **43 123RF.com:** cobalt (circle); Serg_v (sky). **Dreamstime.com:** Christos Georghiou (screws). **44-45 Alamy Stock Photo:** Olga Khomyakova. **46-47 123RF.com:** Dr Ajay Kumar Singh (bc). **46 Alamy Stock Photo:** Nigel Cattlin (cl). **50 Leopold Aichinger:** (c). **51 Leopold Aichinger. 52 DK:** Will Heap / Mike Rose (clb). **53 DK:** Courtesy of Charles Ash. **54-55 DK:** Courtesy of Stefan Diller (c). **59 Alamy Stock Photo:** Arterra Picture Library (cla). **Dreamstime.com:** Elena Frolova (ca). **63 DK:** Emma Shepherd (bc).

64-65 Alamy Stock Photo: Kumar Sriskandan. **67 Science Photo Library:** Matteis / Look at Science (crb); Pan Xunbin (br). **70 Dreamstime.com:** Mikhail Dudarev (bl). **71 Alamy Stock Photo:** Chris Mattison (tc). **74-75 Dreamstime.com:** Mario Lopes. **74 Dreamstime.com:** Christos Georghiou (screws). **75 123RF.com:** cobalt (circle); Serg_v (sky). **Dreamstime.com:** Christos Georghiou (screws). **Thomas Marent:** (c). **76-77 DK:** Courtesy of Thomas Marent (c). **80 National Geographic Creative:** David Liittschwager (clb). **80-81 David Moynahan. 84-85 DK:** Frank Greenaway / Weymouth Sea Life Centre (c). **85 Gabriel Barathieu. 86-87 DK:** Courtesy of The Goldfish Bowl (c). **87 Getty Images:** Helen Lawson (tr). **88-89 DK:** Courtesy of Scubazoo (c). **88 DK:** Courtesy of Scubazoo (tr). **90-91 Alex Mustard. 92-93 Alexander Semenov. 94-95 DK:** Courtesy of The Goldfish Bowl (c). **94 Science Photo Library:** Andrew J, Martinez (ca). **95 Alamy Stock Photo:** Nature Picture Library / WWE (br). **98-99 DK:** Courtesy of The Goldfish Bowl (b). **99 Alamy Stock Photo:** cbimages (crb); Images & Stories (tr); imageBROKER (cra); National Geographic Creative (br). **100-101 Alexander Berg. 102 Alexander Hyde:** (tr). **DK:** Gyuri Csoka Cyorgy (cl); Forrest Mitchell / James Laswel (bc). **naturepl.com:** Julian Partridge (cr). **110-110 Alexander Hyde:** (c). **111 DK:** Frank Greenaway / Natural History Museum, London (tc). **112 DK:** Ted Benton (tr). **113 DK:** Colin Keates / Natural History Museum, London (tl); Koen van Klijken (tc). **Dreamstime.com:** Digitalimagined (tr). **Science Photo Library:** Wim Van Egmond (ca). **115 DK:** Courtesy of Scubazoo (c). **Science Photo Library:** Claude Nuridsany & Marie Perennou (tc). **116-117 naturepl.com:** MYN / Paul Harcourt Davies (c). **117 Getty Images:** Toshiaki Ono / amanaimagesRF (bc). **iStockphoto.com:** Andrea Mangoni (bl). **118-119 FLPA:** Emanuele Biggi (c). **119 Science Photo Library:** Pascal Goetcheluck (tl); Science Picture Co (ca). **120-121 Thomas Marent. 121 Getty Images:** Piotr Naskrecki / Minden Pictures (cr). **naturepl.com:** Nature Production / naturepl.com (tr). **Science Photo Library:** Frans Lanting, Mint Images (br). **125 Alexander Hyde:** (tr, cr). **Thomas Marent:** (br). **126 naturepl.com:** Ingo Arndt (bc). **Science Photo Library:** F. Martinez Clavel (br); Millard H. Sharp (bl). **126-127**

Andreas Kay: (c). **127 Alexander Hyde:** (bl). **DK:** Frank Greenaway / Natural History Museum, London (crb). **naturepl.com:** Nature Production (bc). **130 Alamy Stock Photo:** Christian Ziegler / Minden Pictures (bc). **Dreamstime.com:** Yunhyok Choi (cb). **130-131 Nick Garbutt. 131 Nick Garbutt:** (ca). **132-133 FLPA:** Hiroya Minakuchi / Minden Pictures. **136-137 FLPA:** Malcolm Schuyl. **138 naturepl.com:** Daniel Heuclin (tr). **143 Science Photo Library:** Alexander Semenov (br). **144-145 Dreamstime.com:** Mario Lopes. **144 Dreamstime.com:** Christos Georghiou (screws). **145 123RF.com:** cobalt (circle). **DK:** Courtesy of The Goldfish Bowl (c). **Dreamstime.com:** Christos Georghiou (screws). **146-147 DK:** Courtesy of The Goldfish Bowl (c). **148-149 DK:** Courtesy of The Goldfish Bowl (c). **150-151 naturepl.com:** Krista Schlyer / MYN (c). **153 Alamy Stock Photo:** blickwinkel (cra). **naturepl.com:** Jane Burton (br); Tony Wu (tr); Tim MacMillan / John Downer Productions (crb). **154 Alamy Stock Photo:** Maximilian Weinzierl (bc). **Animals Animals / Earth Scenes:** Kent, Breck P (clb). **Getty Images:** Paul Zahl (cl). **154-155 SeaPics.com:** Steven Kovacs (c). **156-157 AirPano images. 158 Alamy Stock Photo:** Visual&Written SL (bc). **OceanwideImages.com:** C & M Fallows (cl). **158-159 Chris & Monique Fallows / Apexpredators.com. 162 Alamy Stock Photo:** Hubert Yann (cl). **naturepl.com:** Alex Mustard (bl). **162-163 OceanwideImages.com. 163 FLPA:** OceanPhoto (cr); Norbert Wu / Minden Pictures (crb). **naturepl.com:** Alex Mustard (cra). **OceanwideImages.com. 164-165 FLPA:** Reinhard Dirscherl. **166-167 DK:** Courtesy of The Goldfish Bowl (c). **166 DK:** Courtesy of The Goldfish Bowl (tc). **167 FLPA:** Reinhard Dirscherl (cr, br); Colin Marshall (bc). **naturepl.com:** David Fleetham (tr); Alex Mustard (tl). **168 naturepl.com:** David Shale (bl). **168-169 OceanwideImages.com. 170-171 Dreamstime.com:** Mario Lopes. **170 Dreamstime.com:** Christos Georghiou (screws). **171 123RF.com:** cobalt (circle); Serg_v (sky). **Dreamstime.com:** Christos Georghiou (screws). **173 DK:** Twan Leenders (br). **174 iStockphoto.com:** GlobalP (tl). **175 Alamy Stock Photo:** Michael & Patricia Fogden / Minden Pictures (br). **Dreamstime.com:** Isselee (c). **Warren Photographic Limited:** Kim Taylor

(tl). **176-177 Biosphoto:** Michel Loup. **179 Alamy Stock Photo:** Survivalphotos (cla). **180-181 Photoshot:** blickwinkel (c). **181 iStockphoto.com:** stevegeer (cr). **182-183 DK:** Courtesy of Snakes Alive Ltd (c). **182 DK:** Jerry Young (cl). **FLPA:** Jelger Herder / Buitenbeeld / Minden Pictures (bl). **Gary Nafis:** (tl). **183 DK:** Courtesy of Snakes Alive Ltd (tr). **184 Gary Nafis:** (cla). **185 naturepl.com:** MYN / Paul van Hoof (crb). **188-189 Dreamstime.com:** Mario Lopes. **188 Dreamstime.com:** Christos Georghiou (screws). **189 123RF.com:** cobalt (circle); Serg_v (sky). **DK:** Courtesy of Snakes Alive Ltd (c). **Dreamstime.com:** Christos Georghiou (screws). **190-191 DK:** Courtesy of Snakes Alive Ltd (b). **191 123RF.com:** marigranulla (tr); mnsanthushkumar (tl). **192 Alamy Stock Photo:** Ian Watt (cl). **192-193 Chris Mattison Nature Photographics. 194 Science Photo Library:** Edward Kinsman (bc). **194-195 Alamy Stock Photo:** Tim Plowden (c). **196 iStockphoto.com:** Somedaygood (c). **197 iStockphoto.com:** Somedaygood (cb). **Photoshot:** Daniel Heuclin / NHPA (cra). **198-199 Alamy Stock Photo:** Michel & Gabrielle Therin-Weise. **200-201 DK:** Courtesy of Crocodiles of the World (c). **203 Alamy Stock Photo:** Todd Eldred (tr). **206-207 DK:** Courtesy of Snakes Alive Ltd (c). **206 Science Photo Library:** Power and Syred (bl). **208-209 Getty Images:** Joel Sartore / National Geographic Photo Ark. **208 123RF.com:** Molly Marshall (bc). **209 John Marris. 212-213 Alamy Stock Photo:** Nature Picture Library (tl). **Getty Images:** Joe McDonald (c). **213 naturepl.com:** Guy Edwardes (tr). **216 Alamy Stock Photo:** BIOSPHOTO (ca). **216-217 Alamy Stock Photo:** BIOSPHOTO (c). **217 iStockphoto.com:** babel film (tr). **218-219 Dreamstime.com:** Mario Lopes. **218 Dreamstime.com:** Christos Georghiou (screws). **219 123RF.com:** cobalt (circle); Serg_v (sky). **DK:** Courtesy of Eagle Heights (c). **Dreamstime.com:** Christos Georghiou (screws). **220-221 naturepl.com:** MYN / JP Lawrence (c). **221 Alamy Stock Photo:** blickwinkel (cr). **naturepl.com:** Klein & Hubert (crb). **222-223 Science Photo Library:** GustoImages (c). **224 123RF.com:** Jon Craig Hanson (br). **DK:** Courtesy of Eagle Heights (l). **225 123RF.com:** Isselee (br). **FLPA:** Photo Researchers (tc). **226-227 DK:** Courtesy of Eagle Heights. **228-229**

DK: Courtesy of Eagle Heights (c). **230 123RF.com:** Eric Isselee (tr). **232 123RF.com:** Koji Hirando (br). **232-233 iStockphoto.com:** Kenneth Canning (c). **233 iStockphoto.com:** environmantic (cr). **234-235 FLPA:** Martin Willis / Minden Pictures. **236-237 FLPA:** Marion Vollborn, BIA / Minden Pictures. **238 123RF.com:** BenFoto (cl); John79 (bl). **238-239 123RF.com:** BenFoto (c). **239 Getty Images:** Per-Gunnar Ostby (cr). **Gerhard Koertner:** (br). **naturepl.com:** Tim Laman / Nat Geo Creative (cra). **240-241 FLPA:** Jurgen & Christine Sohns (c). **241 Alamy Stock Photo:** Arterra Picture Library (tr); Michael DeFreitas North America (cra); blickwinkel (crb). **FLPA:** Tom Vezo / Minden Pictures (br). **Science Photo Library:** Frans Lanting, Mint Images (cr). **242-245 DK:** Courtesy of Incredible Eggs South East Ltd. **246-247 Alamy Stock Photo:** blickwinkel (c). **247 Alamy Stock Photo:** blickwinkel (cr, crb). **Getty Images:** John Watkins / FLPA / Minden Pictures (tr). **Justin Schuetz:** (bl). **248-249 DK:** Courtesy of Eagle Heights (c). **249 DK:** Peter Chadwick / Natural History Museum, London (br). **250-251 DK:** Courtesy of Eagle Heights (t). **250 Alamy Stock Photo:** Marvin Dembinsky Photo Associates (clb). **Getty Images:** Daniel Hernanz Ramos (bc, br, fbr). **253 naturepl.com:** Edwin Giesbers (tl). **254 Science Photo Library:** Pat & Tom Leeson (br). **255 Alamy Stock Photo:** Arco Images GmbH (br). **256-257 FLPA:** Ernst Dirksen / Minden Pictures. **257 Alamy Stock Photo:** Cultura RM (crb); Hans Verburg (cr). **Dreamstime.com:** Alexey Ponomarenko (br). **258-259 DK:** Frank Greenaway (cb). **259 123RF.com:** Dmytro Pylypenko (tr). **Alamy Stock Photo:** All Canada Photos (ftr); Steve Bloom Images (tl); Minden Pictures (tc). **260-261 naturepl.com:** David Tipling. **262-263 iStockphoto.com:** Rocter (c). **262 123RF.com:** Alexey Sholom (tr). **263 123RF.com:** Andrea Izzotti (cra). **Alamy Stock Photo:** Minden Pictures (crb). **Dreamstime.com:** Stephenmeese (cr). **264-265 Dreamstime.com:** Mario Lopes. **264 Dreamstime.com:** Christos Georghiou (screws). **265 123RF.com:** cobalt (circle); Serg_v (sky). **DK:** Courtesy of Cotswold Wildlife Park (c). **Dreamstime.com:** Christos Georghiou (screws). **266-267 DK:** Courtesy of Animal Magic (c). **266 DK:** Fotolia: Eric Isselee (tc); Jerry Young (tl). **Science Photo Library:**

Ted Kinsman (bl). **268-269 Getty Images:** Joe McDonald (ca). **naturepl.com:** Eric Baccega (tc); Roland Seitre (bc). **269 123RF.com:** Daniel Lamborn (crb). **Alamy Stock Photo:** imagebroker (cra). **Getty Images:** Alex Huizinga / Minden Pictures (tr). **iStockphoto.com:** 2630ben (br). **272-273 naturepl.com:** Jane Burton. **273 Alamy Stock com:** Phasin Sudjai (tl). **274-275 DK:** Courtesy of Animal Magic (c). **275 Alamy Stock Photo:** Panther Media GmbH (cr). **National Geographic Creative:** Joel Sartore (tc). **naturepl.com:** John Cancalosi (crb). **276-277 naturepl.com:** Andy Rouse (tc). **276 FLPA:** Klein and Hubert (br). **277 DK:** Thomas Marent / Thomas Marent (bc). **naturepl.com:** Anup Shah (bl). **278-279 naturepl.com:** Jane Burton (bc). **279 FLPA:** Gerry Ellis / Minden Pictures (tr). **naturepl.com:** ARCO (tl). **280 Ardea:** Adrian Warren (bl). **280-281 naturepl.com:** Andy Rouse (c). **282-283 Science Photo Library:** Christopher Swann (tc). **283 naturepl.com:** Jabruson (tr). **284-285 naturepl.com:** Tony Wu. **286-287 FLPA:** Yva Momatiuk &, John Eastcott / Minden Pictures (tc). **naturepl.com:** Denis-Huot. **288 Getty Images:** Joel Sartore / National Geographic (cl). **288-289 123RF.com:** Robert Eastman (c). **288 DK:** Courtesy of Cotswold Wildlife Park (bl). **289 National Geographic Creative:** Joel Sartore, National Geographic Photo Ark (cr). **290-291 DK:** Wildlife Heritage Foundation, Kent, UK. **291 DK:** Wildlife Heritage Foundation, Kent, UK (tr). **292-293 DK:** Courtesy of Animal Magic (c). **293 Alamy Stock Photo:** Edo Schmidt (tc). **DK:** Corbis image100 (tl). **294-295 DK:** Courtesy of Cotswold Wildlife Park (c). **296 National Geographic Creative:** Joel Sartore. **297 Alamy Stock Photo:** Rick & Nora Bowers (cra); Design Pics Inc (cr); George Reszeter (br). **298-299 Getty Images:** Jeff R Clow (b). **298 Alamy Stock Photo:** Calle Bredberg (bc). **300 DK:** Courtesy of Cotswold Wildlife Park (l). **301 Alexander Hyde:** (cr). **DK:** Courtesy of Colchester Zoo (tl).**FLPA:** Hiroya Minakuchi / Minden Pictures (bl). **naturepl.com:** Daniel Heuclin (tr). **302-303 National Geographic Creative:** Michael Durham / Minden Pictures. **303 DK:** Frank Greenaway / Natural History Museum, London (br); Jerry Young (cb); Jerry Young (bc). **304-305 MerlinTuttle.org**. **306-307 DK:** Courtesy of Animal

Magic (c). **307 Dreamstime.com:** Junnemui (cr). **308-309 DK:** Courtesy of Colchester Zoo (c). **308 naturepl.com:** Ingo Arndt (bc). **310-311 Ardea:** John Daniels. **311 Alamy Stock Photo:** robertharding (br). **Greg Dardagan**. **312-313 DK:** Courtesy of Colchester Zoo. **313 FLPA:** Richard Du Toit / Minden Pictures (cr). **314-315 Getty Images:** Michael Poliza / Gallo Images. **316 Getty Images:** Kent Kobersteen (tr). **316-317 naturepl.com:** Tony Wu (c). **317 naturepl.com:** Tony Wu (bl). **318-319 Dreamstime.com:** Mario Lopes. **318 Dreamstime.com:** Christos Georghiou (screws). **319 123RF.com:** cobalt (circle). **DK:** Courtesy of Scubazoo (c). **Dreamstime.com:** Christos Georghiou (screws). **320 Alamy Stock Photo:** Robert Fried (bc); mauritius images GmbH (clb); David Wall (bl). **Getty Images:** Phil Nelson (br). **321 Alamy Stock Photo:** Hemis (cra); Mint Images Limited (br). **FLPA:** Colin Monteath, Hedgehog House / Minden Pictures (bc). **Getty Images:** Sergey Gorshkov / Minden Pictures (tc); ViewStock (tl); Anton Petrus (tr); Panoramic Images (crb). **Imagelibrary India Pvt Ltd:** James Owler (bl). **322 Alamy Stock Photo:** blickwinkel (cr); Nature Picture Library (cl). **iStockphoto.com:** blizzard87 (bl); Stephane Jaquemet (br). **323 Alamy Stock Photo:** Mint Images Limited (cl); Steve Bloom Images (cr). **DK:** Blackpool Zoo, Lancashire, UK (bl). **iStockphoto.com:** Utopia_88 (br). **324 Getty Images:** Alan Murphy / BIA / Minden Pictures (bl); Phil Nelson (cr). **iStockphoto.com:** jimkruger (br); Ron Thomas (cl). **325 Alamy Stock Photo:** Andrew Cline (cr); Jon Arnold Images Ltd (cl). **Getty Images:** Joe McDonald (br); Ed Reschke (bl). **326 Dreamstime.com:** Rinus Baak (bc); Jnjhuz (bl); Tt (crb). **Getty Images:** Sergey Gorshkov / Minden Pictures (c). **327 Alamy Stock Photo:** Design Pics Inc (c). **Dreamstime.com:** Radu Borcoman (br); Sorin Colac (bl); Steve Byland (cb). **328 Imagelibrary India Pvt Ltd:** James Owler (ca). **iStockphoto.com:** brytta (cb); MaggyMeyer (bl); memcockers (bc). **329 Alamy Stock Photo:** Frans Lanting Studio (cb); hsrana (c). **Dreamstime.com:** Anke Van Wyk (bl). **iStockphoto.com:** RainervonBrandis (bc). **330 Dreamstime.com:** Denis Pepin (crb). **Getty Images:** Andre and Anita Gilden (bl). **naturepl.com:** Gerrit Vyn (c). **331 Alamy Stock

Photo:** mauritius images GmbH (c); Victor Tyakht (bl); Zoonar GmbH (cb). **Getty Images:** M Schaef (br). **332 Alamy Stock Photo:** Robert Fried (cla). **Getty Images:** Kevin Schafer / Minden Pictures (bl); Leanne Walker (c). **332-333 Getty Images:** Jupiterimages (ca). **333 Alamy Stock Photo:** Jan Wlodarczyk (cra). **Dreamstime.com:** Steve Byland (clb); Tinnakorn Srikammuan (crb). **Getty Images:** Ben Horton (bc). **334-335 Getty Images:** Dennis Fischer Photography (ca). **334 Dreamstime.com:** Lynn Watson (bc); Minyun Zhou (clb). **iStockphoto.com:** hackle (cla). **naturepl.com:** David Kjaer (crb). **335 123RF.com:** Christian Musat (cl). **Alamy Stock Photo:** Hemis (cra). **Dreamstime.com:** Kwiktor (cb). **naturepl.com:** Gavin Maxwell (bc). **336 Alamy Stock Photo:** Rick & Nora Bowers (crb); mauritius images GmbH (ca). **FLPA:** Richard Herrmann / Minden Pictures (br). **iStockphoto.com:** KenCanning (bl). **337 Alamy Stock Photo:** Hemis (br). **Dreamstime.com:** Pahham (bl). **Getty Images:** Barcroft (crb); ViewStock (ca). **338 Getty Images:** Patrick Endres / Visuals Unlimited (cb); Anton Petrus (ca). **iStockphoto.com:** mihalizhukov (br). **naturepl.com:** Gerrit Vyn (bl). **339 Getty Images:** Daniel A. Leifheit (bc); Jason Pineau (ca). **iStockphoto.com:** Maasik (bl). **naturepl.com:** Andy Sands (crb). **340 Alamy Stock Photo:** blickwinkel (bl); WaterFrame (crb). **Dreamstime.com:** Outdoorsman (bc). **Getty Images:** Galen Rowell (ca). **341 DK:** Frank Krahmer / Photographers Choice RF (cb). **FLPA:** Colin Monteath, Hedgehog House / Minden Pictures (ca). **Getty Images:** Ralph Lee Hopkins (bl); Visuals Unlimited (br). **342 Alamy Stock Photo:** Nature Photographers Ltd (bc); VPC Animals Photo (crb). **Getty Images:** Alan Majchrowicz (ca). **Science Photo Library:** John Clegg (b). **343 Alamy Stock Photo:** blickwinkel (bl). **Getty Images:** Panoramic Images (ca). **Science Photo Library:** Dante Fenolio (crb); Bob Gibbons (br). **344-345 Alamy Stock Photo:** David Wall (ca). **344 Alamy Stock Photo:** Mark Conlin (crb). **Getty Images:** Daniela Dirscherl (bl); Mauricio Handler (cla). **iStockphoto.com:** NaluPhoto (cb). **345 Alamy Stock Photo:** NOAA (br). **naturepl.com:** David Shale (cb); Tony Wu (clb). **Science Photo Library:** B. Murton / Southampton Oceanography Centre (cra)

Cover images: Front: **123RF.com:** cobalt (inner circle), Kebox (text fill), nick8889 (outer circle), olegdudko cr/ (iguana right arm); **Dreamstime.com:** Amador García Sarduy c, Christos Georghiou (screws), Mario Lopes (background); Back: **123RF.com:** cobalt (inner circle), nick8889 (outer circle), Serg_v c; **Dreamstime.com:** Christos Georghiou (screws), Mario Lopes (background); Spine: **123RF.com:** Kebox (text fll), olegdudko (iguana right arm); **Dreamstime.com:** Amador García Sarduy c, Mario Lopes (background), Pawel Papis (behind iguana)

Endpaper images: Front: **123RF.com:** cobalt cl (inner circle), cr (inner circle), lightpoet cr (monkey), NejroN cra (macaw), nick8889 cl (outer circle), cr (outer circle), olegdudko cl (iguana left arm); **Dreamstime.com:** Amador García Sarduy cl, Christos Georghiou (screws), Mario Lopes (background), Pawel Papis cr; Back: **123RF.com:** cobalt cl (inner circle), cr (inner circle), nick8889 cl (outer circle), cr (outer circle), Serg_v cl (sky), cr (sky); **Dreamstime.com:** Christos Georghiou (screws), Mario Lopes (background);

All other images © DK For further information see:

www.dkimages.com